# THE TALMUD OF BABYLONIA

Program in Judaic Studies
Brown University
BROWN JUDAIC STUDIES
Edited by
Shaye J. D. Cohen, Wendell S. Dietrich,
Ernest S. Frerichs, Calvin Goldscheider, David Hirsch, Alan Zuckerman

**Project Editors (Projects)**

Lenn Evan Goodman, University of Hawaii (Studies in Medieval Judaism)
David Hayes, Coe College (Studia Philonica)

Number 254
THE TALMUD OF BABYLONIA
An American Translation
XXX.B: Tractate Ḥullin
Chapters 3-6

Translated by
Tzvee Zahavy

# THE TALMUD OF BABYLONIA
## An American Translation
## Volume XXX.B: Tractate Ḥullin
## Chapters 3-6

Translated by
Tzvee Zahavy

Scholars Press
Atlanta, Georgia

THE TALMUD OF BABYLONIA
An American Translation
XXX.B: Tractate Hullin
Chapters 3-6

© 1993
Brown University

**Library of Congress Cataloging-in-Publication Data**
(Revised for volume B)

Tractate Hullin.

(The Talmud of Babylonia; 30.A-   ) (Brown Judaic studies; no. 253-   )
Includes bibliographical references and indexes.
Contents: A. chapters 1-2 — B. chapters 3-6.
I. Zahavy, Tzvee.   II. Series: Talmud. English. 1984; 30.   III. Series: Brown Judaic studies; no. 253, 254.
BM499.5.E4   1984 vol. 30   296.1'250521s   92-18378
[BM506.H8]                  296.1'25
ISBN 1-55540-730-7 (cloth: v. A)
ISBN 1-55540-731-5 (cloth)

Printed in the United States of America
on acid-free paper

## Table of Contents

Preface .................................... ix

    1.   Introduction to Tractate Ḥullin .......... 1

    2.   Tractate Ḥullin Chapter Three .......... 19

    3.   Tractate Ḥullin Chapter Four ......... 155

    4.   Tractate Ḥullin Chapter Five .......... 213

    5.   Tractate Ḥullin Chapter Six ........... 245

Abbreviations .............................. 281

Transliterations ............................ 282

Index ...................................... 283

FOR MY FRIEND AND COLLEAGUE

ASSOCIATE DEAN
DR. DAVID GROSSMAN,
FOR HIS WIFE PHYLLIS AND SON SERGE

AND FOR HIS ASSOCIATES IN
CONTINUING EDUCATION AND EXTENSION
AT THE UNIVERSITY OF MINNESOTA

DR. STEPHANIE VAN D'ELDEN
ASSOCIATE DIRECTOR OF INDEPENDENT STUDY

JEFF ZUCKERMAN, EDITOR

DEBORAH HILLENGASS
DIRECTOR OF INDEPENDENT STUDY

WILLIAM VAN ESSENDELFT
CONTINUING EDUCATION SPECIALIST

AND
DEAN HAROLD MILLER
CONTINUING EDUCATION AND EXTENSION

# Preface

I first studied Tractate Hullin with Rav Joseph B. Soloveitchik in preparation for rabbinic ordination at the Rabbi Isaac Elchanan Theological Seminary of Yeshiva University some twenty years ago. That process naturally was an exercise in traditional learning according to the methods employed by Rav Soloveitchik. In conjunction with that analysis I also studied the pertinent laws from the Shulkhan Arukh for preparing meat. For centuries the last stage of preparation for rabbinic ordination has been the study of this tractate of the Babylonian Talmud and of the sixteenth century codification along with all the relevant commentaries. In conjunction with my rabbinic training I also visited a slaughter-house to observe the practice of the acts according to the precepts set forth in the texts.

It quickly will become clear to any reader of the texts of Tractate Hullin that it was not the purpose of those who first redacted this book to provide a code of laws to guide the practical life of the Jew in issues of what is kosher and what is *terefah*. The materials in Bavli Hullin mainly take the form of pure propositions relating to the text of the Mishnah, the Tosefta, other Tannaitic traditions, and to Scripture. Other later compilations, like the Shulkhan Arukh, engage in the application of these concepts of Bavli to the regulation of actual practice in the slaughter-house and in the kitchen.[1] One could say then that Bavli Hullin serves as the statement of the "algebra" of the conceptualization of the law of rabbinic rules for foods and that later documents apply the ideas in "engineering" the rules for application to a rabbinic culture.

I present the translation of this Tractate in three volumes:

*The Talmud of Babylonia: An American Translation. XXX.A: Tractate Hullin. Chapters 1-2,* Brown Judaic Studies. Scholars Press, Atlanta.

---

[1] See for example, S.I. Levin and E. A. Boyden, *The Kosher Code of the Orthodox Jew*, Minneapolis, 1940.

*The Talmud of Babylonia: An American Translation. XXX.B: Tractate Ḥullin. Chapters 3-6,* Brown Judaic Studies. Scholars Press, Atlanta.
*The Talmud of Babylonia: An American Translation. XXX.C: Tractate Ḥullin. Chapters 7-12,* Brown Judaic Studies. Scholars Press, Atlanta.

The theory of this translation follows that of the series as a whole. I adhere closely to the text so that the reader has a sense of the structure and balance of the original. Yet at the same time I convey the flow of the legal arguments and debates, the dramatic unfolding of events in stories, and the sensitivities to words and language in the exegetical texts. I aim to facilitate a smooth conversation between readers and the text so that, without consulting the original Hebrew and Aramaic version, they can appreciate the substantive meaning and recognize some major aspects of the style of the Talmudic text.

With this goal in mind, this English translation is molded in many ways by the complex literary style of the document itself. Some characteristics of the Talmud in particular required that I employ distinctive techniques in my translation to allow me to be literal in my rendering of the text, to avoid having to paraphrase throughout, and yet to maintain a high level of intelligibility for the English reader.

Several distinctive aspects of my translation contribute to making it more of a colloquy. The text is stylized and sometimes terse to an extreme in its style of expression. Accordingly, I interpolate a fair amount of explanatory language into my translation to make it more comprehensible. This additional explication helps me unpack the laconic linguistic style of the document.

By adding explanation *within* the translation I also expand upon the progression of ideas, clarify the arguments of the Talmud, define unfamiliar materials, and generally elucidate the meaning of the text. When adding my own language within the translation, to make it clear where the words of the Talmud end and where my explanations begin, I set off my additional interpolations with brackets, rather than allowing them to stand as indistinguishable parts of a paraphrased rendition of the text.

I follow certain additional conventions in my translation in order to make the nature of the compositions of the composite algebraic propositions of the text of the Talmud more visible and accessible to the reader. Each of those conventions serves an analytical scholarly purpose. The primary advance in this regard is my presentation of the text in paragraphs labelled by capital letter. I mark each larger editorial section with Roman numerals. These markings allow the reader to see the stages of reasoning and of redaction. It also permits the scholar to engage in a

# Preface

more efficient literary and redaction-critical analysis of the text by ready reference to its components. The original text has little if any punctuation or division to demarcate where one sentence or thought ends and another begins. Systematic study based on this more refined schematization in other tractates has already shown that Bavli is not a compiled stream of traditions, as it at first appears, but rather is a carefully crafted sequence of specific propositions.²

A large proportion of the Bavli's concern centers on earlier Tannaitic materials. In this translation I indicate the prior sources of our text, that is the direct citations of Mishnah and Tosefta, by using bold faced type. Careful analysis of numerous tractates has demonstrated that while those traditions dictate the external order and subject matter of interest in Bavli, the ultimate redactors set their own distinctive and coherent agenda for discussion.³ I put quotations from Scripture in quotation marks. Wherever possible I cite verbatim the standard translations of the text.⁴

Bavli makes use of two languages in its presentation. The text intermixes Hebrew, which I represent in normal type face, and Aramaic, which I present in italics.⁵ Studies of Bavli have now shown that the choice of language is by no means arbitrary. Hebrew is the language Bavli's editors use for citations, for normative thought or for rules. Aramaic serves as the language for the editorial and conceptual infrastructure of the document. It is the language most commonly used for argument, inquiry and criticism within the texts of Bavli.⁶

I based my translation on the texts of the standard printed editions and not on either a manuscript or critical edition. Nevertheless, I used and found helpful the critical editions, secondary works and commentaries that I list in the bibliography to the translation that appears

---

²J. Neusner, *The Bavli's One Voice: Types and Forms of Analytical Discourse and their Fixed Order of Appearance*, Atlanta, 1991, and also *The Rules of Composition of the Talmud of Babylonia. The Cogency of Bavli's Composite*, Atlanta, 1991.

³J. Neusner, *The Bavli and its Sources: The Question of Tradition in the Case of Tractate Sukkah*, Atlanta, 1987 and *Making the Classics in Judaism: Three Stages of Literary Formation*, Atlanta, 1990.

⁴J. Neusner, *The Mishnah*, New Haven, 1988, and J. Neusner, et al., *The Tosefta*, New York, 1977-1986, and the Revised Standard Version of the Hebrew Bible in *The Oxford Annotated Bible*.

⁵Because of the complexities of the rendition of the text into English this representation is sometimes approximate at best.

⁶J. Neusner, *Language as Taxonomy. The Rules for Using Hebrew and Aramaic in the Babylonian Talmud*, Atlanta, 1990.

at the end of the last volume of this translation of Bavli Hullin. Among the numerous manuscript variants and traditions discovered in my comparisons of the versions, I have found very few places in the tractate where a divergent reading changes the meaning of a passage. I included these few instances in my translated text, indicating the source of the variant.

The classical commentaries were most valuable for explaining the meaning and background of the legal materials in the text, for explicating the larger context of specific laws and discussions, and for providing rich cross references to other parallel or related units elsewhere in rabbinic literature. Throughout the translation I have used Rashi's commentary more frequently than any other secondary source to help explain the meaning of technical, elliptical, or complex discussions. An unattributed explanation in my translation usually rests on the insights of Rashi. Where I rely on the viewpoint of another commentator, who disagrees with or goes beyond Rashi in his interpretation, I so specify in the translation. Where I refer directly to previous translations I so indicate by noting the name of the translator, e.g., (Cashdan)[7] or (Goldschmidt).[8] Where I refer to the other volumes of this translation I so designate by citing 'Zahavy, *Hullin*,' with the volume and page number.

I added my own brief commentary to my translation of Bavli Hullin. At the end of each section of Talmud, before turning to the next Mishnah selection, I review and summarize the redactional flow of the material just covered and specify the relationship of the preceding Talmudic units of discourse to the concerns of the relevant Mishnah passage. This effort helps bring into focus more sharply the redactional agendum of the editors of the tractate.

I strove to convey the original form and meaning of the text through the translation, and I based the translation on the major classical commentaries, but the framers of the Talmud never conceived nor intended that their books be perused casually in translation. I emphasize that, to fully appreciate the linguistic forms and to comprehend the many nuances of meaning of this complex and elusive text, one must study it in its original along with the numerous creative and comprehensive standard commentaries.

---

[7] Eli Cashdan, *The Babylonian Talmud. Seder Kodashim. Hullin. Translated into English. With Notes, Glossary, and Indices*, London, 1948.

[8] Lazarus Goldschmidt, *Der Babylonische Talmud. Achter Band: Zebahim, Menahoth, Holin*. Haag, 1933.

# Preface

I thank the University of Minnesota for supporting this research in many ways. The Dworsky Center for Jewish Studies and The Dr. and Mrs. Sol Center Fund supported in part the research and publication of this book. My wife, Bernice, encouraged me throughout this project. My children, Yitzhak and Barak, inspired my work as I studied parts of this and other tractates with them every day. I thank also those special students at the University of Minnesota, who inspired me with their devotion and respect and thereby contributed in significant and special ways to this translation.

My former student, friend and colleague, Roger Brooks, Elie Wiesel Professor of Judaic Studies, Connecticut College, served as a critical reader of this volume. His comments saved me from inaccuracies and greatly enhanced the precision of this translation. I thank him for his kindness in taking the time and effort to so thoroughly study this tractate and review this book. I bear responsibility for any shortcomings which may remain in this translation.

I continue to recognize my great debt to my Talmud teachers at Yeshiva University's Rabbi Isaac Elchanan Theological Seminary. I had the honor of studying the Babylonian Talmud as an undergraduate with Rabbi Gershom Yankelewitz and Rabbi Aharon Lichtenstein and the privilege of receiving postgraduate instruction for four years in both the Talmud and Shulkhan Arukh from HaRav Joseph B. Soloveitchik.

Of course, I acknowledge the influence on this translation of the work of my teacher, Jacob Neusner, Graduate Research Professor of Humanities and Religious Studies at the University of South Florida. He has shown us all how to render the wisdom of our sages into our own language through his own lucid and systematic work in his translations of tractates of the Mishnah, the Tosefta, the Talmud of the Land of Israel, the Babylonian Talmud, the Midrash, and in his ongoing work on the documents of rabbinic literature. I am grateful for what he has given us to work with. Without the benefit of Neusner's paradigmatic work, my translation could not have succeeded in whatever small measure it has.

I dedicate this book to my friend Dr. David Grossman, to his wife Phyllis and son Serge. As associate dean of Continuing Education and Extension at the University of Minnesota, he and his valued colleagues created an atmosphere of professionalism and courtesy that has served as an important context for my teaching. For sixteen years they treated me and what I do with respect and with concern. I look forward to many years of continued collegiality and friendship with them.

Tzvee Zahavy<br>
November 23, 1992

# 1

# Introduction to Ḥullin

Ḥullin in the Mishnah deals with issues of meat and food preparation according to the rituals of the rabbis based on Scripture and independent oral traditions. Intuitively we would expect a more practical compilation of rules and rituals for such subjects that were part of the everyday life of the rabbinic Jew. Counter to this expectation, Ḥullin turns out to be one of the more abstract and theoretical tractates of the order. Chapter four in particular deals with the issue of applying the slaughter of the mother to the offspring in the process of birth. The discussions there and in many other instances throughout the tractate focus on the development of hypothetical speculation, not on the detailed specification of law. Accordingly we find numerous finely polished examples in the document of Talmudic logic and inquiry amid far fewer details of practical knowledge of animal anatomy and the techniques of slaughter and meat preparation. The study of this collection of texts would not have served on its own as a useful means of preparing for a profession in food services or supervision.

The tractate before us is by no means a single unitary essay on the subject of slaughter. In his study of Mishnah and Tosefta Ḥullin[1] Neusner describes the varied content of the tractate, analyzes the formal traits of each pericope, the redactional purpose of each larger unit, and the relations of the Tosefta passages to Mishnah. He also takes up the issue of the strata of the development of the Mishnaic law.[2] In the introduction to the former study he discusses the name of the tractate and the overall coherence of the collection:

> While Tosefta's title for the tractate, *Sheḥitat Ḥullin*, the proper slaughter of unconsecrated or secular, non-cultic animals, suggests that the principal subject is the

---

[1] *A History of the Mishnaic Law of Holy Things: Part Three. Ḥullin, Bekhorot. Translation and Explanation*, Leiden, 1979, pp. 12-134. I refer the reader to this work for more detailed critical exegeses of the M. and T. pericopae of this tractate.

[2] Cf. *A History of the Mishnaic Law of Holy Things. Part Six. The Mishnaic System of Sacrifice and Sanctuary*, Leiden, 1980, pp. 109-132.

issue of proper killing of animals, that is, *shehitah* (slaughter), Mishnah's on the surface is more accurate. For, having dealt in Zebahim and Menahot with laws of the food of the Lord's altar in Jerusalem, our Order now gives us a tractate on the parallel laws governing the preparation and use of meat for the table of the ordinary Israelite. Among these, the rules of slaughter are important but not quantitatively predominant. Only the first four chapters are devoted to rules of slaughter; some of these are not immediately and directly germane to that topic, narrowly construed. The next eight chapters present other food rules, in particular, the law against slaughtering the dam and its young on one day, the requirement to cover up the blood of a slaughtered beast, the taboo against the sciatic nerve and against cooking meat with milk, a chapter on food-uncleanness, with special reference to the issue of connection, two chapters on priestly emoluments, first, on what is owed to the priest in an animal which has been slaughtered, second, on the gift to the priest of the first fleece, and finally, ending where the sequence began, a law on letting the dam go from the nest when one takes the eggs. It follows, as I said, that much less than half of the tractate concerns the matter of slaughter. Even here, the real development and amplification of the law takes place after the completion of our tractate, as study of the Babylonian Talmud to Hullin makes amply clear. Still, since Zebahim also bears the title, *Shehitat Qodoshin*, the proper slaughter of consecrated animals, the matched opposite, *Shehitat Hullin*, is not without its symmetry and therefore sense. Indeed, considering that the order as a whole claims to concern itself with Holy Things, that is, with matters of the cult and priesthood, the inclusion of this one in the order, while obviously appropriate from many perspectives, is best justified when we can establish exactly that sort of symmetry as is contained in Tosefta's title. But the fact that the same laws apply to slaughtering animals for the altar as for the domestic table is probably still more compelling argument in favor of the inclusion of the tractate in our order. It is then the first half, rather than the second half, of the tractate which establishes its legitimacy in its present setting, for, as we shall see, some of the taboos of Chapters Five through Twelve (exclusive of Nine) apply at home but not in the Temple.[3]

The act of proper slaughter is a major concern of the first third of the tractate. It is useful to review how it has been defined in later codification of rabbinic law:

> The place of *shehitah* in a living animal is the throat, the whole of which is valid for this purpose. How so? In the gullet it extends from the beginning of that place which, when severed, contracts, and as far as the point where it becomes hairy and begins to be broken up like the stomach. That is the place of *shehitah* in the gullet.... What is the place for *shehitah* in the windpipe? It is from the thyroid cartilage downwards, as far as the top of the lobe of the lung when the animal stretches out its neck to pasture. That is the place for *shehitah* in the windpipe, and the part opposite that place on the outside is called the throat.... The slaughterer should perform *shehitah* in the middle of the throat.... What should be the extent of *shehitah*? It should extend over both organs, the windpipe and the gullet. The preferable extent of *shehitah* is when it severs both of

---

[3]*A History of the Mishnaic Law of Holy Things: Part Three. Hullin, Bekhorot. Translation and Explanation*, pp. 3-4.

them, in either animal or bird, and this should be the slaughterer's aim. If he severs only the major part of one of the organs in a bird or the major part of both organs in a domestic animal or wild beast, the *shehitah* is considered valid.[4]

The following is Neusner's outline of the tractate's divisions with his comments on the sequence and purpose of the redaction.[5]

I. *Rules of slaughtering unconsecrated animals for use at home or in the Temple.* 1:1-4:7

A. *General rules.* 1:1-4(+5-7)

| | |
|---|---|
| 1:1-2 | All slaughter, with anything do they slaughter, at any time do they slaughter, etc. |
| 1:3 | He who slaughters by cutting through the top cartilage ring. |
| 1:4 | The place on the throat at which the act of slaughter is to be located. |
| [1:5-7 | Formal construction: That which is valid in x is invalid in y, and that which is valid in y is invalid in x—six, then five. No relevance to Hullin.] |

B. *Specific regulations. Terefah[6] Rules.* 2:1-6

| | |
|---|---|
| 2:1 | If one cuts one organ in the case of fowl and two in the case of a beast, the act of slaughter is valid. And the greater part of one organ is equivalent to the whole of it. |
| 2:2 | He who slaughters two head of cattle at once—his act of slaughter is valid. |
| 2:3 | If one chopped off the head with a single stroke, it is invalid. Further rules. |
| 2:4 | If one cut the gullet and tore open the windpipe or vice versa, Yeshebab says, It is carrion. Aqiba says, It is *terefah*. <br> Yeshebab: Whatever is invalidated while being slaughtered is carrion. Whatever is properly slaughtered but invalidated for some other reason is *terefah*. |
| 2:5 | He who slaughters a beast from which blood does not exude—it is valid. |
| 2:6 | He who slaughters an animal which was at the point of death—vital signs (dispute). |

---

[4]Maimonides, *Shehitah* 1: 5, 7, 9, translated by L. I. Rabinowitz and Philip Grossman, *The Code of Maimonides. Book Five. The Book of Holiness*, New Haven, 1965, pp. 260-1, cited by Neusner, p. 5.

[5]Pp. 5-9. I have added the verses from Scripture where appropriate.

[6]Neusner explains (p. 4), "A repeated and untranslatable word requires brief attention, *terefah*. Ex. 22:31 uses the word to refer to a beast which is clawed by a wild animal: *You shall be men consecrated to me; therefore you shall not eat any flesh that is torn by beasts in the field; you shall cast it to the dogs.* Now the category of *carrion* already is in hand, that is, a beast which dies without being properly slaughtered. It follows that Ex. 22:31 will be understood to refer to a beast which has not yet died, but which cannot survive. This then produces the notion that beasts which bear some imperfection capable of causing death cannot be eaten by Israelites. Both beasts which die on their own, *carrion*, and those which are going to die because of wounds or imperfections, *terefah*, are prohibited."

## C. Slaughter and illicit sacrifice. 2:7-10

2:7 He who slaughters a gentile's beast in behalf of a gentile—his act of slaughter is valid. Eliezer declares it invalid. (Reprise of M. Zeb. 4:6.)

2:8 He who slaughters for the sake of mountains, valleys, seas, rivers, deserts—his act of slaughter is invalid.

2:9 They do not perform an act of slaughter in such a way that the blood falls into the sea or a river (lest it appear to be an offering).

2:10 He who slaughters an unconsecrated beast outside of the Temple for the sake of a burnt-offering or some other offering which is subject to a vow or given as a freewill offering—it is invalid. Simeon declares valid (reprise of M. Men. 12:3).

## D. Terefah and valid carcasses. 3:1-7

3:1 These are the *terefah*-carcasses among cattle (+15 items).
3:2 And these are the valid carcasses among cattle (+10 items).
3:3 These are the *terefah*-carcasses among fowl.
3:4 And these are valid carcasses among fowl.
3:5 Six sorts of beasts which are valid.
3:6 The tokens by which we know whether animals are fit, of cattle and beasts, have been stated by the Torah, and those of fowl have not been so stated.
3:7 And in locusts.

## E. The effect of valid slaughter on the parts of a beast's body, e.g., on the foetus. 4:1-7

4:1 A beast in hard labor, the offspring of which put forth its hoof and withdrew it, and the beast was properly slaughtered—the offspring is deemed properly slaughtered when the beast is and so may be eaten.
4:2 Continuation of the foregoing, with reference to the rule of the first-born.
4:3 Continuation of the foregoing.
4:4 A beast in hard labor, and the young put forth its hoof, which one cut off, and afterward one slaughtered the beast—the hoof is unclean as carrion but the meat of the offspring in the womb is clean.
4:5 An eight- or nine-month-old foetus found in a beast which has been slaughtered.
4:6 A beast, the hind-legs of which are cut off below the knee is valid. Above, is invalid.
4:7 He who slaughters the beast and found in it an afterbirth—it may be eaten. But it is subject neither to uncleanness as food nor to uncleanness as carrion.

The first of the tractate's two divisions begins where it should, and the first and second units belong exactly where they are. We begin (A) with some important general rules on proper slaughter of animals for domestic use, then proceed to specific regulations on the act of cutting the throat (B). From C onward, it is possible to adduce an argument in favor of the present sequence of ideas. The actual cutting of the throat, B, is suitably carried forward with the issue of the proper motivation in doing so (C), since it is at the moment of the cutting of the throat of the animal ("slaughter") that the issue of intention, hence sacrifice for idolatry, is effective. The next unit, D, reverts to B, supplying lists of defects which invalidate the animal and impose upon it the status of *terefah*, then completing the matter with other complementary lists. The concluding unit, E, brings the subject to a close with

# Introduction

attention to how proper slaughter of an animal renders suitable for Israelite consumption all parts of the animal's body, e.g., even the foetus of a pregnant dam. In all, therefore, the sequence of ideas is logical and orderly.

II. *Other rules on the preparation of food, principally for use at home.* 5:1-12:5

A. *It and its young* ["And whether the mother is a cow or a ewe, you shall not kill both her and her young in one day" (Lev. 22:28)]. 5:1-5

5:1-2   The prohibition against slaughtering on the same day *it and its young* (Lev. 22:28) applies in the Land and abroad, before and after 70, to unconsecrated and consecrated beasts. + 12 exemplifications.
5:3     He who slaughters a beast and it turns out to be *terefah*—Simeon declares exempt from the rule of *It and its young*, since this is not a valid act of slaughter. Sages declare liable.
5:4     Continuation of above.
5:5     Definition of the day referred to in Lev. 22:28.

B. *The requirement to cover up the blood* ["Any man also of the people of Israel, or of the strangers that sojourn among them, who takes in hunting any beast or bird that may be eaten shall pour out its blood and cover it with dust. For the life of every creature is the blood of it; therefore I have said to the people of Israel, You shall not eat the blood of any creature, for the life of every creature is its blood; whoever eats it shall be cut off" (Lev. 17:13-14)]. 6:1-7

6:1     The requirement to cover up the blood applies in the Land and abroad, before and after 70, to unconsecrated but not to consecrated beasts.
6:2     He who slaughters a wild beast or bird and it turns out to be *terefah*—Meir declares liable to covering up the blood (*vs.* Simeon, M. 5:3), and sages declare exempt.
6:3     A deaf-mute, imbecile, and minor who slaughtered under supervision (=M. 1:1)—are liable to cover up the blood (continuation of foregoing).
6:4     If one slaughtered a hundred animals in one place, a single covering of the blood serves for all of them.
6:5     Blood which was mixed with water, if it looks like blood, must be covered up.
6:6     Blood which splashes and which is on the knife must be covered up.
6:7     With what substances do they cover up blood, and with what do they not cover up blood?

C. *The prohibition of the sciatic nerve* ["Therefore to this day the Israelites do not eat the sinew of the thigh, because he touched the hollow of Jacob's thigh on the sinew of the hip" (Gen. 32:32)]. 7:1-6

7:1     The prohibition of the sciatic nerve applies in the Land and abroad, before and after 70, to unconsecrated animals and to consecrated ones.
7:2     A man sends a gentile a hip (thigh) in which the sciatic nerve is located, because its presence is known. How much of the nerve must be removed?
7:3     He who eats an olive's bulk of the sciatic nerve incurs forty stripes.

| | |
|---|---|
| 7:4-5 | A thigh with which the sciatic nerve is cooked, if it imparts a flavor, is prohibited. Construction of three rules in regard to cooking. |
| 7:6 | The prohibition applies to a clean beast, not to an unclean one. |

D. *Milk and meat* ["The first of the first fruits of your ground you shall bring to the house of the Lord your God. You shall not boil a kid in its mother's milk" (Exod. 23:19, 34:26), "You shall not eat anything that dies of itself; you may give it to the alien who is within your towns, that he may eat it, or you may sell it to a foreigner; for you are a people holy to the Lord your God. You shall not boil a kid in its mother's milk" (Deut. 14:21)]. 8:1-6

| | |
|---|---|
| 8:1 | Every kind of flesh is it prohibited to cook in milk, except for that of fish and locusts. |
| 8:2 | One may tie up meat and cheese in a single cloth, so long as they do not touch one another. |
| 8:3 | A drop of milk which fell on a piece of meat, if it imparts flavor—it is prohibited. |
| 8:4 | The meat of clean cattle with the milk of clean cattle may not be cooked. That of unclean cattle and clean cattle may be cooked together. Aqiba: A wild beast and fowl are not subjected to the prohibition. Yosé the Galilean: Fowl are not subjected to the prohibition. |
| 8:5 | Milk in the stomach of a beast slaughtered by a gentile and that in the stomach of carrion, lo this is prohibited. Milk curdled in the skin of the stomach of a validly slaughtered beast, if sufficient to impart a flavor, lo this is prohibited. |
| 8:6 | Comparison of prohibitions of fat and blood. (This last item is relevant only in that M. 8:4 says of milk what M. 8:6 F says of fat.) |

E. *Connection.* 9:1-8

| | |
|---|---|
| 9:1 | The hide, grease, sediment, flayed-off flesh, bones, sinews, horns, hooves are included together to make up the volume for imparting uncleanness as food, but not to make up the volume to impart uncleanness as carrion. |
| 9:2 | The skin is deemed one with the flesh, so is susceptible to uncleanness even after flaying, in the case of man, domestic pig, etc. |
| 9:3 | The skin counts as connected to the carcass in what concerns uncleanness—definitions. |
| 9:4 | If there remained an olive's bulk of meat on the hide, and a man touched a shred that jutted forth. |
| 9:5 | Touching the marrow bone of a corpse, whether stopped up or hollowed out, makes a man unclean. If it is a carcass of a creeping thing, if stopped up, he is clean, but if hollowed out, he is unclean. |
| 9:6 | Egg of a creeping thing in which the young is fashioned is clean. |
| 9:7 | Hanging flesh or parts of the body are susceptible as food while they continue in place. |
| 9:8 | Hanging flesh or part of the body of man is clean. |

F. *The shoulder, two cheeks, and maw, which are given to the priest* ["And this shall be the priests' due from the people, from those offering a sacrifice, whether it be ox or sheep: they shall give to the priest the shoulder and the two cheeks and the stomach" (Deut. 18:3)]. 10:1-4

# Introduction

10:1      The shoulder, two cheeks, and maw apply in the Land and abroad, before and after 70, to unconsecrated animals but not to Holy Things.

10:2      Any animals which are blemished before dedication and are redeemed are subject to the law of the firstling and priests' dues.

10:3      If a firstling was confused among a hundred other beasts and a hundred and one people slaughtered them all, all are exempt from priests' dues.

10:4      If a proselyte had a cow and it was slaughtered before he converted, he is exempt from the priests' dues. Afterward, he is liable.

G. *First fleece goes to the priest* ["The first fruits of your grain, of your wine and of your oil, and the first of the fleece of your sheep, you shall give him" (Deut. 18:4)]. 11:1-2

11:1      The law of the first of the fleece applies in the Land and abroad, before and after 70, for unconsecrated animals but not for animal-offerings.

11:2      How many sheep must one own to be liable to the gift of the first of the fleece?

H. *The law of letting the dam go from the nest when taking the young* ["If you chance to come upon a bird's nest, in any tree or on the ground, with young ones or eggs and the mother sitting upon the young or upon the eggs, you shall not take the mother with the young, you shall let the mother go, but the young you may take to yourself; that it may go well with you, and that you may live long" (Deut. 22:6-7)]. 12:1-5

12:1      The law of letting the dam go applies in the Land and abroad, before and after 70, to unconsecrated birds but not to bird-offerings.

12:2      The law does not apply to an unclean bird.

12:3      If a dam hovered over the nest and the wings touched the nest, the man must let her go, but if they do not touch the nest, he is not bound to do so, since she is not regarded as sitting on the young.

12:4      If a man took the dam and the young, Judah says, He is smitten but then may keep the dam. Sages say, He must let the dam go but is not smitten.

12:5      A man may not take the dam and her young even for the sake of cleansing the leper.

In the second division of the tractate it is difficult to account for the sequence of topics, although all together they do have their logical place in that second division. Obviously there is a certain symmetry between A and H, but I cannot argue that the redactor deliberately placed one at the beginning, the other at the end. There is a further, obvious effort to follow a single thematic pattern at A, B, C, D, F, G, and H. None of the units, except for E, presents a rich repertoire of ideas. I certainly cannot explain why E is located where it is. Had it followed I.E, it would have been in no more logical a location, since its topic, the connection which subjects one part of a beast to the status of some other part of the beast or which makes of the diverse segments of a carcass a single volume of edible matter, exhibits no logical ties to anything in the opening division of the tractate.[7]

---

[7]Neusner further explains: "Indeed, in the entire Order, its basic problem—uncleanness and cleanness—arises only here. If I had my way, I would move it to Mishnah-tractate Tohorot, for example, after M. Tohorot Chapter Three. But it is where it is, and the earliest witnesses, Tosefta and Babli, know it

It is useful to cite here Neusner's introductions to the Mishnah, chapters three to six.

## Chapter three:[8]

The chapter is composed of a set of lists of *terefah* and valid, carcasses. The redactor has brought the lists into line with one another at M. 3:1-2, M. 3:3-4, and M. 3:7, which continues M. 3:4 and depends on it. The lists specify those traits which render a beast *terefah* (M. 3:1), as against those which do not (M. 3:2); the same for fowl (M. 3:3-4); and, as a brief and uninformative appendix (M. 3:7), the valid kinds of locusts and fish. M. 3:5, 6 are singletons.... The intent is to present six lists, even though, to do so, the tradent of M. 3:7 has had to pretend he has in hand a list which in fact he lacks. This Ushan chapter does not cite M. 2:4; its lists of *terefah*-animals and birds and valid ones are based on the capacity of the animals or birds to survive certain faults (M. 3:1 L). Surely assumed, however, is Yeshebab's principle, since none of our items pertains to faults in the act of slaughter but only to faults external to that act. It follows that we have an extensive amplification by Ushans of a principle assigned to a Yavnean.

## Chapter four:[9]

The principal interest of the chapter is in the rule that if a beast is properly slaughtered, whatever is contained within its body is deemed affected by the same act of slaughter and to require no additional act of slaughter (M. 4:5). The matter,

---

exactly here. I cannot explain why the redactor put it there. Raising the same question, Qahaty (to Hullin 9:1, Pinhas Qahaty, *Seder Qodoshim*, Jerusalem, 1976, p. 217) claims that Chapter Nine reverts to the issues of Chapter Four, the distinction between imparting uncleanness as food and as carrion, having been interrupted by the intervening sequence of Chapters Five through Eight. Each of those chapters is introduced because something in the preceding chapter has alluded to its topic, he says. Thus M. 4:5 refers to liability to the law of *It and its dam*, accounting for the inclusion of Chapter Five. Then, in that Chapter, we refer to an act of slaughter which is inappropriate, so we introduce the matter of covering up the blood, Chapter Six, which pertains specifically to the law of slaughter which is inappropriate. Since covering of the blood applies to wild beasts but not to fowl, we turn to the prohibition of the sciatic nerve, Chapter Seven. Since M. 7:4 alludes to the mixture of prohibited with permitted food, we turn to Chapter Eight, which addresses itself to mixtures of meat and milk. All these matters having been spelled out, Qahaty says, we return at Chapter Nine to the continuation of Chapter Four. But Qahaty does not tell us why Chapters Ten, Eleven, and Twelve belong after, and not before Chapter Nine; considerations important in his argument in behalf of the present location of Chapters Five through Eight surely occur in Chapters Ten through Twelve. While it is certainly attractive to imagine that we have the best of all possible Mishnahs, I find Qahaty's argument not entirely compelling, even though I can propose nothing better."

[8]*A History of the Mishnaic Law of Holy Things: Part Three. Hullin, Bekhorot. Translation and Explanation*, p. 46.

[9]*Op. cit.*, pp. 58-59.

# Introduction

however, is taken for granted, and secondary and tertiary problems of its application come under discussion. The opening unit consists of M. 4:1-3, in which the stated theme is joined to others not relevant to our tractate's interests but highly pertinent to the issue of the status of the offspring in the process of parturition. The three inaugural units of the set, at M. 4:1 A, M. 4:2 A, and M. 4:3 A, begin, X-*which*, followed by apocopation, and the units secondary to them rely upon implied-*ifs*. The first deals with a beast in hard labor. The offspring puts forth its hoof and draws it back. If the dam is then properly slaughtered, we deem the hoof to be part of the dam, even though it has been put forth for a moment. If, on the other hand, the head is put forth, even though later withdrawn, it is deemed to have been born, therefore not affected by the slaughtering of the mother. One may cut off a piece of the offspring in the womb, and it may be eaten if the dam is properly slaughtered; but one may not, of course, cut off a piece of the body of the dam itself. M. 4:2 deals with a beast which, in hard labor, gives birth to its first-born. If one chops off pieces of the offspring, they are not deemed to be sanctified as part of a first-born and may be thrown to the dogs. But if the greater part of the offspring (= M. 4:1's head) comes forth, it is to be buried and the beast is free of obligation to the law of the first-born. M. 4:3, finally, deals with a beast whose offspring dies in the womb. The offspring is deemed an integral part of the body of the beast, therefore does not impart corpse-uncleanness to the shepherd who touches it. The unit closes with consideration of the same problem in the case of a woman whose offspring dies in the womb.

The supposition of the foregoing — that the offspring is part of the dam, therefore is subject to the act of slaughtering of the dam itself — is subject to discussion at M. 4:4. If a beast is in hard labor, and the offspring puts forth a hoof, which is cut off, the remaining flesh of the offspring, in the womb, is deemed subject to the act of slaughter of the dam. If the beast is slaughtered, the flesh of the offspring in the womb is clean. If one slaughtered the dam, after the offspring has put forth its hoof and did not withdraw it, and one then cut off the protruding hoof, Meir holds that the flesh of the offspring in the womb is unclean for having had contact with carrion, namely, the protruding hoof (compare Yosé, M. Kel. 27:9-10). Sages hold that it is clean. A brief debate follows. At that point the supposition of both parties, that slaughtering a *terefah*-beast renders it clean (Aqiba, T. 2:9), is provided with an excellent set of arguments. M. 4:5 carries forward the interest of M. 4:4 in the status of the offspring in the womb of the dam, and M. 4:7 completes the matter, with attention to the status of the afterbirth. At this point the established principles of M. 4:1, 2, 4, and 5 are brought to bear on the matter.

The inclusion of M. 4:6, which deals with a beast the legs of which are cut off, if explicable along these same lines, that is, as an exercise in the application of the established principles. On the surface, the pericope belongs in a chapter on the matter of *terefah*, and, indeed, T. alludes to it in its exposition of Chapter Three. But the redactor's reasons are entirely clear and beyond reproach. Accordingly, the chapter as a whole consists of two primary units, M. 4:1-3, and M. 4:4-5, and two secondary ones, M. 4:6, and... M. 4:7, attached for clearly discernible reasons.

## Chapter five:[10]

This brief chapter deals with the prohibition against slaughtering the dam and its offspring on the same day (Lev. 22:28). There is little to be said about the rule, so the

---

[10]*Op. cit.*, p. 71.

chapter commences with a huge formal construction, M. 5:1-2, introducing variations on the rule, deriving from the status of the dam and the offspring, on the one side, and the location of slaughter, on the other. If they are unconsecrated and are slaughtered outside of the Temple, then one who slaughters both on one day effects a valid act of slaughter but is liable to forty stripes because of slaughtering the offspring on the same day as the mother. If he slaughters Holy Things inside, the first animal is validly slaughtered; the second is not because it is subject to the stated prohibition and cannot be offered. M. 5:1-2 develop twelve variations on the intersecting rules just now stated. Obviously, the principal interest is in the formal traits of the consequent pericope.

M. 5:3 A-I raise the interesting question of whether an improper act of slaughter is subject to the stated prohibition. Simeon holds that it is not, and sages, whose view is expressed, T. shows, at M. 5:1-2, maintain that it is. T. further makes clear that the authority of M. 5:1-2 is Meir. In any event, if there is no act of slaughter at all, the prohibition is not invoked. The other three issues of the pericope, extending through M. 5:4, concern (1) who takes precedence in a case where one man has the dam, the other the offspring; (2) the possibility of slaughtering more than a single offspring and the consequent punishment; and (3) the times at which one must inform the purchaser that there is a possibility that the mother and offspring will be slaughtered on the same day. M. 5:5 defines the *day* on which the two are not to be slaughtered. In all... the topic does not provide a rich intellectual repertoire.

## Chapter six:[11]

In the model of the foregoing chapter the present one deals with the requirement to cover the blood with dirt after the act of slaughter has been effected (Lev. 17:13). The requirement to do so applies to a bird and a wild beast, not to domesticated cattle. The principal part of the chapter M. 6:1-2 unfolds along the lines of M. 5:1, 3; omitting M. 5:1-2's extensive exercise in the variations consequent upon slaughtering cattle in the Temple and outside. The remainder deals with conceptions distinctive to the chapter's theme, M. 6:4, 6, 7. M. 6:3 is secondary to M.1:1, which is applied to M. 6:2, and M. 6:5 is familiar from M. Zeb. 8:6. These chapters — Five through Seven, Ten through Twelve — are essentially secondary and artificial constructions, intended to make a tractate out of disparate materials.

As expected, the elucidation of Mishnah is the main concern of the Talmud's agendum in these four chapters.

## Outline of Bavli Hullin chapters three through six:
M. 3:1

Chapter three is a large-scale composite that resembles a code of rules rather than an extended discourse on principles. It bears more characteristics of a list of laws than an extended essay. Few of the topics in the present text are discussed or cross-referenced elsewhere in the Talmud. And furthermore the rules of this chapter can have profound implications in the actual regulation by the rabbis of meat consumption

---

[11]*Op. cit.*, p. 79.

Introduction

in their communities. For these reasons the chapter is considered to be one of the most difficult in the Talmud.

I.1 Begins by seeking a basis in the Torah for Mishnah's definition of *terefah*. It goes on to discuss the number of categories of *terefah*-animals.

II.1-3 Continue the above inquiry with specific questions regarding the categories of *terefah*-animals. The next few sections closely adhere to the agenda of Mishnah and mainly clarify its meaning.

III.1-2 Give rules about a pierced gullet.

IV.1 States rules for a thorn in the gullet.

V.1-2 Provide rules for the pharynx and discussion of their application.

V.3 Delineates the extent of the gullet as a place for the incision of slaughtering.

V.4 Gives the rule for slaughter in a detached pharynx.

VI.1 Relates to Mishnah's rule for the torn windpipe. This leads into a second-level discussion of the responsibilities and consequences for sages who rule on the status of an animal.

VII.1 Investigates the operative principle of combining holes together to constitute a sign of a *terefah*-animal.

VII.2 Clarifies the rule regarding a slit in the windpipe.

VII.3 Identifies the appropriate area of the neck for the incision of slaughter.

VIII.1 Discusses Mishnah's rule regarding defects caused by piercing the membranes of the brain. This is followed by secondary materials relating to the brain.

IX.1-2 Again adhering to Mishnah's operative concerns, the unit takes up Mishnah's rule regarding defects caused by piercing the heart. A rule for the aorta follows.

X.1 Analyzes Mishnah's rule regarding defects of the spinal cord.

X.2 Gives other rules for spinal liquids.

X.3-4 Discuss where the spinal cord ends.

XI.1-3 Investigate Mishnah's rule for a defect of the liver. More rules for the liver follow.

XII.1-5 Clarify Mishnah's rule for a defect of the lung. Secondary materials about the lung follow that.

XIII.1-5 Specify procedures for inspecting the lung. The Talmud then turns to derivative rules for judging the status of ulcerations of the lung.

XIV.1-2 Give rules relating to a needle in the lung.

XV.1-3 Append rules relating to defects of the lung.

XVI.1 Takes up Mishnah's concern with a defect in the bronchial tubes.

XVII.1 Addresses Mishnah's rule regarding a defect in the belly.

XVIII. Gives rules for fats and forbidden liquids.

XIX.1 Investigates Mishnah's rule for a defect in the intestine. The text then adds a secondary rule for mourning.

XX.1-2 Provide us with principles and rules for comparing operative defects to one another.

XX.3 Deals with the rule for a defect in the rectum.

XXI.1 Exposits Mishnah's rule for a defect in the rumen.
XXII.1-2 Clarify Judah's rule in Mishnah. Rules follow for judging the size of a defect that has operative implications.
XXIII.1 Takes up Mishnah's rule for a defect in the reticulum. The text cites Tosefta and then a precedent to clarify Mishnah.
XXIV. Examines Mishnah's rule for a defect where an animal fell. The Talmud follows this with related second-level rules regarding hidden injuries due to the trauma of a fall, a blow, or to stress (1-3). Then it raises similar issues for birds (4-5).
XXV.1-3 The pattern of the text continues the sustained and predictable program of defining and amplifying the operative concerns stated in Mishnah. It takes up Mishnah's rule for a defect due to broken ribs. More rules for ribs follow.
XXVI Clarifies Mishnah's rule for a defect due to mauling. Various derivative rules on the subject follow this.
XXVII Provides us with precedents and additional rules with regard to mauling.
XXVIII Comments on Mishnah's concluding principle. The units throughout present no surprises as they persistently and directly amplify the rules of Mishnah.

M. 3:2

These units adhere predictably closely to Mishnah's operative agenda.

I.1 Explores the implications of Mishnah's general statement in comparison with that of M. 3:1.
I.2 Comments on a lemma cited in I.1.
II.1 Discusses Mishnah's measure of size.
II.2 Takes up general issues regarding measures of size. The unit cites a complementary Tannaite rule from Mishnah Kelim for its illustrations.
III.1 Comments on a rule of Mishnah in light of the premises of M. 4:1.
IV.1 Directly elucidates Mishnah's rule regarding kidneys.
IV.2 Provides a discussion regarding the comparison of defects of one organ with those of another, secondary to the Mishnah.
V-VI Provide brief glosses to clarify Mishnah's rules.
VII.1 Glosses Mishnah's rule and adds a further discussion regarding the inspection of the lung.
VIII.1 Expands on Mishnah's rule by citing related materials including the Tosefta-passage relevant to the text.
VIII.2 Examines a secondary issue raised in the preceding discussion — how much and which hide counts? The unit cites a related Tosefta-passage from Zebahim and examines its implications.

M. 3:3

These units engage in close Mishnah-criticism and rarely venture far from the Mishnah's narrowly stated operative concerns.

I.1 States the procedure for inspecting for defects specified in Mishnah and correlates this with related views.

# Introduction

| | |
|---|---|
| I.2 | Gives rulings related to the preceding and correlates this with the relevant Tosefta-passage. |
| I.3-5 | Provide further inspection procedures and precedents. |
| II.1-2 | Delineates the minimum needed for Mishnah's next ruling. Secondary rules related to Mishnah's concern follow. |
| III.1 | Comments on Mishnah's rule. |

**M. 3:4**

The materials adhere closely to Mishnah's operative considerations and issues.

| | |
|---|---|
| I.1 | Supplies a precedent that relates to Mishnah's primary concern. It goes on to a secondary discussion of that tradition in comparison with Mishnah and then to a related rule. |
| II.1 | Comments on Mishnah's rule and cites Scripture related to it. B suggests an alternative application of the verse. |
| II.2 | Provides a colorful proof that a defect listed by Mishnah need not be lethal. |
| III.1-2 | Give precedents and rulings that relate to Mishnah's next rule and to defects in fowl in general. |
| IV.1 | Provides a precedent to illustrate Mishnah's rule. It then goes off on a tangential discussion. |
| V.1 | States some general principles of signs of *terefah*-defects. G-V takes up the status of the by-products, eggs of a *terefah*-bird. It cites independent Mishnah-sources and invokes in the discussion the principle of a product of two antecedent causes. |
| VI.1 | Cites secondary rules and a story derivative of the preceding. |
| VII.1 | Introduces an unrelated rule based on an independent Mishnah-source. |
| VIII.1 | Cites a precedent that has general relevance to Mishnah's rule in E-4. |
| IX.1 | Returns to cite another Mishnah-source that complements our Mishnah and then briefly discusses its relevance. |

**M. 3:5**

| | |
|---|---|
| I.1 | Invokes a rule of Samuel and the text of Tosefta to elucidate to Mishnah. The text continues with related rules and precedents. |

**M. 3:6-7**

These units introduce Tosefta text in the criticism of Mishnah 3:6-7. They also provide several secondary digressions and intricate and technical discussions of the biblical sources.

| | |
|---|---|
| I.1 | Cites the appropriate verse and a relevant Tosefta-rule and discusses the tokens of clean and unclean animal species. |
| II.1 | Invokes Tosefta's rule to further clarify Mishnah and examines a related rule regarding fats of a wild beast. |
| II.2 | Digresses from the topic with several stories. |
| III.1-3 | Supply further digressions unrelated to Mishnah. |
| IV.1 | First returns to comment on a term in the verse that lists the categories of clean species. Then it digresses. |
| V.1-3 | Expand upon Mishnah's generalization on tokens of clean fowl. |

| | |
|---|---|
| V.4-5 | Go on to a secondary issue concerning the identification of birds valid for a sacrifice. |
| V.6-8 | Give a catalogue of varieties of birds and their respective rules and related traditions. |
| V.9-10 | Provides extended discussion of the number of categories of the unclean birds. |
| V.11 | Concludes with secondary matters on clean birds. |
| V.12 | Now that the primary considerations have been exposed the unit introduces the new issue of tokens for clean eggs. It gives a variant of Tosefta's text on the subject and a second Tosefta-text. |
| V.13-15 | Provide additional materials regarding the rules for eggs. |
| VI.1 | Reverts to Mishnah's rules relating to birds and cites the relevant Tosefta-texts. |
| VII.1-2 | Directly comments on locusts, the next issue in Mishnah, cites Tosefta, and comments and expounds on the verse regarding categories of locusts. |
| VIII.1 | Cites material directly relevant to Mishnah's rule regarding tokens for clean fish. |
| VIII.2 | Comments and expounds upon at length the verses regarding clean fish. |
| VIII.3-5 | State several of the rules for worms and the like. The materials continue the established program closely investigating the Mishnah-text with few digressions or deviations from the line of inquiry. |

M. 4:1

| | |
|---|---|
| I.1 | Analyzes the reasoning of the rules of Mishnah. |
| I.2 | Extends the inquiry and aligns the rules of Mishnah with a Tosefta-text and additional Tannaite and Amoraic materials. |
| I.3-5 | Compare the premises of our Mishnah paragraph with intersecting premises of different rules. |
| I.6 | Translates the process of Mishnah-criticism into a quest for a statement of a legal premise. |
| I.7 | Extends and explores Mishnah's premises and principles by proposing a series of theoretical cases. |
| II.1 | Seeks the scriptural basis for the rule of Mishnah and then aligns the rules with those of other Tannaite authorities. |

M. 4:2

| | |
|---|---|
| I.1 | Contrasts the premise of our Mishnah paragraph with parallel concerns of different rules, working through the same problem in different ways. |
| I.2 | Clarifies and spells out the implications of the rule of Mishnah. |
| I.3 | Poses a series of questions probing the premises and principles of Mishnah. |

M. 4:3 A-E

| | |
|---|---|
| I.1 | Explores the scriptural and logical bases of the Mishnah. |
| II.1 | Moves to a second-level issue out of the foregoing. |

## M. 4:3 F-G

I.1 Identifies the principle behind the rule of Mishnah, seeks its scriptural basis, enters into a sustained inquiry of its premises and extends the discussion to related principles and their logical bases.
I.2 Enters into a second level of the issue deriving from the preceding.

## M. 4:4

I.1 Analyzes the reasoning of Mishnah's authorities and invokes Tannaite complements in establishing the premises.
II.1 Gives a principle in support of one view of Mishnah.
III.1 Continues the exposition of the Mishnah-paragraph on its own terms.
IV.1 Extends the dispute of Mishnah to another related issue and works out the implications.
IV.2 Continues the foregoing, extending it to a second-level issue.
IV.3 Provides further inquiry into the theme.
V.1 Returns to the subject of Mishnah and explores its assumptions.
V.2 Concludes with a secondary matter.

## M. 4:5

I-II Explore various extensions of the rules of Mishnah.
III-IV Inquire into intersecting rules, based on the principles of the rule of Mishnah, cite complementary Tannaite rules and work through the problem in different ways.
V.1 Continues the inquiry into the premises of Mishnah.
VI.1 Reverts to the text and extends the rule of Mishnah.
VI.2 Further clarifies the position of Simeon b. Shezuri.

## M. 4:6

I.1 Begins with an exercise in Mishnah-criticism that clarifies the correct reading and meaning before us.
II.1 Further clarifies Mishnah's terms and rules.
II.2-3 Extend the rule of Mishnah and define it.
III.1 Analyzes a dispute based on the rule of Mishnah.
IV.1 Cites a Tannaite complement to M. and clarifies its meaning.
IV.2 Adds cases related to the foregoing and examines their premises.

## M. 4:7

I.1 Provides scriptural basis for the rules of Mishnah.
II-VI Clarify the meaning and underlying principles of Mishnah.

## M. 5:1-2

I.1 Engages in a detailed analysis of the scriptural basis for the rule of Mishnah.
I.2 Cites an intersecting secondary rule regarding the legal ramifications of the genetic relation of the sire to the offspring.
I.3-4 Move to a tertiary level of discourse.
I.5 Returns to the primary thematic level citing a relevant Tosefta-text. In this long and tight composition, the framers make reference to the secondary premises [e.g., at F] and work through all the alternatives.

I.6 Cites a brief secondary expansion on the subject of the *koy*-animal.
I.7 Discusses a tertiary concern.
II.1 Engages in the familiar process of clarifying the authorship of Mishnah.
II.2 Presents an ostensible Tannaite contradiction to the rule of Mishnah.
II.3 Picks up on a principle evoked in II.1 and seeks to align the Tannaite premises.

M. 5:3 A-I
I.1 Analyzes the premises of the rule of Mishnah.
II.1-2 Provide an exercise in Mishnah-criticism. The units cite relevant Tannaite sources and criticize the working of the Mishnah-paragraph.

M. 5:3 J-L
I.1 Identifies Mishnah's operative principle.

M. 5:3 M-Q
I.1 Explores the premises of the scriptural and logical bases of Mishnah's rules.
II.1 Identifies the operative principle of the view of Sumkhos in Mishnah and explores its application to secondary cases.
II.2 Cites a related rule from a Tosefta-text and seeks to align its views with those of our Mishnah.
II.3 Continues this inquiry.

M. 5:3 R-V, M. 5:4
I.1 Extends the rule of Mishnah.
II.1 Derives a minor point from a criticism of the Mishnah-paragraph.
III.1 Makes a brief inquiry into the premises of Mishnah.

M. 5:5
I.1 Clarifies the premise of the Mishnah.

M. 6:1
I.1 Identifies the premise and logic of the rule of Mishnah in a sustained inquiry.
II.1 Explores a second level of issues.
III.1-4 Add related insight on the value of moderation. The unit concludes citing the relevant Tosefta-text and exploring its premises.

M. 6:2
I.1 Aligns various views of Mishnah and sets forth a sustained inquiry into the scriptural and logical bases for the rule.
I.2 Takes up the premises of the preceding and explores them independent of the criticism of our Mishnah-text.
II.1 Has no bearing on the elucidation of the Mishnah until F relates the inquiry to I.1 A.

M. 6:3
I.1 Identifies the nature and premises of the dispute of Mishnah.
II.1 Turns to the second-level issue of what is the definitive rule that derives from the Mishnah?

*Introduction*

M. 6:4 A-D
I.1     Establishes a scriptural basis for the rule of Mishnah.
II.1    Examines a second-level issue — regulations for reciting blessings over acts of slaughter and covering the blood.

M. 6:4 E-G
I.1     Sets forth a scriptural basis for the rules of Mishnah and several further expositions of the verse in A-C. D-K moves to a second-level issue derivative of the primary consideration of the nature of the commandment to cover the blood.
II.1    Contrasts the premise of the Mishnah-paragraph with an intersecting premise of a different rule.
III.1   Engages in a brief criticism of the premise of the rule of the Mishnah.

M. 6:5-6
I.1     Clarifies the premises of Mishnah.
I.2     Progresses to a second-level issue.
II.1    Reverts to the Mishnah-text and sets forth the scriptural and logical bases for the rules.

M. 6:7
I.1     Defines the terms of Mishnah.
II.1    Finds a scriptural basis for the rule of Mishnah.
II-III  Give further inquiries extending the rule of Mishnah.
IV.1    Adds secondary materials with no bearing on the elucidation of Mishnah but developed out of the general theme of the discussion.
V.1-2   Presents homilies on the same general theme.
VI.1    Concludes with a rule related to Mishnah in a brief appendix.

# 2

## Bavli Ḥullin Chapter Three

## Folios 42A-67B

### 3:1

- A. These are the *terefah* [carcasses] among cattle:
- B. (1) one in which the gullet is pierced,
   (2) and one in which the windpipe is torn.
- C. (3) [If] the membrane of the brain is pierced,
   (4) [if] the heart is pierced up to the cavity thereof;
   (5) [if] the backbone is broken so that the spinal cord is severed;
   (6) [if] the liver is removed [missing], so that nothing whatsoever remains of it.
- D. (7) The lung that is pierced or lacking [any part thereof].
- E. R. Simeon says, "[It is not *terefah*] until its bronchial tubes are pierced."
- F. (8) [If] the belly [abomasum] is pierced,
   (9) [if] the gallbladder is pierced,
   (10) [if] the intestines are pierced;
   (11) [if] the innermost belly [rumen] is pierced.
- G. (12) The greater part of the outer [exterior coating] which is pierced.
- H. R. Judah says, "In the case of a large [animal], a handbreadth, and in the case of a small one, its greater part."
   (13) The omasum or the second stomach [reticulum] which are pierced on the outer side [exterior].
- I. (14) [If] it fell from the roof,
   (15) [if] the greater number of its ribs are broken.

J.  And one which has been mauled by a wolf.
K.  R. Judah says, "One mauled by a wolf, in the case of a small beast, and one mauled by a lion in the case of a large beast, one mauled by a hawk, in the case of small fowl, and one mauled by a falcon, in the case of large fowl."
L.  This is the general principle: Any the like of which does not live is *terefah*.

I.1
A.  Said R. Simeon b. Laqish, "Where in the Torah is there an allusion to [the prohibition of eating an animal that is] *terefah*?" Where [is there an allusion? There is an explicit rule]: "You shall not eat any flesh that is torn by beasts in the field" (Exod. 22:31). [Hence this rule is explicit.]

B.  Rather [what did Simeon ask about]? Where in the Torah is there an allusion to [the principle that] a *terefah* is not considered to be alive? *As it was taught in the last text of the Mishnah,* [**This is the general principle:**] **Any the like of which does not live is *terefah*** [M. Hul. 3:1 L]. From there we may derive the principle that a *terefah* is not considered to be alive.

C.  *What is the source [in the Torah] of this assertion?* "[Say to the people of Israel], These are the living things which you may eat [among all the beasts that are on the earth]" (Lev. 11:2). What is living, you may eat. What is not living, you may not eat. *You may derive the principle* that a *terefah* is not considered to be alive.

D.  *And according to the authority who holds the view that a terefah is considered to be alive, what is the source of this assertion? We derive it from,* "These are the living things which you may eat." [This implies that] "*These* are the living things" you may eat. Other living things you may not eat. *You may derive the principle* that a *terefah* is considered to be alive.

E.  *And how does the other authority [who holds that it is not considered to be alive] interpret this [word in the verse],* "These"? *It is necessary [for the verse to use the word] in accord with that which the House of R. Ishmael taught.*

Bavli Ḥullin Chapter Three. Folios 42A-67B

F. For the House of R. Ishmael taught: "These are the living things which you may eat" — this teaches us that the Holy One blessed be He held up one of each of the species and showed them to Moses and said to him, "This you may eat. This you may not eat."

G. *And does the other authority not need to interpret the verse in accord with that which the House of R. Ishmael taught? Of course. Accordingly what then is the source of the assertion that* a terefah *is considered to be alive?*

H. *You may derive it from another teaching of the House of R. Ishmael. For the House of R. Ishmael taught, "Between the living creature that may be eaten and the living creature that may not be eaten"* (Lev. 11:47) — *these [varieties of creatures] are the eighteen categories of* terefot *that were addressed to Moses at Sinai.*

I. *And are there no more [categories]? But lo there are the four more [categories in the Mishnah based on Tannaitic authority alluded to by a mnemonic] and the seven [additional categories] that were taught [by Amoraic authorities (Rashi)].*

J. [42b] *This makes perfect sense according to the Tanna of our Mishnah. We can say that the Tanna taught [the rules in our Mishnah] and omitted [the other categories]. They are then subsumed in the* **general principle [M. Hul. 3:1 L].**

K. *But according to the Tanna of the House of R. Ishmael who said* there are eighteen categories of terefot and no more, but lo there is [another category referred to in the following]: **A beast, the [hind] legs of which are cut off [below the knee, is valid. If they are cut off] above the knee, it is invalid [M. 4:6 A-B].**

L. He [the Tanna] holds in accord with the view of R. Simeon b. Eleazar who said, **[If the bone broke and the juncture of the thigh-sinews is removed, it is invalid (M. Hul. 4:6). And R. Simeon b. Eleazar declares valid,] because it can be cauterized and recover [T. 3:6 B-C].**

M. But even if **it can be cauterized and recover**, according to whom are we stating matters? According to the Tanna of the House of

Ishmael. And the Tanna of the House of Ishmael reasons that a *terefah* is considered to be alive.

N. Rather he must reason in accord with the view of R. Simeon b. Eleazar who said that it is valid. [The justification that it can be cauterized and recover is not essential to the view that it is valid.]

O. *But lo there is* [another category of *terefah* — an animal that has an] abnormal deficiency of the spine. *As it was taught on Tannaite authority in the Mishnah,* **How much is deemed a deficiency in the spine [of a skeleton so that it does not render unclean objects in a tent]? The House of Shammai say, "Two vertebrae." And the House of Hillel say, "One vertebra"** [M. Ohal. 2:3].

P. And said R. Judah, said Samuel, "And the same [rule of deficiency in the spine applies] for [rendering the animal] a *terefah*."

Q. [Count this deficiency of the spine as another category. Accordingly in order to preserve eighteen as the number of categories] **The omasum or the second stomach [reticulum which are pierced on the outer side]** [M. 3:1 H] *that you reckoned as two [categories], you should reckon them as one [category]. You take one out and add one in.*

R. *But lo there is* [another category of *terefah* — an animal that] **has lost its hide [having been flayed]** [M. 3:2 E]. You can reason in accord with the view of R. Judah who declares it valid.

S. *But lo there is* [another category of *terefah* — an animal whose] **[lung] is dried naturally** [M. 3:2 D].

T. **[If] the gallbladder [is pierced]** [M. 3:1 F], *who taught this rule? R. Yosé b. R. Judah [cf. b. 43a]. You can take out the gallbladder [from the list of eighteen] and put in [the animal whose lung] **is dried naturally**.*

U. *But lo there are* [other categories of *terefah*, namely] the seven that were taught [by Amoraic authorities as follows]:

Bavli Ḥullin Chapter Three. Folios 42A-67B

V. (1) For said R. Matna, "*This [case of an animal whose] femur slipped out of its socket [Cashdan] is* terefah."

W. (2) And said Rakhish bar Pappa in the name of Rab, "[An animal that was] *diseased in one kidney is* terefah."

X. (3) *And it was taught in the Mishnah on Tannaite authority,* **[if] the spleen is removed [M. 3:2 C]** it is valid. And said R. Avira in the name of Raba, "They taught this rule only in the case where it was removed. But if it was pierced, it is *terefah*."

Y. (4) And said Rabbah bar bar Hannah, said Samuel, "[If one of the throat] organs was for the most part [torn away and] dangling, it is *terefah*."

Z. (5) And said Rabbah bar R. Shila, said R. Matna, said Samuel, "If a rib was torn away from its socket, [the animal] is *terefah*."

AA. (6) And [if] the skull that was for the most part shattered, [the animal is *terefah*].

BB. (7) And [if] the membrane that covers the rumen [that was for the most part torn], it is *terefah*.

CC. [How then do we maintain a list of eighteen categories of *terefah*?] *The eight [categories of terefah caused by] puncturing should be reckoned as one [category]. Take out seven and add seven others.*

DD. *If so then [the cases in M. of] severing are two categories that should be reckoned as one. You are then short [of eighteen by] one category.*

EE. *And further, the case of R. Avira in the name of Raba [above at X] is also an instance of puncturing [and should be subsumed into this one category leaving us two categories short of eighteen].*

FF. **[43a]** *Rather those two categories that you took out [above at Q and T] —you should not take them out.* [Then you are left with eighteen categories.]

II.1
A. Said Ulla, "Eight kinds of *terefot* were stated to Moses at Sinai: [An animal with an organ that was damaged when it was] pierced, or severed, [or if the organ was] missing, or deficient, torn, or mauled, [or if the animal] suffered a fall, or suffered a fracture."

B. *This excludes [as a category unto itself the case of] a diseased kidney, stated by Rakhish bar Pappa [above at I.1 W].*

C. Said Hiyya bar Rab [var. Raba], "There are eight [sub-categories of] *terefot* subsumed under the category of [an organ that was] pierced [enumerated in M. 3:1 B-H]."

D. *And if you say [by way of objection] that there are nine [categories enumerated there, I can respond that the category of M. 3:1 F,] the gallbladder [that was pierced is terefah, only] R. Yosé b. R. Judah taught that one.*

E. *As it was taught on Tannaite authority,* If the belly [abomasum] was pierced, or if the intestines were pierced, it is *terefah*. R. Yosé b. R. Judah says, "Even if the gallbladder was pierced [it is *terefah*]."

F. [A mnemonic is given.] Said R. Yitzhak b. R. Joseph, said R. Yohanan, "The law follows in accord with R. Yosé b. R. Judah."

G. And said R. Yitzhak b. R. Joseph, said R. Yohanan, "*What did the colleagues say in response to R. Yosé b. R. Judah?*" [They cited this verse where Job proclaimed], "He pours out my gall on the ground" (Job 16:13). And Job went on living! [It is not a lethal wound and should not render an animal *terefah*.]

H. He said to them, "You cannot cite miraculous events [as proof regarding the laws of *terefah*]. *For if you do not state matters in this way* [then consider the first part of the verse], 'He slashes open my kidneys, and shows no mercy.' *Could someone live [with such a wound]? [Rather it must have been a miracle that Job lived with a wound to his kidney.] And miracles are subject to different expectations. As it was written,* '[And the Lord said to Satan, Behold, he is in your power;] only spare his life' (Job 2:6). Here too [in the case of

*Bavli Ḥullin Chapter Three. Folios 42A-67B* 25

his gallbladder] you say that miracles are subject to different expectations [and that is why Job went on living].

**II.2**

A. And said R. Yitzhak b. R. Joseph, said R. Yohanan, "The law [concerning the liver that was removed (M. 3:1 C6)] is in accord with the authority who says [if] an olive's bulk [of the liver remains it is valid]."

B. And did R. Yohanan say this? But lo, said Rabbah bar bar Hannah, said R. Yohanan, "The law is in accord with the anonymous teaching in the Mishnah."

C. *And it was taught in the Mishnah on Tannaite authority,* **[If] the liver is removed so that nothing whatsoever remains of it [M. 3:1 C]** [it is *terefah*]. Lo, if something remained it would be valid even if it was not an olive's bulk.

D. [Accordingly we must say that on this issue] *there is an Amoraic dispute about [the ruling of] R. Yohanan.*

**II.3**

A. And said R. Yitzhak b. R. Joseph, said R. Yohanan, "A gallbladder that was pierced and the liver [rested on it and] closed it up, it is valid."

B. And said R. Yitzhak b. R. Joseph, said R. Yohanan, "If the gizzard was pierced and its membrane was intact, it is valid."

C. *They posed the question:* "If the gizzard was pierced and its membrane was intact, what is the law?" *Come and take note:* For said R. Nahman, "If this one was pierced [i.e., the gizzard] but not the other [i.e., the membrane], it is valid."

**III.1**

A. Said Raba, "The gullet has two layers of skin. The exterior one is red and the interior one is white. If this one was pierced but not the other, it is valid."

B. *Why must I state* that the exterior one is red and the interior one is white? [That has no bearing on the piercing of the organ.]

[Because] if they are reversed in color [the organ is deemed defective and the animal is] *terefah*.

C. *They posed the question: If the two of them [i.e., the skins of the gullet or the gizzard and its membrane] were pierced, but not opposite one another, what is the law? Said Mar Zutra in the name of R. Pappa, "In the case of the gullet, it is valid. In the case of the gizzard, it is not valid."*

D. *R. Ashi raised an objection to this. The contrary [conclusion makes more sense]. With regard to the gullet, the animal eats through it and breathes through it, and it contracts and expands. At times [the holes] may line up with one another [so it should not be valid]. The gizzard, that is always still, remains as it is [and the holes will not line up, so it should be valid].*

E. Said to him R. Aha the son of R. Joseph to R. Ashi, "This is what we have stated in the name of Mar Zutra who said in the name of R. Pappa in accord with your view."

### III.2

A. And said Rabbah, "A membrane that formed as a result of an injury to the gullet is not considered to be a membrane [with regard to the law of piercing]."

B. And said Rabbah, "There is no valid external inspection of the gullet. It must be internal." *In what case does this make a difference?* [43b] For the case of an animal about which there is a doubt whether it was mauled.

C. There once was a case of an animal about which there is a doubt whether it was mauled. *It was brought before Rabbah. Rabbah was inspecting the gullet externally.* Said to him Abayye, "Was it not the master [i.e., you] who said, 'There is no valid external inspection of the gullet. It must be internal?'"

D. *Rabbah turned it and inspected it [internally] and found on it two drops of blood and declared it to be* terefah. *And Rabbah did this [external inspection initially] in order to test the sharpness of Abayye's acumen.*

## IV.1

A. Said Ulla, "If a thorn was lodged in its gullet we do not suspect that perhaps it [had pierced the gullet but then the wound] healed."

B. [A mnemonic is given.] And according to the view of Ulla why is this case different from the case of a doubt as to whether the animal had been mauled? Ulla reasons that, "We are not concerned with the possibility of a case of a doubt as to whether the animal had been mauled."

C. *And what is the difference between this [case of doubt whose significance he rejects] and [the case of doubt] concerning [two pieces of fat] — one of forbidden fat and one of permitted fat? There we have a definite presumption that a forbidden substance was present. [Here regarding the doubt about mauling, we are not sure that any forbidden substance exists.] And what is the difference between this case and the case of one who slaughters with a knife and afterward finds that it was defective? There the taint arose in the knife [not in the animal]. And what is the difference between this case and the case of doubt concerning uncleanness in a private domain? [It should be deemed equivalent to that.] And a case of doubt in this instance is deemed to be unclean.*

D. *But according to your logic we should compare this to a case of doubt concerning uncleanness in a public domain. And such a case of doubt is deemed to be clean. But there [in the case of these principles regarding doubt about uncleanness] we derive the rule from analogy to the laws for the suspected woman [see 9b above].*

E. *A rabbi was sitting before R. Kahana. And he sat and he said, "[The law of A] was stated for a case where it [i.e., the thorn] was found [in the hollow of the gullet]. But where it was set [in the wall of the gullet] we do suspect [that perhaps it had pierced the gullet but then the wound healed]."*

F. *Said to him R. Kahana, "Pay no attention to him. [The law of A] was stated for a case where it was set [in the wall of the gullet]. But where it was found [in the hollow of the gullet], it was not necessary to state for Ulla [the rule] because [as a rule] all beasts that graze eat some thorns."*

**V.1**

A. *It was stated:* [To render the animal *terefah* the amount that must be pierced in] the pharynx [lit., the forecourt of the gullet (Cashdan), is a matter of dispute]. Rab said, "Any amount." And Samuel said, "The majority."

B. Rab said, "Any amount" because it is a valid place [in the neck] to slaughter the animal. And Samuel said, "The majority" because it is not a valid place [in the neck] to slaughter the animal.

C. *What is this* pharynx? Said Mari bar Mar Uqba, said Samuel, "Any place [in the gullet] where the opening widens as you cut, that is the pharynx. [Any place in the gullet] where the opening stays as it is as you cut, that is the gullet itself."

D. Said to him R. Pappi, "The master did not state matters in this manner." And who was [that master]? R. Bibi bar Abayye. Rather [he said], "[Any place in the gullet] where the opening stays as it is as you cut it, that is the pharynx." Where then is the gullet itself? Any place where the opening contracts as you cut it.

E. Jonah said [in the name of] Zira, "*Where it swallows* [that is the pharynx]."

F. And how far [into the gullet does the pharynx extend]? Said R. Avya, "*Less than the length of a grain of barley and more than the length of a grain of wheat.*"

**V.2**

A. *There was an ox that belonged to the children of R. Uqba that they started to slaughter in the pharynx and completed [the incision] in the gullet itself. Said Raba, "I impose upon it the stringencies of the rulings of Rab and the stringencies of the rulings of Samuel and I rule that it is* terefah."

B. *The stringencies of the rulings of Rab* — for Rab said, "Any amount [of piercing renders it terefah]." But did Rab not say that it is a valid place [in the neck] for slaughter? This accords with the rule of Samuel who says that it is not a valid place for slaughter.

C. *If you hold in accord with the view of Samuel, then did he not say [it is* terefah *only if he cut],* "A majority"? *This accords with Rab who said,* "Any amount" *[renders it* terefah]. *They went around and around on this matter [and there seemed to be no resolution].*

D. *They brought it before R. Abba. He said to them, "Both in accord with Rab and in accord with Samuel an ox [slaughtered in this fashion] is permitted. Go and tell [Raba] the son of R. Joseph bar Hama to pay the value of the ox to the owner."*

E. Said Mar the son of Rabina, "I can pose an objection to the enemies of Raba [from the following text]:"

F. In general the law is in accord with the House of Hillel. But one who wishes to act [consistently] in accord with the words of the House of Shammai may do so. [One who wishes to act consistently in accord with] the words of the House of Hillel may do so. [One who wishes to act in accord with] the leniencies of the House of Shammai and the leniencies of the House of Hillel is evil. [44a] [One who wishes to act in accord with] the stringencies of the House of Shammai and the stringencies of the House of Hillel, about him Scripture says, "The fool walks in darkness" (Qoh. 2:14). But [it is proper] if one follows the House of Hillel [to follow both] their leniencies and their stringencies and if one follows the House of Shammai [to follow both] their leniencies and stringencies [T. Suk. 2:3]. [The version in B. has the names reversed.]

G. *But this text itself contains a contradiction. It states,* In general the law is in accord with the House of Hillel. *And then it teaches,* But one who wishes to act [consistently] in accord with the words of the House of Shammai may do so.

H. *This is not a contradiction. This [latter statement that one may follow the House of Shammai was made] prior to the issuance of the heavenly echo [that proclaimed the law follows the House of Hillel]. And that [former statement that in general the law follows the House of Hillel was made] after the issuance of the heavenly echo.*

I. *And if you prefer* [both statements were made] *even after the issuance of the heavenly echo. And this accords with the view of R. Joshua who said, "We do not pay heed to a heavenly echo."*

J. In any case the objection stands [against Raba for ruling in accord with the stringencies of both Rab and of Samuel].

K. Said R. Tabot, "[Raba] acted entirely in accord with the view of Rab." For when Rami bar Ezekiel came [from Israel] he said, "Pay no attention *to these principles that Judah my brother brought in the name of Rab. This is what Rab said,* 'For [defining the location of] the gullet the sages prescribed a fixed measure.'" *We may derive* [from this statement] the rule that the pharynx is not a valid place [in the neck] for slaughtering. And it states, "Any amount [makes it *terefah*]." [Accordingly Raba rules consistently in accord with Rab.]

V.3
A. At the top [of the gullet] how far [does the place valid for slaughter extend]? Said R. Nahman, "Up to [the place where there is enough left over] for the hand to grasp [the gullet at the top]."

B. At the bottom [of the gullet] how far [does the place valid for slaughter extend]? Said R. Nahman, said Rabbah bar Abbuha, "Up to the place where it has hair [i.e., villi (Cashdan)]."

C. *Is this the case? Lo,* said Rabina, said Geniva in the name of Rab, "The lower handbreadth in the gullet near the rumen, this is called the inner rumen." *How* [could you say that the place where it has hair is a valid place for slaughter]? When he slaughters [the animal at that place] he is slaughtering in the rumen! *It makes sense to maintain* that the handbreadth in the rumen near the gullet, this is called the inner rumen.

D. *If you prefer — what Rab spoke of was in reference to an ox where there is more hair* [higher up on the gullet].

V.4
A. Said R. Nahman, said Samuel, "[In an animal even if] the pharynx is completely detached from the jaw, it is valid." And

our Tanna teaches in accord with this: **And these are the valid [carcasses] among cattle: ... [if] the lower jaw is removed [M. 3:2].**

B. *R. Pappa objected [to the rule of Samuel], "But lo, there is [in such a case the defect of] the organs that are torn out." But according to R. Pappa is there not a contradiction from the Mishnah itself:* **And these are the valid [carcasses] among cattle: ... [if] the lower jaw is removed?**

C. *It is consistent to say that the Mishnah does not contradict the view of R. Pappa. Here [in the case where we declare it to be invalid, the jaw] was torn away with force along with the surrounding flesh]. And here [in the case where we declare it valid, the jaw] was torn away but remains embedded in the flesh near the organs.*

D. *But according to Samuel the contradiction remains. [I.e. —] do not say that all of it [was detached]. Say rather that a majority [was detached].*

E. But lo, said Rabbah bar bar Hannah, said Samuel, "[In a beast where the] organs were dangling, detached in the major part, it is *terefah*."

F. Said R. Shisha the son of R. Idi, "Here [where we say it is valid] it was stripped apart [from the animal in a contiguous fashion]. Here [where we say that it is invalid] it was broken away [in various places from the flesh of the animal]."

## VI.1

A. **[These are the *terefah* (carcasses) among cattle: (1) one in which the gullet is pierced,] (2) and one in which the windpipe is torn.** It was taught: How much constitutes a torn windpipe? A majority. And how much is a majority? Rab said, [44b] "A majority of the thickest part." And others say, "A majority of [the circumference of] its cavity."

B. *An animal with a torn windpipe was brought before Rab. He sat and inspected it to see if a majority of the thickest part [was torn]. Said to him R. Kahana and R. Assi to Rab, "Did not our master instruct us that [it is rendered invalid if it was torn] in a majority of its cavity?"*

C. *He sent it before Rabbah bar bar Hannah who inspected it [to determine if it was torn through] a majority of its cavity. And he declared it valid. And he bought from it thirteen ordinary istirae's worth of meat.*

D. But how could he have done this [reversing another sage's decision]? *For lo it was taught on Tannaite authority,* **Once a sage has declared something unclean his colleague is not permitted to declare it clean. [Once a sage has] declared something forbidden his colleague is not permitted to declare it permitted** [T. Ed. 1:5].

E. *This case is different because Rab did not declare it forbidden.* [The general rule does not pertain to it.]

F. [Now what about the conflict of interest?] *Since the sage [Rabbah] issued a ruling concerning [the meat], how could he [buy] and eat from it?* [Do we not worry that his interest will influence his decision?]

G. But lo, it is written, "Then I said, 'Ah Lord God! behold, I have never defiled myself; from my youth up till now I have never eaten what died of itself or was torn by beasts, nor has foul flesh come into my mouth'" (Ezek. 4:14). "Behold, I have never defiled myself," [means that I was so pious that] I never reflected during the day about becoming unclean at night. "From my youth up till now I have never eaten what died of itself or was torn by beasts," [means, I was so pious that] I never in my life ate meat [from an animal at the point of death that was slaughtered in haste as they cried out], "Slaughter it, slaughter it." "Nor has foul flesh come into my mouth," [means] that I never ate from an animal [about whose validity there was some question and] a sage pronounced it [was valid].

H. In the name of R. Nathan they said [the last phrase means], "I never ate from an animal whose [priestly] gifts had not been given." [This was an act of piety because as a priest he could have eaten it anyway.]

I. *This concern [that it is an act of piety not to eat meat that a sage pronounced valid] applies to a case [where there was a question and he declared it valid] based on an issue of logical reasoning.*

Bavli Hullin Chapter Three. Folios 42A-67B

J.     *Rabbah bar bar Hannah [in C above] provided [additional] support [for his decision to reverse the ruling and to permit the meat].*

K.    *But let us exclude this [justification] because there is a suspicion [that he was taking compensation for a favorable ruling]. As it was taught on Tannaite authority,* **[A judge] after he rendered the judgment, declared [the material] exempt or liable, unclean or clean, prohibited or permitted, and the witnesses who testified, all of them are permitted to purchase [a portion of the material about which they rendered judgment]. But the sages said, "Make yourself distant from what is ugly or what appears ugly"** [T. Yeb. 4:7 and ARN 2].

L.    *This concern applies to something that one purchases through an appraisal [of the approximate value of the object]. Here [in the case of meat] its [precise] weight is the evidence [that he receives no benefit from his ruling].*

M.   *[This case above] is similar to the case of Rabbah, who permitted [by his ruling the consumption of an animal that was thought to be] a terefah and he purchased meat from it. Said to him the daughter of R. Hisda, "My father permitted [by his ruling the consumption of an animal that was] a firstling but he did not buy meat from it." He said to her, "This concern applies to a firstling that is sold by appraisal. Here [in the case of terefah] its weight is the evidence [that I received no benefit from my ruling]. What other [suspicion] is there? [Might they suspect] that I received the best cut [of the meat]? [That is not a pertinent suspicion.] Every day they sell me the best cut [of the meat out of respect]."*

N.    Said R. Hisda, "Who is considered a [true] disciple of the sages? He who sees [that it is proper to rule] that his own animal is *terefah.*" And said R. Hisda, "Who is [the true subject of the verse], '[He who is greedy for unjust gain makes trouble for his household, but] he who hates bribes will live' (Prov. 15:27)? He who sees [that it is proper to rule] that his own animal is *terefah.*"

O.    Mar Zutra expounded in the name of R. Hisda, "Anyone who [while studying] recites the Scripture and repeats the Mishnah and who sees [that it is proper to rule] that his own animal is *terefah*, and who serves disciples of the sages, about him Scripture says, 'You shall eat the fruit of the labor of your hands; you shall be happy, and it shall be well with you' (Ps. 128:2)."

P. R. Zebid said, "He [who acts in this manner] merits and inherits both worlds — this world and the world to come. 'You shall be happy,' in this world. 'And it shall be well with you,' in the world to come."

Q. *When they sent something to R. Eleazar from the Patriarch's house, he would not take it. And when they invited him [for a meal] he would not go. He said, "The master [by doing this shows that he] does not want me to live. For it is written, 'He who hates bribes will live' (Prov. 15:27)."*

R. *When they sent something to R. Zira [from the Patriarch's house,] he would not take it. But when they invited him [for a meal] he would go. He said,* **[45a]** *"They receive honor by honoring me [so when I go it is not a bribe for me]."*

### VII.1

A. Said R. Judah, said Rab, "If [upon inspection they find that the windpipe] was pierced [with a number of perforations] like a sieve, they combine them together to constitute a majority [and render the animal a *terefah*]." [Holes combine to constitute the measure for a tear in the windpipe.]

B. R. Jeremiah *posed a question*, "And regarding a skull that has one long hole [this is a sign the animal is *terefah*]. Or if there were many holes, they combine them together to constitute [the minimum measure of the size of] a drill hole. It seems [logical to conclude] that since the [minimum] measure is [the size of] a drill hole, they combine together to constitute [a measure the size of] a drill hole. Here as well [with regard to the measure of a hole in the windpipe that constitutes a *terefah*] since its [minimum] measure is [the size of] an *issar* [a small coin], they combine together to constitute [a measure the size of] an *issar*." [He argues that you should reckon holes in regard to the measure for holes, not the measure for a tear in the windpipe.]

C. *He [Jeremiah] must have neglected that said by R. Helbo, said R. Hama bar Goria, said Rab*, "Holes resulting from a loss [of a piece of bone or cartilage] combine together to constitute [a measure the size of] an *issar*. [Holes] not resulting from a loss [but rather from a piercing] combine together to constitute a majority [of the circumference, that is a tear that would invalidate the windpipe]." [Judah in A referred to a case of the latter kind of piercing.]

D. Said Rabbah bar bar Hannah, said R. Joshua b. Levi, "If he removed a strip [from the windpipe], it combines [with other holes] to constitute [a measure] the size of an *issar* [to invalidate the animal]."

E. R. Yitzhak bar Nahmani *asked* R. Joshua b. Levi, "If [the windpipe] was pierced [with a number of perforations] like a sieve, what is the law?"

F. He said to him, "Lo, they said, 'Holes resulting from a loss [of a piece of bone or cartilage] combine together to constitute [a measure the size of] an *issar*. [Holes] not resulting from a loss [but rather from a piercing] combine together to constitute a majority.'"

G. *What is the law for fowl?* [What is the minimum measure for holes that result from a loss in its windpipe?] Said R. Yitzhak bar Nahmani, "This was interpreted for me by R. Eleazar. [He cuts around all the holes in the windpipe until he can fold over the tissue with the holes.] He folds the tissue and places it over the opening of the windpipe. If it covers the majority of the windpipe, it is *terefah*. And if not then it is valid."

H. Said R. Pappa, "And the mnemonic [for this interpretation is]: a sieve. [When he folds the tissue with the holes over the opening it looks like a sieve.]"

I. If it [the windpipe] was slashed [in three ways so that the tissue was hanging] like a door — said R. Nahman, "[It is *terefah* if there is enough room in the opening] so that an *issar* could pass through it across the width [of the opening, but not if it can pass through only diagonally]."

## VII.2

A. If it [the windpipe] was slit lengthwise — said Rab, "Even if there remained only one ring intact at the top and one ring intact at the bottom [but all the other rings were split] it is valid."

B. They said this *before* R. Yohanan. He said, "What is [the need for] this ring [to be intact at the top] and what is [the need for] this ring [to be intact at the bottom] that Rab spoke of? Rather it makes sense to maintain that even if there remained any amount [intact] at the top and any amount at the bottom, it is valid."

C. *They said this before R. Yohanan in this regard in the name of R. Jonathan. Thus he did say to them, "Those Babylonian associates know how to interpret things in a logical way."*

## VII.3

A. R. Hiyya bar Joseph *taught* in the name of R. Yohanan, "Any place in the neck is valid for slaughtering, from the large ring until the bottom lobe of the lung."

B. Said Raba, "The bottom [lobe actually] means the upper [lobe that is found at the bottom]. For I say that [you may slaughter anywhere that is accessible] as it [naturally] extends its neck to graze. But you may not force it [to extend its neck to find additional accessible places to slaughter]."

C. R. Hanina *posed a question. And alternatively:* R. Hanania. "What is the law if it forced itself [to extend its neck]?" *The question stands unresolved.*

D. R. Yohanan and R. Simeon b. Laqish were sitting [in session] and they jointly issued the following rule of law: If [an animal] was forced [to stretch] its organs and he slaughtered [at a place in the neck ordinarily inaccessible] it is invalid. If the windpipe was pierced below in the breast, it is judged to be [a puncture] in the lung.

E. *Our rabbis taught on Tannaite authority,* **What is the breast? Whatever is visible from [i.e., faces] the ground and upward, through to the neck, and downward through to the belly. One cuts it off and removes it from between the two walls on either** side [T. 9:13 A-C]. And this is the breast that is given to the priests.

**VIII.1**

A. [If] **the membrane of the brain is pierced [M. 3:1 C].** Rab and Samuel, the two of them said, "*[This rule refers to a case where] the exterior membrane [was pierced, the dura mater (Cashdan)], even if the interior membrane [pia mater (Cashdan)] was not pierced [it is terefah].*"

B. *And there are those that say [it is not terefah] unless the interior membrane is pierced.*

C. Said R. Samuel bar Nahmani, "Your mnemonic for this is: The sack in which the brain rests." [The word for sack, *hyyt'*, resembles the word for living, *hy*.]

D. Said Rabbah bar bar Hannah, said R. Joshua b. Levi, "The same [structure of interior and exterior membranes] is observable in the [animal's] testicles."

E. Said R. Simeon b. Pazzi, said R. Joshua b. Levi, in the name of Bar Qappara, "The brain is defined as all that is found in the cranium. Where it starts to draw away [from the cranium] that is defined as the spinal cord."

F. *And from what point* does it start to draw away? Said R. Yitzhak bar Nahmani, "R. Joshua b. Levi's [rule] was explained to me. There are two bean [shaped objects, i.e., the occipital condyles that articulate the cranium to the first vertebra (Cashdan)] **[45b]** attached at the cranial opening. From the place of these beans and inside [the cranium] is defined as part of the [brain] inside. And from the place of these beans and outside [the cranium] is defined as [the spinal cord] outside. And at the place of these beans themselves, I do not know [the law]. But it makes sense that they are [defined as part of the brain] inside."

G. R. Jeremiah examined a fowl and found objects like two beans attached at the cranial opening.

IX.1
A. **[If] the heart is pierced up to the cavity thereof [M. 3:1 C].** R. Zira posed the question: [Does this mean] the small cavity [the atrium] or the large cavity [the ventricle]? Said to him Abbaye, "What is your question? Was it not taught [in an analogous case] in the Mishnah on Tannaite authority, **R. Simeon says, '[It is not** *terefah*] **unless its bronchial tubes are pierced'** [M. 3:1 E]?"

B. And said Rabbah bar Tahlifa, said R. Jeremiah bar Abba, said Rab, [this means], "Unless its large bronchial tube is pierced."

C. [Zira answered], "*Are these cases comparable? There it is taught,* **Bronchial tubes,** [lit., the housing of the tubes, which implies] *to the place where the bronchial tubes all converge. And here it is taught,* **The cavity,** [lit., the housing of the heart]. What is the difference to me if it refers to the large cavity or the small cavity?" [In either case it is *terefah*.]

IX.2
A. [Concerning a piercing of] the main artery of the heart [i.e., the aorta] — Rab says, "Any amount [renders the animal *terefah*]." And Samuel says, "A majority [renders the animal *terefah*]."

B. *Where is* the aorta? Said Rabbah bar Yitzhak, said Rab, "It is the fat [artery] adjacent to the walls [of the chest cavity]."

C. The walls? *Does that make sense?* Rather [say that it is the artery that is] adjacent to the walls of the lung [i.e., the mediastal cavity (Cashdan)].

D. Said Amemar in the name of R. Nahman, "*There are three [large] arteries. One diverges to the heart [i.e. the aorta]. One diverges to the lungs [i.e., the windpipe, not an artery]. And one diverges to the liver [i.e., the vena cava inferior (Cashdan)]. The one that diverges to the lung is considered to be part of the lung [with regard to defects in the animal]. The one that diverges to the liver is considered to be part of the liver. The one that diverges to the heart, is the subject of a dispute.*"

E. *Mar bar Hiyya taught the reverse,* "The one that diverges to the lung is considered to be part of the liver [with regard to defects in the animal]. The one that diverges to the liver is considered to be part of the lung. The one that diverges to the heart, is the subject of a dispute."

E. R. Hiyya bar Joseph went and recited the teaching of Rab in front of Samuel. He said to him, "If this is what Abba [Rab] said, then he knew nothing about [the laws of] terefot."

X.1
A. [If] the backbone is broken [so that the spinal cord is severed] [M. 3:1 C]. *It was taught on Tannaite authority,* **If the spinal cord was snapped [Talmud here adds:] through a majority of the cord, [it is invalid, (Talmud adds):] the words of Rabbi. R. Jacob says, "Even if it [the spinal cord] was perforated, [it is invalid] [T. 3:1 F-G]."**

B. Rabbi taught [that the law was] in accord with R. Jacob. Said R. Huna, "The law is not in accord with R. Jacob."

C. And how much constitutes a majority [of the cord]? Rab said, "A majority of its skin [i.e., its membrane]." *And some say,* "A majority of its inner matter [i.e., of the medulla (Cashdan) even if the membrane is intact]."

D. *According to the authority who says [it is* terefah *if severed in],* "A majority of its inner matter," *certainly [it is terefah if severed in],* "A majority of the skin" [because once the membrane breaks the spinal matter will cease to be intact].

E. *But according to the authority who says [it is* terefah *if severed in],* "A majority of its skin," *what is the law [if it is severed in],* "A majority of its inner matter?"

F. *Come and take note:* For said Nivli, said R. Huna, "The majority about which they spoke refers to the majority of the skin. [Severing] this inner matter makes no difference at all."

G. R. Nathan bar Abin was sitting [in session] before Rab. He inspected [a spinal cord for severance] of the majority of its skin and he inspected it [for severance] of a majority of its inner matter. He [Rab] said to him, "If the majority of the skin is intact, [severing of] this inner matter makes no difference at all."

### X.2

A. Said Rabbah bar bar Hannah, said R. Joshua b. Levi, "[If the spinal matter] turned into liquid, it is invalid. [If the spinal matter] turned soft, it is invalid." What is the definition of "turned into liquid"? And what is the definition of "turned soft"? "Turned into liquid" [means] *it flows like liquid.* "Turned soft" [means] it cannot stand [on its own without a container].

B. R. Jeremiah *posed the question:* If it cannot stand [on its own] because of its own weight, *what is the law? The question stands unresolved.*

C. The House of Rab say, "If it turned soft, it is invalid. If it disintegrated [in part], it is valid."

D. *They posed this objection:* R. Simeon b. Eleazar says, "An animal whose spinal matter disintegrated is *terefah.*" [They responded:] That was stated [actually where it] turned soft.

E. *Really? [Does that make sense?] But lo, Levi was sitting in the baths. He saw a person who hit his head [and injured his spine]. He said [about him], "This man's spine has disintegrated." Did he not imply [by saying this that because of the injury] the man could not continue to live? Said Abayye, "No. He meant to say that he was rendered impotent [as a result of such an injury]."*

### X.3

A. *How long is the spinal cord [as far as the laws of defects are concerned]?* Said R. Judah, said Samuel, "[It extends] to the place where the [sacral] nerves branch off."

B. *R. Dimi bar Yitzhak had to go to Be Huzai. He came before R. Judah. He said to him, "Will the master please show me where is the place where the nerves branch off?" He said to him, "Go fetch me a kid and I will show you." He brought him a fattened kid. He said to him, "[The nerves] are embedded too much [in the fat] and I cannot identify them." He brought him a thin kid. He said to him, "[The nerves] are protruding too much [and are too close to the bones] and I cannot identify them." He said to him, "Come and I will teach you the rule [in any case even though I cannot demonstrate it for you]. This is what Samuel said, '[Any severing of the cord] up to the first branch [of* the nerves] is *terefah*. After the third branch, it is valid. In the second branch, I do not know [the law].'"

C. R. Huna the son of R. Joshua *posed a question:* **[46a]** [Does Samuel in his ruling mean] up to and including [that place in the spinal cord] or perhaps [he means] up to but not including [that place]?

D. R. Pappa *posed a question:* If you wish to say that [Samuel means] up to but not including [that place], then what is the law with regard to [severing at] the point it branches off? [Cashdan: the point in the cord where the first pair of sacral nerves is given off.]

E. R. Jeremiah *posed a question:* If you wish to say that [Samuel means] up to and including [that place], then what is the law with regard to [severing in] the point it branches off itself?

F. *Come and take note:* The branch is judged [to have the same rules] as the meat [of the animal, not as an organ]. *Does this not mean* the first or the second [point of] branching? No, [it means] the third [point of] branching.

X.4

A. In a fowl [up to what point in the spinal cord does severing render it *terefah*]? R. Yannai says, "[Any place in the cord down to the area] below the wings [i.e., the bottom of the wings]." And Resh Laqish says, "Until [the area of the cord parallel to the area] between the wings [i.e., the top of the wings]."

B. Said Ulla, "I was standing before Ben Pazzi and they brought before him a fowl. And he inspected it [for defects of the spinal cord] up to the area between the wings. And the House of the Patriarch sent for him [before he could inspect any further]. He got up and went off. And I did not know if [he stopped inspecting the cord] because he held the view that you do not have to inspect [the cord for defects] any further or [whether he stopped inspecting at that point] out of respect to [the summons of] the House of the Patriarch."

XI.1

A. **[If] the liver is removed [missing], so that nothing whatsoever remains of it [M. 3:1 C].** Lo [this implies] that if any amount [of the liver] remains, it is valid, even if it was not equivalent to the volume of an egg's bulk. But lo, *it was taught on Tannaite authority,* **[It is valid if] the liver is removed, but an olive's bulk of which remains [M. 3:2 C]**! Said R. Joseph, *"This is not a contradiction. One is the ruling of R. Hiyya and the other is the ruling of R. Simeon bar Rabbi. [Regarding an animal with less than an olive's bulk of liver] like this case, R. Hiyya used to discard it [because he ruled it was* terefah*], and R. Simeon b. Rabbi would dip it* [i.e., eat it because he ruled that it was valid. Rashi interprets the views in reverse. R. Hiyya used to discard the liver. Accordingly he was lenient in rules regarding any defects in it. But R. Simeon used to dip the liver and eat it for his health. Accordingly he was stricter in rules regarding defects in the liver. But this is contradicted by the following.]"

B. A mnemonic [for these rulings]: *the wealthy are stingy* [i.e., R. Simeon b. Rabbi was more lenient even though he could have afforded to discard the animal].

XI.2
A. *There was a regiment that came to Pumbedita. Rabbah and R. Joseph fled. R. Zira met them. He said to them, "You who flee [should remember this teaching]: the olive's bulk about which they spoke [in the Mishnah] refers to [that amount] in the area of the gall-bladder."* [Perhaps this was an indirect reference to the rabbis who did not remain in the town where it was bitter because of the occupation by a regiment.]

B. R. Ada bar Ahavah said, "[The olive's bulk referred to in the Mishnah is that amount] in the vital area [of the liver, i.e., by the falciform ligament (Cashdan)]."

C. Said R. Pappa, "Therefore [because of these two rulings] we require [for the animal to be valid both] an olive's bulk in the area of the gall-bladder and an olive's bulk in the vital area [of the liver]."

D. R. Jeremiah *posed a question:* What is the rule in the case of [an animal that has an olive's bulk of liver, but only] if he collects [smaller portions of liver together]? What is the rule in the case

*Bavli Ḥullin Chapter Three. Folios 42A-67B*

[of an animal that has] an olive's bulk [of liver in the thin shape] of a lace?

E. R. Ashi *posed a question:* What is the rule in the case of [an animal that has an olive's bulk of liver] that is flattened out? *These questions remain unresolved.*

### XI.3

A. *R. Zeriqa posed a question to R. Ammi: What is the rule in the case of an animal whose liver was dangling, but still attached to the diaphragm? He said to him, "I do not know [what problem there is] concerning this [case of a liver that is] dangling. If we hold in accord with the authority who says [to be valid the animal must have an olive's bulk of liver] in the area of the gall-bladder, lo, you have it. And it we hold in accord with the authority who says [to be valid the animal must have an olive's bulk of liver] in the vital area, lo you have it."*

### XII.1

A. **The lung which is pierced... [M. 3:1 D].** Rab and Samuel and R. Assi say, "The exterior membrane [must be pierced to render it invalid]." *And others say about this,* "The interior membrane [must be pierced]."

B. Said R. Joseph bar Manyomi, said R. Nahman, "A mnemonic: *The red coat in which the lungs are situated* [i.e., the interior membrane, parenchyma pulmonis (Cashdan)]."

C. *It is obvious that if the exterior membrane is pierced and the interior membrane is not pierced, the interior membrane will protect [the lung]. This accords with the rule of Rabbah.* For said Raba, "This [animal whose] lung had [its exterior membrane] peeled off so that it looked like **[46b]** a red date is valid."

D. *If the interior membrane was pierced but the exterior membrane was not pierced, does it protect [the lung] or not? R. Aha and Rabina disputed. One said it does not protect and one said it does protect. And the law follows in accord with the authority who says it does protect [the lung].*

E. *And this is in accord with the view of R. Joseph.* For said R. Joseph, "A lung that hisses [with a leak of air when inflated] — if we know where it is hissing, we put on it a feather or some saliva or straw, and if it bubbles [or wobbles, the animal] is terefah. If it does not, it is valid. And if we do not know where it is hissing, we bring a tub of warm water and we immerse [the lung] in it [to locate the leak]. It cannot be hot water because this would cause contraction [and we could not locate the leak]. It cannot be cold water because this would cause hardening [and the membrane might crack]. But we immerse it in warm water and we inflate it. If it bubbles, it is terefah. If it does not, it is valid. [We conclude in the latter case that] the interior membrane is pierced and the exterior membrane is not pierced. And the hissing sound is air flowing between the membranes."

XII.2
A. [A mnemonic is given.] *Reverting to the body of the prior text [XII.1 C]: Said Raba, "This [animal whose] lung had [its exterior membrane] peeled off so that it looked like a red date is valid."*

B. And said Raba, "[If an animal's] lung that turned partially red, it is valid. [If it turned] completely red, it is terefah." Said Rabina to Raba, "On what basis [do we rule that if it turned] partially [red it is valid]? Because [an animal that has such a condition] will [ordinarily] return to health. [An animal with a lung that turned] completely [red] will also [ordinarily] return to health."

C. Was it not taught on Tannaite authority, "[If one wounded on the Sabbath] other creeping or crawling animals [he is not liable for violating the Sabbath] unless they bleed." [This implies that if the creature turned red without bleeding it is not considered an injury of any consequence.]

D. But if you maintain that we compare [our issue of a defect in the lung with the Sabbath law for] the eight [kinds of] creeping animals [this will also lead to an inconsistency]. For it was taught on Tannaite authority, If [he caused a wound so that] the blood coalesced [under the skin], even if it did not bleed [he is liable for violating the Sabbath]. If [you compare our case to this one] then [you should conclude] that even if [the lung turned red] partially it also [should be deemed terefah]. Rather [in regard to the status of the animal whose lung turned either partially or completely red] there is no difference. [Some commentators interpret that this means in either case the animal is deemed valid. Some say, *terefah*.]

## XII.3

A. And Raba said, "An [animal with a] lung that dried up partially is *terefah*." And how much [must dry up for it to be deemed *terefah*]? Said R. Pappi in the name of Raba, "[Dry enough] so that [scraping it with] a fingernail will crack it."

B. *In accord with what authority is this rule? In accord with R. Yosé b. Ha-Meshullam. For it was taught on Tannaite authority,* **What is the meaning of 'dried up' [in reference to the ear of a firstling that is deemed a blemish]? Such that if it is pierced it does not produce a drop of blood. R. Yosé b. Meshullam says, "'Dried' means that it crumbles [by scraping it with] a fingernail [M. Bekh. 6:1 C-E]."**

C. *You can even say [that the rule for a dried lung is consistent with the rule of] the rabbis [regarding a firstling]. [You can argue that] with regard to the ear of a firstling that is exposed to the air, [even a partially dried ear] will not return to health. But a [partially dried] lung that is not exposed to the air will return to health.*

D. And Said Raba, "A lung that had scabs all over it, black spots all over it, white spots all over it, it is valid."

E. Said Amemar in the name of Raba, "We do not make comparison tests of cysts." [If a burst cyst is found on the lung we do not compare it to another on the lung to determine whether it constitutes a defect.]

F. And said Raba, "[Animals that have] these two lobes of the lung that adhere to one another cannot be inspected [without thereby tearing the tissue]."

G. *And we say this only with regard to [lobes that adhered to one another] that were not aligned properly. But concerning those [that adhered to one another] that were in their proper alignment, this is effective [for them to prevent defects].*

H. [47a] And said Raba, "These two cysts [on the lung] that are adjacent to one another are not subject to inspection. [They are definite symptoms of an underlying defect.]

I. *"If there is one [cyst] that looks like two, we take a thorn and lance it. If [the fluid] flows from one to the other, it is one [cyst] and it is valid. If not, it is two [cysts] and it is terefah."*

J. *And said Raba, "The lung has five lobes. Facing the animal, there are three on the right and two on the left. If there are fewer or more or they are reversed, it is terefah."*

K. *These [lungs of an animal with] an added lobe were brought before Meremar [for a ruling]. R. Aha was sitting at the gate. He [Aha] said to him [the one who inquired], "What did he say to you?" He said to him, "He declared them valid." He said to him, "Take them before him again [for another ruling]." He [Meremar] said to him [the inquirer], "Go tell the one who sits at the gate that the law does not follow in accord with Raba with regard to a case of an additional lobe [in the lung]."*

L. *And this concern applies where it is found in among the lobes. But if it was found between the lungs, it is terefah. These [lungs of an animal with an added lobe] between the lungs were brought before R. Ashi [for a ruling]. R. Ashi reasoned that he should declare them terefah. Said to him R. Huna Mar bar Avya, "All healthy grazing animals have this lobe. And the butchers call it the fragile little rose lobe."*

M. *And this concern applies when [the added lobe between the lungs] is found in the front.* **[47b]** *But when it is found behind [the lungs], even if it is [as small as] a myrtle leaf, it is terefah.*

N. *Said Rafram, "This lung that resembles wood is terefah." Some say [this means like wood] in appearance. Some say, in texture. Some say, pale [like wood]. Some say, hard [like wood]. Some say, smooth [like wood] with no indentations in the lobe.*

O. *And said Raba, "If it [the lung] is blue, it is valid. But if it is inky black, it is terefah." For said R. Hanina, "A black [lung is but a] red [lung] that was diseased."*

P. *A green [lung] is valid in accord with the view of R. Nathan. A red [lung] is valid in accord with the view of R. Nathan.*

*Bavli Ḥullin Chapter Three. Folios 42A-67B*

Q. *As it was taught on Tannaite authority*: R. Nathan says, "Once I went to the towns by the sea. A woman came before me who had circumcised her first son and he died. [She circumcised] her second son, and he died. Her third son she brought before me [for a ruling]. I observed that he was flushed red. I said to her, 'My daughter. Wait until his blood is circulating better.' She waited for him [to improve], and then she circumcised him and he lived. And they named him after me, Nathan the Babylonian.

R. "And another time I went to the province of Cappadocia. A woman came before me who had circumcised her first son and he died. [She circumcised] her second son, and he died. Her third son she brought before me [for a ruling]. I observed that he was greenish [anemic (Cashdan)]. I examined him and determined that he did not have blood suitable for circumcision. I said to her, 'My daughter. Wait until his blood pressure improves.' She waited for him [to improve], and then she circumcised him and he lived. And they named him after me, Nathan the Babylonian."

### XII.4

A. Said R. Kahana, "[A lung that looks in its color] like a liver is valid. [If it looks] like flesh, it is *terefah*." And a mnemonic for this [rule is the verse where the words flesh and *terefah* appear together], "Therefore you shall not eat any flesh that is torn by beasts in the field (*terefah*)" (Ex. 22:31).

B. *Said R. Sama the son of Raba*, "A lung that looks [in color] like cuscuta or like a crocus or like an egg [yolk] is terefah. Rather what is the definition of the green color that is [for a lung] valid? Green like a leek.

### XII.5

A. *Said Rabina*, "[If there is] an obstruction in the lung, they take a knife and cut into it. If pus exudes then it is surely on account of the pus [that there was an obstruction, not another defect] and it is valid. And if none exudes then they place upon it a feather or some saliva. If it flutters or bubbles [because air passes through], then it is valid. And if not, it is terefah [because this is a substantive defect of the lung]."

B. Said R. Joseph, "A membrane that forms as a result of an injury to the lung is not [a valid] membrane [and the animal is *terefah*]."

C. *And said R. Joseph, "A lung that hisses [with a leak of air when inflated] — if we know where it is hissing, we put on it a feather or some saliva or straw, and if it bubbles [or wobbles, the animal] is terefah. If it does not, it is valid. And if we do not know where it is hissing, we bring a tub of warm water and we immerse [the lung] in it [to locate the leak]. It cannot be hot water because this would cause contraction [and we could not locate the leak]. It cannot be cold water because this would cause hardening [and the membrane might crack]. But we immerse it in warm water and we inflate it. If it bubbles, it is terefah. If it does not, it is valid. [We conclude in the latter case that] the interior membrane is pierced and the exterior membrane is not pierced. And the hissing sound is air flowing between the membranes."* [See above XII.1 E.]

D. Said Ulla, said R. Yohanan, "A lung whose tissue flows like liquid [inside of its membranes] is valid. *It seems [logical to conclude] that he reasons that a defect inside [the tissue of the lung] does not have the status of a defect* [that renders the animal *terefah*]."

E. R. Abba raised an objection to Ulla, "[The Mishnah says], **The lung which is pierced or lacking [any part thereof].** What does **lacking** mean? If you say it means lacking on the exterior, that is the same as **pierced**. So does it not mean lacking on the interior. And so we may derive from this that any lack on the interior has the status of a lack [that renders the animal *terefah*]."

F. No. [This objection does not stand.] It is consistent to say that **lacking** refers to the exterior. And what [about what] was stated [as an objection that this is redundant because] that is the same as **pierced**? It is necessary [to state both] in accord with the view of R. Simeon who said, **"[It is not *terefah*] until its bronchial tubes are pierced."** This concern applies to a hole [puncture] that does not lack [any tissue, i.e., that it must go deep.] But with regard to a hole that does lack [tissue] even R. Simeon agrees [that it is *terefah* even if it does not pierce the bronchial tubes].

G. *R. Hanina became infirm. R. Nathan and all of the great rabbis of the generation came up to visit him. They brought before him [for a ruling] a lung whose tissue flowed like liquid [inside of its membranes] and he declared it valid.*

Bavli Ḥullin Chapter Three. Folios 42A-67B

H. Said Raba, "And this [is the rule in an instance where] the bronchial tubes are intact."

I. *Said R. Aha the son of Raba to R. Ashi, "How do we determine [whether they are intact]?" He said to him, "They bring a glazed pot and they pour [the liquified lung matter] into it. If there are white streaks in it, it is terefah. And if not, it is valid."*

J. Said R. Nahman, "A lung whose tissue liquified but whose membranes are intact is valid." *It was taught on Tannaite authority also in this regard,* A lung whose tissue liquified but whose membranes are intact, even if it [the cavity caused by the change] had the volume of a quarter *log*, it is valid.

K. If its womb was missing **[48a]**, it is valid. If its liver became worm-infested [the law is unclear]. [Regarding] this [case] was an incident where the residents of Asia Minor came up on three occasions to Yavneh [seeking a ruling on the matter]. On the third [occasion a decision was rendered] that permitted [such a case] for them.

XIII.1
A. Said R. Joseph bar Manyomi, said R. Nahman, "[Regarding] a lung that adjoins the wall [of the chest cavity], we are not concerned [that it is a sign of a *terefah*]. If ulcerations erupted [on the lung near the place it adjoins the chest], we are concerned [that this indicates it is a *terefah*]."

B. Mar Judah in the name of Abimi said, "In both [of the above] cases we are concerned [that the animal is *terefah*]."

C. *What is the procedure* [for determining whether it is a sign of a *terefah*]? Said Raba, "Rabin bar Sheba explained to me that we bring a sharpened knife [i.e., a scalpel] and we detach it [the lung from the wall of the chest]. If there is a taint on the wall (Cashdan), we then presume that [some secretion from] the chest wall caused [the lung to adhere to the wall]. And if not, then [some secretion] from the lung caused [the adhesion] and it is terefah."

D. [And this is the case] even if air does not escape [from the lung after it is detached from the chest wall. Most MSS omit this last phrase.]

**XIII.2**

A. *R. Nehemiah the son of R. Joseph inspected it [the lung detached from the chest wall] in warm water. Said Mar Zutra, the son of R. Huna, the son of R. Pappi to Rabina, "Do you cite this [procedure] of R. Nehemiah the son of R. Joseph in connection with this case? We cite it in connection with [this case taught by] Raba. For said Raba, '[Animals that have] these two lobes of the lung that adhere to one another cannot be inspected to render them fit [without thereby tearing the tissue]' [above, XII.3 F]."*

B. *[And we cite the teaching:] R. Nehemiah the son of R. Joseph inspected it [the lung with two adhering lobes] in warm water. R. Ashi raised an objection [to citing this teaching in connection with this latter case]. What is the use of applying this rule here? It makes sense [to apply the rule] here [in the case of a lung that adhered to the wall of the chest]. [If we find a hole in the lung] we can attribute its cause to [adhesion resulting from a defect in] the wall and [the animal will be deemed] valid. But there [in the case of the lung with two adhering lobes], if this one [lobe] has a hole, it is* terefah, *and if that one [lobe] has a hole, it is* terefah.

C. *And did R. Nahman say this? [I.e., If ulcerations erupted [on the lung near the place it adjoins the chest], we are concerned [that this indicates it is a* terefah] *[XIII.1 A].] Lo, said R. Joseph bar Manyomi, said R. Nahman, "A lung that was pierced and the wall of the chest seals it [the hole], it is valid."*

D. *There is no contradiction. There [where we declare that it is valid, the hole is located] in a place they naturally abut. Here [where we declare that it is terefah, the hole is located] in a place they do not naturally abut. [Though the wall seals off the hole in the lung, in this latter circumstance they likely will separate.]*

E. *And where is the place that they naturally abut? Where the lobes split off [at the top of the chest].*

**XIII.3**

A. *Reverting to the body of the previous text [C, above]:* Said R. Joseph bar Manyomi, said R. Nahman, "A lung that was pierced and the wall of the chest seals it [the hole], it is valid." Said Rabina,

Bavli Ḥullin Chapter Three. Folios 42A-67B

"[And that is so] where it fused into the flesh [and there was a symphysis of the lung and intercostal muscles (Cashdan)]."

B. Said R. Joseph to Rabina, "And if they did not fuse what is the law? It is terefah. It seems [logical to conclude] that we say it is deemed to be pierced [prior to fusing]. When it has fused it should also [be deemed to be pierced]. For lo, it was taught on Tannaite authority, If [a man's penis] was pierced he is invalid because he is languid [in ejaculating semen]. If it was closed up, he is valid because he can inseminate. And this is a defect [that renders invalid] that can return to validity [T. Yeb. 10:4 E-G]."

C. [What does the phrase] "And this is" exclude? Does it not exclude a case like this one [of a defect in the lung of an animal sealed up by contact with the chest wall]? No, it excludes [the case of] a membrane that formed as a result of an injury to the lung. For this is not deemed to be a valid membrane.

D. R. Uqba bar Hama raised an objection to this, "If it was pierced in the chest wall at that spot, what would be the law? It would be deemed terefah. Let it teach [in the Mishnah the case of] the chest wall that was pierced [as one of the animals that is deemed terefah]."

E. And according to your view that which R. Yitzhak bar Joseph said in the name of R. Yohanan [cf. II.1 E-F, above], "[If] the gallbladder was pierced and the liver seals it up, it is valid." If the liver was pierced at that spot what would be the law? It would be deemed terefah. Let it teach [the case of] the liver that was pierced. Rather it must be that a case where if it was pierced [i.e., in the liver] not in this circumstance [where it seals a hole in another organ, such a hole does not render the animal terefah and accordingly such a case] is not taught. Here as well because it is a case where [if it was pierced in the chest wall] not in this circumstance [where the chest seals a hole in the lung, such a hole does not render the animal terefah and accordingly such a case] is not taught.

XIII.4

A. Rabbah bar bar Hannah posed a question to Samuel, "If ulcerations erupt [on the lung] what is the law?" He said to him, "It is valid." He said to him, "I also say this. But the students balked [at the ruling] in this matter."

B. For said R. Matna, "If they [the ulcerations] are filled with pus, it is terefah. [If they are filled with] clear water, it is valid."

C. He [Samuel] said to him, "This rule was stated with regard to the kidneys."

XIII.5
A. *R. Yitzhak bar Joseph was following R. Jeremiah through the butcher's market. He saw some lungs that had upon them ulcerations. He said to him, "Does not the master want a fine piece?" He said to him, "I have no money." He said to him, "I'll vouch for you [that your credit is good]." He said to him, "What will I do with you? [You are so persistent.]"* [But he gave no indication of his view on the matter.]

B. *When such [cases of lungs with ulcerations] came before R. Yohanan [for a ruling] he would send them before R. Judah b. R. Simeon who ruled regarding them in the name of R. Eleazar b. R. Simeon to permit them [for consumption]. But he [Yohanan himself] did not reason in accord with that view.*

C. *Said Raba, "When we walked behind R. Nahman in the leather market* **[48b]**, *and some say [this took place] in the scholars' market, we saw those [lungs] that had large growths on them. And he did not say anything to them [to indicate that he deemed these* terefah]."

D. *R. Ammi and R. Assi were traversing the market in Tiberias. They saw those [lungs] that had gigantic growths. And they did not say anything to them [to indicate that they deemed these* terefah].

XIV.1
A. It was stated: If a needle was found in the lung, R. Yohanan and R. Eleazar and R. Hanina declared it valid. And R. Simeon b. Laqish and R. Mani bar Patish and R. Simeon b. Eliakim declared it *terefah*.

B. *Let us say that they disputed this [principle of law]. Those masters [who say it is invalid] reason* that a lack internal [to the lung] has the status of a lack [that renders it invalid]. And *those masters [who say it is valid] reason* that a lack internal [to the organ] does not have the status of a lack [that renders it invalid].

C. *No. All parties agree that a lack internal [to the organ] does not have the status of a lack [that renders it invalid]. And here it is over this [principle] that they dispute. Those masters [who say it is valid] reason it [could have] entered through the bronchial tubes [and not pierce the organ]. And those masters [who say it is invalid] reason it [must have] pierced the organ as it entered [the lung].*

D. *A certain needle that was found in a slice of a lung. They brought it before R. Ammi [for a ruling]. He reasoned he could declare it valid. R. Jeremiah objected and some say R. Zeriqa [objected based on the text of the Mishnah]:* **The lung which is pierced or lacking [any part thereof] [M. 3:1 D].** *What does* **lacking** *mean? If you say it means lacking on the exterior, that is the same as* **pierced***. So does it not mean lacking on the interior? And so we may derive from this that any lack on the interior has the status of a lack [that renders the animal terefah]. [See above XII.5 E.]*

E. *They then sent it before R. Yitzhak Nappaha [for a ruling]. He reasoned he could declare it valid. R. Jeremiah objected and some say R. Zeriqa [objected based on the text of the Mishnah]:* **The lung which is pierced or lacking [any part thereof] [M. 3:1 D].** *What does* **lacking** *mean? If you say it means lacking on the exterior, that is the same as* **pierced***. So does it not mean lacking on the interior? And so we may derive from this that any lack on the interior has the status of a lack [that renders the animal terefah].*

F. *They then sent it before R. Ammi and he declared it* terefah. *They said to him, "But lo the Rabbis have declared it valid." He said to them, "They who declared it valid know for what reason they declared it valid. On what basis shall we declare it valid? Perhaps if the entire lung was in front of us we would find that it was pierced."*

G. *The basis [for his declaring it* terefah*] was that it was not there [before him]. Lo [this implies that] if it was there before him and was not pierced, it would be valid. But lo said R. Nahman, "This bronchial tube of the lung that was pierced, it is* terefah.*" This was stated for [a case of] one next to another [at a branch point].*

H. *But lo said R. Nahman, "This colon of an intestine that was pierced where it is next to another, it protects it [and seals the hole and so it is valid.]."*

I. *Can you compare [defects that render animals]* terefot *to one another? We do not say concerning [defects that render animals]* terefot *that this one resembles that one. For lo you may cut from this place [on an animal] and it will die. You may cut from here [an identical amount in another place on the animal] and it will live.*

### XIV.2
A. *A certain needle was found in the main bronchial tube of the lung. They brought it before the rabbis who declared* terefah *[other cases of a needle found in the lung]. They did not declare it prohibited or permitted [in this instance]. They neither declared it permitted in accord with our account [above]. Nor did they declare it prohibited because it was found in the main bronchial tube [and not in the lung]. It made sense to say that it entered through the bronchial tube [and not through the esophagus].*

B. *A certain needle was found in a slice of liver. Mar the son of R. Joseph reasoned that he should declare it* terefah. *Said to him R. Ashi, "If such an object was found lodged in the flesh of the animal would our master declare it* terefah? *[The same should apply to the liver.]"*

C. *Rather said R. Ashi, "Let us take a look. If the head of the needle points toward the exterior [of the liver], then we may say that it pierced [other organs as it entered and the animal is* terefah]. *If the head of the needle points toward the interior [of the liver], then we may say that it entered through the tube [i.e., the ductus choledocus (Cashdan)]. And this concern applies in the case of a large needle. But in the case of a small needle it makes no difference whether the head points toward the exterior or toward the interior. [We presume that] it pierced [organs] as it entered."*

D. *And why is this different from the case of a needle that was found* **[49a]** *in the thick wall of the reticulum? [With regard to that we say if it protrudes] from one side it is valid; from two sides it is* terefah. *And we do not say let us take a look to see whether the head points toward the exterior or toward the interior. We may say there that because food and drink pass through, it makes sense to say that the food or drink pushed it [into the wall of the reticulum and it is not of any use to inspect to see whether the head points inward or outward. It is* terefah *only if it pierced all the way through].*

*Bavli Ḥullin Chapter Three. Folios 42A-67B*

E. *A certain needle was found in the large portal vein of the liver [of an animal]. Huna the master the son of R. Idi declared it terefah. R. Ada bar Manyomi declared it valid. They went and asked Rabina [which view to follow]. He said to them, "Take the mantles [of authority] off those who declared it terefah."*

F. *A certain [date] pit was found in the gallbladder [of an animal]. Said R. Ashi, "When I was in the house of R. Kahana he said this [object] certainly came in through the portal vein. Even though it cannot exit [naturally from the vein], the movements [of the animal as it walks] move it along [in the vein]. And this case applies to the pit of a date. But the pit of an olive surely can pierce [organs and lodge in the vein like a needle (Rashi)]."*

**XV.1**

A. Said R. Yohanan, "Why do they call [the lung] *ry'h*? Because [of the play on the Hebrew words]: it lights up [*m'yrh*, from the same root] the eyes [of the person who eats it]."

B. *They posed a question*: [Does the statement that the lung lights up the eyes mean] eating [the lung] or [applying it to the eyes along] with medications?

C. *Come and take note:* For said R. Huna bar Judah, "A whole goose [may sell for] one zuz. But its lung [alone may sell for] four zuz." And if you wish to conclude that [a lung helps the eyes] through eating, then buy it [the whole goose] for a zuz and eat it! Rather it must be that [it helps the eyes if applied] with medications.

**XV.2**

A. If the lung was pierced in a place where the butcher [normally] handles it, do we impute [the defect to his handling] or not? R. Ada bar R. Nathan says, "We impute it [to him]." Mar Zutra the son of R. Mari said, "We do not impute it [to him]." And the law is that we do impute it [to him].

B. Said R. Samuel the son of R. Abahu, "My father was one of the head [spokesmen] of Rafram's seminars. And he said [the law is] that we do impute it [to the butcher]."

C. *They stated this before Mar Zutra the son of R. Mari and he would not accept this [as binding]. Said R. Mesharshayya, "It makes sense to accept the view of my father's father. For we [hold the view that we may] impute [damage to intestines that are dragged away] to a wolf [cf. M. 1:1, I.17 C, Zahavy, Hullin, vol. I, p. 51]."*

XV.3
A. A worm [that bored a hole in the lung of an animal] — *there is a dispute over this matter between R. Joseph bar Dostai and the rabbis. One said [we may presume that] it bored through before the animal was slaughtered [and so the defect is of consequence]. And the other said [we may presume that] it bored through after the animal was slaughtered [and so the defect is of no consequence]. And the law follows the view [that we presume] it bored through after the animal was slaughtered.*

XVI.1
A. **R. Simeon says, "[It is not *terefah*] until its bronchial tubes are pierced [M. 3:1 E]."** *Said Rabbah bar Tahlifa, said R. Jeremiah bar Abba, "[This means] until the major bronchial tube is pierced."*

B. *R. Aha bar Abba sat [and taught] before R. Huna. He sat and said, "Said R. Malokh, said R. Joshua b. Levi, 'The law is in accord with the view of R. Simeon.' He said to him, 'You are stating the view of Malokh of Arabia. He has stated that the law is not in accord with R. Simeon.'"*

C. *When R. Zira departed [to Israel] he found R. Bibi sitting [in session] and stating, "Said R. Malokh, said R. Joshua b. Levi, 'The law is in accord with R. Simeon.'" He said to him, "By the master's life! For I and R. Hiyya bar Abba and R. Assi came to R. Malokh's place and we said to him, 'Did the master say that the law followed in accord with the view of R. Simeon?' And he said to us, 'The law does not follow in accord with the view of R. Simeon.' And we [Bibi] said [to Zira], 'And what [tradition] do you have in your hand?' And he said to him as follows: 'Said R. Yitzhak bar Ammi, said R. Joshua b. Levi, 'The law follows in accord with R. Simeon.'"*

D. *And the law does not follow in accord with R. Simeon.*

## XVII.1

A. **[If] the belly [abomasum] is pierced [M. 3:1 F].** Said R. Yitzhak bar Nahmani, said R. Oshaia, "The fat attached to the abomasum, the priests were accustomed to treating it as permitted [for eating] in accord with the view of R. Ishmael, who stated the matter in the name of his ancestors."

B. And your mnemonic [for this teaching] is, "Ishmael the priest helps support the priests." *What makes you say this? [We see that Ishmael supports the priests from the following.]* For it was taught on Tannaite authority, "Thus you shall bless the people of Israel" (Num 6:23). R. Ishmael says, "We learned [from this phrase in the verse] of a blessing for Israel from the mouths of the priests. [A blessing] for the priests themselves we do not learn about [from this phrase]. When the verse states, 'And I will bless them' (Num. 6:27) you could say [that means] that the priests bless Israel and the Holy One blessed be He blesses the priests."

C. R. Aqiba says, "[From the first verse] we derived that there was a blessing for Israel from the mouths of the priests. We did not derive that there was a blessing for Israel from the mouth of the Almighty [from that verse]. When the verse states, 'And I will bless them,' you could say [that means] the priests bless Israel and the Holy One blessed be He concurs with them."

D. Then *where* [in Scripture] according to the view of R. Aqiba do we find that there is a blessing for the priests? Said R. Nahman bar Yitzhak, "From 'I will bless those who bless you' (Gen. 12:3)."

E. [If there is support according to both for a blessing for the priests, then] *in what way does R. Ishmael support the priests? In that he upholds the view that the [evidence for the] blessing for the priests is in the same place [in Scripture] as the blessing for Israel.*

F. *What is the point of [the teaching of] R. Ishmael who stated the matter in the name of his ancestors? As was taught on Tannaite authority,* **"And all the fat that is on the entrails" (Lev. 3:3): [49b] "This is the fat which is on the abomasum," the words of R. Aqiba. R. Ishmael says, "The fat which is on the maw." [And sages did not concur with him.] [T. 9:14 E-G.]**

G. *And they raised a contradiction:* "And all the fat that is on the entrails" (Lev. 3:3): R. Simeon [var. Ishmael] says, "Just as that fat that is on the entrails is encased in a membrane and easily peeled away, likewise any [fat that is prohibited is] encased in a membrane and is easily peeled away." [This includes as prohibited the fat that is on the abomasum in contradiction to Ishmael's teaching at F.]

H. R. Aqiba says, "Just as that fat that is on the entrails is layered [across the organ], encased in a membrane and easily peeled away, likewise any [fat that is prohibited is] layered, encased in a membrane and is easily peeled away."

I. *Sent Rabin in the name of R. Yohanan, "This is the correct presentation of the [views in the] Mishnah [i.e., the teachings of G-H]. And you must reverse the [attributions of the views] in the first [teachings, in F]."*

J. *Why is it more fitting to reverse [the attributions of the views] in the first [text]? Reverse [them in] the last [i.e., the second text]? That one is different because it teaches [more fully, spelling out the rule using the language], "Just as..." [hence] it is [more] specific.*

K. *If so* [why does it say above at A that they ruled leniently] in accord with the view of R. Ishmael, it is in accord with the view of R. Aqiba? Said R. Nahman bar Yitzhak, "[The pericope in A hedges the attribution by saying] he stated the matter in the name of his ancestors. [This implies that] he himself did not reason in accord with this view."

## XVIII.1
A. Said Rab, "Clean [i.e., permitted] fat can seal [a hole in an organ]. Unclean [i.e., forbidden] fat cannot." And R. Sheshet, "Both can seal [a hole]."

B. R. Zira posed a question: What about fat from a wild beast? [Can it seal a hole?] Did it state specifically that clean fat can seal up a hole and this too is clean fat? Or perhaps [clean fat can seal up a hole] because it is sticky. And this [fat from a wild beast] is not sticky [enough to seal a hole].

*Bavli Ḥullin Chapter Three. Folios 42A-67B*     59

C.     *Said Abayye, "What is his question? [Even] if it is permitted for eating, [if] it is not sticky [then it is not effective in sealing a hole]."*

D.     *There was [an organ with] a hole that had been sealed up by unclean [forbidden] fat that was brought before Raba [for a ruling]. Said Raba, "What shall we be concerned with? First, lo R. Sheshet [at A] said that unclean fat also can serve to seal a hole. And furthermore [we have a principle that] the Torah had mercy on the money of an Israelite."*

E.     Said R. Pappa to Raba, "[We should be concerned with two things. First there is the contrary view of] Rab. [And furthermore this is a case that involves] a prohibition based on the authority of the Torah. *And yet you say* [we should invoke the principle that] the Torah had mercy on the money of an Israelite!"

**XVIII.2**
A.     *Manyomin, the pot merchant, left a pot of honey uncovered. They brought it before Raba [for a ruling]. He said, "What shall we be concerned with? First, it was taught in the Mishnah on Tannaite authority,* **Three [kinds of] liquids are forbidden [for consumption] on account of [danger of poisoning in an instance of being discovered in a vessel that is] uncovered: (1) water, (2) wine, and (3) milk. [But all other liquids are permitted for consumption, even if left uncovered]** [M. Ter. 8:4]. And furthermore, [we should invoke the principle that] the Torah had mercy on the money of an Israelite."

B.     Said R. Nahman bar Yitzhak to Raba, "[We should be concerned. First there is the contrary view of] R. Simeon. [And furthermore this is a case that involves] a life threatening danger. *And yet you say* [we should invoke the principle that] the Torah had mercy on the money of an Israelite!"

C.     *What [contrary view] of R. Simeon [do they refer to above]? That which was taught on Tannaite authority,* **Five [liquids] are not subject to [the prohibition of consumption on account of danger of poisoning in an instance of being discovered in a vessel that is] uncovered: brine, vinegar, oil, honey and** *muries.* **And R. Simeon says, "Even among these there are those [instances]** when they are [prohibited for consumption on account of being discovered] uncovered [T. Ter. 7:12, variant version]."

D. And said R. Simeon, "I saw a serpent drink brine in Sidon." They said to him, "That snake was a blockhead. And you cannot adduce proof from the actions of blockheads."

E. *He [Raba] said to him [Nahman], "Admit I am right at least with regard to brine [that a serpent cannot poison it]. For lo R. Pappa and R. Huna the son of R. Joshua and the rabbis when they had [an instance of liquid that was uncovered] they would pour into it brine [to neutralize any poisons]."*

F. *He [Nahman] said to him [Raba], "Admit I am right at least with regard to honey [that a serpent can poison it]. For R. Simeon b. Eleazar upholds his [i.e., Simeon's] view. For it was taught on Tannaite authority:* And likewise R. Simeon b. Eleazar used to prohibit honey [that was left uncovered]."

## XVIII.3

A. Said R. Nahman, "Forbidden fat [on an organ] in the shape of a hat does not serve to seal up [a hole]." *What is this [fat]? Some say this is the fat nodules of the rectum. And some say that this is the pericardium (Cashdan).*

B. *Said Raba, "I heard two rulings from R. Nahman regarding the himsa-fat and the bar-himsa-fat [on the abomasum]. [He rules that] one sealed [up a hole] and the other did not seal. And I do not know which is which."*

C. R. Huna bar Hinnena and R. Huna the son of R. Nahman said, "*Bar-himsa*-fat seals and *himsa*-fat does not seal."

D. Said R. Tabot, "And the mnemonic for this is: 'The strength of the son [i.e., *bar-himsa*-fat] is superior to that of the father.'"

E. *Which is the himsa and which is the bar-himsa? Come and take note: For said R. Nahman, "They [in Israel] eat it.* **[50a]** *For us, should it not serve to seal [a hole]?"*

F.  [The fat of the abomasum] on the greater curvature, everyone agrees that it is forbidden [to eat it]. Concerning what do they dispute? [Concerning the fat] on the lesser curvature. [See above, the dispute at XVII.1 F.]

G.  There are those that state [another version of the tradition]: [Concerning the fat] on the lesser curvature, everyone agrees that it is permitted [to eat it]. Concerning what did they dispute? [Concerning the fat] on the greater curvature.

H.  This [F] follows in accord with that which was said by R. Avya, said R. Ammi, "They pare [away a thin layer of the fat and may eat the rest]." And so said R. Yannai in the name of one elder, "They pare [away a layer]."

I.  Said R. Avya, "I was waiting on R. Ammi. They pared away [a layer] and gave him [from the remaining fat] and he ate it."

J.  The attendant of R. Hanina was waiting on him. He said to him, "Pare away [a layer]. Bring me [from the remaining fat] so that I may eat it." He saw that [the attendant] was balking. He said to him, "You are a Babylonian [and hold the view that it is all forbidden fat]. Carve it all away and toss it out."

### XIX.1

A.  *It was taught on Tannaite authority:* **Rabban Simeon b. Gamaliel says, "The intestines which were perforated, but which the fluid stops up — it is valid [T. 3:11 A].** *What* is the fluid? Said R. Kahana, "[It is] the liquid that can be squeezed out of the intestines."

B.  *The associate of R. Abba learned from R. Abba. And who was this? R. Zira. And some say the associate of R. Zira learned from R. Zira. And who was this? R. Abba. Said R. Abba the son of R. Hiyya bar Abba, "This was said by R. Hiyya bar Abba, said R. Yohanan, 'The law follows in accord with the view of R. Simeon b. Gamaliel with regard to terefah [i.e., declaring a perforated intestine valid if the fluid sealed the hole]. And [the law follows] R. Simeon with regard to mourning.'"*

C. The law follows in accord with the view of R. Simeon b. Gamaliel with regard to *terefah as we stated* [in A that a perforated intestine is valid if the fluid sealed the hole].

D. And what is [the case where the law follows] R. Simeon with regard to mourning? *As it was taught on Tannaite authority,* **During the first three days [of mourning] he who came from a nearby place counts [the days of mourning] with them [the other mourners]. [If he came] from a distant place he counts [the days] for himself. From that point onward [after the third day] even if he came from a nearby place, he counts for himself. R. Simeon says, "Even [if he comes] on the seventh day, he who came from a nearby place counts with them [b. M.Q. 21b]."**

E. *Someone once said, "May I merit that I may go [to Israel] and learn the tradition from the mouth of the master." When he did go [to Israel] he found R. Abba the son of R. Hiyya bar Abba. He said to him, "Did the master say that the law follows in accord with the view of R. Simeon b. Gamaliel with regard to* terefah?" *He said to him, "Lo, the law does not follow [in accord with the view of R. Simeon b. Gamaliel]."* [He said], *"They say, '[The law follows] in accord with R. Simeon with regard to mourning.' What about that?" He said to him, "That is a matter of dispute. For it was stated, 'R. Hisda said the law follows [in accord with R. Simeon]. And likewise R. Yohanan said the law follows [in accord with R. Simeon]. But R. Nahman said the law does not follow [in accord with R. Simeon]."*

F. And the law does not follow in accord with the view of R. Simeon b. Gamaliel with regard to *terefah*. But the law does follow in accord with the view of R. Simeon with regard to mourning. For said Samuel, "The law follows in accord with the lenient view in matters of mourning."

XX.1
A. [The Talmud now continues a matter taken up at the end of XIV.1.] Said R. Shimi bar Hiyya, "They may compare [defects] of the intestines [to determine if the defect arose before or after the animal was slaughtered]."

B. *There were intestines brought before Raba [for a ruling]. He compared them [with others] and they were not similar. R. Mesharshayya his son came and manipulated them until they were similar. He [Raba] said to him, "Where do you get [the idea that you may manipulate them to make them appear similar]?" He said to him, "How many hands manipulated these before they came before the master [for a ruling]?" He said to him, "My son is as learned in [the laws of] terefot as R. Yohanan."* [See b. 28b, M. 2:1, VI.3 N.]

XX.2

A. R. Yohanan and R. Eleazar *both said*, "They may compare [defects of] the lung." Said Raba, "They said this only [for defects in lungs] of the same side [right or left]. But from one side to the other they may not [compare defects]."

B. *And the law is* [that they may compare defects] even from one side to the other [in the same animal], from one small animal to another, or from one large animal to another. But they may neither [compare defects of the lung] from a large animal to a small animal, nor from a small animal to a large animal.

C. *Abayye and Raba both said*, "They may compare [defects of] the windpipe." Said R. Pappa, "They said this only [for defects in the windpipe] of the same cartilage-region. But from one region to another they may not [compare defects]."

D. *And the law is* [that they may compare defects] even from one cartilage-region to another and from one membrane-region to another. But they may not [compare defects of the windpipe] from a cartilage-region to a membrane-region or from a membrane-region to a cartilage-region.

XX.3

A. Said Ziri, "If the rectum was pierced it is valid because the hips support it."

B. And how much [must be pierced before it is deemed *terefah*]? Said R. Ilai, said R. Yohanan, "In the part [of the rectum] that is attached [to the hip it must be torn in] a major portion. In a part that is not attached, any amount [that is torn renders it *terefah*]."

C. *The rabbis stated this before Raba in the name of R. Nahman. He said, "Has not someone told you not to attribute* **[50b]** *nonsensical views to him?" This is what R. Nahman said, "In the part that is attached [to the hip] even if it is entirely torn away, it is valid as long as there remained a part that can be grasped."*

D. *And how much is this? Said Abayye, "As [much as] the size of a finger [suffices even in the largest] ox."*

XXI.1
A. [If] the innermost belly [rumen] is pierced [M. 3:1 F]. Said R. Judah, said Rab, "Nathan **Ben Shila, head of the butchers of Sepphoris, testified** before Rabbi in the name of R. Nathan, 'This is the mucal sieve' [cf. T. 3:2 E]."

B. And so said R. Joshua b. Levi, "This is the mucal sieve." R. Ishmael said, "It is the stomach [entrance] of the rumen."

C. R. Assi said R. Yohanan, "This is a narrow part of the rumen. But I do not know which one." Said R. Nahman bar Yitzhak, "The rumen might as well have fallen into a well. [This last statement clarifies nothing.]"

D. Said R. Aha bar R. Ava, said R. Assi, "From where it narrows and below [that is the innermost belly]." R. Jacob bar Nahmani, said Samuel, "In the part that has no furry lining." R. Abina, said Geniva in the name of Rab, "The part of the windpipe within a handbreadth of the rumen is the inner rumen."

E. *They said in the West in the name of R. Yosé bar Hanina, "The entire rumen is called the inner rumen. And what then is the outer rumen? The fleshy membrane that covers the major part of the rumen." Rabbah bar R. Huna said, "[The outer rumen is] the exposed part." What is the exposed part? Said R. Avya, "That part which is exposed by the butcher [when he slits open the abdomen to remove the intestines]."*

F. *In Nehardea they acted in accord with Rabbah bar R. Huna. R. Ashi said to Amemar, "What do we do with all the other views?" He said to him, "They are all subsumed in the view of Rabbah bar R. Huna." [He said], "But [what about the view] of R. Assi said R. Yohanan [in C]?"*

*Bavli Hullin Chapter Three. Folios 42A-67B* 65

He said to him, "That was explained by R. Aha bar Ava [in D]." [He said], "[But what about the views] of R. Abina [D] and the people of the West [E]?" He said to him, "These views are certainly in dispute [with Rabbah bar R. Huna]."

### XXII.1

A. R. Judah says, "In the case of a large animal, a handbreadth, and in the case of a small one, its greater part [M. 3:1 H]." Said R. Benjamin bar Yapet, said R. Eleazar, "Neither does large mean actually in a large animal. Nor does small mean actually in a small animal. But in any case where if the size of a handbreadth was torn and this did not constitute the major part, this is what we meant by, In the case of a large animal, a handbreadth. [And in any case where if] a major part was torn and this did not constitute the size of a handbreadth, this is what we meant by, In the case of a small one, its greater part."

B. [The case where if] a major part was torn and this did not constitute the size of a handbreadth, *this is obvious* [that it is *terefah*]! *It is necessary to state it. For this is where it was [torn through a major part and would have been torn through] a handbreadth with just a small amount more. What might you have said? Until it is torn a handbreadth it is not terefah. It makes the point [that even so it is terefah].*

### XXII.2

A. Said R. Assi, "If it [a circular part of the rumen] was cut out in the size of a large coin, it is *terefah*. For if you stretch it out [the circumference] will equal a handbreadth."

B. Said R. Hiyya bar Abba, "*The teaching of Geniva was explained to me on the bridge of Nehardea*: [If a hole was found] as large as a large coin, it is valid. Larger than a large coin, it is *terefah*." And how much is more than a large coin? Said R. Joseph, "*Big enough for three date pits with fruit on them to pass through with pressure, or without fruit on them to pass through with space.*"

### XXIII.1

A. **The omasum or the second stomach [reticulum] which are pierced on the outer edge [M. 3:1 H].** *The rabbis taught,* **A needle which is found in the thick wall of the reticulum [M. Hul. 3:2**

C6], when it protrudes from one side, it [the animal] is valid. [When it protrudes] on both sides, it is invalid. If there is in its place a coagulated drop of blood, [51a] one may be certain that [the needle was in place] before slaughter. [If] there is not in its place a coagulated drop of blood, one may be certain that [the needle was in place] after slaughter. [If] the surface of a wound formed a scab, one may be certain that [it was there] three days before slaughter. [If] the surface of a wound did not form a scab, [then] he who makes a claim against his fellow must bring proof [that the animal is invalid] [T. 3:11 B-D].

B. *And why is this [case of the needle in the reticulum] different from all other [instances of] piercing where even if there is no blood the master may declare it terefah?*

C. *There [in the other cases] there was nothing [for the blood] to adhere to. Here [in our case] since there is a needle [in the hole], if it was there before the slaughtering, [the blood] would surely have adhered to it.*

D. Said R. Safra to Abayye, "Has the master seen the great rabbi who came from the West and says his name is R. Avira? And he said it once happened that a [case of a] needle that protruded from one side of the thick wall of the reticulum came before Rabbi [for a ruling]. And he declared it *terefah*. He sent for him [Avira]. But he did not come to him. He [Abayye] himself went to him [Avira]. He was standing on the roof. He [Abayye] said, 'Come Down Master.' He did not come down. He [Abayye] went up to him. He said to him, 'Tell me what were the main points of the incident.'"

E. "He said to him, 'I was at the back of the assembly of the most high great Rabbi. And R. Huna from Sepphoris and R. Yosé of Medea were sitting before him. And there came to Rabbi [a case for a ruling] of a needle found in the thick wall of the reticulum [protruding] from one side. And Rabbi turned it over and found on it a coagulated drop of blood and declared it *terefah*. And he said, "If there is no wound there, where did the coagulated drop of blood come from?"'"

F. *He [Abayye] said to him, "You put me through so much trouble [with this lengthy story to relate such an obvious rule]. It is in the Mishnah:* **The omasum or the second stomach [reticulum] that are pierced on the exterior [M. 3:1 H].**"

*Bavli Ḥullin Chapter Three. Folios 42A-67B*        67

**XXIV.1**

A.      **[If] it fell from the roof [M. 3:1 I].** Said R. Huna, "If he left an animal above [on the roof] and came and found it below [on the ground], we do not suspect there is any [hidden] injury to its limbs." [If we did suspect we would require that he wait for twenty-four hours before slaughtering the animal.]

B.      *Rabina had a kid [on his roof]. It saw peeled barley through the skylight [in the house]. It jumped and fell from the roof to the ground.*

C.      *He [Rabina] came before R. Ashi [for a ruling]. He said to him, "Lo, R. Huna said, 'If he left an animal above [on the roof] and came and found it below [on the ground], we do not suspect there is any [hidden] injury to its limbs.' [Is this] because it had something [i.e., the wall of the house] to rub against [to slow it as it fell]. But here [because it jumped through a skylight] it had nothing to rub against. Or perhaps [we do not suspect injury where it jumped from the roof] because it estimated itself [that it could make the jump safely] and here too it estimated itself [that it could make the jump safely]."*

D.      *He said to him, "[It was that we do not suspect injury where it jumped from the roof] because it estimated itself [that it could make the jump safely] and here too it estimated itself [that it could make the jump safely]."*

E.      *In R. Habiba's house there was a ewe that dragged its hind legs behind it. Said R. Yemar, "This one is afflicted with sciatica." [But it is not terefah.] Rabina objected, "Perhaps its spine is broken."*

F.      *They inspected it and found [its spine was broken] in accord with Rabina. And even so the law follows in accord with R. Yemar [because] sciatica is common but [a broken] spine is not common.*

G.      Said R. Huna, "[In the case of] rams that butt one another we do not suspect there is any [hidden] injury to its limbs. *Even though they groan in pain [we generally may assume that] the intensity of the contest has overcome them. If they fall to the ground [as a result of the butting] then we certainly should suspect [they suffered serious injury]."*

H. Said R. Menashe, "These rams that were stolen by burglars [who must have dropped them over an enclosure to steal them] — we do not suspect that there is any [hidden] injury to their limbs. What is the basis for this [conclusion]? When they throw them [over the enclosure], they throw them on their sides [so they will not be injured and] so they will be ready to run. If they threw them [the rams] back [to the enclosure], we certainly suspect [injury because under such circumstances the burglars would not care about them]. And this is the case only where they threw them back out of fear [of being caught with stolen goods]. But where they threw them back out of remorse [over the burglary, we assume that because of their] remorse they would do so in the best way they could [without injuring the animals].

### XXIV.2

A. Said R. Judah, said Rab, "If he hit it [an animal] on its head and it [the reflex from the blow] traveled to its tail, or if he hit it on the tail and it traveled to the head, or if [the reflex went] through the entire spine, we do not suspect there is any [hidden] injury to its limbs. *And if [he hit an animal] with a thick stick [on the back] we suspect that he broke the back [of the animal]. And if [the stick] has on it nodes, we suspect [there is hidden injury to its limbs]. And if [he hit the animal with a stick that] is fresh [i.e., not brittle], we suspect the spine was broken.*"

B. Said R. Nahman, "[As a result of a newborn passing out of] the womb, we do not suspect there is any [hidden] injury to its limbs."

C. Said Raba to R. Nahman, "*There is a Tannaite teaching that supports your view:* **An infant one day old [51b] becomes unclean on account of his seminal flow [M. Nid. 5:3 C].** And if you might have concluded that [we do suspect] there is [hidden] injury to its limbs, then we should apply here the verse, "[When any man has a discharge] from his body, [his body is unclean]" (Lev. 15:2) [which implies he does not become unclean] because of [emission that may be attributable to] another force."

D. *In that case [in M. Nid.] what are we dealing with? The case in question may be one where [the offspring was born] by caesarian section.*

E. *Come and take note:* A calf that was born on the festival, they may slaughter it on the festival [b. Shab. 136a, b. Bes. 6b]. [This implies that we do not suspect there was any hidden injury to the animal.] *Here too the case in question may be one where [the offspring was born] by caesarian section.*

F. *Come and take note:* And they agree [concerning a firstling] that if he is born with a blemish on him, this is [a case of an animal] that is ready [for eating on the festival] [b. Bes. 26b]. *And if you say that this too is a case of an animal born through caesarian section, is an animal born through caesarian section sanctified [as a firstling]?*

G. But lo, said R. Yohanan, "R. Simeon agreed with regard to Holy Things, that [a firstling born through caesarian section] is not holy [b. Nid. 40a]." [So we must reject the suggestion that the animal had no serious injury because it was born by caesarian section.]

H. *In that case what are we dealing with?* Where the animal [after birth] placed its hooves on the ground [to stand up]. [This demonstrates that it had no serious injury.]

I. And said R. Nahman, "In the slaughter house [if an animal falls] we do not [suspect that] there is any [hidden] injury to its limbs."

J. *A certain ox fell [in the slaughter house] and the sound of its groaning was heard [when it fell]. R. Yitzhak bar Samuel bar Marta went up and bought the choicest cuts [of meat from this animal]. Said to him the rabbis, "On what basis do you do this?" He said to them, "Here is what Rab said, 'It digs in its hooves [to break the fall] prior to reaching the ground.'"*

### XXIV.3

A. Said R. Judah, said Rab, "If [an animal that had fallen] stood up, it is not necessary to wait twenty-four hours [to see if it suffered a serious injury in the fall]. *It certainly requires an inspection.* If it walked [after falling], it is not even necessary to perform an inspection."

B. R. Hiyya bar Ashi said, "In both cases it is necessary to perform an inspection [to see if there was a serious injury]."

C. Said R. Jeremiah bar Aha, said Rab, "If it stretched forth its foreleg to stand, even if it did not stand [that is enough of a sign that there was no serious injury]. If it lifted up its hind leg to walk, even though it did not walk [that is enough of a sign that there was no serious injury]."

D. And R. Hisda said, "If it stirred as if to stand, even though it did not stand [that is enough of a sign that there was no serious injury]."

E. *And the law is for an animal that fell off a roof and he did not know [how it fell], if it stood but did not walk, it is necessary to inspect it, but it is not necessary to wait twenty-four hours. And if it walked, it is not necessary even to inspect it.*

F. Said Amemar in the name of R. Dimi from Nehardea, "The animal that fell about which they spoke, it is necessary to inspect it [for injury] near the intestines."

G. Said to him Mar Zutra, "Here is what they said in the name of R. Pappa, 'It is necessary to inspect all the internal areas.'"

H. Said Huna Mar the grandson of R. Nehemiah to R. Ashi, "*What about* the throat organs?" He said to him, "[You do not need to inspect the animal.] The throat organs are too hard to be injured by a fall."

XXIV.4
A. Said R. Judah, said Samuel, "A bird that accidently fell into the water — if it propelled itself one body length, that is enough [to show that there was no serious injury]. " And they said this only in the case of where [it propelled itself] from downstream to upstream. But upstream to downstream [we may say] *the water propelled it. And if the water was still [with no current], then it makes no difference [which way the bird goes]. And if it was littered with twigs and [the bird] overtook them [even while going downstream], it overtook them [and this is a sign that there was no serious injury to the bird].*

B. *And if there was a sheet stretched out [and a bird flew into it] we suspect [there is hidden injury to its limbs]. If it was not taut, we do* not suspect. And if it was folded [and stretched taut], we do not suspect [because it cannot be made taut enough to do serious injury to the bird].

C. [A bird that flew into] a tightly knotted net, we do suspect [there is injury to its limbs]. [If it flew into] a loosely knotted net, we do not suspect."

D. [A bird that flew into the top of] a bundle of flax, we do suspect [injury]. [If it flew] into one side or the other [of the bundle], we do not suspect [injury]. [If it flew into] a bundle of reeds, we do suspect [injury]. [If it flew into] flax that was pounded and corded, we do not suspect injury. [If it flew into flax that was] pounded, but not corded, we do suspect [injury]. [If it flew into flax] that had seed pods, because it has in it knots, we do suspect [injury]. [If it flew into] coarse tow (Cashdan), we do suspect [injury]; fine tow, we do not suspect. Dried bark, we do suspect; crushed bark, we do not suspect. Sifted ashes, we do suspect [because it hardens]; unsifted ashes, we do not suspect. **[52a]** Fine sand, we do not suspect; coarse sand, we do suspect. Dirt from the road, we do suspect [because it too hardens].

E. [If it flew into] straw that was bundled into sheaves, we do suspect [injury]; [straw that was] not bundled, we do not suspect. [If it flew into stacks of] all the various types of wheat, we do suspect [injury]. All the various types of barley, we do suspect injury [some var.: we do not or the phrase is omitted].

F. All the various types of legumes — they are not subject to [suspicion that if a bird flew into a pile of them] there is hidden injury to its limbs, except for fenugreek. For chick peas, we do not suspect there is hidden injury to its limbs. For lentils, we do suspect there is hidden injury to its limbs. This is the general rule for this issue: For any goods that are slippery, we do not suspect there is hidden injury to its limbs. For any good that are not slippery, we do suspect there is hidden injury to its limbs.

**XXIV.5**
A. [A bird whose wings are] clipped [Rashi interprets that its wings were attached to a slat to prevent it from flying off] — R. Ashi permits [consumption of the bird if it crashed to the ground when it tried to fly off and might have injured itself in the process]. Amemar

prohibits [consuming it since he suspects there is hidden injury to its limbs].

B. [If the case is that it was clipped] in one wing, all the authorities would agree that [if it tried to fly and crashed] it is permitted [to eat this bird for there is not sufficient cause to assume it was injured]. Where to they dispute? In [a case where] both wings were clipped [and the bird tried to fly and crashed]. The authority who declares it prohibited [to eat the bird] would say to you, "How can it stay aloft [with its wings clipped]?" And the authority who declares it permitted [to eat it] would say to you, "It is possible for it to stay aloft [by the force created] at the joint of its wing [even if they are clipped at the ends]."

C. Another version: [If the case is that it was clipped] in both wings, all the authorities would agree that [if it tried to fly and crashed] it is prohibited [to eat this bird for there is sufficient cause to assume it was injured]. Where do they dispute? In [a case where] one wing was clipped [and the bird tried to fly and crashed]. The authority who declares it permitted [to eat the bird] would say to you, "It is possible to fly with one wing clipped." And the authority who declares it prohibited [to eat it] would say to you, "Since with one wing it cannot fly [because it is clipped], with the other it cannot fly [either]."

D. And the law is [a bird that is clipped] in both wings [and tried to fly and crashed] is prohibited [for consumption because of suspicion of injury]. [A bird that is clipped] in one wing [and tried to fly and crashed] is permitted [for consumption].

XXV.1
A. **[If] the greater number of its ribs are broken [M. 3:1 I].** *Our rabbis taught:* These constitute the majority of the ribs. Six on one side and six on the other. Or eleven on one side and one on the other. [Twelve of the twenty-two ribs must be broken.]

B. Said Ziri, "[The ribs must be broken] in that half nearest the spine." Said Rabbah bar bar Hannah, said R. Yohanan, "[The ribs that must be broken are] those big ribs that have in them marrow."

C. Said Ulla, Ben Zakkai said, "If the majority [of the ribs] were dislocated on one side [or] if the majority [of the ribs] were broken on both sides [it is *terefah*]." R. Yohanan said, "Whether [we deal with a case of ribs that were] dislocated or broken [it must be] a majority of them on both sides."

D. Said Rab, "If a rib was dislocated along with its vertebra, it is *terefah*." Said R. Kahana and R. Asi to Rab, "If the rib on both sides were dislocated and the vertebra remains intact, what is the law?" He said to them, *"You have stated the case [equivalent in the law to the case] of the cleaved animal* [cf. b. 21a, M. 1:4, V.2 C]." [The rule there is that the animal is deemed to be carrion.]

E. *But has not Rab also stated [a case equivalent in the law to the case of] the cleaved animal? Rab stated [a case of the dislocation of] a rib without its vertebra. But lo he stated, "A rib along with its vertebra." [Rab's statement was], "A rib along with half its vertebra." We may derive the rule that R. Kahana and R. Asi stated [a case of the dislocation of] a rib without its vertebra. And he [Rab] stated to them [that it was equivalent to a case of] the cleaved animal. [This would not be a valid objection.]*

F. But lo, said Ulla, Ben Zakkai said, "If the majority [of the ribs] were dislocated on one side [or] if the majority [of the ribs] were broken on both sides [it is *terefah*]." He would say to you, "There [where we require a majority, the case is where the ribs are] not opposite one another. Here [where we say it is equivalent to a case of a cleaved animal and is carrion, the case is where the ribs are] opposite one another."

G. [But this leads to an inconsistency.] For said R. Yohanan [in C], "[It must be] a majority of them on both sides." And in [the case of] a majority of them on both sides *it is impossible that there not be at least one pair of ribs that [are broken that are] opposite one another.*

H. [We can explain that this is not a direct contradiction.] *There [in the case referred to by Yohanan he speaks of the dislocation of] the rib but not its facet. Here [in the case of Kahana and Asi they speak of the dislocation of] the rib with its facet. If so [this leads to another inconsistency, to wit] this is Rab's [rule]! [We can respond that indeed it is but that] they had not heard Rab's [rule].*

I. *Why did they not pose the question to them as they did to Rab [as in D-E above]? They reasoned they would pose to him one question that would lead to an explanation of two matters. For if they posed to him a question about [the case of] one [rib that was dislocated] it would settle the matter [as follows]. If he said it is* terefah *[in the case of one rib] then certainly [in the case of] two [ribs it would be* terefah*]. [But] if he said it is valid [in the case of one rib] then the case of two ribs would still be a problem for us.*

J. *But if this is the case, then even now that they have posed to him the question regarding the case of two [ribs] it would settle the matter [as follows]. If he said it is valid [in the case of two ribs], then certainly [in the case of] one [rib it would be valid]. [But] if he said it is* terefah *[in the case of two ribs], then the case of one rib would still be a problem for us.*

K. *They reasoned [that if they posed the question in this way] he would become angry [and answer them concerning both, to wit], "If one [is dislocated and declared]* terefah, *is there any question concerning [the case of] two [dislocated ribs]?" But lo they did state matters to him in this way and he did not get angry with them. [Actually he did get angry.] When he said to them, "You have stated the case of an animal that was cleaved," this was his way of expressing anger to them.*

### XXV.2

A. Said Rabbah bar Rab Shila, said R. Matna, said Samuel, "If a rib was dislocated from its socket, or if a majority of the skull was shattered, or if a majority of the membrane that covers the rumen [was torn], it is *terefah*."

B. "If a rib was dislocated from its socket... it is *terefah*." *And they raised in contradiction to this:* [52b] *[As it was taught on Tannaite authority in the Mishnah],* **How much is deemed a deficiency in the spine [of a skeleton so that it does not render unclean objects in a tent]? The House of Shammai say, "Two vertebrae." And the House of Hillel say, "One vertebra"** [M. Ohal. 2:3]. And said R. Judah, said Samuel, "And the same [rule of deficiency in the spine applies] for [rendering the animal] a *terefah*." [Cf. b. 42b, M. 3:1, I.1 O-P.]

Bavli Hullin Chapter Three. Folios 42A-67B

C. [There is no contradiction.] *Here [the case is] a rib [dislocated] without its vertebra. There the vertebra [is dislocated] but not its rib.*

D. *It is consistent [to say the case of a dislocated] rib without its vertebra does occur. But where does it occur that a vertebra [is dislocated] without its rib? In the lumbar region (Cashdan: where there are vertebrae but no ribs).*

E. *R. Oshaia raised an objection to this: This case should be taught as one of the lenient rulings of the House of Shammai and one of the stringent rulings of the House of Hillel.*

F. *Said to him Raba, "When this was brought up [as a dispute] it was brought up as an issue of [whether the spine with a missing vertebra transmits] uncleanness where it is the case that the House of Shammai rule more stringently [that the spine is complete enough to transmit uncleanness]."*

XXV.3
A. [Said Rabbah bar Rab Shila, said R. Matna, said Samuel, "If a rib was dislocated from its socket,] or if a majority of the skull was shattered... [XXV.2 A]. R. Jeremiah *posed a question,* "[Does this mean] the majority of the diameter or of the circumference?" *The question remains unresolved.*

B. "... or if a majority of the membrane that covers the rumen [was torn], it is *terefah* [XXV.2 A]." R. Ashi *posed a question,* "[Does this mean] the majority was torn or the majority was removed?" *Let us resolve this from what was taught on Tannaite authority,* **[If] the innermost belly [rumen] is pierced or the greater part of the outer [exterior coating] is pierced [M. 3:1 F-G].** And they said in the West in the name of R. Yosé bar Hanina, "The entire rumen is called the inner rumen. And what then is the outer rumen? The fleshy membrane that covers the major part of the rumen [above XXI.1 E]."

C. *But the basis for [posing a question regarding] this matter [is not according to Yosé bar Hanina]. Rather it is according to Samuel. And lo, said R. Jacob bar Nahmani, said Samuel, "[The innermost belly is] in the part that has no furry lining [XXI.1 C]." [Because* the Mishnah does not refer to the membrane it cannot be used as proof.]

### XXVI.1
A. **And one which has been mauled by a wolf [M. 3:1 J].** Said R. Judah, said Rab, "For beasts [that were mauled, the Mishnah means] by a wolf or [by any animal] larger than that [in size]. And for birds [that were mauled, the Mishnah means] by a hawk or [by any bird of prey] larger than that [in size]."

B. *What does this [statement] exclude? If it excludes [the case of] a cat [that mauls] it was taught,* **And one which has been mauled by a wolf.** *And if you wish to say this [particular statement of the Mishnah] makes the novel point that a wolf can maul even a large animal* [but as to a cat we might assume it could maul a small animal], *but lo, it was taught on Tannaite authority,* **R. Judah says, "One mauled by a wolf, in the case of a small beast, and one mauled by a lion in the case of a large beast [M. 3:1 K]."**

C. *And if you wish to say that R. Judah is in dispute* [with M. 3:1 J], lo *said R. Benjamin bar Yefet, said R. Ila* [var. Eleazar], *"R. Judah only comes to interpret the words of the sages* [not to dispute them]."

D. *There is a contradiction between the teachings of this man [Rab] and that man [Ila or Eleazar].* [Rab assumes that Judah does dispute J of M. Accordingly he teaches the rule of A to exclude animals smaller than a wolf that maul small cattle.]

E. *If you prefer another possibility: It is consistent [to say that the Mishnah] excludes [mauling by] a cat. What might you have said? That it just taught the more common [case of a wolf]. It comes to make the novel point [that it means specifically a wolf and that a cat is excluded].*

### XXVI.2
A. Said R. Amram, said R. Hisda, "Mauling by a cat or a marten [renders the animal *terefah*] in the case of goats and lambs. Mauling by a weasel [renders the animal *terefah*] in the case of fowl."

B. *They raised an objection:* Mauling by a cat, hawk or marten [does not render an animal *terefah*] until it pierces the abdominal cavity. But [this implies that] the mauling [itself without piercing] *does not render it [terefah].*

C. *And how do you make sense of this? Is a hawk not capable of mauling? But lo it is taught on Tannaite authority,* **One mauled by a hawk [M. 3:1 K].** *Lo this is not a contradiction. This one [in M.] refers to fowl and this one [in B] refers to goats and lambs.*

D. *But in any case it does contradict the view of R. Hisda. For he stated matters in accord with this Tanna. For it was taught on Tannaite authority,* Beribbi says, "They only stated [that a cat] does not maul in an instance where there is no one trying to save [the animal or bird. For then the cat is not as vicious.] But in an instance where there is someone trying to save [the animal or bird, a cat becomes more vicious and] does maul."

E. [But is it true that cat] does not maul in an instance where there is no one trying to save [the animal or bird]? *But lo [consider this case]: There was a chicken in the house of R. Kahana. A cat ran after it and it went into a room and the door slammed in the cat's face and it scratched the door in anger. And they found on it five drops of blood* [Rashi: the poison of five fingers of the cat, indicating that the cat could have mauled the chicken]. [We can respond to this objection that when the animal tries] to save itself, it is the same as if others tried to save it [from the mauling].

F. And [how do we explain this poison on the door in accord with the view of] the rabbis [who say that a cat does not maul]? [They say that a cat] *has poison but that it does not contaminate* [enough to constitute a mauling of the organs that would render the animal or bird *terefah*].

G. *There are those that say [that R. Hisda says that even where no one tries to save the animal, it can be classified as a mauling. And the Mishnah specifies a wolf for a case of mauling of large sheep. And the baraita that says it must pierce the abdominal chamber] in accord with whom is this [rule that it must penetrate]? In accord with Beribbi.*

H. *For it was taught on Tannaite authority:* Beribbi says, "They only stated [that a cat] does maul in an instance where there is someone trying to save [the animal or bird. For then the cat is vicious.] But in an instance where there is no one trying to save [the animal or bird, a cat becomes less vicious and] does not maul."

I. [But is it true that a cat] does not maul in an instance where there is no one trying to save [the animal or bird]? *But lo [consider this case]: There was a chicken in the house of R. Kahana. A cat ran after it and it went into a room and the door slammed in the cat's face and it scratched the door in anger. And they found on it five drops of blood* [Rashi: the poison of five fingers of the cat, indicating that the cat could have mauled the chicken]. [We can respond to this objection that when the animal tries] to save itself, it is the same as if others tried to save it [from the mauling].

### XXVI.3

A. R. Kahana *posed a question* to Rab, **[53a]** "Does the rule of mauling [that renders an animal *terefah*] apply to a cat or not?" He said to him, "The rule of mauling applies even to a weasel." [He said to him,] "Does the rule of mauling apply to a weasel?" He said to him, "The rule of mauling does not apply even to a cat." [He said to him,] "Does the rule of mauling apply to a cat or to a weasel or not?" He said to him, "The rule of mauling applies to a cat but not to a weasel."

B. *And all this is not contradictory.* That which he said, "The rule of mauling applies even to a weasel," [refers to a case where it mauled] birds. That which he said, "The rule of mauling does not apply even to a cat," [refers to a case of] large sheep. That which he stated, "The rule of mauling applies to a cat but not to a weasel," [refers to a case of] kids and lambs.

### XXVI.4

A. R. Ashi *posed a question,* "Does the rule of mauling apply to other kinds of unclean birds [of prey] or not?" Said R. Hillel to R. Ashi, *"When I was in the house of R. Kahana he said that the rule of mauling applies to other unclean birds."*

B. *But lo we have taught on Tannaite authority,* **One mauled by a hawk in the case of small fowl [M. 3:1 K].** [That means] the mauling of a hawk [renders *terefah* a bird] *even its own size. But other [birds render* terefah *by mauling] only those birds that are smaller than them.*

C. *And some say:* [That means] the mauling of a hawk [renders *terefah* a bird] *even larger than its own size. But other [birds render* terefah *by mauling] up to their own size.*

**XXVI.5**

A. Said R. Kahana in the name of R. Shimi bar Ashi, "The rule of mauling does not apply to a fox."

B. *Is it not the case [that the rule does apply]? But lo when R. Dimi came [from Israel] he said,* "There was an instance where a fox mauled a ewe in the bath house of Bet Hini. And the instance came before the sages [for a ruling]. And they said that the rule of mauling does apply [to the case of a fox]."

C. Said R. Safra, "This was [a case of] a cat [that mauled a ewe]."

D. *Another version:* Said R. Kahana in the name of R. Shimi bar Ashi, "The rule of mauling does apply to a fox."

E. *Is it not the case [that the rule does apply]? But lo when R. Dimi came [from Israel] he said,* "There was an instance where a fox mauled a ewe in the bath house of Bet Hini. And the instance came before the sages [for a ruling]. And they said that the rule of mauling does not apply [to the case of a fox]."

F. Said R. Safra, "This was [a case of] a dog [that mauled a ewe]."

G. Said R. Joseph, "We obtained that the rule of mauling does not apply to a dog." Said Abayye, "We obtained that the rule of mauling applies only [where the animal mauled with its] fore leg." *This excludes [any case where it clawed with] its hind leg [where the rule of mauling] does not apply.*

H. The rule of mauling only applies [where the animal mauled with its] claw. *This excludes [any case where it bit with] its teeth [where the rule of mauling] does not apply.*

I. The rule of mauling only applies [where the animal mauled] with intent. *This excludes [any case where it tore] without intent [where the rule of mauling] does not apply.*

J. The rule of mauling only applies [where the animal mauled] while alive. *This excludes [any case where it mauled by falling on the prey] after it died [where the rule of mauling] does not apply.*

K. *They said there: You said [any case where it mauled] without intent [the rule of mauling] does not apply. Is it necessary to state [that in any case where it mauled by falling on its prey] after it died [the rule of mauling does not apply]? [This appears to be redundant.]*

L. *No. It is necessary [to state both rules so as to include under the rule of mauling the case of an animal that] mauled and then its leg was cut off [before it could withdraw the leg from the animal]. What would you like to say? That in the act of mauling it injects the poison [into the prey]. [By teaching both rules] it makes the novel point that in the act of withdrawing [its leg from the prey] it injects the poison [that kills the prey].*

### XXVI.6

A. Said Rabbah bar R. Huna, said Rab, "If a lion entered the midst of a herd of oxen and then a claw was found in the back of one of them, we are not concerned that perhaps the lion mauled it." *What is the basis [for this conclusion]?* [It is based on the principle that] the majority of lions do maul and the minority do not maul. And for any [species of] animal that mauls, its nail is not likely to come off [even if that particular animal is not wont to maul].

B. And this [ox] — since a nail was found in its back, we should say that it rubbed up against a wall [and a nail of a lion that had become stuck in the wall, became lodged in the back of the ox].

C. *But the opposite conclusion is more reasonable [based on another principle, namely]* the majority of oxen rub [their back] and the minority do not rub. And any animal that rubs [its back], it is not likely that a nail will remain lodged in its back. And this one since it has a nail lodged in its back, we should say that [it became lodged there when] a lion mauled it.

D. *There is a basis to say [the inference must be drawn in accord with] this [line of reasoning in B] and there is a basis to say that [the inference must be drawn in accord] with that [line of reasoning in C]. Let us uphold the [validity of] the animal according to its presumptive status. It then is a case of an animal about which there is a doubt whether it was mauled. And Rab rules in accord with his own view [elsewhere]. For he said, "We are not concerned with the possibility of a case of a doubt as to whether the animal had been mauled." [Cf. b. 43b, IV.1 B.]*

E. Said Abayye, "We only said [that we are not concerned if in the animal's back they found] a nail. But if [they found a wound on the animal's back] the size of a nail, then we are concerned [that the animal was mauled]."

F. *And with regard to the nail itself [that was found in the animal's back] we only said [that we are not concerned it was mauled] if it was moist [with blood and it is unlikely that a vital nail would come loose even during a mauling]. But if it was dried out, it is likely to be dislodged [from the animal's claw during a mauling].*

G. *And with regard to a moist nail we only said [that we are not concerned it was mauled] in the case where [they found in the animal's back] one nail. But where they found two or three [nails in its back] we are concerned [that it was mauled]. And this applies only where they were [lodged in the back] in a row, like a claw.*

## XXVII.1

A. It was stated: Rab said, "We are not concerned with the possibility of a case of a doubt as to whether the animal had been mauled." And Samuel said, "We are concerned with the possibility of a case of a doubt as to whether the animal had been mauled."

B. *They all agree [regarding an animal that mauls, that in a case where] there is a doubt whether or not it went up [into the herd], it makes sense to say it did not go up. Where there is a doubt [about an instance of mauling] whether it was done by a dog or a cat, it makes sense to* say that it was done by a dog. If it went up quietly and lay down among them, it makes sense to say that it made peace [with them and did not harm any of the herd]. If it decapitated one of them [it makes sense to say that its fierceness then subsided.

C. [And they all agree that] if it [the lion] was roaring and they [the oxen] were lowing [that means] they are facing off against one another [and no mauling has taken place yet]. Where do they dispute? Where it [the lion] is quiet and they [the oxen] are lowing. One authority [Samuel] reasons that [we must conclude the lion] has done the deed [i.e., attacked]. And the other authority [Rab] reasons that they are doing so as a response [to the presence of the lion but he has not yet attacked them].

D. Said Amemar, "The law follows in accord with the view that we are concerned with the possibility of a case of a doubt as to whether the animal had been mauled."

E. Said R. Ashi to Amemar, "What about this opinion of Rab?" He said to him, "I did not hear it." That is to say, "I do not reason in accord with it."

F. And if you prefer, Rab retracted his view in favor of Samuel's. For there was a basket of birds about which there was a doubt as to whether they had been mauled that came before Rab [for a ruling]. They sent it before Samuel. He strangled them and threw them into the river. And if you conclude that he [Rab] did not retract his view [that they were not to be deemed as if they were mauled] then he should have declared them permitted [for consumption]. Rather what [should he have done if he had retracted his view]? He should have declared them prohibited [on his own]. But this case was in the jurisdiction of Samuel [and Rab wanted to allow him to render the opinion].

G. Why did he have to strangle them? Why not throw them into the river as they were? Because they might fly off [and be consumed by another Israelite]. And why did he not leave them and wait twelve months [to see if they would live]? He might thereby transgress [in the interim by consuming them]. And why did he not sell them to an idolater? He might go and sell them back to an Israelite. And why did he not strangle them and throw them into the trash? And on this basis you could allow him to throw them to the dogs. [That is correct.] But [he threw them into the river] to publicize his prohibition.

## XXVII.2
A. A duck that was at the house of R. Ashi went up into the reeds. It came out with its neck covered with blood. Said R. Ashi, "Did we not say, 'Where there is a doubt [about an instance of mauling] whether it was done by a dog or a cat, it makes sense to say that it was done by a dog'? Here too [we should say], 'Where there is a doubt [about an instance of mauling] whether it was done by a reed or a cat, it makes sense to say that the injury was done by a reed.'"

B. Said the sons of R. Hiyya, "The mauled animal that they spoke of must be inspected around its intestines." Said R. Joseph, "This rule of R. Joseph was already specified by Samuel." For said Samuel in the name of R. Haninah b. Antigonus, "The mauled animal that they spoke of must be inspected around its intestines."

## XXVII.3
A. *Ilfa posed a question:* Does the rule of mauling apply to the organs [of the throat] or not? Said R. Zira, "The rule for that question which Ilfa posed was already specified by R. Hanan bar Raba." For said R. Hanan bar Raba, said Rab, "The mauled animal that they spoke of must be inspected around the entire abdominal cavity including the organs [of the throat]."

B. *Ilfa posed a question:* Concerning the organs [of the throat] that were dangling: how much [must they dangle out of their normal position to render the animal *terefah*]? Said R. Zira, "The rule for the question which Ilfa posed was already specified by Rabbah bar bar Hannah." For said Rabba bar bar Hannah, said Samuel, "Concerning the organs that were dangling: a majority [that dangles renders the animal *terefah*]."

C. *R. Ammi posed a question:* What is the rule regarding putrefaction [of the animal's flesh caused by mauling]? Said R. Zira, "The rule for the question which R. Ammi posed was already specified by R. Judah." For said R. Judah, said Rab, "In regards to an animal that was mauled [there is no consequence unless the flesh around the intestines turns red. If the flesh putrefied we regard it as if it were not there at all."

D. *What is the definition of putrefaction?* Any instance [of non-vital tissue] in which the physician would scrape it away to help restore the living flesh.

E. *Said R. Ashi, "When we were in the house of R. Kahana they brought before us [for a ruling] a lung that when it was set down it sat perfectly well. But when they lifted it up it disintegrated. And we declared it terefah in accord with the rule of R. Huna the son of R. Joshua."*

### XXVII.4
A. R. Nahman said, "A thorn — [the animal is not *terefah*] unless it has pierced the abdominal cavity. A mauling — [The animal is *terefah*] when the flesh around the intestines turns red."

B. R. Zebid taught as follows, "A mauling — [The animal is *terefah*] when the flesh around the intestines turns red. The organs [of the throat] — [the animal is not *terefah*] until the organs themselves turn red."

C. Said R. Pappi, "R. Bibi bar Abayye *posed the question*: [54a] The gullet — any amount of piercing at all [renders it *terefah*]. Any amount of mauling at all [renders it *terefah*]. The windpipe — a piercing the size of an *issar* [renders it *terefah*]. How much mauling [renders it *terefah*]?"

D. *After he posed the question, he then answered it:* In either case any amount at all [of mauling renders it *terefah*]. What is the basis for this view? The venom [of the animal from the mauling] will continue to burn [a larger hole even after the mauling itself].

### XXVII.5
A. R. Yitzhak bar Samuel bar Marta sat [in session] before R. Nahman and he sat and said, "The mauled animal that they spoke of must be inspected around its intestines." [See above XXVII.2 B.]

B. R. Nahman said, "By God! Rab ruled concerning it [that an animal must be inspected] from the pan to the hips [so Cashdan]." *What is the [location of the] pan? If you say the pan of the fore-leg, this is [the same as saying] around the intestines. Rather [it must mean] from the pan of the brain to the hips.*

C. When R. Hiyya bar Joseph departed [for Israel] he found R. Yohanan and R. Simeon b. Laqish who were sitting and saying, "The mauled animal that they spoke of must be inspected around its intestines."

D. He said to them, "By God! Rab ruled concerning it [that an animal must be inspected from the pan to the hips." *Said to him Resh Laqish, "Who is Rab? Who is Rab? I do not know who he is." Said R. Yohanan, "Do you not remember that student who served the Great Rabbi and R. Hiyya? And by God! All those years that student [sat and] served in the academy, I served standing up. And in what [subject] was his strength? He was strong in all [subjects]."*

E. Resh Laqish immediately spoke and said, "To be sure. I remember this man well. For a teaching was stated in his name: [If an organ of the neck was found] dislocated and slaughtered, it is valid. For it is impossible to slaughter a dislocated organ. [Thus it must have been dislocated after it was slaughtered.]"

F. And R. Yohanan says, "Let him bring it and compare it [to a properly slaughtered organ before he declares it valid]."

G. Said R. Nahman, "They only taught this law in regard to a case of one who did not take hold of the organs of the neck. But in the case of one who did take hold of the organ and slaughtered, it is possible that a displaced organ can be slaughtered. [Thus we have no proof that it was slaughtered prior to the organ becoming displaced.]"

## XXVIII.1

A. **This is the general principle: [Any the like of which does not live is *terefah*] [M. 3:1 L].** *What does this statement encompass? It encompasses the seven categories [of terefot] that were taught [on Amoraic authority, see above b. 42b].*

B. *Members of the house of Joseph the trapper used to hit [the animal on] the sciatic nerve to kill [their catch]. They brought this case before R. Judah b. Betera for a ruling. He said to them, "Is there a need to add to the [list of those circumstances that render animals] terefot? You only need [to enumerate] those [cases] that the sages specified."*

C. *[Some versions: Members of the house of] R. Pappa bar Abba the trapper used to hit [the animal on] the kidneys to kill [their catch]. They brought this case before R. Abba for a ruling. He said to them, "Is there a need to add to the [list of those circumstances that render animals] terefot? You only need [to enumerate] those [cases] that the sages specified."*

D. *But lo we can see that it dies [from a blow to the kidneys]! We learn from this that if you applied medication to it, it would live. [Therefore it is not included with the other conditions that render animals terefot].*

This chapter is a large-scale composite that resembles a code of rules rather than an extended discourse on principles. It bears more characteristics of a list of laws than an extended essay. Few of the topics in the present text are discussed or cross-referenced elsewhere in the Talmud. And furthermore the rules of this chapter can have profound implications in the actual regulation by the rabbis of meat consumption in their communities. For these reasons the chapter is considered to be one of the most difficult in the Talmud.

Unit I.1 begins by seeking a basis in the Torah for Mishnah's definition of *terefah*. It goes on to discuss the number of categories of *terefah*-animals. II.1-3 continue the above inquiry with specific questions regarding the categories of *terefah*-animals. The next few sections closely adhere to the agenda of Mishnah and mainly clarify its meaning. III.1-2 give rules about a pierced gullet. IV.1 states rules for a thorn in the gullet. V.1-2 provide rules for the pharynx and discussion of their application. V.3 delineates the extent of the gullet as a place for the incision of slaughtering. Then V.4 gives the rule for slaughter in a detached pharynx.

VI.1 relates to Mishnah's rule for the torn windpipe. This leads into a second-level discussion of the responsibilities and consequences for sages who rule on the status of an animal. VII.1 investigates the operative principle of combining holes together to constitute a sign of a *terefah*-animal. VII.2 clarifies the rule regarding a slit in the windpipe. VII.3

identifies the appropriate area of the neck for the incision of slaughter. VIII.1 discusses Mishnah's rule regarding defects caused by piercing the membranes of the brain. This is followed by secondary materials relating to the brain.

Again adhering to Mishnah's operative concerns, IX.1-2 take up Mishnah's rule regarding defects caused by piercing the heart. A rule for the aorta follows. X.1 analyzes Mishnah's rule regarding defects of the spinal cord. X.2 gives other rules for spinal liquids and X.3-4 discuss where the spinal cord ends. XI.1-3 then investigate Mishnah's rule for a defect of the liver. More rules for the liver follow. XII.1-5 clarify Mishnah's rule for a defect of the lung. Secondary materials about the lung follow that.

XIII.1-5 specify procedures for inspecting the lung. The Talmud then turns to derivative rules for judging the status of ulcerations of the lung. At XIV.1-2 rules relating to a needle in the lung follow. XV.1-3 append rules relating to defects of the lung. XVI.1 then takes up Mishnah's concern with a defect in the bronchial tubes. XVII.1 follows this with concern for Mishnah's rule regarding a defect in the belly. XVIII.1-3 state rules for fats and forbidden liquids. XIX.1 investigates Mishnah's rule for a defect in the intestine. The text then adds a secondary rule for mourning.

XX.1-2 provide us with principles and rules for comparing operative defects to one another. XX.3 deals with the rule for a defect in the rectum and XXI.1 exposits Mishnah's rule for a defect in the rumen. XXII.1-2 clarify Judah's rule in Mishnah. Rules follow for judging the size of a defect that has operative implications. XXIII.1 takes up Mishnah's rule for a defect in the reticulum. The text cites Tosefta and then a precedent to clarify Mishnah. XXIV.1-5 examine Mishnah's rule for a defect where an animal fell. The Talmud follows this with related second-level rules regarding hidden injuries due to the trauma of a fall, a blow, or to stress (1-3). Then it raises similar issues for birds (4-5).

The pattern of the text continues the sustained and predictable program of defining and amplifying the operative concerns stated in Mishnah. XXV.1-3 take up Mishnah's rule for a defect due to broken ribs. More rules for ribs follow. XXVI.1-6 clarify Mishnah's rule for a defect due to mauling. Various derivative rules on the subject follow this. XXVII.1-5 provide us with precedents and additional rules with regard to mauling. Finally, XXVIII.1 comments on Mishnah's concluding principle. The units throughout present no surprises as they persistently and directly amplify the rules of Mishnah.

### 3:2

A. And these are the valid [carcasses] among cattle:
(1) [if] the windpipe is pierced or is slit [lengthwise] —

B. How large may the hole be? Rabban Simeon b. Gamaliel says, "So much as an Italian *issar*" —

C. (2) [if] the skull is damaged, but the membrane of the brain is not pierced,
(3) [if] the heart is pierced, but not up to the empty space [cavity] thereof,
(4) [if] the backbone is broken, but the spinal cord is not severed,
(5) [if] the liver is removed, but an olive's bulk of it remains,
(6) the omasum or the second stomach [reticulum] that are pierced [so that the holes lead] one into the other,
(7) [if] the spleen is removed,
(8) [if] the kidneys are removed,
(9) [if] the lower jaw is removed,
(10) [if] the womb is removed.

D. (11) And one [the lung] of it is dried naturally.

E. (12) One that has lost its hide [having been flayed] —

F. R. Meir declares valid.

G. And sages declare invalid.

### I.1

A. *It was stated:* R. Yohanan said, **These are the *terefah* [carcasses] [M. 3:1 A]** *specifies* [precisely these cases and no others]. And R. Simeon b. Laqish said, **These are the valid [carcasses]** *specifies* [precisely these cases].

B. *Concerning what did they dispute? Concerning the rule of R. Matna. For said R. Matna, "This [case of an animal whose] femur slipped out of its socket [Cashdan] is* terefah" [M. 3:1, I.1 V].

C. R. Yohanan said, **These are the *terefah* [carcasses] [M. 3:1 A]** specifies [precisely these cases]. The Mishnah taught, **These are the *terefah* [carcasses] [M. 3:1 A]**, and it taught, **This is the general principle [M. 3:1 L].** [54b] *And it seems reasonable for the rule of R. Matna to be subsumed in* **the general principle.**

## Bavli Ḥullin Chapter Three. Folios 42A-67B

D. *What is the basis for this conclusion? Because it resembles a case where [an organ] was removed [from the animal rendering it* terefah]. *The Tanna taught* **These are the** *terefah* **[carcasses]** *[to teach us] these are* terefah. *That case of [the rule of] R. Matna is valid.*

E. And R. Simeon b. Laqish said, **These are the valid [carcasses]** specifies [precisely these cases]. The Mishnah taught, **These are the** *terefah* **[carcasses] [M. 3:1 A]**, and it taught, **This is the general principle [M. 3:1 L]**. *And it seems reasonable for the rule of R. Matna not to be subsumed in* **the general principle.**

F. *What is the basis for this conclusion? Because it does not resemble a case where [an organ] was pierced. Nor does it resemble a case where [an organ] was severed. And neither does it resemble a case where [an organ] was removed. The Tanna taught,* **These are the valid [carcasses]** *[to teach us] these are valid. That case of [the rule of] R. Matna is terefah.*

I.2
A. *Reverting to the body of the prior text: Said R. Matna, "This [case of an animal whose] femur slipped out of its socket is terefah." And Raba said, "It is valid. But if its ligaments were severed it is terefah."*

B. *And the law is: if they were severed it is valid anyway, unless they [the ligaments] disintegrated.*

II.1
A. **How large may the hole be? [Rabban Simeon b. Gamaliel says, "So much as an Italian** *issar* **(B)."]** *Said Ziri, "You who are not familiar with this measure [of an Italian issar] may take the measure of a Gordian dinar. And that is the same as a small peshitta [coin]. And it is found [circulating] among the peshittas of Pumbedita."*

B. *Said R. Hanna the money changer, "[Yohanan] bar Nappaha was standing before me. And he asked me for a Gordian dinar to measure [the size of a defect that might render an animal] terefah. And I wanted to stand up before him [as a sign of respect]. And he would not let me. He said to me, 'Sit my son, sit.' Professionals [such as money changers] are not permitted to stand up on account of* disciples of the sages while they are engaged in their professional activities."

C. But are they not [supposed to stand up before a sage]? *For lo it was taught in the Mishnah on Tannaitic authority,* **All of the craftsmen [of Jerusalem] stand before them and greet them [saying], "Brothers, men of such and such a place, you have come in peace" [M. Bik. 3:3 J-K].**

D. Said R. Yohanan, "Before them [those who bring first fruits to the Temple] they stand up. Before disciples of the sages, they do not have to stand up."

E. Said R. Yosé bar Abin, "Come and see how beloved is the performance of a commandment in its proper time. For lo, 'Before them [those who bring first fruits to the Temple] they stand up. Before disciples of the sages, they do not have to stand up.'"

F. *But why draw this conclusion? Perhaps [they acted in this way] so as not to discourage them [from bringing the first fruits] in the future. [It does not prove that one who brings first fruits is inherently more deserving of respect than a sage.]*

II.2
A. Said R. Nahman, "[A measure] the size of a *sela* [exactly] is treated as if it were larger than a *sela*. [A measure] the size of an *issar* [exactly] is treated as if it were larger than an *issar*." *It seems [logical to conclude] that R. Nahman reasons in accord with the principle that in measures of size, 'So much as' a certain size means not equal to [that size].*

B. *Raba raised an objection to R. Nahman,* **The rope that hangs over from [the webbing of] the bed — up to five handbreadths is clean [if the bed itself becomes unclean. M. Kel. 19:2 A-B].** *Do we not conclude that five [handbreadths] is the same as any amount below this measure? No. [We conclude that] five [handbreadths] is the same as any amount above this measure.*

C. *Come and take note:* **From five handbreadths up to ten is unclean [M. Kel. 19:2 C].** *Do we not conclude that ten [handbreadths is the* *same as any amount below [this measure]? No. [We conclude that] ten [handbreadths] is the same as any amount above this measure.*

D. *Come and take note:* **[As to] the smallest [size] of earthenware vessels: their [rimmed] bottoms or their sides [that can] set without supports [are unclean if]** [55a] **their measure is as much [oil as needed for] anointing a small finger of a child. [And this measurement applies to vessels that, when whole, hold] up to a** *log* **[M. Kel. 2:2 A].** *Do we not conclude that a log is the same as any amount below this measure? No. [We conclude that] a log is the same as any amount above this measure.*

E. *Come and take note:* **[If, when whole, such vessels held] from a** *log* **to a** *seah,* **[the uncleanness will persist if the remnant may hold] a quarter-***log* **[M. Kel. 2:2 B].** *Do we not conclude that a seah is the same as any amount below this measure? No. [We conclude that] a seah is the same as any amount above this measure.*

F. *Come and take note:* **From a** *seah* **to two** *seahs,* **a half-***log* **[M. Kel. 2:2 C].** *Do we not conclude that two seahs is the same as any amount below this measure? No. [We conclude that] two seahs is the same as any amount above this measure.*

G. *But lo it was taught on Tannaite authority,* [In rulings regarding the uncleanness of vessels, exactly] *a* log *is the same as any amount below this measure.* [Exactly] *a* seah *is the same as any amount below this measure.* [Exactly] *two* seahs *is the same as any amount below this measure.*

H. *There [in ruling regarding the uncleanness of utensils] we judge in accord with the more strict alternative. For said R. Abbahu, said R. Yohanan, "All of the measures specified by the sages are meant to accord with the stricter alternative except for the [measure of] the size of a bean for [blood stains on] test rags [used for determining menstrual uncleanness where the measure is meant] to accord with the more lenient view."*

I. *And you may derive this as well from this that was taught on Tannaite authority concerning the matter,* **[Exactly] five is the same as any amount above this measure.... [Exactly] ten is the same as any** amount below this measure [T. Kel. B.M. 9:3 C, E, commenting on M. Kel. 19:2, cited above at B].

III.1
A. (7) [If] the spleen is removed [M. 3:2 C] [according to Meir, it is valid]. And said R. Avira in the name of Raba, "They taught this rule only in the case where it was removed. But if it was pierced, it is *terefah*" [see above M. 3:1 I.1 X, b. 42b].

B. R. Yosé bar Abin, and some say it was R. Yosé bar Zabeda, posed a question, [If] one cuts off part of the offspring which is in its womb — it [that which is cut off and left inside the mother when it is slaughtered] is permitted to be eaten. [If he cut off] part of the spleen or kidneys [of the beast itself], it is prohibited to be eaten [M. 4:1 D-F]. Lo [this implies that if he cut from the spleen] the animal itself is permitted. [No.] The law is that even the animal itself is also prohibited. Since the former text taught, it is permitted to be eaten, the latter text taught, it is prohibited to be eaten. [But it does not mean that only the parts of the spleen that are cut off are prohibited. The animal is *terefah* because he cut off from the spleen.]

C. And if you prefer [we could argue that the animal itself is not terefah. The rule for] piercing [the organ] is independent, and [the rule for] cutting [the organ] is independent.

IV.1
A. (8) [If] the kidneys are removed [M. 3:2 C]. Said Rakhish bar Pappa in the name of Rab, "If the animal was diseased in one kidney, it is *terefah*." They said in the West [in Israel], "And this is the case only if the disease reached [55b] the hilum."

B. And where is the hilum? [Cashdan:] At the white calyces in the middle of the kidney immediately below the loins.

C. Said R. Nehuniah, "I inquired of those who issue rulings from the West [regarding the defects that render an animal] terefah. And they said to me, 'The law follows in accord with the view of Rakhish bar Pappa. And the law does not follow in accord with the view of R. Avira.'"

Bavli Ḥullin Chapter Three. Folios 42A-67B

D. *We say this only [if the spleen was pierced] in its thin section. But if it was [pierced] in its thick section, it is* terefah *[in accord with Avira]. And if there remained [in the spleen some thickness not pierced] as much as the thickness of a gold dinar, it is valid.*

IV.2
A. *They said in the West [in Israel]: All that renders unfit in regard to the lung is valid in regard to the kidney. For lo, a hole renders unfit in regard to the lung and it is valid in regard to the kidney. And all the more so that which is valid in regard to the lung, is valid in regard to the kidney.*

B. *R. Tanhuma raised this by way of contradiction: Is this the general rule? But lo, consider the case of pus that is valid in regard to the lung and unfit in regard to the kidney. But lo, [consider on the other hand the case of] clear water that is considered valid in both [if found in either the lung or the kidney].*

C. *But said R. Ashi, "Can you compare [defects that render animals]* terefot *to one another? We do not say concerning [defects that render animals]* terefot *that this one resembles that one. For lo you may cut from this place [on an animal] and it will die. You may cut from here [an identical amount in another place on the animal] and it will live [b. 48b, XIV.1 I]."*

D. *And in the case of clear water we only say [it is valid] if the water is unclouded. But if it was murky it is unfit. And even if it is unclouded we do not say that it is valid unless it was not foul. But if it was foul, it is unfit.*

E. The [rule concerning the] kidney that shrunk — for a small beast [it is valid unless it shrank smaller than] a bean; for a large beast [it is valid unless it shrank smaller than] a medium size grape.

V.1
A. [This passage is omitted in some editions.] **(9) [If] the lower jaw is removed [M. 3:2 C]** [according to Meir, it is valid]. Said R. Zira, *"They taught this only where it could survive by force feeding. But where it could not survive by force feeding [such a case is terefah]."*

## VI.1

A. **(10) [If] the womb is removed [M. 3:2 C]** [according to Meir, it is valid]. *It was taught,* The womb, that is the *tarpahat*, that is the *šlpwhyt* [cf. b. 48a above].

## VII.1

A. **(10) And one whose [lung] dried naturally — is valid. [M. 3:2 D].** *Our rabbis taught,* What is the case of a dried [lung]? Any animal whose lung shrunk [cf. T. 3:12]. [If it] dried naturally it is valid. [If it was dried] by human intervention it is *terefah*.

B. R. Simeon b. Eleazar says, "Even if it was [dried out] by the intervention of any creature [it is *terefah*]."

C. *They posed a question: Does R. Simeon b. Eleazar's statement apply to the former text and state a lenient rule? Or does it apply to the latter text and state a stricter rule? [The translation at B follows in accord with this second alternative.]*

D. *Come and take note: It was taught on Tannaite authority,* If it dried out by human intervention, it is *terefah*. R. Simeon b. Eleazar says, "Even if it was [dried out] by the intervention of any creature [cf. T. 3:6 D-E]."

E. *Rabbah bar bar Hannah was walking in the wilderness. He found some rams whose lungs were shrunk. He went and asked [for a ruling regarding them] in the house of study. They said to him, "In the summer [this is the procedure to determine if the animals are valid]. Bring white glazed basins and fill them with cold water and put [the lungs] in them for twenty-four hours. If they return to normal [then they were shrunk] by natural causes and they are valid. And if not, they are* terefah. *In the winter [this is the procedure]. Bring dark glazed basins and fill them with warm water and put [the lungs] in them for twenty-four hours. If they return to normal, they are valid. And if not, they are* terefah."

## VIII.1

A. **(12) One that has lost its hide [having been flayed] [M. 3:2 E].** *Our rabbis taught:* **One that lost its hide — R. Meir declares valid. And sages declare invalid [M. 3:2 E-G].** And Eleazar the

Bavli Hullin Chapter Three. Folios 42A-67B

scribe and Yohanan b. Gudguda already testified concerning the animal that lost its hide that it is invalid.

B. Said R. Simeon b. Eleazar, "R. Meir retracted his view on this." We may derive the conclusion that according to R. Simeon b. Eleazar R. Meir did [earlier] dispute [the view of sages regarding] one that lost its hide.

C. *But lo it was taught on Tannaite authority,* **R. Simeon b. Eleazar said, "R. Meir and sages did not dispute concerning one which has lost its hide, that it is invalid." R. Oshaia the son of R. Judah [T.: Judah b. Isaiah] the spice maker already testified before R. Aqiba, speaking in the name of R. Tarfon, concerning one which has lost its hide, that it is invalid [T. 3:7 B-C].**

D. But if there remained on it [hide] the size of a *sela* it is valid.

E. Said R. Nahman bar Yitzhak, "What does it mean that they did not dispute? [They did not disagree originally, but it means that] R. Meir did not stand by his [conflicting view] in dispute [with sages]."

VIII.2
A. Said the master: But if there remained on it [hide] the size of a *sela* it is valid [D above]. *Where [must there remain this amount]?* Said R. Judah, said Samuel, "All along the backbone [of the animal]."

B. *They posed a question: [Does this mean] a long and thin [piece of hide along the backbone] that when combined adds up to the size of a* sela? *Or perhaps does it mean [there must be a strip of hide] the width of a* sela *along the entire backbone?*

C. *Come and take note: R. Nehorai explained in the name of Samuel, "[There must be a strip of hide] the width of a* sela *along the entire backbone."*

D. Rabbah bar bar Hannah said, "At the top of each joint [there must be hide the size of a *sela*.]"

E. R. Eleazar b. Antigonus in the name of R. Eleazar b. R. Yannai said, "At the navel [there must be hide the size of a *sela*]."

F. R. Yannai b. R. Ishmael *posed a question*: If the [hide] was removed along the length of the backbone and the rest [of the hide] was intact; if the [hide] was removed from the navel and the rest was intact; if the [hide] was removed from the tops of the joints and the rest was intact, what is the law? *The question stands unresolved.*

G. Said Rab, "Any of the hide serves to rescue [the animal] from the status of **one that has lost its hide** except for the hide on the hooves." And R. Yohanan said, "Even the hide on the hooves serves to rescue it."

H. R. Assi posed a question of R. Yohanan, "What is the rule with regard to whether the hide of the hooves rescues it from the status of **one that has lost its hide**?" He said to him, "It rescues it." He said to him, "But our master taught us, 'These are the places where the hide has the status of the flesh: the hide of the hooves [b. 122a]." He said to them, "Stop annoying me. For I teach this as my personal view."

I. *For it was taught on Tannaite authority,* **He** who slaughters the burnt-offering [with the intention] to eat [var. to offer] an olive's bulk of the hide from under the tail outside of its proper place [M. Zeb. 2:2 E], it is unfit and there is for this no punishment of extirpation. [If he did so with intention to eat or offer it] after its proper time, it is refuse. And they are liable on its account to the punishment of extirpation [T. Zeb. 2:3 A-D].

J. Eliezer b. Judah of Eiblayim said in the name of R. Jacob, and so R. Simeon b. Judah of [Kefar] Akkum says in the name of R. Simeon, "The same applies to the hide of the hooves, or the soft skin of the head of a calf, or the skin under the tail, or all [the places] that were listed by the sages regarding uncleanness whose hide has the same status as the flesh [of those places] [cf. T. Zeb. 2:3 F-G]."

K. [56a] This includes [by inference] the skin of the pudenda [of an animal that he slaughtered with intention to eat or offer it] outside of its proper place, it is invalid but there is for this no punishment of extirpation. [If he did so with intention to offer it] after its proper time, it is refuse and they are liable to punishment on account of extirpation [cf. T. Zeb. 2:3 H-I].

These units adhere predictably closely to Mishnah's operative agenda. I.1 explores the implications of Mishnah's general statement in comparison with that of M. 3:1. I.2 comments on a lemma cited in I.1. II.1 discusses Mishnah's measure of size. II.2 takes up general issues regarding measures of size. The unit cites a complementary Tannaite rule from Mishnah Kelim for its illustrations.

III.1 comments on a rule of Mishnah in light of the premises of M. 4:1. IV.1 directly elucidates Mishnah's rule regarding kidneys. IV.2 provides a discussion regarding the comparison of defects of one organ with those of another, secondary to the Mishnah. V.1 and VI.1 give us brief glosses to clarify Mishnah's rules. VII.1 glosses Mishnah's rule and adds a further discussion regarding the inspection of the lung. VIII.1 expands on Mishnah's rule by citing related materials including the Tosefta-passage relevant to the text.

Finally, VIII.2 examines a secondary issue raised in the preceding discussion — how much and which hide counts? The unit cites a related Tosefta-passage from Zebahim and examines its implications.

3:3

A. And these are the *terefah* [carcasses] among fowl:
(1) one the gullet of which is pierced,
(2) one the windpipe of which is torn.

B. (3) [If] the weasel pierced its head at a point which renders it *terefah*;
(4) [if] the gizzard is pierced;
(5) [if] the small intestines are pierced.

C. (6) [If] it fell into the fire and the intestines were scorched — if they are green, they are invalid. If they are red, they are valid.

D. (7) [If] one trampled it or knocked it against the wall,

E. or [if] a beast trampled on it, and it flutters — if it remains alive for twenty-four hours, and one [then] slaughtered it, it is valid.

### I.1

A. *Rab and Samuel and Levi said, "He inserts his hand inside and inspects it [i.e., the mouth of a bird whose head was pierced by a weasel]. If it oozes [from a hole in the skull] it is terefah. And if not, it is valid."*

B. This is reasonable according to the authority who holds the view [that it is not *terefah*] *unless the interior membrane is pierced* [b. 45a]. But according to the authority who holds the view that [it is terefah] *if the exterior membrane is pierced even though the interior membrane is not pierced*, we should suspect that perhaps [in our case] the exterior membrane was pierced but the interior membrane was not pierced. [That is why there is no oozing from the skull. Accordingly, this form of inspection would not be an effective means to determine if the animal is *terefah*.]

C. *[This is not likely.] If it is the case that the exterior membrane is pierced, the interior membrane on account of its delicacy will surely rupture.* [Thus the inspection is valid.]

### I.2

A. Said Ziri, "There is no effective inspection for [piercing by] a weasel because its teeth are thin." *But what difference does it make if its teeth are thin?*

B. Said R. Oshaia, "[There is no effective inspection for piercing by a weasel] because its teeth are thin and curved." [There will be no oozing because the holes it makes in the two membranes do not align.]

C. *When he departed to Nehardea he sent to them,* "The matters that I spoke before you were errors on my part. In fact this is what they said in the name of R. Simeon b. Laqish, 'They inspect [for signs of piercing by] a weasel by hand, but not with a nail [or needle or straw].' And R. Yohanan said, '[They may inspect] even with a needle.'"

D. *And this is [the same as] the dispute between R. Judah and R. Nehemiah. One inspected by hand and one inspected with a needle. The one who inspected by hand would say to the one who inspected with a needle, "How long will you go on losing money for Israel?"* [The inspection with a needle resulted in the discovery of many more signs of defects.] *Said the one who inspected with a needle to the one who inspected by hand,* "How long will you go on feeding the Israel carrion? [Your method of inspection does not discover the defects.]"

E. Is it carrion? But lo the animal was slaughtered [and should not be categorized as carrion in any case]! Rather [he means] *terefah* for perhaps the membrane of the brain was pierced.

F. *We have proof that R. Judah was the one who inspected by hand. For it was taught on Tannaite authority,* **R. Simeon b. Eleazar says in the name of R. Judah, "They inspect [the weasel] by hand, but they do not inspect it with a needle. If the bone is pierced, [it is invalid, and if not, it is valid] [T. 3:15 D]"** even if the membrane of the brain was not pierced. *This is proof.*

G. *Lo the body of this text itself contains a contradiction. It says,* **They inspect [the weasel] for signs of piercing by hand, but not with a nail.** *It seems [logical to conclude from this] that it you need to inspect [for the defect]. And then it teaches,* **If the bone is pierced [it is invalid]** *even if the membrane of the brain was not pierced. It seems [logical to conclude from this] that you do not need to inspect it.*

H. [You can explain that there is no contradiction.] *The latter text refers to a water bird since it has no membrane. Can you conclude that it has no membrane? Rather because its membrane is delicate [it would rupture if you inspected it].*

I.3
A. *Said R. Nahman to R. Anan, "Did not the master say, 'Samuel inspected by hand and declared it valid [if he found no defect].' And did not Huna our associate say, 'Rab inspected by hand and declared it valid.' But Levi taught, 'The terefot that the sages enumerated for an animal all have equivalents for a fowl. There is an additional one for fowl:* **If the bone is pierced [it is invalid]** *even if the membrane of the brain was not pierced.'"*

B. *He [Anan] said to him, "The latter text refers to a water bird since it has no membrane. Can you conclude that it has no membrane? Rather because its membrane is delicate [it would rupture if you inspected it]."*

**I.4**

A. *A certain hen that was in the house of R. Hana [and] they sent [it for a ruling] before R. Matna [because it fell under the rule of]:* **If the bone is pierced [it is invalid]** *even if the membrane of the brain was not pierced. And he declared it valid! They said to him, "But lo Levi taught, 'The terefot that the sages enumerated for an animal all have equivalents for a fowl. There is an additional one for fowl:* **If the bone is pierced [it is invalid]** *even if the membrane of the brain was not pierced.'"*

B. *He [Matna] said to him, "The latter text refers to a water bird since it has no membrane. Can you conclude that it has no membrane? Rather you should maintain because its membrane is delicate [it would rupture if you inspected it]."*

**I.5**

A. *R. Shizbi inspected [the membrane for signs of piercing] in the sun. R. Yemar inspected it [for leaks] in water. R. Aha bar Jacob inspected it with a* **[56b]** *stalk of wheat [i.e., as they did with a nail or needle].*

B. *Said R. Shizbi, "Our geese are like water birds [with respect to this rule]."*

**II.1**

A. **[If] it fell into the fire [and the intestines were scorched — if they are green, they are invalid. If they are red, they are valid]** **[M. 3:3 C]**. Said R. Yohanan in the name of R. Yosé b. Joshua, "The [minimum] quantity that must turn green [to render it invalid] is the same as the [minimum] quantity that must be pierced [to render it invalid]. Just as the [minimum quantity that must] be pierced [to render it invalid] is any amount at all, the [minimum quantity that must] turn green [to render it invalid] is any amount at all."

B. R. Joseph the son of R. Joshua b. Levi *posed a question to* R. Joshua b. Levi: If the liver near the intestines turned green, what is the law? He [Joshua] said to him, "It is *terefah*." [Joseph asked,] "Should it not be treated as if it were removed [and thus valid]?" Said Raba, "Because the liver near the intestines turned green, we know that it fell into the fire and that the intestines were scorched and it is *terefah*."

## II.2

A. *Rabbi Joshua b. Levi had a certain hen [that had fallen into a fire] that he sent before R. Eleazar Haqqappar Beribbi [for a ruling]. He said to him, "They are green." And he declared them valid. But lo we were taught,* **If they are green, they are invalid.** [This is not a contradiction.] *They only said,* **If they are green, they are invalid** *regarding the gizzard, the heart and the liver.*

B. *It was also taught on Tannaite authority in this regard: For these internal organs they stated the matter — for the gizzard, the heart and the liver.*

C. *R. Yitzhak bar Joseph had a certain hen [that had fallen into a fire] that he sent before R. Abbahu [for a ruling]. He said to him, "They [the intestines] are red." And he declared them* terefah. *But lo we were taught,* **If they are red, they are valid.** [This is not a contradiction.] *He said to him, "Red ones that turned green or green ones that turned red are* terefah. *They only said that red ones are valid regarding the heart, the gizzard and the liver."*

D. Said R. Samuel bar Hiyya, said R. Mani, "Red ones [intestines] that turned green [after the hen fell into the flame] and he boiled them and they turned red again are valid." *What is the basis for this rule? Smoke had contaminated them [and made them look green].*

E. Said R. Nahman bar Yitzhak, "Even we said, 'Red ones that had not turned green [after the hen fell into the flame] and he boiled them and they turned green are *terefah*." *What is the basis for this rule? Their true status is revealed [by boiling them].* Said R. Ashi, "Therefore a person should only eat [from a hen that fell into a fire if he checks the intestines they are] boiled."

F. *But this is not the case! We do not surmise the presence of a taint [that would render the animal defective].*

## III.1

A. **[If] one trampled it or knocked it against the wall, or [if a beast trampled on it...]** [M. 3:3 D-E]. Said R. Eleazar b. Antigonus in the name of R. Eleazar b. R. Yannai, "In any case it must be inspected [for defects that would render it *terefah*]."

These units engage in close Mishnah-criticism and rarely venture far from the Mishnah's narrowly stated operative concerns. I.1 states the procedure for inspecting for defects specified in Mishnah and correlates this with related views. I.2 gives rulings related to the preceding and correlates this with the relevant Tosefta-passage. I.3-5 provide further inspection procedures and precedents.

II.1-2 delineates the minimum needed for Mishnah's next ruling. Secondary rules related to Mishnah's concern follow. The section concludes with III.1, a brief lemma commenting on Mishnah's rule.

### 3:4

A. And these are valid [carcasses] among fowl:
(1) [if] the windpipe is pierced or severed [lengthwise],

B. (2) [if] the weasel pierced its head at a point which does not render it *terefah*,

C. (3) [if] the crop was pierced,

D. Rabbi says, "Even if it is removed" —

E. (4) [if] the intestines protrude but are not pierced,
(5) [if] its wings are broken,
(6) [if] its legs are broken,
(7) [if] its wing feathers are plucked.

F. R. Judah says, "If the fuzz is removed, it is invalid."

### I.1

A. *Our rabbis taught on Tannaite authority:* Once [*m'sh b*] R. Simai and R. Zadok went to intercalate the year in Lod and they spent the Sabbath in Ono. And they ruled regarding [defects in a bird's] womb in accord with the view of Rabbi regarding [defects in a bird's] crop.

B. *They posed a question [concerning this teaching at A]:* Did they rule to prohibit [regarding defects] in a womb in the same manner that Rabbi ruled to permit [regarding defects] in a crop? Or perhaps, did they rule to permit [regarding defects] in a womb in the same manner that rabbi ruled [to permit regarding defects] in a crop? But [at the same time] did they not reason in accord with the view of Rabbi [regarding defects in a] crop? *The question stands unresolved.*

C. Said Rabbah *and some say* R. Joshua b. Levi, "The top of the crop is treated with regard to the law as if it were part of the gullet."

*Bavli Ḥullin Chapter Three. Folios 42A-67B*

*Where is [the top of the crop]? Said R. Bibi bar Abayye, "Any part of it that contracts along with [the gullet]."*

**II.1**

A. **(4) [If] the intestines protrude [but are not pierced] [M. 3:4 E].** Said R. Samuel bar R. Yitzhak, "They taught this only where he did not twist them. But if he twisted them, it is *terefah*." *As it is written*, "[Is not he your father, who created you,] who made you and established you?" (Deut. 32:6). This teaches us that the Holy One, blessed be He, established order [in the organs] in a person. And if one of them should become twisted, he cannot live.

B. *It was taught on Tannaite authority:* R. Meir used to say, "[The verse], '[Is not he your father, who created you,] who made you and established you?' (Deut. 32:6) [implies that the people of Israel are like] a village that has it all. From it come its priests, prophets, officers and kings. As it states, "Out of them shall come the cornerstone, out them the tent peg, out of them the battle bow, out of them every ruler" (Zech. 10:4).

**II.2**

A. *A certain illusionist [lit.: Aramean; alt.: Roman] saw a certain man fall from the roof to the ground. His abdomen burst and his intestines protruded. He brought the man's son and created the illusion that he was slaughtering him [the son] before him [the father].* **[57a]** *He [the father, upon seeing the apparition,] swooned and sighed deeply and drew [his intestines] back into his abdomen and they stitched up his belly.*

**III.1**

A. **(6) [If] its legs are broken [M. 3:4 E].** *A certain basket of crippled birds was brought before Raba [for a ruling]. Raba inspected them at the nexus of the sinews and he declared them fit.*

B. Said R. Judah, said Rab, "[A case of] a dislocated fore-leg in an animal is valid. [Some versions add this item: A case of] a dislocated femur in an animal is *terefah*. [A case of] a dislocated femur in a bird is *terefah*. [A case of] a dislocated wing in a bird is *terefah*. [In that case] we suspect that perhaps the lung was pierced."

C. And Samuel said, "Let it [i.e., the lung of a bird with a dislocated wing] be inspected." And so said R. Yohanan, "Let it [i.e., the lung of a bird with a dislocated wing] be inspected."

D. Hezekiah said, "There are no [defects that render *terefah* in the] lungs in a bird." And R. Yohanan said, "There are. And they are like the petals of a rose between the wings."

E. *What does it mean*: There are no [defects that render *terefah* in the] lungs in a bird? *If you say it means that they have none at all, but lo we can see that they do have. Rather it must mean that they are not rendered terefah by [defects in] them.*

F. *But lo, Levi taught,* "The *terefot* that the sages enumerated for an animal all have equivalents for a fowl. There is an additional one for fowl: **If the bone is pierced [it is invalid]** even if the membrane of the brain was not pierced" [M. 3:3 I:3 A, b. 56a].

G. Rather what does it mean? There are no [defects in the lungs in a bird that affect its status], neither if it falls [from a roof], nor if it is scorched [in a flame]. *What is the basis for this view? Said R. Hanna,* "Because the majority of its ribs protect them [from becoming defective]." But lo what [is the implication of what] R. Yohanan said [in D], "There are. And they are like the petals of a rose between the wings?" *We may derive from this the conclusion that Hezekiah reasons that they have no [lungs].*

H. *But they said in the West [Israel] in the name of R. Yosé b. R. Hanina,* "From the words of Beribbi [i.e., Hezekiah] it is understood that he is not knowledgeable in [the anatomy of] fowls [i.e., chickens]."

### III.2

A. Said R. Huna, said Rab, "[A case of] a dislocated femur in a bird is valid." Said to him Rabbah bar R. Huna to R. Huna, "*But lo the rabbis who came from Pumbedita said [that] R. Judah in the name of Rab said, '[A case of] a dislocated femur in a bird is terefah.'*"

B. *He said to him, "My son. Every river runs its own course." [Every place has its own customs.]*

*Bavli Ḥullin Chapter Three. Folios 42A-67B* 105

C. R. Abba went and found R. Jeremiah bar Abba inspecting the nexus of the sinews. He [Abba] said to him, "Why is the master doing all this?" But lo [said] R. Huna, said Rab, "[A case of] a dislocated femur in a bird is valid."

D. He [Jeremiah] said to him, "I know a Mishnah-passage [that says], **A beast, the [hind] legs of which are cut off below the knee, is valid. [If they are cut off] above the knee, it is invalid. And so [if] the juncture of the thigh sinews was removed [it is invalid] [M. 4:6 A-C]**." And Rab said regarding this, "The same applies to a bird."

E. *If this is the case, then we have a contradiction between one statement of Rab [cited in C] and the other [cited in D]. He [Jeremiah] was silent. He [Abba] said to him, "Perhaps he [Rab] differentiated between a dislocated [femur] and one that had been cut." He [Jeremiah] said to him, "Are you explaining the teaching of Rab? Rab said explicitly, 'A dislocated [femur] is valid. A cut [femur] is invalid.' And do not be surprised [by these rules]. For lo, you may cut from this place and [the animal] will die. You may cut this [other] place and [the animal] will live."* [Cf. M. 3:1 XIV.1 I, b. 48b.]

F. *When R. Abba departed [for Israel] he found R. Zira sitting and saying, "Said R. Huna, said Rab, '[A case of] a dislocated femur in a bird is terefah.'" He said to him, "By the master's life! Since the time you departed to come here* **[57b]** *we had a chance to speak before R. Huna. And we asked him [about this matter]. And he said to us, '[A case of] a dislocated femur in a bird is valid.' And we also found R. Jeremiah bar Abba who was sitting and inspecting the nexus of the sinews. And we asked him, 'Does not the master reason in accord with that which R. Huna said in the name of Rab: [A case of] a dislocated femur in a bird is valid?'"*

G. *He said to us, "I know a Mishnah-passage [that says],* **A beast, the [hind] legs of which are cut off below the knee, is valid. [If they are cut off] above the knee, it is invalid. And so [if] the juncture of the thigh sinews was removed [it is invalid]. [M. 4:6 A-C].**" *And Rab said regarding this, "The same applies to a bird."*

H. *And we said to him, "If this is the case then we have a contradiction between one statement of Rab and the other." He [Jeremiah] was silent.*

*And we asked him, "Perhaps he [Rab] differentiated between a dislocated [femur] and one that had been cut." He [Jeremiah] said to me, "Are you explaining the teaching of Rab? Rab said explicitly, 'A dislocated [femur] is valid. A cut [femur] is invalid.'"*

I. *And what more do you [Zira] have [to contribute to this discussion]? [He said,] "This is what R. Hiyya bar Ashi said, said Rab, '[A case of] a dislocated femur in a bird is terefah.' And so said R. Jacob bar Idi, said R. Yohanan, '[A case of] a dislocated femur in a bird is terefah.'"*

J. *And said R. Jacob bar Idi, "If R. Yohanan had been in that place when the associates ruled that it was permitted, he would not dare to raise a finger to oppose the ruling [because of the greatness of those sages]."*

K. For said R. Hanina, said Rabbi, "[A case of] a dislocated femur in a bird is valid." And R. Hanina had a hen that had a dislocated femur. And he brought it before Rabbi [for a ruling]. And he ruled to permit it to him. And R. Hanina pickled it [to keep it as an exhibit]. And he would teach the law to his students with it [saying], "This is what Rabbi ruled to permit for me. This is what Rabbi ruled to permit for me."

L. *And the law does not follow in accord with any of these teachings. Rather [it is in accord] with what R. Yosé b. Nehorai asked R. Joshua b. Levi, "How large must the hole be in the windpipe [to render it terefah]?" He said to him, "We learned an absolute [rule in the] Mishnah about this:* **So much as an Italian** *issar* **[M. 3:2 B]."**

M. He [Yosé] said to him, "But there was a lamb in our neighborhood that had a hole in its windpipe and they made for it a tube of a reed [and inserted it in the windpipe] and it lived [that way]."

N. He [Joshua] said to him, "*But can you rely on that [single case as proof of the law]?* But lo the law was disseminated in Israel that, '[A case of] a dislocated femur in a bird is *terefah*.' And [yet] R. Simeon b. Halafta had a hen whose femur was dislocated. And they made for it a tube of a reed [as a splint to reinforce it] and it lived [that way]."

Bavli Ḥullin Chapter Three. Folios 42A-67B    107

O.  *But what can you say regarding this [latter case]? It [lived] less than twelve months [that way]. Here too [in the former case] it [lived] less than twelve months.* [And the principle is that if it cannot live a full twelve months with an injury it is *terefah*.]

IV.1

A.  They said concerning R. Simeon b. Halafta that he was an inventor. And he performed an act to dissuade R. Judah [from his view]. For R. Judah used to say, **If the fuzz is removed, it is invalid [M. 3:4 F].** And R. Simeon b. Halafta had a hen whose fuzz had been removed. And he put it in an oven and he dressed it in a leather apron of bronze workers [that is constantly hot]. And it grew more new feathers than it had originally.

B.  But perhaps [this was not valid proof that the condition is not a severe enough defect to render the bird *terefah* because] R. Judah reasons that a *terefah* may show [temporary] signs of improvement. *But is this so [that it would improve] in the very manner in which it became terefah?* It grew more new feathers than it had originally!

C.  What does it mean that he was an inventor? Said R. Mesharshayya, "As it is written, 'Go to the ant, O sluggard; consider her ways, and be wise. Without having any chief, officer or ruler, she prepares her food in summer, and gathers her sustenance in harvest' (Prov. 6:6-8). *He [Simeon] said, 'I will go and see if it is true that he [the ant] has no ruler.'* He went at the season of Tammuz [the summer solstice] and spread his cloak [over an ant hill]. One of them came out. He marked it with a sign. It went back in and said to them [the other ants], 'The shade has descended.' They all came out. He removed his cloak [from the hill] and the sun shined upon them. So they pounced on that ant [that misled them like a mob] and killed him. He [Simeon] said, *'We may derive from this that they have no ruler. For if they had, would they not have had to seek the authority of the ruler [before killing that ant]?'"*

D.  *Said R. Aha the son of Raba to R. Ashi, "But perhaps there was a ruler among them. Or perhaps they did have the authority of the ruler. Or perhaps it was between the reign of one ruler and another. As it is written, 'In those days there was no king in Israel; every man did* what was right in his own eyes' (Jud. 17:6). [No. You must reject all these alternatives.] *Rather, you must rely on Solomon's integrity* [in his statement about the ants. Accordingly, it must be that they had no king.]"

**V.1**

A. Said R. Huna, "A sign [that an animal with a physical defect is *not* to be deemed a] *terefah* [is that it lives] twelve months [after developing the defect]."

B. *They posed an objection:* [Another source says,] A sign [that an animal with a physical defect is to be deemed a] *terefah* [is that] it does not give birth. [That is, if it gives birth, it is not deemed to be a *terefah*.] Rabban Simeon b. Gamaliel says, "If its health improves, we know that it is valid. If its health deteriorates, we know that it is *terefah*."

C. Rabbi [var. R. Meir] says, "A sign [that an animal with a physical defect is *not*] *terefah* [is that it lives] thirty days." They said to him [by way of objection], "But lo, many live two or three years."

D. This [issue] is the [principle behind] a Tannaite dispute. *For it was taught on Tannaite authority:* And regarding a skull that has one long hole [this is a sign the animal is *terefah*]. Or if there were many holes, they combine them together to constitute [a sign that it is *terefah* if they exceed the minimum measure of the size of] a drill hole [b. 45a, M. 3:1 VII.1 B].

E. Said R. Yosé b. Meshullam, "Once at Ayn Ibl a person's skull was broken. And they used a gourd hull as a splint for it. And he lived." Said to him R. Simeon b. Eleazar, "From this we have no proof. It was during the summer. [The weather was mild and there was no stress on the person.] As soon as winter came, he died."

F. Said R. Aha bar Jacob, "The law is in accord with the view that [an animal with a physical defect may be deemed a] *terefah* [even if] it gives birth or if its health improves."

G. Said Amemar, "*Regarding these eggs laid by a bird that was deemed* terefah **[58a]**: *the first batch [produced after the bird became* terefah]

*Bavli Ḥullin Chapter Three. Folios 42A-67B* 109

are prohibited. *[Any eggs produced] thereafter are deemed to fall under the principle of two antecedent causes [i.e., the prohibited-mother and permitted-father produce the offspring] and [therefore the eggs] are permitted."*

H. *R. Ashi raised an objection to Amemar,* "[The Mishnah rules:] **But they agree that an egg from a bird that is *terefah* is forbidden, since it grew in what was forbidden [M. Ed. 5:1 F].**" [That ruling makes no distinction between the first and subsequent batches.]

I. [We can explain that the Mishnah refers to a case where the hen] was impregnated by [rubbing in] the soil. But why not explain that [rule refers to] the first batch [of eggs]? In that case [the Mishnah should not have stated,] it grew. It should have [stated,] it finished [growing].

J. *Rather [consider] this that was taught on Tannaite authority:* **[Concerning] the offspring of [an animal that was deemed] *terefah* — R. Eliezer says, "It is not to be offered [as a sacrifice] on the altar." And R. Joshua [M.: sages] says, "It may be offered [M. Tem. 6:5 B-D]."** *Concerning what [circumstance] do they dispute?* Where [the animal] first became *terefah* and then became pregnant. R. Eliezer reasons [in accord with the principle that] where there are two antecedent causes [one permitted and one prohibited] we rule the result is prohibited. And R. Joshua reasons [in accord with the principle that] where there are two antecedent causes [one permitted and one prohibited] we rule the result is permitted.

K. *If this is the case then why is the dispute formulated in relation to consecrated [animals]? They ought to dispute regarding ordinary [animals]. This will inform you of the authority of R. Joshua. For even in regard to consecrated [animals we rule in accord with his view that the offspring of a* terefah-*animal] is permitted.*

L. *But why is the dispute not formulated in relation to ordinary [animals]? And this would inform you of the authority of R. Eliezer. For even in regard to ordinary [animals we rule in accord with his view that the offspring of a* terefah-*animal] is prohibited. [The reason we do not formulate it in this way is that we follow the principle that] the*

M. And they agree that the egg produced by a *terefah*-bird is prohibited [where the hen] *was impregnated by [rubbing in] the soil because there is one antecedent cause [in that case, i.e., the forbidden mother bird].*

N. *R. Aha reasons in accord with the view of R. Aha bar Jacob [F] and taught the ruling of Amemar as was stated above [G]. Rabina did not reason in accord with the view of R. Aha bar Jacob and accordingly taught this version of the ruling of Amemar:* Said Amemar, "Regarding these eggs laid by a bird about which there was a doubt whether it was terefah: the first batch [produced after the bird became terefah] *must be held in abeyance. If she goes on to lay more eggs, they are permitted. And if not, they are forbidden.*"

O. *R. Ashi raised an objection to Amemar,* "[The Mishnah rules:] **But they agree that an egg from a bird that is** *terefah* **is forbidden, since it grew in what was forbidden [M. Ed. 5:1 F].**"

P. *He [Amemar] said to him,* "[We can explain that the Mishnah refers to] *the first batch [of eggs]. In that case [the Mishnah should not have stated],* **it grew.** *It should have [stated],* **it finished [growing]**.

Q. *[Indeed] you should teach [the version],* **It finished [growing]**.

R. *Rather [consider] this that was taught on Tannaite authority:* **[Concerning] the offspring of [an animal that was deemed]** *terefah* **— R. Eliezer says, "It is not to be offered [as a sacrifice] on the altar." And R. Joshua [M.: sages] says, "It may be offered [M. Tem. 6:5 B-D]."** *Concerning what [circumstance] do they dispute? Where [the animal] first became pregnant and then became terefah. R. Eliezer reasons [in accord with the principle that as regards to the law] the foetus is considered to be a thigh of the mother [and thus it too is terefah]. And R. Joshua reasons [in accord with the principle that] the foetus is not considered to be a thigh of the mother.*

S. *If this is the case then why is the dispute formulated in relation to consecrated [animals]? They ought to dispute regarding ordinary* [animals]. *This will inform you of the authority of R. Joshua. [For even in regard to consecrated (animals we rule in accord with his view that the offspring of a* terefah-*animal) is permitted.]*

T. *But why is the dispute not formulated in relation to ordinary [animals]? And this would inform you of the authority of R. Eliezer. [For even in regard to ordinary animals we rule in accord with his view that the offspring of a* terefah-*animal is prohibited. The reason we do not formulate it in this way is that we follow the principle that] the authority of the rule that permits takes precedence [over the authority of the rule that prohibits].*

U. And they certainly agree that the egg produced by a *terefah*-bird is prohibited *where it was part of the first batch. On what basis? It is part of the [mother's] body.*

V. And the law is for a male [it is deemed *terefah* if it lives less than] twelve months. And for a female [it is deemed *terefah* if it] does not give birth.

**VI.1**
A. Said R. Huna, "Any creature that does not have a bone [i.e., an invertebrate] does not live longer than twelve months."

B. Said R. Pappa, "We may derive from the statement of R. Huna the following [rule]: For said Samuel, 'A cucumber that was infested with worms while on the vine — it is forbidden [to eat it because the worms have the status of forbidden crawling creatures].'

C. [58b] "Those [worm-infested-] dates in a barrel after twelve months of a year they are permitted [because the worms could not have entered the dates while on the tree and then lived that long]."

D. Said Rab, "No gnat lives more than a day. No fly lives more than a year."

E. Said R. Pappa to Abayye, "Lo, the folk tell [this story]: For seven years the female gnat bickered with the male gnat. She said to him, 'I have seen a person from Mehoza who was bathing and came out of the water and wrapped himself in a sheet. And you alit on him and sucked his *blood and did not tell me about it.'"* [Apparently, gnats can live more than a day.]

F. *He [Abayye] said to him, "According to your logic [consider this tale]. Lo, the folk tell [this story]: Sixty minas [weight] of iron can be hung from the proboscis of a gnat. Could this be for real? By itself how much does it weigh? Rather [what is the explanation of this statement]? It refers to their scale of mina-weights [of the gnats]. Here too [regarding the first story] it must refer to their measure of years [i.e., much less than ours]."*

**VII.1**

A. *It was taught there in the Mishnah on Tannaite authority:* **A beast with five legs or that has only three... lo these are deemed blemishes [M. Bekh. 6:7].** *Said R. Huna, "They taught this only if a fore-leg was missing or added. But if a hind-leg was missing or added, it is also deemed to be a* terefah.*" One what basis? [It is based on the principle that] we treat every added limb like a missing limb [and that renders the animal* terefah*].*

B. *A certain animal had two inner rumens. They brought it before Rabina [for a ruling]. And he declared it* terefah *on the basis of the ruling of R. Huna. But if [the two rumens] empty from one to the other it is valid [i.e., we treat them as if they were one].*

C. *A certain tube that went from the reticulum to the omasum — R. Ashi reasoned to declare it* terefah. *Said R. Huna mar bar Hiyya to R. Ashi, "All grazing animals have this."*

D. *A certain tube that went from the reticulum to the rumen — Mar bar R. Ashi reasoned to declare it valid. Said to him R. Oshaia, "Will you weave all [the laws] together into one fabric? Where it is stated [that the law deems it valid], it is stated. And where it is not stated, it is not stated."*

**VIII.1**

A. *Nathan bar Shila, the chief butcher of Sepphoris, testified before Rabbi that if two intestines protrude from an animal at the same time it is* terefah. *And the equivalent case for a bird is valid. Under what circumstances? If they protrude from two different places. But if* they protrude from the same place and end within a finger's breadth of each other, it is valid.

B. R. Ammi and R. Assi dispute [regarding the interpretation of "end within a finger's breadth"]. One said, "They must merge back together." And the other said, "Even if they do not merge back together."

C. *Now this is consistent according the authority that holds the view that [to be valid] they must merge back together that they taught [this must be] "within a finger's breadth." But according to the authority that holds the view that [to be valid it is acceptable] even if they do not merge back together, what is the meaning of the stipulation, "within a finger's breadth?" It means, "within a finger's breadth below [i.e., near the rectum they must merge (Rashi)]."*

IX.1
A. **R. Judah says, "If the fuzz is removed, it is invalid" [M. 3:4 F].** Said R. Yohanan, "R. Judah and R. Ishmael said the same thing. R. Judah, as we stated [in the Mishnah]. And R. Ishmael, *as it was taught in the Mishnah on Tannaite authority,* **R. Ishmael says, 'The down joins together [i.e., the fuzz combines with other parts of the carcass to constitute the minimum quantity to render unclean and to contract uncleanness, M. Toh. 1:2 B].'"**

B. *Said Raba, "Perhaps this is not a valid assertion. On this point only regarding the matter of* terefah *R. Judah stated [that the fuzz is significant because without it] there is nothing to protect the bird [from the elements and it will die]. But with regard to matters that spoil the animal [i.e., uncleanness] he holds in accord with the view of the rabbis. And on this point only regarding the matters that spoil the animal [i.e., uncleanness] R. Ishmael stated [that the fuzz is significant]. But with regard to the matter of rendering the animal terefah [he would argue that] it does not afford any protection [for the bird and thus is of no consequence]."*

Again the materials adhere closely to Mishnah's operative considerations and issues. I.1 supplies a precedent that relates to Mishnah's primary concern. It goes on to a secondary discussion of that tradition in comparison with Mishnah and then to a related rule. II.1 comments on

Mishnah's rule and cites Scripture related to it. B suggests an alternative application of the verse.

II.2 provides a colorful proof that a defect listed by Mishnah need not be lethal. III.1-2 give precedents and rulings that relate to Mishnah's next rule and to defects in fowl in general. IV.1 provides a precedent to illustrate Mishnah's rule. It then goes off on a tangential discussion. V.1 states some general principles of signs of *terefah*-defects. G-V take up the status of the by-products, eggs of a *terefah*-bird. They cite independent Mishnah-sources and invokes in the discussion the principle of a product of two antecedent causes. VI.1 cites secondary rules and a story derivative of the preceding.

VII.1 introduces an unrelated rule based on an independent Mishnah-source. VIII.1 cites a precedent that has general relevance to Mishnah's rule in E-4. IX.1 returns to cite another Mishnah-source that complements our Mishnah and then briefly discusses its relevance.

### 3:5

A.     (1) **[A beast which suffers from] congestion of blood,**
        **(2) and one [which has suffered from] smoke,**
        **(3) and one [which has suffered from] cold,**
        **(4) and one which has eaten oleander,**
        **(5) and one which has eaten chicken excrement,**
        **(6) or which has drunk dirty water**

B.     **is valid.**

C.     **[If] it ate deadly poison, or if a snake bit it, it is permitted [to eat it] in respect to [the laws of] *terefah*, but it is prohibited as a danger to life.**

### I.1

A.     Said Samuel, "If it chewed asafoetida, it is *terefah*." *On what basis? [On the assumption that it is so strong it] perforated [the animal's] internal organs.*

B.     *R. Shizbi posed an objection:* **[A beast which suffers from] congestion of blood, and one [which has suffered from] smoke, [and one which has suffered from cold, and one which has eaten oleander, and one which has eaten chicken excrement, or which has drunk dirty water]** [M. Hul. 3:5A] — [if] one force fed it asafoetida, root of crowfoot, **oleander,** deadly poison, [or] chicken excrement — it is valid. One bitten by a snake, or bitten by a rabid dog in respect to *terefah* it is permitted, but it is prohibited as a danger to life [M. Hul. 3:5 C] [T. 3:19 A-C].

C. *There is a contradiction with regard to asafoetida [between Samuel's rule and T.] And there is a contradiction with regard to deadly poison [between M. and T.].*

D. *We may explain that there is no contradiction with regard to asafoetida. This one [Samuel] refers to the extract [that is potent] and this one [T.] refers to the leaves [that are milder].*

E. *We may explain that there is no contradiction with regard to deadly poison. This one [T.] refers to [a beast that ate] animal-poison and this one [M.] refers to [a beast that ate] human-poison [that poses danger if one eats the animal that ingested it].*

F. *But animal-poison is oleander! [The text of T. is repetitive if we accept this interpretation.] [We can say] there are two distinct kinds of animal-poison [listed by T.].*

G. *What is the root of crowfoot [listed by T.]? Said R. Judah,* **[59a]** *"The root of succory (Cashdan)."*

H. *Said R. Judah, "Any person who eats three* tiqlas *of asafoetida on an empty stomach will shed his skin (Cashdan)." Said R. Abbahu, "It once happened to me that I ate one* tiqla *of asafoetida and had I not immersed in water I would have shed my skin. So I fulfilled for myself the verse, '[For the protection of wisdom is like the protection of money; and the advantage of knowledge is that] wisdom preserves the life of him who has it' (Qoh. 7:12)."*

I. *Said R. Joseph, "Any person who eats sixteen eggs, forty nuts, and seven caperberries, and who drinks a quarter [log] of honey during the season of Tammuz [i.e., the summer] on an empty stomach — he will have a heart attack [lit.: snaps his heart strings asunder (Cashdan)]."*

J. *A certain young deer whose hind legs had been broken was brought before the Exilarch [for a ruling]. Rab inspected it at the nexus of the sinews and declared it valid. He planned to eat it barbecued. Said to him Samuel, "Does not the master suspect it might have been bitten [by a snake and the poison will pose a danger to you if it is not cooked properly]?"* He said to him, *"What is the procedure [I must follow to see if this is the case]? [He said to him,] "Let us put it into the oven [to cook]. For [if it has poison in it] it will become evident."* They put it in and it fell apart. Samuel recited concerning Rab, *"No ill befalls the righteous, [but the wicked are filled with trouble]"* (Prov. 12:21). And Rab recited concerning Samuel, *"[O Belteshazzar, chief of the magicians, because I know that the spirit of the holy gods is in you and that] no mystery is difficult for you, [here is the dream which I saw; tell me its interpretation]"* (Dan. 4:9).

I.1 invokes a rule of Samuel and the text of Tosefta to elucidate to Mishnah. The text continues with related rules and precedents.

### 3:6

A. The tokens [by which we know whether or not animals are deemed clean or fit] of cattle and wild beasts have been stated by the Torah (cf. Lev. 11:3).

B. And the tokens of fowl have not been so stated.

C. But sages have ruled: "Any fowl that seizes is unclean. Any [fowl] that has an extra talon [the hallux] and a craw, and the skin of the stomach of which [can] be stripped off is clean."

D. R. Eleazar b. Sadoq says, "Any bird that parts its toes evenly [two in front and two in back] is unclean" (Lev. 11:3).

### 3:7

A. And among locusts [these are valid]: Any that has (1) four legs, (2) four wings, and (3) jointed legs (Lev. 11:21), and (4) the wings of which cover the greater part of its body.

B. R. Yosé says, "And (5) the name of which is locust."

C. And among fish: Any that has fins and scales.

D. R. Judah says, "Two scales and a single fin [are sufficient]."

E. And what are scales?

F. Those that are immovable.

G. And fins?

H. Those with which it swims [but not propelling itself on dry land with them].

## I.1

A. *Our rabbis taught on Tannaite authority:* **These are the tokens of cattle [by which we know whether or not animals are deemed fit]** [M. Hul. 3:6A]: "Whatever parts the hoof and is cloven-footed and chews the cud among animals you may eat" (Lev. 11:3). **Whatever chews the cud [we know] has no upper teeth** [T. 3:20 A-B] and it is clean.

B. *But is this the rule? For lo, [consider by way of counter example] the camel. For it chews the cud and has no upper teeth and is unclean! [The reason for this is] the camel has canines (Cashdan). But lo, [consider] the young camel that does not even have canines! And furthermore [consider as support for the rule that] the rock-badger and the hare chew the cud and they have upper teeth and they are unclean.*

C. *And moreover [why should this rule be stated at all]? Are teeth even mentioned in the Torah [as a sign of a clean or unclean animal]?*

D. *Rather here is what you should say:* Any animal that does not have upper teeth, we know that it chews the cud and it has split hooves and is clean.

E. *But why not just inspect the hooves? [What is the value of this generalization?] The case in question may be one where the hooves were cut up. And this accords with the view of R. Hisda. For said R. Hisda,* "If he was walking in the wilderness and came across an animal whose hooves were cut up [so that he could not determine if they were split], he should inspect its mouth. If it does not have upper teeth, we know that it [chews the cud and it has split hooves and] is clean. And if not, then we know it is unclean."

F. [This rule applies] as long as he is able to identify a camel [since that is an exception to the rule]. *But a camel has canines!* [We should say then,] as long as he is able to identify a young camel [that has no canines and is unclean].

G. *Do you not state that there is another kind [of animal] like the young camel [with no upper teeth that is unclean]?* No. You cannot have concluded that. For the house of R. Ishmael taught: "[Nevertheless among those that chew the cud or part the hoof, you shall not eat these:] The camel, because it chews the cud [but does not part the hoof, is unclean to you]" (Lev. 11:4). He who rules over the world knows that the only [kind of animal] that chews its cud and is unclean is the camel. Therefore Scripture singles it out [with the pronoun] "it."

H. And said R. Hisda, "If he was walking in the wilderness and came across an animal whose mouth was mangled, he should inspect its hooves. If it has split hooves, we know that it is clean. If it does not, we know that it is unclean."

I. [This rule applies] as long as he is able to identify a swine [since that is an exception to the rule]. *Do you not state that there is the swine [that is an exception to the rule]? Are there not other kinds that are like the swine? No. You cannot have concluded that. For the house of R. Ishmael taught:* "And the swine, because it parts the hoof and is cloven-footed [but does not chew the cud, is unclean to you]" (Lev. 11:7). He who rules over the world knows that the only [kind of animal] that parts the hoof and is unclean is the swine. Therefore Scripture singles it out [with the pronoun] "it."

J. And said R. Hisda, "If he was walking in the wilderness and came across an animal whose mouth was mangled, and whose hooves were cut up, he should inspect its flesh [under its tail]. If it [has a pattern that is] criss-cross, we know that it is clean. If not, we know that it is unclean."

K. [This rule applies] as long as he is able to identify the wild ass. *Do you not state that there is the wild ass [that is an exception to the rule]? Are there not other kinds that are like the wild ass? We have a tradition that there are not.*

L. *And where does he inspect [the flesh]? Said Abayye, and some say, R. Hisda, "[In the hind quarter] under the tail."*

II.1
A. **The tokens [by which we know whether or not animals are deemed clean or fit of cattle and] wild beasts [M. 3:6 A].** *Our Rabbis taught on Tannaite authority:* **What are the tokens [by which we know whether an animal is] a wild beast? [Any that has horns and (pointed) hooves] [T. 3:21 A-B].** *Are not the wild*

beasts subsumed in the [same] rules as cattle with regard to the tokens [that signify whether they are clean]?

B. Said R. Zira, [59b] "[We stipulate separate rules for wild beasts] so as to render it permissible to use their fats." *So here is what you should say [in the rule in T.]:* **What are the tokens [by which we know whether an animal is] a wild beast,** whose fats are permissible? **Any that has horns and [pointed] hooves.**

C. R. Dosa says, "If it has horns you do not have to look for its [pointed] hooves. If it has [pointed] hooves, you still need to look for its horns."

D. And the antelope, even though it has only one horn, [its fat] is permitted.

E. *Is this a fixed rule [that the fats from an animal with horns and pointed hooves is permitted]? Behold the goat has horns and [pointed] hooves and its fats are forbidden. You must have layered [horns on the animal to be a valid sign that the fats are permitted]. But behold an ox has layered [horns] and it fats are forbidden. You must have notched [horns]. But behold the goat has notched [horns] and its fats are forbidden. You must have branched [horns, i.e., antlers]. But behold the deer does not have branched [horns] and its fats are permitted. [Cashdan: this may refer to the pronghorn antelope.] You must have pointed [horns, alt.: cylindrical].*

F. *Therefore where [the animal has] branched [horns] there is not the slightest doubt [that it is a wild beast]. Where [the animal] does not have branched [horns], you must have [horns that are] layered, pointed and notched. And the notches must intersect with one another.*

G. *And this Karkuz goat [possibly: gazelle] is a case of doubt. [Rashi: It has the signs of a wild beast but it is called a "goat."] A certain Karkuz goat was [slaughtered] in the house of the Exilarch. A basket full of fat was removed from it. R. Ahai prohibited [its use]. R. Samuel the son of R. Abbahu ate from it. He recited about himself, "From the fruit of his mouth a man is satisfied; [he is satisfied by the yield of his lips]"* (Prov. 18:20). *[Based on the ruling he learned, he had a good meal.]*

H. *They sent forth [the ruling]: The law follows in accord with the view of Samuel the son of R. Abbahu. But take care [to account for the view of] R. Ahai. For he lights up the eyes [of the Jews who live in] the exile.*

II.2
A. And the antelope, even though it has only one horn [its fat] is permitted [II.1 D above]. Said R. Judah, "The antelope is [called] the deer in Be Ilai. The tiger is [called] the lion in Be Ilai."

B. *Said R. Kahana, "There were nine cubits between the ears of the lion of Be Ilai." Said R. Joseph, "The lion of Be Ilai was sixteen cubits long."*

C. *Said the Caesar to R. Joshua b. Hananiah, "Your God is like a lion. As it is stated, 'The lion has roared; who will not fear? [The Lord God has spoken; who can but prophesy?]' (Amos 3:8)."* What is exceptional about this? Any horseman can kill a lion. He [Joshua] said to him, "He is not like any lion. He is like the lion of Be Ilai." He said to him, "You must show it to me." He [Joshua] said to him, "You cannot see it. [That lion is too terrifying.]" He said to him, "Really! Show it to me!"

D. He [Joshua] prayed. It was uprooted from its place [and started to be transported toward them]. When it was four hundred parsangs away it gave out a single roar. All of the pregnant women of Rome miscarried [from fright] and all the walls fell down [from the vibrations]. When it was three hundred parsangs away it gave out another roar. All of the teeth of the people [of Rome] fell out [of their mouths from the impact of the sound]. And he [Caesar] himself fell from his throne to the ground. He said to him [Joshua], "I beg you. Pray that it go back to its place." He prayed and it went back to its place.

E. The Caesar said to R. Joshua b. Hananiah, "I want to see your God." He said to him, "You cannot see Him." He said to him, "Really! **[60a]** Show him to me!" He went and pointed him towards the sun during the season of Tammuz [i.e., the summer]. He [Joshua] said to him, "Look at it." He said, "I cannot." He said, "The sun is one of the attendants that attend the Holy One, blessed be He. You say you cannot look at it. All the more [is it impossible to look at] the Divine Presence."

## Bavli Ḥullin Chapter Three. Folios 42A-67B

F. *The Caesar said to R. Joshua b. Hananiah, "I want to make a dinner for your God." He said to him, "You cannot." [He asked,] "Why not?" [He said,] "Because he has too many in his entourage." [He said,] "Really! [I insist!]" [He said,] "Go set it up on the widest banks of the great sea." He worked for the six months of the summer [preparing the dinner]. A storm came up and washed it all into the sea. He worked for the six months of the winter. The rains came and washed it all into the sea. He said to him, "What is the meaning of this?" He [Joshua] said to him, "These [storms] are like the [workers] who sweep and wash in preparation for his arrival." He said to him, "If that is the case, then I cannot do it."*

G. *The daughter of the Caesar said [mockingly] to R. Joshua b. Hananiah, "Your God must be a carpenter. For it is written, 'Who hast laid the beams of thy chambers on the waters, [who makest the clouds thy chariot, who ridest on the wings of the wind]' (Ps. 104:3). Tell him to make a spool for me." He said, "On my life!" He prayed and she was smitten with leprosy. They took her into the market place of Rome and they brought her a spool. For it was the custom that in Rome they brought a spool to anyone who was smitten with leprosy. And they sat her in the market place and she wound skeins of yarn so that people would see this and pray for her. One day he [Joshua] was passing there and she was sitting and winding skeins of yarn in the market place of Rome. He said to her, "Did my God give you a good spool?" She said to him, "Tell your God to take back what he gave me." He said to her, "Our God gives but does not take back."*

III.1
A. *Said R. Judah, "An ox has a wide belly and wide hooves, a large head and a large tail. And the ass has the opposite." What difference does it make [to know this]? For buying and selling [one needs to know the signs of identification].*

B. *And said R. Judah, "The ox that Adam offered had one horn on its forehead. As it says, 'This will please the Lord more than an ox or a bull with horns and hooves' (Ps. 69:31)."*

C. *[But] 'With horns' implies two. Said R. Nahman, "It is written defectiva (mqrn) [implying there was a single horn]."*

D. And said R. Judah, "The ox that Adam offered produced horns before it produced hooves. As it says, 'This will please the Lord more than an ox or a bull with horns and hooves' (Ps. 69:31)." [It states,] 'With horns' *first and then* 'hooves.'

E. *This supports the view of R. Joshua b. Levi.* For said R. Joshua b. Levi, "All the creatures formed at the beginning were created fully mature in size, in accord with their own will, and in accord with the form they desired." As it says, "Thus the heavens and the earth were finished, and all the host of them" (Gen. 2:1). Do not read the word *sb'm*, "all the host of them." Rather read it *sbywnm*, "with the form they desired."

F. R. Hanina bar Pappa interpreted [the verse], "May the glory of the Lord endure for ever, may the Lord rejoice in his works" (Ps. 104:31). This verse the Angel of the World spoke. [Why?] At the time that the Holy One, blessed be He said, "[Let the earth put forth vegetation, plants yielding seed, and fruit trees bearing fruit in which is their seed,] each according to its kind, [upon the earth]" (Gen. 1:11). [He juxtaposed "Each according to its kind"] to the trees. The plants argued for themselves *a fortiori*: If the Holy One, blessed be He wants disarray [in the species] why did he say regarding the trees, "Each according to its kind?" And furthermore it is an argument *a fortiori*. What is the case? Regarding the trees that normally do not emerge in disarray, the Holy One, blessed be He said, "Each according to its kind." Regarding us [the plants] how much more so [should he say this]! Immediately each one emerged according to its kind. And the Angel of the World uttered, "May the glory of the Lord endure for ever, may the Lord rejoice in his works" (Ps. 104:31).

G. *Rabina posed a question:* If a person grafted two kinds of plants [60b] what would the status of the product be according to the view of R. Hanina bar Pappa? *Since he did not write about them,* "Each according to its kind" *will he not be liable* [for a transgression]? *Or perhaps because he assented to their [logic] is it as if he wrote about them,* "Each according to its kind?" *The question stands unresolved.*

Bavli Ḥullin Chapter Three. Folios 42A-67B

**III.2**

A. R. Simeon b. Pazzi raised a contradiction: It is written, "And God made the two great lights." And it is written, "The greater light [to rule the day], and the lesser light [to rule the night; he made the stars also]." (Gen. 1:16). Said the moon to the Holy One, blessed be He, "Master of the Universe, is it possible to have two kings serve with one crown?" He said to her, "Go and be smaller." She said to him, "Master of the Universe, [is it fair that] because I said to you something that is proper, that I have to make myself smaller?" He said to her, "Go and rule over both the day and the night."

B. *She said to him, "What is the purpose of this? What good is a lamp in the daylight?" He said to her, "Go so that Israel will be able to calculate through you the days and the years." She said to him, "It is not possible to calculate the seasons without the sun too. For it is written, 'Let them be for signs and for season and for day and for years" (Gen. 1:14).*

C. *[He said to her,] "Go forth. And righteous men shall be called by your name." [The moon was named the "lesser light," i.e., the small light. Jacob the Patriarch, the Tanna Samuel and King David were called "small."]* Jacob was called small ["When they had finished eating the grass of the land, I said, 'O Lord God, forgive, I beseech thee! How can Jacob stand? He is so small!'" (Amos 7:2)]. Samuel [the Tanna was called] the small one. David was called small ["David was the youngest (i.e., smallest); the three eldest followed Saul" (I Sam. 17:14)].

D. *He saw that she was not placated.* Said the Holy One, blessed be He, "May I attain atonement because I made the moon smaller."

E. *And about this said R. Simeon b. Laqish,* "What is different about the goat offering for the new moon? For it is said regarding it, '[Also one male goat for a sin offering] to the Lord; [it shall be offered besides the continual burnt offering and its drink offering]' (Num. 28:15). Said the Holy One, blessed be He, 'This goat shall be my atonement because I made the moon smaller.'"

III.3
A. R. Assi raised a contradiction: It is written, "The earth brought forth vegetation" (Gen. 1:12) on the third day of the week. And it is written, "When no plant of the field was yet in the earth" (Gen. 2:5) at the end of the week. This teaches us that the plants came forth but remained just beneath the surface of the ground until Adam came and prayed for them. And rain fell and they sprouted forth. This will teach you that the Holy One, blessed be He, yearns for the prayers of the righteous.

B. R. Nahman bar Pappa had a garden. He planted in it seeds but they did not grow. He prayed. It rained. And they grew. He said, "This is what R. Assi meant."

IV.1
A. Said R. Hanan bar Raba, "The šsw'h is another category of creature unto itself." [The verse is: "Yet of those that chew the cud or have the hoof cloven (the Hebrew is hšsw'h, taken to mean another type of creature) you shall not eat these: the camel, the hare, and the rock badger, because they chew the cud but do not part the hoof, and are unclean for you" (Deut. 14:7).] It has two backs and two back bones. [And how did Moses know about all the creatures?] Was Moses our Rabbi a hunter or was he an archer [who would know all this]? This serves as a refutation of anyone who says that the Torah is not divinely inspired.

B. Said R. Hisda to R. Tahlifa bar Abina, "Go and write homilies about the [Greek term for] 'hunter' and the [Latin term for] 'archer' and interpret the terms." [Cashdan: R. Tahlifa was advised to note these words as foreign words.]

C. [And consider another verse that uses a foreign term:] "There are five rulers of the Philistines, those of Gaza, Ashdod, Ashkelon, Gath, and Ekron, and those of the Avvim" (Josh. 13:3). It states there are five and lists six! Said R. Jonathan, "They had five potentates."

D. Said R. Hisda to R. Tahlifa bar Abina, "Go and write a homily about the [term for] potentate ['rwnqy] and interpret the term."

E. *And this view disputes the view of Rab. For said Rab, "The Avvim came from Yemen." There is another teaching to this effect, "The Avvim came from Yemen. And why were they called Avvim? [Based on these plays on the Hebrew name.] Because they despised ['wtw] their place."* Another matter: [They were called] Avvim because they lusted ['yww] for many gods. Another matter: [They were called] Avvim because anyone who saw them was seized by shivering ['wyt]. *And said R. Joseph, "Every one of them had sixteen rows of teeth."*

F. Said R. Simeon b. Laqish, "There are many verses that seem to merit suppression [lit.: burning] but they are essential to the Torah."

G. [For example:] "As for the Avvim, who lived in villages as far as Gaza, [the Caphtorim, who came from Caphtor, destroyed them and settled in their stead]" (Deut. 2:23). *What do we derive from this verse? Because Abimelech swore to Abraham,* "Now therefore swear to me here by God that you will not deal falsely with me or with my offspring or with my posterity, [but as I have dealt loyally with you, you will deal with me and with the land where you have sojourned]" (Gen. 21:23). *Said the Holy One, blessed be He, "Let the Kaftorim take [the land] from the Avvim, who are the Philistines. And let Israel take [the land] from the Kaftorim."*

H. In the same manner you should state [regarding this verse]: "For Heshbon was the city of Sihon the king of the Amorites, who had fought against the former king of Moab and taken all his land out of his hand, as far as the Arnon" (Num. 21:26). *What do we derive from this verse? For the Holy One, blessed be He said to Israel,* "And the Lord said to me, 'Do not harass Moab [or contend with them in battle, for I will not give you any of their land for a possession, because I have given Ar to the sons of Lot for a possession]' (Deut. 2:9). *Said the Holy One, blessed be He, "Let Sihon take [the land] away from Moab. And let Israel take [the land] away from Sihon."*

I. *And about this R. Pappa stated, "[The territories of] Ammon and Moab were made clean [for conquest by Israel] through [the conquest of that land by] Sihon."*

J. [Regarding this verse:] "The Sidonians call Hermon Sirion, [while the Amorites call it Senir]" (Deut. 3:9), *it was taught,* Senir and Sirion are names of mountains of the Land of Israel. This teaches that every one of the nations of the world went and built for itself a great city and named it after a mountain of the Land of Israel. This teaches you that even the mountains of the Land of Israel are beloved to the nations of the world.

K. In the same manner [you may interpret this verse:] "And as for the people, he removed them to the city [from one end of Egypt to the other]" (Gen. 47:21). *What do we derive from this verse? So that [the Egyptians] will not call his brothers [exiles, since they themselves were moved from their cities].*

V.1
A. **And the tokens of fowl have not been so stated [M. 3:6 B].** *Have they not? But lo it was taught on Tannaite authority,* "The eagle" (Lev. 11:13) — **[61a]** just as the eagle is distinctive in that it does not have an extra claw, [and it does not have] a crop, and [the skin of] its gizzard cannot be peeled off, and it mauls [its prey] and eats it, [and the eagle is] unclean. So too all [birds] similar to it are unclean.

B. "Turtle doves" (Lev. 1:14) — they have an extra claw, [and they have] a crop, and [the skin of] its gizzard can be peeled off, and they do not maul [their prey] and eat it, [and they are] clean. So too all [birds] similar to it are clean. [Apparently, the tokens of clean fowl are in the Torah.]

C. Said Abayye, "The specifics [of the tokens] were not matters stated in the Torah. Rather they were matters stated by the scribes."

D. *Taught R. Hiyya,* "A bird that has one token is clean, because it does not resemble the eagle." [We reason as follows:] *The eagle that has none [of the tokens], that is the [kind of bird] that may not be eaten. Lo, if there is one [kind of bird] that has one [token of cleanness] it may be eaten.*

E. *But why not derive the rule from [the principle regarding] turtle doves? [And let us reason as follows:] What is the case regarding turtle doves?*

*Bavli Ḥullin Chapter Three. Folios 42A–67B*

*They have all four [tokens of cleanness]. So these too [may be eaten] only if they have all four [tokens of cleanness].*

F. *If this is the case [that we follow this line of reasoning] then what is the purpose of [listing] all of the other unclean birds that are written in the Torah? Let us derive the inference from these [listed birds]. What is the case regarding those that have three [tokens]? We do not eat them. So all those with three [tokens] we do not eat. And all the more so [in the case of a bird that has only] two [tokens] or one [token].*

G. *If this is the case, then what purpose is served by the Torah stating [as unclean] the raven [that has two tokens]? Now those that have three [tokens], we do not eat them. Must we state the rule for [a bird] that has only two [tokens]?*

H. **[61b]** *Then let us derive [the rule] from the [inclusion of the] raven. What is the case there? [A bird that has] two [tokens of cleanness] we do not [eat]. So all those with two [tokens] we do not [eat]. If so, "The vulture and the osprey" (Lev. 11:13), that the Torah stated [are unclean], why must we have these [specified]? Now those that have two [tokens], we do not eat them. Must we state the rule for [a bird] that has only one [token]?*

I. *Then let us derive [the rule] from the [inclusion of the] vulture and the osprey. If this is the case, then why do we need to have the Torah state [that] the eagle [is unclean]? Now those that have one [token], we do not eat them. Must we state the rule for [a bird] that has none?*

J. *Rather [it must be the case that] an eagle that has no [tokens] at all, [that is the type of bird] we do not eat. But lo, one that has one [token], we do eat!*

K. *But [it must be the case] that the reason the Torah states the eagle [is unclean is because] if it did not so specify I would have reasoned that we derive the rule from [the specification in the verse] of the vulture and the osprey. But the [references to the] vulture and the osprey [come under the principle of] concurrent scriptural references [that teach the same rule]. And [we say that from] concurrent scriptural references [that teach the same rule] we do not derive any conclusions [about other cases].*

L. *[But we may argue that they do not teach exactly the same rule.] We have a tradition that [the token] that is present in this one [bird] is not present in that one. And [the token] that is present in that [bird] is not present in this one.*

M. *[But we may object to this solution.] Consider: there are twenty-four unclean birds [specified in the Torah]. It is not possible that one [token] that is present in some is missing in all the others. So it would be [certain that we have an instance of] concurrent scriptural references [that teach the same rule]. [Thus we should not be able to derive any conclusions at all about other cases from this list.]*

N. *[But we may argue that they do not teach exactly the same rule.] We have a tradition that there are twenty-four unclean birds and there are four tokens. Three are present in all [twenty-four as follows]: Twenty have all three of them; two are present in the raven; one of these is present in the vulture and one in the osprey. The one that is present in this one is absent in that one. [Accordingly one of these is not "concurrent" in that it has a token unique from the others.]*

O. *It would make sense to say that we should derive from this one [some general conclusion about the others]. [But we do not because] the Torah wrote concerning the eagle. [You conclude from this that] the eagle that has no [tokens] at all you may not eat. Lo any [bird] that has one [token] you may eat.*

P. *But then why did the Torah write about turtle doves? Said R. Uqba bar Hama, "[To teach us which bird may be brought as a] sacrifice. [But not to teach us anything in regard to tokens of uncleanness.]"*

**V.2**

A. Said R. Nahman **[62a]**, "[To] one who is knowledgeable of them [i.e., the various kinds of birds] and their names, [a bird that has] one token is deemed clean. To one who is not knowledgeable of them and their names, [a bird that has] one token is deemed unclean. [A bird that has] two tokens is deemed clean."

B. [And that is so] as long as he can identify a raven. [Does this mean that he needs to be able to identify] just a raven and no other [kind of bird]?

C. *But lo, it was taught on Tannaite authority:* "Every raven [according to its kind]" (Lev. 11:15) — this means the raven itself. "[Every raven] according to its kind" — R. Eliezer says, "This subsumes [under the category of the raven] the starling." They said to R. Eliezer, "But lo, the people of the village of Tamrata in Judea used to eat [starlings] because they have crops." [The raven does not have this token.]

D. He said to them, "In the future they will have to be judged [for this questionable action]."

E. Another version: "[Every raven] according to its kind" — "this subsumes [under the category of the raven] the white bellied swallow," the words of R. Eliezer. They said to him, "But lo, the people of the Upper Galilee used to eat them because their gizzards can be peeled." [The raven does not have this token.]

F. He said to them, "In the future they will have to be judged [for this questionable action]." Rather [the verse specifies] the raven [and subsumes under that] every kind of raven.

V.3
A. Said Amemar, *"The law is* that any bird that has one token is deemed clean as long as [in addition] it does not maul its prey."

B. *Said R. Ashi to Amemar, "Lo, what of the rule of R. Nahman [V.2 A]?" He said to him, "I did not hear it." That is to say [he meant], "I do not reason in accord with it."*

C. For which ones are there [that we should be concerned with identifying]? The vulture and the osprey. But they are not common in settled areas.

V.4
A. Said R. Judah, "A bird that can scratch [with its talon] is valid [for the sacrifice one must bring] for the purification of the leper. And this is the white bellied swallow about which there is a dispute between R. Eliezer and the sages."

B. *Said Amemar, "Concerning the white bellied [swallow] there is a consensus that it is permitted. Where do they dispute the matter?*

*Regarding the green bellied [swallow]. R. Eliezer prohibits and the sages permit. And the law follows in accord with R. Eliezer."*

C. *Mar Zutra taught as follows: With regard to the green bellied [swallow] there is a consensus that it is prohibited. Where do they dispute? Regarding the white bellied [swallow]. R. Eliezer prohibits and the sages permit. And the law follows in accord with the sages who permit.*

D. *It is consistent, according to the authority who holds the view that they disputed over the status of the white bellied [swallow], with that stated above [in A], "This is the white bellied swallow [about which there is a dispute between R. Eliezer and the sages]."*

E. *But according to the authority who says that [Eliezer and sages] disputed over the status of the green bellied [swallow] what [can we say to harmonize this with A that says,] "This is the white bellied swallow [about which there is a dispute between R. Eliezer and the sages]?" This [dispute over the white bellied swallow] excludes the black house swallow [that is prohibited according to both authorities].*

V.5
A. Said Rehaba, said R. Judah, "The tasil-dove is invalid [for a sacrifice requiring] a turtle dove. But it is valid [for a sacrifice requiring] a young pigeon. Dazipe and the Rehaba-doves are valid [for a sacrifice requiring] a turtle dove. But they are invalid [for a sacrifice requiring] a young pigeon."

B. R. Daniel bar R. Qatina *posed a question:* **All the fowl [62b] render unfit [the purification water if they drink from it] except for the dove, because it sucks it up [not drooling into it] [M. Parah 9:3 C-D].** *And if you accept this [rule in A] then it should teach,* **Except for the dove and the tasil-dove.**

C. Said R. Zira, "This one [the tasil-dove] sucks it up and drools [and thereby renders the water unfit]. This one [the ordinary dove] sucks it up and does not drool."

D. Said R. Judah, "These Zuzinian doves (Cashdan) are valid [as sacrifices] upon the altar. And these are identical with Rehaba-doves."

E. *They posed this objection: "[And the priest shall take cedarwood and] hyssop [and scarlet stuff, and cast them into the midst of the burning of the heifer]"* (Num. 19:6) — *and not Greek hyssop, and not blue hyssop, and not Roman hyssop, and not desert hyssop, and not any kind of hyssop that has a distinct name.*

F. Said Abayye, "Any kind that had different names [for its various kinds] before the giving of the Torah [at Mt. Sinai], and the Torah was consistent about [using the generic name in all instances] — [then a kind] that has a distinct name — it is invalid. *But these [doves] did not have different names [for the various kinds] before the giving of the Torah."* [Accordingly, all kinds are valid.]

G. *Raba said, "The Zuzinian doves are called ordinary doves in their native locale."*

**V.6**

A. *Said R. Judah, "The winged creatures of the rushes are permitted. Those of the cabbages are prohibited."* [Rashi interprets: locusts. Tosafot: birds.]

B. Said Rabina, "And [if one eats them] *he is flogged on account* of violating the prohibition (Lev. 9:23) against the creeping things that fly."

C. *And said R. Judah, "The linnet [zrd'] is permitted. The white jay [brd'] is prohibited. And the mnemonic is: let not the linnet [br mynyh]."* [As to the] *moor-cock [mrd'] there is a doubt.*

D. Said R. Assi, "There are eight cases of doubt [regarding these kinds of birds]: the crested lark, the lark, the wren, the mountain chaffinch, the wood lark, the moor-hen, the black woodpecker, and the partridge."

E. *And what doubt is there about them?* Clean birds have gizzards that can be skinned. Unclean birds have gizzards that cannot be skinned. And these have gizzards that can be skinned with a knife [but not by hand].

F. But lo, there was a duck in the house of Mar Samuel whose gizzard could not be skinned. So they left it out in the sun. And as soon as it softened, it could be skinned. [The circumstances are different in that case.] There as soon as it softened it could be skinned by hand. Here even after it softened it could be skinned only with a knife.

G. Said Abayye, "The moor-cock is one of the eight cases of doubt [listed in D]. For it is in the same category as the moor-hen."

H. Said R. Pappa, "The moor-cock is prohibited. The moor-hen is permitted. And the mnemonic is: An 'Amonite' (Deut. 23:4) [is prohibited from entering the congregation of Israel] and not an Amonitess."

I. Meremar interpreted, "The moor-hen is prohibited. We can see that it mauls and eats its prey. And this is also called the giruta."

J. Said Rab, "The domesticated parrot is permitted. The wild (Hebrew: prwz) parrot is prohibited. And its mnemonic is: Peroz is evil."

K. Said R. Huna, "The penguin is permitted. The sea-mew is prohibited. [A mnemonic is given.]" Said R. Pappa, "A moor-hen that stands and eats is permitted. A moor-hen that bends over and eats is prohibited. And the mnemonic for this is: 'For you shall bow down to no other God' (Exod. 34:14)."

L. Said Samuel, "The redwing thrush [lit.: wine-drinker] is prohibited. And the mnemonic for this is: 'Those [priests] drunk with wine are invalid' (b. San. 22b)." And said Samuel, "The lapwing is prohibited. [63a] And the stock pigeon is permitted. And the mnemonic for this is: the power of the offspring is greater than the power of the father [b. 49b]." [The literal meaning of the Hebrew names are: wine-mixer and daughter of the wine-mixer.]

M. Said R. Judah, "The pink flamingo with long legs is permitted. And the mnemonic for this is: murzama [i.e., another permitted pink bird with long legs (Rashi)]. And the pink flamingo with short legs is prohibited. And the mnemonic for this is [the legal principle]: **the dwarf is invalid [M. Bekh. 7:6 T(5)]**. The green flamingo with long legs is prohibited. And the mnemonic for this is: **If they are green — they are invalid [M. 3:3 C(6)]**."

N. Said R. Judah, "The cormorant (Lev. 11:17), this is [a bird] that snatches fish from the sea. The hoopoe (Lev. 11:19), this is [a bird] with a double crown."

O. *It was taught on Tannaite authority in accord with this:* The hoopoe (Lev. 11:19), this is [a bird] with a double crown. And this is the bird that brought the shamir-worm to the Temple [b. Git. 68b]. When R. Yohanan would see a cormorant he would recite, "Thy judgments are like the great deep" (Ps. 36:6). And when he saw an ant he would recite, "Thy righteousness is like the mountains of God" (ibid).

P. Said Amemar, "The pelican and the gannet *are permitted.* The bustard and the black gannet — in a place where they are accustomed to eat them, they may eat them. In a place where they are not accustomed to eat them, they may not eat them." *Is it that the matter depends on the custom [and not on the law]? Yes. And there is no contradiction [between the two customs]. This one [custom that prohibits] is in a place where the vulture and the osprey are common [and we fear lest they confuse the birds and eat a prohibited kind]. This one [custom that permits] is in a place where the vulture and the osprey are not common [and we have no such fear].*

Q. *Said Abayye, "The large screech owl and the small screech owl are prohibited. The owl is permitted. In the West [Israel] they gave lashes [to one who ate it] and they called it the night screecher."*

R. *Our rabbis taught on Tannaite authority:* The *tnšmt* [RSV: the water hen (Lev. 11:18)] is the ugliest of the birds [Rashi: the bat; Cashdan: the night bird or owl]. Do you say it is the ugliest of the birds? Or do you say that it is the ugliest of the creeping things? [The same name is used to describe one of the prohibited kinds of creeping things in Lev. 11:30. RSV translates the chameleon.] You may say we may go forth and determine this from [one of] the thirteen principles by which the Torah is interpreted: [This is] a matter that may be determined from its context. Of what is Scripture speaking? Of birds. This too [must refer to] birds.

S. *It was taught also with regard to creeping things in the same manner:* The *tnšmt* is the ugliest of the creeping things. Do you say it is the ugliest of the creeping things? Or do you say that is it the ugliest of the birds? You may say we may go forth and determine this from [one of] the thirteen principles by which the Torah is interpreted: [This is] a matter that may be determined from its context. Of what is Scripture speaking? Of creeping things. This too [must refer to] creeping things.

T. *Said Abayye, "The ugliest of the birds is the bat and the ugliest of the creeping things is the mole."* Said R. Judah, "The *q't* is the sea crow. The *rhm* is the vulture." Said R. Yohanan, "Why is it called the *rhm* [meaning mercy, but implying rain]? Because when the *rhm* comes [around it is a sign that] rain [lit. mercy] will come to the world."

U. Said R. Bibi bar Abayye, "[The coming of the vulture is a sign] *if he sets down someplace and squawks. And we have a tradition that if he sets down on the land and squawks the messiah will come.* As it says, 'I will signal [lit. squawk] for them and gather them in, [for I have redeemed them, and they shall be as many as of old]' (Zech. 10:8)."

V. *Said R. Ada bar Shimi to Mar bar R. Idai, "But lo, this one [vulture] set down on a plowed field and squawked. And a stone rolled down on it and split open its head."* He said to him, "This one [vulture] was a quack."

V.7

A. *Our rabbis taught on Tannaite authority:* [The verse says, "Every raven according to its kind" (Lev. 11:15).] "Raven" is the raven itself. "Every raven" includes [in the category] the raven of the valley. "According to its kind" includes [in the category] the raven that travels in front of the doves.

B. Said the master, "[You said], 'Raven' is the raven itself. *It is right here before us. Rather you should say:* 'Raven' is the black raven. And so it says [in the verse], "His head is the finest gold; his locks are wavy, black as a raven" (Song of Songs 5:11).

C. The raven of the valley [in A, that is] the magpie [a white spotted raven]. And so it says [in the verse], "[The priest shall examine it, and if the hair in the spot has turned white] and it appears deeper than the skin, [then it is leprosy, it has broken out in the burn, and the priest shall pronounce him unclean; it is a leprous disease]" (Lev. 13:25). As [they say]: the appearance of sun is deeper than shade. [This is a play on the words for valley and deep from 'mq. The white raven is the deeper- or the valley-raven.]

D. [And concerning] the raven that travels in front of the doves [in A]: *Said R. Pappa, "Do not maintain that it means it travels in front of the doves. Rather [maintain that it means] its head resembles that of a dove* [i.e., the cuckoo (Cashdan)]."

V.8
A. *Our rabbis taught:* [The verse says, "The hawk according to its kind" (Lev. 11:16).] "The hawk" is the hawk itself. "According to its kind," this includes the *bar hyry'*. What is the *bar hyry'*? Said Abayye, "It is the falcon."

B. Said R. Judah, "'The stork, [the heron according to its kind, the hoopoe, and the bat]' (Lev. 11:19): This is the white stork. And why is it called the *hsydh* [lit. merciful]? Because it performs merciful acts for its fellows."

C. The *'nph* is the heron. And why is it called *'nph* [lit. angry]? Because it is quarrelsome with its fellows.

V.9
A. Said R. Hanan bar R. Hisda, said R. Hisda, said R. Hanan the son of Raba, said Rab, "There are twenty-four [categories of] unclean birds." Said R. Hanan bar R. Hisda to R. Hisda, "*Where are they? If you refer to Leviticus, there are twenty [categories there]. If you refer to Deuteronomy, there are twenty-one [categories] there. And if you maintain that [you should take the category of] the kite (Lev. 11:14) that is written in Leviticus but not written in Deuteronomy and add it to the others [that are listed], you still have only twenty-two!*"

B. He [Hisda] said to him, "*This is what your mother's father said in the name of Rab, '[You must count as separate categories] the four times [in chapter 11] that it says, After its kind.' There are your other four.*"

C. *[He said,] "If this is so then you have twenty-six [categories]!" Said Abayye, "The kite (d'h, Lev. 11:13) and the buzzard (r'h, Deut. 14:13) are one category. For if you wished to conclude that they are two [categories],* **[63b]** *then let us consider this. Deuteronomy [repeats the laws] so as to add to them. Why then there [in Leviticus] does it write d'h and there [in Deuteronomy] does it write r'h but not d'h? Rather we must derive from this that they are one category."*

D. *You still have twenty-five [categories]! Said Abayye, "Just as d'h and r'h are one category, so too 'yh [RSV: the falcon, Lev. 11:14] and dyh [RSV: the kite, Deut. 14:13] are one category. For if you wished to conclude that they are two [categories], then let us consider this. Deuteronomy [repeats the laws] so as to add to them. Why then there [in Leviticus] does it write 'according to its kind' regarding the 'yh and there [in Deuteronomy] does it write 'according to its kind' regarding the dyh? Rather we must derive from this that they, 'yh and dyh, are one category."*

E. *And after we concluded that 'yh and dyh, are one category why then does it need to write both 'yh and dyh? As it was taught on Tannaite authority:* Rabbi says, "I call it *'yh. Why then does it say dyh? So as not to give an opening for lawyers to dispute the law. So that you do not call it one name, and he call it the other, or vice versa. Therefore it is written in Deuteronomy, 'The buzzard, the kite (hr'h w't h'yh whdyh lmynh) after their kinds' (Deut. 14:13)."*

F. *They raised a question: Why were they [i.e., the lists of clean and unclean animals] repeated [i.e., in Leviticus and Deuteronomy]? For [the list of prohibited] beasts, it was on account of the addition of the šsw'h. And for [the list of prohibited] birds, it was on account of the addition of the r'h. Is it not the case that regarding [the list in Deuteronomy of unclean] beasts that it adds [a new category]? [In the list in Deuteronomy of unclean] birds does it not also add [a new category]? No. There [for beasts] it adds. Here [for birds] it explains [a category that was already stated].*

G. *And this disputes the view of R. Abbahu. For said R. Abbahu, "The r'h is the same as the 'yh. And why was it called that? Because it has acute eyesight [a reference to the Hebrew root for seeing, r'h]. And so*

*Bavli Ḥullin Chapter Three. Folios 42A-67B* 137

it says [in the verse], 'That path no bird of prey knows, and the falcon's ['yh] eye has not seen it' (Job 28:7)."

H. *It was taught,* "It can be in Babylonia and see carrion in the Land of Israel."

I. *Since we said r'h is identical to 'yh, we may derive the rule that d'h is not identical to r'h. Then let us consider this. Deuteronomy [repeats the laws] so as to add to them. Why then there [in Leviticus] does it write d'h and there [in Deuteronomy] does it not write d'h? Rather we must derive from this that they, d'h, r'h and 'yh, are one category."*

J. *And since r'h is identical to 'yh we may derive the rule that dyh is not identical to 'yh. What then is the difference between the verse there that writes* according to its kind *in regard to 'yh and the verse here that does not write* according to its kind *for 'yh, but only for dyh? Rather we must derive from this that they, d'h, r'h, dyh and 'yh, are one category.*

V.10

A. *It was taught on Tannaite authority:* Isi b. Judah says, "There are one hundred categories of unclean birds in the East and all of them are kinds of *'yh."*

B. *Taught Abimi the son of R. Abbahu,* "There are seven hundred kinds of [unclean] fish and eight hundred kinds of [unclean] locusts. And there is an infinite number of the kinds of [unclean] birds." *[But we learned in V.9 A that] there are twenty-four [kinds of unclean birds]! [You should say that it means here that] there is an infinite number of clean birds.*

C. *It was taught on Tannaite authority:* Rabbi says, "It is apparent to the Creator that the [categories of] unclean beasts outnumber the [categories of] clean beasts. Therefore Scripture listed the clean beasts. It was apparent to the Creator that the [categories of] clean birds outnumber the [categories of] unclean birds. Therefore Scripture listed the unclean birds."

D. *What novel point does this make? In accord with R. Huna in the name of Rab [it makes a novel point]. And some say, in accord with R. Huna* in the name of Rab in the name of R. Meir, "A person should always teach something to his student in the most concise way possible."

V.11
A. Said R. Yitzhak, "A clean bird may be eaten on the basis of the received tradition. The hunter is trusted to say, 'This bird is clean. My master passed the tradition on to me.'"

B. Said R. Yohanan, "And this is the case if he is expert in [identifying] them and their names."

C. R. Zira posed a question: [Does the rule of A apply if] his master was a sage or [does it apply only if] his master was a hunter? Come and take note of what R. Yohanan said, "And this is the case if he is expert in [identifying] them and their names."

D. It is consistent if you say that his master was a hunter. Then it makes perfect sense [to say that he was an expert in identifying them and their names]. But if you say his master was a sage, it is consistent to conclude that he was learned in their names. But [is it consistent to assume] that he knew how to identify them. Rather must we not then derive that his master was a hunter? We must derive it.

V.12
A. Our rabbis taught on Tannaite authority: They may buy eggs from idolaters anywhere. And they need not suspect that they are from carrion nor from *terefot*. But perhaps they are from an unclean bird? Said the father of Samuel, "[This rule applies] where he [the seller] said, 'They are from such-and-such a bird that is clean.'"

B. But [why not] let him say, "They are from a clean bird?" If he does this, he might prevaricate. [Later he might be tempted to change his story (Rashi)].

C. But why not let him [the buyer] inspect for the tokens [of cleanness]? For it was taught on Tannaite authority: The tokens [of cleanness] for eggs are like the tokens for fish. *Does it make sense to conclude that they are like [the tokens for] fish? The Torah said [the tokens for] fish are] fins and scales!* Rather say, [The tokens of cleanness for birds' eggs] are like the tokens [64a] for fish roe.

Bavli Hullin Chapter Three. Folios 42A-67B   139

D. *And it was taught on Tannaite authority with regard to eggs:* These are the tokens [of cleanness] for eggs: Any [egg] that is arched and rounded, [that is] with one end broad and one end narrow, is clean. [Any eggs that have] both ends broad or both ends narrow are unclean. [Any egg] with the white on the outside and the yolk on the inside, is clean. [Any egg] with the yolk on the outside and the white on the inside, is unclean. [Any egg] with the yolk and the white mixed together is known to be and egg of an [unclean] creeping thing. **[T. has this version: Any [egg] that is arched (on top, not pointed) and rounded, one may be certain, derives from an unclean bird, and any that is not arched and rounded, one may be certain, derives from a clean bird [T. 3:23 C].]**

E. [If we have tokens of cleanness for eggs, why then does the hunter need to state that the eggs come from a clean bird?] *It is necessary for him to state it for eggs that were cut up [and the external tokens would not be visible anymore]. But then let him inspect the white and the yolk [to see if the egg is clean]. [He cannot do this if we speak of a case where the eggs were already] scrambled in a bowl.*

F. *But because of this very matter do we buy [eggs] from them [i.e., gentiles]? For lo it was taught on Tannaite authority:* **[They purchase eggs from any source and do not scruple lest they are of carrion- or *terefah*-birds.] They do not sell eggs [of carrion-birds or] of *terefah*-birds to a gentile unless they were cracked open into a dish. Therefore they said, "They do not purchase from a gentile eggs that are cracked open into a dish [T. 3:24 A-C]."**

G. *But said R. Zira, "The tokens [for eggs] do not derive from the authority of the Torah. For if you do not maintain this view, lo [consider] that which R. Assi said, 'There are eight cases of doubt [regarding these kinds of birds]...' [above V.6 D]. [In those cases] let him inspect their eggs [and if they have the tokens of cleanness, then the birds are clean]. But we may derive from this [i.e., from the fact that they do not suggest this course of action] that the tokens [of cleanness for eggs] do not derive from the authority of the Torah."*

H. *Then [if they are not based on the authority of the Torah] what is the legal implication [of the statement of these tokens for eggs]? This is how you should state the matter:* If both its ends were broad or both its ends were narrow, or if the yolk was on the outside and the white on the inside, it is surely unclean. If one end was broad and one end was narrow, or if the white was on the outside and the yolk on the inside, and he said to you, "This comes from such-and-such a bird and it is clean," you may rely on them [i.e., the tokens along with the statement].

I. *In ordinary circumstances [where he says nothing] you may not rely on them [i.e., the tokens alone are not sufficient]. For there are eggs from a raven that resemble the eggs of a dove.*

V.13
A. Said the master, "[Any egg] with the yolk and the white intermingled, it is known that this is an egg from [an unclean] creeping thing [D, above]." *What is the legal implication of this [statement that it is from a creeping thing]? Said R. Uqba bar Hama, "This tells us that if [the embryo in the egg] formed and [the shell] was pierced, it conveys uncleanness in [any amount more than] a lentil's-bulk."*

B. *Rabina posed an objection, "But perhaps it is [the egg of] a serpent [and that does not convey uncleanness]." Rather said Raba, "If it [the embryo] formed and he ate it, he is flogged for eating it on account of [the prohibition against eating] any creeping thing that crawls on the earth."*

C. *If this is the case, then why specify that it is an unclean [creeping thing]? [If he eats from] even a clean one [he should be flogged].*

D. *For it was taught on Tannaite authority:* "Every creeping thing that crawls upon the earth" (Lev. 11:41) — [64b] this [use of the word 'all'] includes [under the prohibition] chicks whose eyes are not yet opened. [But this is not probative.] *[The ruling is] based on the authority of the rabbis and the verse is merely a [secondary] support for it.*

V.14
A. *Our rabbis taught:* **[Clean eggs] boiled together with [unclean] eggs are permitted [because the unclean eggs do not contaminate the clean ones in this manner (Rashi)].... Eggs that**

were addled [by the mother] — one with a strong constitution may eat them. If a drop of blood was found upon it, he may wipe away the blood and eat the rest [T. Ter. 9:5 D, K-L].

B. Said R. Jeremiah, "And this is so if [the drop of blood] was found on its knot [in the tip of the white of the egg (Rashi)]."

C. *Taught Dostai the father of R. Aptoriqi, "They taught this [rule] only where it [the blood] was found in its white. But if it was found in its yolk, all of the egg is prohibited." What is the basis for this? The taint has spread throughout [the egg].*

D. *Said R. Gabihah of Be Katil to R. Ashi, "A Tanna taught the opposite before Abayye. But Abayye rejoined him [in accord with our rule]."*

V.15
A. Said Hezekiah, "What is the source of the assertion that an unclean egg is prohibited by the Torah?" As it states, "The ostrich" (Lev. 11:16) [*bt hy'nh*, lit.: the daughter of the Ya'anah]. And does the Ya'anah have a daughter? [No.] But what then is this [that the verse refers to]? This is an unclean egg.

B. *But perhaps this is the name [of a kind of bird]. No, you cannot have concluded that. For it is written, "[Even the jackals give the breast and suckle their young,] but the daughter of my people has become cruel, like the ostriches [y'nym, not bt y'nym] in the wilderness" (Lam. 4:3).*

C. Is it not the case [that a verse does refer to *bt*, the daughter]? *But lo, it is written, "For this I will lament and wail; I will go stripped and naked; I will make lamentation like the jackals, and mourning like the ostriches [here: bnwt, daughters]" (Micah 1:8). [That does not prove it is the name of a kind of bird. It could mean here]: as the ostrich that mourns over its offspring.*

D. *But lo, it is written, "[But wild beasts will lie down there, and its houses will be full of howling creatures;] there ostriches [here again: bnwt, daughters] will dwell, [and there satyrs will dance]" (Isa. 13:21). [It could mean here]: as the ostrich that dwells with its offspring.*

E. *But lo, it is written,* "The wild beasts will honor me, the jackals and the ostriches [again: *bnwt*]; [for I give water in the wilderness, rivers in the desert, to give drink to my chosen people]" (Isa. 43:20). [Now this must be the name of a kind of bird.] *For if you wish to conclude that this is an egg, can an egg sing [praise]?*

F. *But it is written both ways [in that verse, i.e., two scribal alternatives]: the Ya'anah and the daughter of the Ya'anah. And this case is different because the scribe left a space between the two words. And since the scribe left a space* **[65a]** *between the two words, we may derive from this that there are two separate names [in the verse].*

G. *But then consider this:* "[In the days of Amraphel king of Shinar, Arioch king of Ellasar,] Ched-or-laomer [king of Elam, and Tidal king of Goiim]" (Gen. 14:1), *where the scribe left a space between the two words, will you say that here too there are two separate names [in the verse]? You could say [there is a difference between the two examples]. Here he left a space between the two words. He did not put them on two separate lines. But there he even put them on two separate lines. [So there is more justification in the former case to say they are separate names.]*

## VI.1

A. But sages have ruled: "Any fowl that seizes is unclean. Any [fowl] that has an extra talon [the hallux] and a craw, and the skin of the stomach of which [can] be stripped off is clean" [M. 3:6 C]. *It was taught on Tannaite authority:* **Rabban Simeon b. Gamaliel says, "Any fowl that has an extra talon [and a craw, and the skin of the stomach of which can be stripped off] is clean. Any fowl that seizes [prey] is unclean"** [M. Hul. 3:6 C]. **R. Eleazar bar Sadoq says, "They stretch out a cord for it. Any that, when placed on a cord divides [its toes], two before it and two behind it, is unclean"** [M. Hul. 3:6 D]. [Any bird that divides its toes] three on one side and one on the other, is clean [T. 3:22 A-C].

B. R. Simeon b. Eleazar says, "Any bird that can catch in mid-air [an object thrown to it] is unclean." *[But consider:] A hummingbird also can catch [an object in mid-air]! Said Abayye, "We speak of [the ability of the bird] to catch [food in mid-air] and to eat it."*

C. Others say, "That which nests among unclean [birds] and is like unclean [birds] is unclean. That which nests among clean ones and is like clean ones is clean" [T. 3:22 D]. *In accord with whose view is this? In accord with R. Eliezer. For it was taught on Tannaite authority:* R. Eliezer says, "It is not an accident that the starling [nests] near the raven. But it is because it is of the same kind [as the raven]." *You might even maintain that this is in accord with the view of the Rabbis. For we speak of nesting among and looking like [unclean birds].*

**VII.1**

A. **And among locusts: Any that has (1) four legs, (2) four wings, and (3) jointed legs (Lev. 11:21), and (4) the wings of which cover the greater part of its body [M. 3:7 A].** *What is the greater part of its body?* Said R. Judah, said Rab, "The greater part of its length." *And some say,* "The greater part of its circumference." Said R. Pappa, "Therefore, we must have [them cover both] the greater part of its length and the greater part of its circumference."

B. *Our rabbis taught on Tannaite authority:* [R. Eleazar bar Yosé says,] "[If] it does not now have [these signs] but is going to produce them after a while, for example, the *zahal*, it is valid [T. 3:25 E]."

C. R. Eleazar b. R. Yosé says, "'[Yet among the winged insects that go on all fours you may eat] those which have legs [above their feet, with which to leap on the earth]' (Lev. 11:21) — even though it does not now have them, but is going to produce them after a while." [The verse is written *l'*, that is, have no legs, but is read *lw*, that is, have legs. Eleazar's rule accounts for both, that is, now it has none but later it will.]

D. *What is the* zahal? Said Abayye, "The *'sqrn*."

**VII.2**

A. *Our rabbis taught on Tannaite authority:* "Of them you may eat: the locust according to its kind, the bald locust according to its kind, the cricket according to its kind, and the grasshopper according to its kind" (Lev. 11:22). [Following Cashdan who relies on Lewysohn:] "The locust," this is the migratory locust. "The bald locust," this is the bald locust. "The cricket," this is the green grasshopper. And "the grasshopper," this is the cricket.

B. What does it come to teach by repeating "according to its kind" four times? To include [in the rules] the vine-hopper, the Jerusalem *ywhn'*, the *'rzwby'*, and the *rzbnyt*.

C. *The House of R. Ishmael taught*: Some of these are general rules added to general rules. And some of these are specific rules added to specific rules. [Here is how you should interpret the verse.] "The locust," this is the migratory locust. "According to its kind" includes [65b] the vine-hopper. I only have [a rule that includes a locust] that migrates and is not bald. Based on what [would I have a rule for a locust] that migrates and is bald? It comes to teach, "The bald locust [*sl'm*]," this is the *nypwl*. "According to its kind" includes the *'yškp* [that is bald]. I only have [a rule that includes a locust] that migrates and is not bald, or that migrates and is bald. Based on what [would I have a rule for a locust] that migrates and has no tail or that migrates and has a tail? It comes to teach, "The cricket," that is the *ršwn*. "According to its kind" includes the *krspt* and the *šlhpt* [that have tails]. I only have [a rule that includes a locust] that migrates and is not bald, or that migrates and is bald or that migrates and has no tail or that migrates and has a tail. Based on what [would I have a rule for a locust] that migrates and has not got a long head or that migrates and has got a long head?

D. *State then*, lo you should deduce this from the generative principle of all three. The locust does not resemble [in all its features] the cricket. And the cricket does not resemble the locust. And the two of them do not resemble the bald cricket. And the bald cricket does not resemble the two of them. The common denominator of all of them is that they have four legs and four wings and jointed legs and wings that cover the greater part of their bodies. So all those that have four legs and four wings and jointed legs and wings that cover the greater part of their bodies.

E. But do not the *zarzor* have four legs and four wings and jointed legs and wings that cover the greater part of their bodies? You might infer that it is permitted. It comes to teach us [with a fourth category], "the grasshopper" [that includes in the rule] any that is called a grasshopper [in ordinary parlance]. If it is called a grasshopper, you might infer that [it comes under the rule] even if it does not have all these tokens [as discussed]. It comes to teach us, "according to its kind" [it does not come under the rule] unless it has all these tokens.

F. R. Ahai asked, "What about those that do not have a long head? And if you maintain that since they match four of the tokens, we may subsume it [in the rule] and we may not question [its appropriateness], then [based on this logic] the cricket as well that matches them [in the other tokens], let it not be written [in the verse], and derive it from the locust and the bald locust. But you can question [this inference as follows:] what is the case regarding those? It is the case that they have no tails. Here too [in our case] we can question [this inference on the basis that] what is the case regarding those? It is the case that their heads are not long."

G. But said R. Ahai, "[Including in the verse] the bald locust is superfluous. The Torah need not have written the bald locust and we could have derived it by inference from the inclusion of the locust and the cricket. For what question did you have? What is the case regarding the locust? It is not bald. Lo, we have the cricket that is bald. What is the case regarding the cricket? It has no tail. Lo, we have the locust that has a tail. The bald locust that the Torah wrote, why do I need [to state it]? If it is not a matter stated for its own sake, then apply it to the matter of [a case of a locust] whose head is long."

H. [66a] On what principle do the Tanna from the house of Rab [in F-G] and the Tanna of the house of Ishmael [VII.2 C] dispute? In the case of [a locust that has] a long head they dispute. The Tanna of the house of Rab reasons [as follows]: "[Yet among the winged insects that go on all fours you may eat] those which have legs above their feet, [with which to leap on the earth]" (Lev. 11:21) — this is a general rule. "[Of them you may eat:] the locust according to its kind, the bald locust according to its kind, the cricket according to its kind, and the grasshopper according to its kind" (Lev. 11:22) — this is a specification [of the rule]. Where you have a general rule and a specification of the rule, you can only subsume under the rule what you have in the specifications. [This then means] *if it is of the same kind, yes* [*you may subsume it under the rule*]. *But if it is not* of the same kind, no [you may not subsume it]. And we encompass [in the rule] all [kinds] that match it in all manners.

I. *The Tanna of the House of Ishmael reasons [as follows]:* "[Yet among the winged insects that go on all fours you may eat] those which have legs above their feet, [with which to leap on the earth]" (Lev. 11:21) — this is a general rule. "[Of them you may eat:] the locust ... the bald locust ... the cricket ... and the grasshopper..." (Lev. 11:22) — this is a specification [of the rule]. "According to its kind" — this is another general rule. Where you have a general rule and a specification of the rule, and another general rule, you may judge [what is subsumed] only according to the specifications. *And we encompass [in the rule] all [kinds] that match it in one manner.*

J. *But lo, here the first general rule does not match the latter general rule. According to the first rule, the Torah said, "Those which have legs above their feet." [This implies that] those that have [legs], you may eat. Those that do not have, you may not eat. According to the latter general rule [you cannot eat them] unless they match in the four tokens [of cleanness].*

K. *The House of R. Ishmael explicates [issues] based on general rules and specifications like this very matter. And what we say in general that the House of R. Ishmael explicates [issues] based on general rules and specifications like this very matter, [we derive that statement] from this instance here.*

L. Said the master [see E above]: If it is called a grasshopper, you might infer that [it comes under the rule] even if it does not have all these tokens [as discussed]. It comes to teach us, "according to its kind" [it does not come under the rule] unless it has all these tokens.

M. If it does not have all these tokens — *from what source could we derive this inference? It is written:* the locust... and the cricket. *If it did not also write,* the bald locust, *[we might have concluded] as you said. Now that it did write,* the bald locust, *[does it make sense to maintain] this comes to encompass [a locust whose] head is long? It makes sense to maintain that it comes to encompass any [match of the tokens] at all. It makes the novel point [that this is not the case].*

N. *What is the difference between that version that states* the bald locust, that is the *ršwn;* the cricket, that is the *nypwl, and this version that states* the bald locust, that is the *nypwl;* and the cricket, that is the *ršwn? This master follows [the interpretation of] his locality. And this master follows [the interpretation of] his locality.*

### VIII.1

A. **And among fish: Any that has fins and scales [M. 3:7 C].** *Our rabbis taught on Tannaite authority:* If [a species of fish has no fins and scales] now but is going to grow them later on, for example, the sultanit fish and the aphis fish, lo, this [species of fish] is permitted. If it has [fins and scales] now but is going to slough them off when it is taken out of the water, for example, **[66b]** the colias, scomber, swordfish, anthias, and tunny, it is permitted [b. A.Z. 39a (Neusner's translation)].

B. *It was taught there on Tannaite authority:* **Whatever has scales has fins, but there is that which has fins and does not have scales [M. Nid. 6:9 A].** Whatever has scales and has fins is a clean fish. If it has a fin but does not have scales, it is an unclean fish. *Since we rely on the presence of scales, why did the Torah have to make mention of fins at all?*

C. *If the Torah had not made reference to fins, I might have supposed that the word translated as scales refers to fins, so even an unclean fish would be permitted. It was necessary for the Torah to refer explicitly to both fins and scales.*

D. *And now that the Torah has written both fins and scales, how do we know that the word translated as scales actually means a covering? As it is written,* "[He had a helmet of bronze on his head,] and he was covered with a coat of mail [*qsqsym*], [and the weight of the coat was five thousand shekels of bronze]" (I Sam. 17:5).

E. *So why did the Torah not write just scales and there would have been no need to make mention of fins at all?* Said R. Abbahu, and so taught a Tannaite authority of the house of R. Ishmael, "To magnify his teaching and make it glorious" (Isa. 42:21).

## VIII.2

A. *Our rabbis taught on Tannaite authority:* From what was stated that one may eat [those fish] that do have them [fins and scales], I derive that one may not eat those that do not have them. And from what was stated that one may not eat those that do not have them, I derive that one may eat those that do have them. *So why did it teach both? [To inform us that if he eats a fish that is prohibited] he transgresses for that both a positive and a negative commandment.* [The verses are: "These you may eat, of all that are in the waters. Everything in the waters that has fins and scales, whether in the seas or in the rivers, you may eat. But anything in the seas or the rivers that has not fins and scales, of the swarming creatures in the waters and of the living creatures that are in the waters, is an abomination to you" (Lev. 11:9-10).]

B. "These you may eat, of all that are in the waters" — what does this come to teach us? You might have inferred that since it permitted specific [water creatures] and permitted them in general, just as when it permitted them in specific it permitted only those that were [grown] in vessels, so too when it permitted them in general it permitted only those that were [grown] in vessels. On what basis do we include [the rule] that from cisterns, ditches and caverns one may bend down and not refrain from drinking [even though he may swallow a creature from the water]? It comes to teach [in the verse], "These you may eat, of all that are in the waters."

C. *In what source does it permit [water creatures] found in vessels? As it is written,* "These you may eat, of all that are in the waters. Everything in the waters that has fins and scales, whether in the seas or in the rivers, you may eat." *Those that have [fins and scales], you may eat. Those that do not have, you may not eat. Lo, those that are found in vessels, even though they do not have [fins and scales], you may eat them. But it makes [just as much] sense to say those that are found in vessels, even though they do have [fins and scales], you may not eat them. No, you cannot have concluded that. For it is written,* "But anything in the seas or the rivers that has not fins and scales, of the swarming creatures in the waters..." — *[that implies] whatever is in the seas or the rivers that does not have [fins and scales], you may not eat. Lo, those that are found in vessels, even though they do not have [fins and scales], you may eat them.*

D. *But it makes sense to say that* "in the waters" *is a general rule,* "in the seas or the rivers" *is a specification. Where there is a general rule and a specification of the rule, there can be in the general rule only those features that are found in the specifications.* [You should then conclude that] *yes,* [it refers to creatures] *in the seas or the rivers, but no,* [it does not refer to creatures] *in gutters or trenches.* [Scripture says,] "That are in the waters," *once again stating a general rule. These then are two general rules that are juxtaposed to one another.*

E. *Said Rabina, "This is what they stated in the West* [i.e., Israel]: *In every instance where you find two general rules juxtaposed to one another* **[67a]**, *you may place the specifications between them and treat this as if it constituted a general rule, a specification and a general rule."* [Accordingly here you have] "in the waters" *that is a general rule;* "in the seas or the rivers" *that is a specification;* "that are in the waters" *that is once again a general rule.* [Where you have] *a general rule, a specification and a general rule* [the principle we follow is that] *you can only subsume under the rule what you have in the specification. What does the specification define? That you have flowing water. So all* [instances where you have] *flowing water. What does this subsume?* [Creatures without fins and scales that are found in] *gutters and trenches that are prohibited. And what does it exclude?* [Creatures without fins and scales that are found in] *cisterns, ditches or caverns that are permitted.*

F. *But why does it not make sense to say* [the following]? *What does the specification define? That you have water that emanates from the ground. So all* [instances where you have] *water that emanates from the ground. What does this subsume?* [Creatures without fins and scales that are found] *in cisterns, ditches or caverns that are prohibited. And what does it exclude?* [Creatures that are in] *vessels* [that are permitted].

G. [*This alternative line of reasoning in F does not make sense because you could object to it:*] *If this is the case, what is the implication of the phrase,* "you may eat?"

H. *The Tannaite authority of the house of R. Ishmael taught,* "In the waters... in the waters," [it is written] *two times. This does not* represent a general rule followed by specification, but rather, an inclusionary and exclusionary usage [b. Bekh. 51a (Neusner)].

I. [Accordingly here you have] "in the waters" that is an inclusionary usage; "in the seas or the rivers" that is an exclusionary usage; "that are in the waters" that is once again an inclusionary usage. Where it stated an inclusionary usage, an exclusionary usage and an inclusionary usage, it included all [possibilities in the rule]. *What does this subsume? [Creatures without fins and scales that are found in] gutters and trenches that are prohibited. And what does it exclude? [Creatures without fins and scales that are found in] cisterns, ditches, or caverns that are permitted.*

J. *But why does it not make sense to say [the following]? What does this subsume? [Creatures without fins and scales that are found in] cisterns, ditches or caverns that are prohibited. And what does it exclude? [Creatures that are in] vessels [that are permitted].*

K. *[This alternative line of reasoning in F does not make sense because you could object to it:] If this is the case, what is the implication of the phrase, "you may eat?"*

L. *And why not let me teach the opposite? In accord with that taught by Mattiah. For taught Mattiah bar Judah, "Why did you see fit to include [creatures without fins and scales that are found in] gutters and trenches that are permitted? And [why do you see fit] to exclude [creatures without fins and scales that are found in] cisterns, ditches or caverns that are prohibited? I prefer to include [creatures without fins and scales that are found in] gutters and trenches because they are closed up [and hence] in the same category with vessels. And I prefer to exclude [creatures without fins and scales that are found in] cisterns, ditches or caverns because they are not closed up like vessels."*

M. *In which phrase is it [referring back to B, permitted to eat the creatures without fins and scales found in vessels] in general and in which phrase is it [permitted] in specific? There is a dispute regarding this between R. Aha and Rabina. One authority said, "There is a specific, but not a general [permission]." And the other authority said, "There is no specific, but there is general [permission]."*

N. *What is the basis for the view of the authority who holds there is a specific [permission]? He would say to you, "From [the verse] itself we derive the permission [for creatures found] in vessels."*

O. *What is the basis for the view of the authority who holds there is a general [permission]? [He would say to you,] "This one [verse] demonstrates what the other one means. For if we derived it from the other [verse] alone, I would have reasoned that in regards to [creatures found in] vessels even if they have [fins and scales], you should not eat them."*

## VIII.3

A. *Said R. Huna, "A person should not pour his beer through a filter at night lest a worm fall off from the filter into the cup. And he would thereby transgress* [the prohibition in Scripture against eating it, to wit], 'Every swarming thing that swarms upon the earth is an abomination; it shall not be eaten' (Lev. 11:41)." [Once the worm crawls on the filter it is forbidden to eat it.]

B. *If this is the case then even [when he pours it without filtering directly] into the container [it should be forbidden because we should fear] lest [a worm] fell off onto the side of the container and then fell into the container itself. [It crawls when it falls on the side of the container.] This is the normal process [of pouring the liquid and so we do not consider that the worm separated from the liquid and crawled on the surface].*

C. *And based on what source do I say this? From what was taught on Tannaite authority:* On what basis do we include [the rule] that from cisterns, ditches and caverns one may bend down and not refrain from drinking [even though he may swallow a creature from the water]? It comes to teach [in the verse], "These you may eat, of all that are in the waters." [Cf. above, VIII.2 B.]

D. *And why not suspect that perhaps [a worm] fell off onto the side of the container and then fell [back into the container itself]. But [we say] this is the normal process [and a worm that falls on the side of the container does not take on the status of a creature that creeps on the ground]. Here too it is the normal process [when he pours the beer and we say that we do not take into account the possibility that the worm would crawl on the side of the container].*

E.     *Said R. Hisda to R. Huna, "There is a teaching on Tannaite authority that supports you: 'Every swarming thing that swarms upon the earth is an abomination; it shall not be eaten' (Lev. 11:41) — this includes [in the rule of forbidden creatures] insects [gnats found in wine (Rashi)] after it was strained. The basis for this is that he strained it [and the insects crawled on the strainer before they entered back into the wine]. Lo, if he did not strain it, it is permitted [to drink these insects]."*

F.     Said Samuel, "A cucumber that became infested with worms [67b] while growing on the vine is prohibited on account of [the verse], 'Every swarming thing that swarms upon the earth is an abomination; it shall not be eaten' (Lev. 11:41)."

G.     *Let us say there is support for this view as one Tanna taught on Tannaite authority: '[Every swarming thing that swarms] upon the earth [is an abomination; it shall not be eaten' (Lev. 11:41)] — this excludes the mites in lentils, and the mosquitoes in peas, and the worms in the dates and the dried figs.*

H.     *And there is another teaching on Tannaite authority: 'Every swarming thing that swarms upon the earth is an abomination; it shall not be eaten' (Lev. 11:41) — this includes [as prohibited] the worms that are found in the roots of olive trees and in the roots of grape vines.*

I.     *What then [can we say to explain the apparent contradiction between these two teachings]? Both refer to [insects found in] produce. And this one [refers to produce] still growing and the other refers to [produce] no longer growing.*

J.     *No. Both refer to [produce] still growing. And there is no contradiction. This one refers to [insects found in the] produce [and that is prohibited]. And this one refers to [insects found in the] tree [and that is permitted].*

K.     *Let us revert to the body of the prior text [H]: You may derive this as well from what was taught, "The worms that are found in the roots of olive trees and in the roots of grape vines." You may indeed derive this [conclusion because it refers to roots].*

## VIII.4

A. R. Joseph posed questions [regarding the definition of a prohibited creeping thing]: If it [i.e., an insect] detached [from the produce] and died [without ever crawling on the ground], what is the law? If part [of the insect detached and crawled on the ground], what is the law? [If it detached, but a person ate it before it touched the ground, i.e.,] while in mid-air, what is the law? *These questions stand unresolved.*

B. R. Ashi posed questions [regarding the definition of a prohibited creeping thing]: [If it crawled from the inside of the fruit] to the surface of a date, what is the law? [If it crawled] to the surface of the date pit, what is the law? [If it crawled] from one date into another [without going outside], what is the law? *These questions stand unresolved.*

C. Said R. Sheshet the son of R. Idi, "Parasites [found in an animal or in a fish] are prohibited." *What is the basis for this rule? [It is because] they came [into the animal or fish] from the exterior [and must have crawled in the process]. [If so] they should be found in the intestinal passages [where we presume they entered the animal].*

D. *Another version:* Said R. Shisha the son of R. Idi, "Parasites [found in an animal or in a fish] are permitted." *What is the basis for this rule? [It is because] they grow within [the animal] spontaneously.* Said R. Ashi, "This is obvious. For if they came in from the exterior, they should be found in the intestinal passages."

E. *And the law is that parasites are prohibited. What is the basis for this rule? When the animal is asleep they may enter through its snout [and accordingly they would not be found in the intestinal passages].*

F. *Worms [Cashdan: maggots; Lewysohn: gadfly] under the skin [of an animal] are prohibited. [Worms found] in fish are permitted.* Rabina said to his mother, "Hide them for me [in the fish] and I will eat them."

G. Said R. Mesharshayya the son of R. Aha to Rabina, "*What is the difference [between this case] and that taught on Tannaite authority,* '[They shall remain an abomination to you; of their flesh you shall not eat,] and their carcasses you shall have in abomination'

(Lev. 11:11) — this serves to include [in the prohibition] maggots that are found in a beast."

H. *He said to him, "Are these cases [of meat and fish] comparable? A beast is made permitted through the act of slaughter. But [concerning] these [maggots on the beast they grow before the beast is rendered permitted]. Since the act of slaughter has no effect on them, they remain prohibited. But fish are made permitted [for eating] by the mere act of catching them. And [so concerning] these [maggots on a fish], when it grows them, it grows them after it was rendered permitted."*

### VIII.5

A. *Our rabbis taught on Tannaite authority:* "[Scripture states: Whatever goes on its belly, and whatever goes on all fours, or whatever has many feet, all the swarming things that swarm upon the earth, you shall not eat; for they are an abomination" (Lev. 11:42).] "Whatever goes on its belly" — this includes the snake; "whatever" — this includes the earthworm and any like it; "on all fours" — this is the scorpion; "and whatever goes" — this includes the beetle and any like it; "has many feet" — this is the centipede; "or whatever" — this includes any like it or any like those that are like it.

B. *It was taught on Tannaite authority:* R. Yosé b. Durmasqet says: The Leviathan is a clean fish as it says, "His back is made of rows of shields" (Job 42:15 RSV)... "His underparts are like sharp potsherds" (Job 42:30 RSV). "His back is made of rows of shields" — these are its scales. "His underparts are like sharp potsherds" — these are the fins with which it propels itself.

These units introduce Tosefta text in the criticism of Mishnah 3:6-7. They also provide several secondary discussions of the biblical sources. I.1 cites the appropriate verse and a relevant Tosefta-rule and discusses the tokens of clean and unclean animal species. II.1 invokes Tosefta's rule to further clarify Mishnah and examines a related rule regarding fats of a wild beast. II.2 digresses from the topic with several stories. III.1-3 supply further digressions unrelated to Mishnah. IV.1 first returns to comment on a term in the verse that lists the categories of clean species. Then it digresses. V.1-3 expand upon Mishnah's generalization on tokens of clean fowl. V.4-5 go on to a secondary issue concerning the identification of birds valid for a sacrifice. V.6-8 give a catalogue of varieties of birds and their respective rules and related traditions. V.9-10 provide extended discussion of the number of categories of the unclean birds. Then V.11 concludes with secondary matters on clean birds.

Now that the primary considerations have been exposed, V.12 introduces the new issue of tokens for clean eggs. It gives a variant of Tosefta's text on the subject and a second Tosefta-text. V.13-15 provide additional materials regarding the rules for eggs. VI.1 reverts to Mishnah's rules relating to birds and cites the relevant Tosefta-texts. VII.1-2 directly comment on locusts, the next issue in Mishnah, cites Tosefta, and comments and expounds on the verse regarding categories of locusts. VIII.1 cites material directly relevant to Mishnah's rule regarding tokens for clean fish. VIII.2 comments and expounds upon at length the verses regarding clean fish. Finally, VIII.3-5 state several of the rules for worms and the like. The materials continue the established program closely investigating the Mishnah-text with few digressions or deviations from the line of inquiry.

# 3

# Bavli Ḥullin Chapter Four

# Folios 68A-78A

**4:1**

A. A beast that was in hard labor, and its offspring put its hoof out and withdrew it —

B. [when the dam is properly slaughtered], it [the offspring] is permitted to be eaten. [Not being deemed born, it is not a living beast that itself must be slaughtered before being eaten.]

C. [If] it put forth its head, even though it withdrew it, lo, this is [deemed] as fully born.

D. [If] one cuts off part of the offspring that is in its womb —

E. it [what is cut off] is permitted to be eaten.

F. [If he cut off] part of the spleen or kidneys [of the beast itself], it is prohibited to be eaten.

G. This is the general principle:
(1) Something that is part of its [the dam's] body is prohibited.
(2) Something that is not part of its body is permitted.

I.1
A. Said R. Judah, said Rab, "And the limb itself [that the animal put out and withdrew] is prohibited." *What is the basis for this? Because Scripture said,* "You shall not eat any meat that is torn by beasts in the field" (Exod. 22:31). As soon as the meat [of the limb] went outside of the confines [of the womb] it became prohibited.

B. *It was taught on Tannaite authority in the Mishnah:* **A beast that was in hard labor, and its offspring put its hoof out and withdrew it — [when the dam is properly slaughtered], it [the offspring] is permitted to be eaten [M. 4:1 A-B].** *Is it not the case that this [rule granting permission] refers to the limb? No, it may refer to the [entire] offspring. If it pertains to the offspring, why specify that it* **withdrew it***? Even if it did not withdraw it, it also [should be permitted to eat the animal]. The same conclusion pertains even if it did not withdraw it. But because it was necessary to teach in the latter text of the Mishnah,* **[If] it put forth its head, even though it withdrew it, lo, this is [deemed] as fully born [M. 4:1 C],** *it taught also in the former text of the Mishnah that it* **withdrew it.**

C. *And what novel point does the latter text of the Mishnah make? As soon as its head goes forth [from the womb] that is considered the birth of the animal. [However, consider that] it was taught on Tannaite authority,* **Who is a firstborn in respect to inheritance and not a firstborn in respect to the priest? He who comes after an untimely birth whose head emerged alive, or [after] a nine-month-old birth the head of which emerged [but which was] dead [M. Bekh. 8:1 E-F].** *The basis for this rule is that his head emerged [and the offspring was] dead. Lo, if his head emerged [and the offspring was] alive, those that come after it [in birth] are not deemed firstborn in respect to inheritance either.*

D. *And if you [wish you may say that it is consistent to] maintain that we were instructed [of the rule there] in respect to human [birth] and that we derive the novel point [here] in respect to the [birth of] beasts, because we cannot deduce [the rule] for humans from [the rule] for beasts, because beasts have no entrance-way [to the womb]. And we cannot deduce [the rule] for beasts from [the rule] for humans, because [the emergence of] a human's face is decisive [in determining the emergence of the head]. Lo, it also was taught on Tannaite authority in the Mishnah:* **An afterbirth, part of which emerged, is prohibited to be eaten. It is a token of [the birth of] an offspring in a woman, and the token of [the birth of] an offspring in a beast [M. 4:7 E-F].** *[The rules for humans and beasts are parallel.]*

E. *If you wish to say that it is consistent to maintain that [the stipulation]* **it withdrew** *stated in the former text is specific to that case [and not stated on account of the rule of the latter text, then we could maintain* *that] it was taught in the latter text on account of [the fact that it was taught] in the former text. But if you wish to say that neither is [the stipulation of* it withdrew*] specific to the former text nor is [the stipulation of* it withdrew*] specific to the latter text, why then must I teach it at all?*

F. No [this is not the correct line of reasoning]. It is consistent to say that [the rule granting permission applies to] the offspring. And [it accords with the view] stated by R. Nahman bar Yitzhak, "It was only necessary [to state the rule so as to render permitted for eating] the place of the incision [in the limb of the animal]." Here also [we may say], "It was only necessary [to state the rule so as to render permitted for eating] the place of the incision [in the limb of the animal]."

I.2
A. *Come and take note:* **A beast that was in hard labor, and its offspring put its hoof out and withdrew it — and afterward he slaughtered its mother, it [the offspring] is permitted to be eaten.** If he slaughtered its mother and afterward it **withdrew it,** one is prohibited to eat it [cf. T. 4:3 B].

B. **If it put its hoof out and he cut it off, and afterward he slaughtered its mother,** what was outside [the mother at the time it was slaughtered] **is unclean and prohibited.** What was inside [the mother at the time of slaughter] **is clean and permitted. [If]** he slaughtered its mother and afterward cut it off — [68b] "**the meat [of the offspring] is in the status of that which has touched carrion** [namely, the hoof, which, located outside the womb, is unaffected by the slaughter of the mother]," **the words of R. Meir. And sages say, "[It is in the status of that which has] touched** *terefah* **that has been slaughtered.** [After the act of slaughter, the animal, including the hoof, no longer has the status of carrion. However the hoof takes on the status of *terefah* and renders unclean the rest of the animal through contact with it.] [M. 4:4 A-E]."

C. *It was taught on Tannaite authority in respect to this in the first text of the Mishnah:* [**A beast that was in hard labor, and**] **its offspring put its hoof out and withdrew it — when the dam is properly slaughtered, it [the offspring] is permitted to be eaten**

[M. 4:1 A-B]. *Is it not the case that this [rule granting permission] refers to the limb? No it may refer to the [entire] offspring. If it pertains to the offspring, then consider the latter text: If he slaughtered its mother and afterward it withdrew it, one is prohibited to eat it. And if this refers to the offspring, why is it prohibited? It should be in accord with the view stated by* R. Nahman bar Yitzhak, "It was only necessary [to state the rule so as to render permitted for eating] the place of the incision [in the limb of the animal]." Here also [we may say], "It was only necessary [to state the rule so as to render permitted for eating] the place of the incision [in the limb of the animal]." [See I.1 F.]

D. *Is this the case? But lo when Abimi came from Be Huzai, he came and brought this Mishnah with him:* "[Based on his inference from Deut. 14:6 where the words hoof and hooves are stated—] If it withdrew a hoof, you may eat it. If it withdrew hooves, you may eat it." *What then is the explanation?* "If it withdrew a hoof, you may eat" — [does it mean you may eat] the hoof? No. [It means,] If it withdrew the hoof, you may eat the offspring.

E. *If it refers to the offspring then why does it specify that it **withdrew** it? Even if it did not withdraw it, it also [should be permitted to eat the animal].* Said R. Nahman Bar Yitzhak, "It was only necessary [to state the rule so as to render permitted] the place of the incision [in the limb of the animal]."

F. *But lo, two texts are brought to bear upon this issue. What then [should we infer]? One [to teach us the rule] for the limb and one [to teach us the rule] for the place of the incision? No. One [to teach us the rule] for the place of the incision and one [to teach us the rule] for the case of a foetus with uncloven hooves in the womb of the mother [that it is permitted].*

G. *And this accords with the view of* R. Simeon. For said R. Simeon, "A foetus with uncloven hooves that is the offspring of a cow is prohibited." *This concern applies where it* emerged [from the womb] to the light of day. But if it is yet in the womb of the mother, *it is permitted.*

I.3
A. [Said] Ulla, said R. Yohanan, "And the limb itself is permitted." Said R. Judah to Ulla, "But lo, Rab and Samuel *both said*, 'The limb itself is prohibited.'" *He said to him, "Who will give us the dust of Rab and Samuel so that we may fill our eyes with it? [We are not worthy enough even to sit at their feet as students.]"*

B. *But this is what R. Yohanan said, "All [the rules] were subsumed in the general rule,* 'Therefore you shall not eat any flesh that is torn by beasts in the field' (Exod. 23:31). When Scripture specified the rule for the sin-offering that went beyond its enclosure [in the Temple] and returned [back within], that it is prohibited, *[only the prohibition] for the sin-offering did Scripture specify. But for all other concerns [of cases where the object went beyond its enclosure and then returned], once it returned it is permitted."*

I.4
A. *They posed a question:* "Therefore you shall not eat any flesh that is torn by beasts in the field" (Exod. 23:31). What does this come to teach [by stating *"terefah"*]? Because we maintain regarding second tithes and first fruits, that even if they go beyond their prescribed enclosures [in Jerusalem] and return, they are permitted, you might wish to infer that even this [case of an offspring that put its hoof out and withdrew it] is the same. It comes to teach us [that it is not by adding], *"terefah."*

B. *How do you derive this inference?* Said Rabbah, "It is like a *terefah* [in this way]. What is the rule for a *terefah*-animal? Once it is deemed *terefah*, there is no way after that to permit it. So even the flesh [of a limb] that went beyond its enclosure [in the womb], there is no way after that to permit it." *This question raised concerning the view of Ulla is a decisive question [to refute this view].*

I.5
A. Said the master: Because we maintain regarding second tithes and first fruits, [that even if they go beyond their prescribed enclosures in Jerusalem and return, they are permitted, I.4 A] — where do we maintain this? *As it is written,* "You may not eat within your towns the tithe of your grain or of your wine or of your oil, or the firstlings of your herd or of your flock, or any of

your votive offerings which you vow, or your freewill offerings, or the offering that you present" (Deut. 12:17). [You may deduce that,] "Within your towns" that is where you should not eat it. But if they [these offerings] go beyond their prescribed enclosures and return, they are permitted.

I.6
A. *In the West [Israel] they taught as follows:* Rab said, "Limbs can be born [on their own]." And R. Yohanan said, "Limbs cannot be born [on their own]." *What is the matter of the dispute between them? The dispute between them is the matter of whether to prohibit the lesser part of the limb that is inside the animal [where the major part of the limb already emerged].*

B. *[Regarding this dispute] they posed a question:* According to the authority who says, "Limbs cannot be born [on their own]," [what if] the offspring put out its limb and withdrew it and then again put out [another part of] its limb and withdrew it until it had done this for the major part [of the limb]. What is the law? *Do we say, lo the major part [of the limb] did go out? Or perhaps since it withdrew [the limb], it has been withdrawn [in respect to its legal status]?*

C. *If you wish to say, since it withdrew [the limb], it has been withdrawn [in respect to its legal status], [then consider the case where]* the offspring put out its limb and he cut it off and then again it put out [another part of] its limb and he cut it off until it had done this for the major part of the animal. What is the law? *Do we say, lo the major part has emerged [and the animal was born]? Or perhaps we must have a major part [emerge] at one time [to result in birth]?*

D. Come and take note: **[69a] This is the general principle: Something that is part of its [the dam's] body is prohibited. Something that is not part of its body is permitted [M. 4:1 G].** *What does* **Something that is not part of its body** *encompass? Does it not encompass this very matter? No. It encompasses [the case of]* an animal with uncloven hooves in the womb of the cow. And this is in accord with the view of R. Simeon.

E. For even though R. Simeon said, "A foetus with uncloven hooves that is the offspring of a cow is prohibited [I.2 G]," *this concern*

*Bavli Ḥullin Chapter Four. Folios 68A-78A* 161

*applies to an instance where it emerged to see the light of day. But as long as it remains in the womb of the mother it is permitted.*

I.7
A. R. Hanania posed a question: If the offspring [of a peace-offering] put forth its limb while [the mother was] in the Temple court, what is the law? Do we reason that since [the Temple court] is an enclosure for Holy Things, it serves as such for this [offspring] as well [and when the mother is slaughtered, the offspring is rendered permitted]? Or perhaps [we reason] what with regard to this case [the Temple court] does not serve as an enclosure. For the enclosure for an offspring [with regard to the effectiveness of slaughter for the mother upon the offspring] is its mother.

B. Said to him Abayye, "According to your logic you should have posed a question regarding Lesser Holy Things in Jerusalem. Why did you not pose a question regarding Lesser Holy Things in Jerusalem? For the enclosure for an offspring [with regard to the effectiveness of slaughter for the mother upon the offspring] is its mother. Here too [in our case] the enclosure for an offspring [with regard to the effectiveness of slaughter for the mother upon the offspring] is its mother."

C. Ilfa posed a question: If the offspring put out its limb between [the actual slaughter of] one organ [of the neck] and the other, what is the law? Do we reason that the [slaughter of the] first organ combines with that of the second organ to render it clean of the status of carrion? Or do we not [reason in this manner]?

D. Said Raba, "[It may be derived from an argument] *a fortiori*. If the first organ effectively [combines in an ordinary instance] with the second to render it permitted for eating, does it not effectively [combine in our case] to render it clean of the status of carrion?"

E. R. Jeremiah posed a question: What is the law with regard to taking into account the seed [of the offspring that had put forth its limb and that was born alive after the slaughter of the mother in determining the status of the progeny]? What is the situation? If we say that it went and mated with a normal cow, why specify this case that has a prohibited limb that it put out of the mother's womb? Why not consider also even the more general case of an offspring that was born alive [with no protruding limb] after the slaughter of the mother?

F. *For said R. Mesharshayya, "According to the view of those who say we take into account the seed of the father [in determining the status of the progeny], if an offspring that was born alive after the slaughter of the mother mates with a normal cow, there is no redress for the offspring."*

G. *It is not necessary [to raise this issue because our case is where] it mated with an offspring that was born alive after the slaughter of the mother, just like [the father] itself. What [is the law]? [Do we say] each limb [in the parent] produces the equivalent [in the offspring]? Then he can cut it off [i.e., cut off the limb of the offspring equivalent to that of the parent that was outside its mother when it was slaughtered] and it is permitted [i.e., the rest of the animal]. Or perhaps [we say] the seed [of the parents] is mixed together [in the offspring]?*

H. *He responded and said, "It is obvious that the seed is mixed together. For if not then a blind one would give birth to a blind offspring and a lame one would give birth to a lame offspring. Rather it is obvious that the seed is mixed together."*

I. *So this is how we should phrase the question: Does not an ordinary animal result from the [elements in the seed of the father] of forbidden fats and blood [mixed together with all the other genetic materials] and it is permitted [to eat an ordinary animal]? Here too [where the father is an animal born alive after the mother was slaughtered and while it had a protruding limb, it] should make no difference [if the forbidden substance is mixed together with the rest of the seed]? Or perhaps we say that two prohibited elements [are acceptable] but that three prohibited elements are not?*

J. *And in accord with whose view do we say this? If in accord with the view of R. Meir, then we do have the prohibition against forbidden fats and blood. But we do not have the prohibition against [the animal born alive after the slaughter of the mother with the limb that] protrudes. And if it is in accord with the view of R. Judah then we do have the prohibition against [the animal born alive after the slaughter of the mother with the limb that] protrudes. But we do not have the prohibition against forbidden fats and blood.* [Some var. omit 'and blood.']

K. *For it was taught on Tannaite authority: "[The prohibition of] the sinew of the hip applies to the foetus, and its fat is prohibited," the words of R. Meir. R. Judah says, "It does not apply to the foetus. Its fat is permitted [T. 7:2 A-B]."*

L. *But [on the contrary in general] we do state that all [that are derivatives] of elements [that are prohibited] are [themselves] permitted. So here is how we should phrase the question: [With regard to an offspring whose foot was protruding and was born alive after the slaughter of the mother], what about drinking its milk? Is not [taking from an animal] ordinary milk like [taking] a 'limb' from a live animal and still it is permitted? In this case too it should make no difference. Or perhaps there [in the case of milk from an ordinary animal], there is redress for its prohibition [as a 'limb' from a live animal] through slaughtering. Here there is no redress for its prohibition through slaughtering. [It remains prohibited.] The question stands unresolved.*

II.1

A. **[If] one cuts off part of the offspring which is in its womb [M. 4:1 D].** *What is the basis in Scripture for this rule? As it is written,* "Every animal that parts the hoof and has the hoof cloven in two, and chews the cud, among the animals, you may eat it" (Deut. 14:6). *[It repeats,]* "animal" *and* "among the animals" *to include the offspring [under the rules].*

B. *But on this basis they should be able to make a substitution with it. Why then was it taught on Tannaite authority,* **They do not substitute limbs for foetuses or foetuses for limbs, or limbs and foetuses for whole beasts, or whole beasts for them [M. Tem. 1:3 A-B]**?

C. *Rather said Scripture,* "Every animal" *to include the offspring [under the rule, that is, it is included in this rule but they are not identical with regard to the rule of substitution].*

D. *If this is the case then even if one cuts off from the spleen or the kidneys it also [should be permitted based on this verse]. Why then was it taught in the Mishnah on Tannaite authority,* **[If] one cuts off part of the offspring that is in its womb — it [what is cut off] is permitted to be eaten. [If he cut off] part of the spleen or** kidneys [of the beast itself], it is prohibited to be eaten [M. 4:1 C-E]?

E. Scripture said, "[You may eat] it." [You may eat it] whole but not if it is missing parts.

F. *But on this basis [consider the following]:* One who slaughters a beast and finds inside it [a foetus] the shape of a dove, *it should be permitted! Why then [does it say]:* Said R. Yohanan, "One who slaughters a beast and finds inside it [a foetus] the shape of a dove, it is prohibited to eat it."

G. [69b] *It must have split hooves. And there are none here.*

H. *But on this basis consider the case of a foetus with uncloven hooves in the womb of a cow. Let it be prohibited. Lo, taught the House of R. Ishmael in accord with R. Simeon b. Yohai,* "[Every animal that parts the hoof and has the hoof] cloven in two, [and chews the cud], among the animals, you may eat it" (Deut. 14:6).

I. R. Shimi bar Ashi said, "It is invariably as you stated earlier. And that question you raised [in B] that they do not substitute [limbs for foetuses or foetuses for limbs, or limbs and foetuses for whole beasts, or whole beasts for them] *in accord with whose view is this [a question]? In accord with R. Simeon's view.* For he juxtaposes the laws of substitution with those of tithes. What is the case regarding tithes? [The obligation to tithe] does not apply to limbs and foetuses. Similarly [the rules of] substitution do not apply to limbs and foetuses."

J. *And on what basis do you say this? As it was taught on Tannaite authority in the Mishnah,* **Said R. Yosé, "Is it not so that in the case of animals that have been consecrated, he who says, 'The foot of this is a burnt-offering' — the whole beast is a burnt-offering? Also, when he will state, 'The foot of this is instead of that' — the whole of it should be a substitute in its stead [M. Tem. 1:3 D-E].**" *To whose view does he [Yosé] respond? If you say that it is to [the views of] R. Meir and R. Judah, do they hold this [contrary] view?*

K. *But lo, it was taught on Tannaite authority,* You might infer that one who says, 'This is the foot of a burnt-offering' that the whole beast will become a burnt-offering. It comes to teach us [in the verse], "[If it is an animal such as men offer as an offering to the Lord,] all of such that any man gives to the Lord is holy" (Lev. 27:9). [This implies some] "of all" will become holy, but not that "all" of it will become holy.

L. You might infer that [in such a case the animal] will revert to being unconsecrated. It comes to teach us [in the verse], "is." [That implies] it will retain its status [b. Tem. 11b].

M. *Lo, what then is the procedure?* "Let the [animal] be sold for the purpose of bringing burnt-offerings. And its monetary value will be available for unconsecrated purposes excluding the value of the limb," the words of R. Meir. And R. Judah, R. Yosé, and R. Simeon say, "What is the basis for the rule that **one who says, 'This is the foot of a burnt-offering' that the whole beast becomes a burnt-offering**? It comes to teach us [in the verse], 'is.' That [word] includes all of it."

N. *In accord with whose view is this stated? If you wish to maintain that it is in accord with the view of R. Meir or R. Judah, do they hold in accord with this view? But rather it must be in accord with the view of R. Simeon. No [this need not be the conclusion]. R. Yosé [in the M. cited in J] expressed his own view [and not in accord with any other Tanna].*

I.1 analyzes the reasoning of the rules of Mishnah. I.2 extends the inquiry and aligns the rules of Mishnah with a Tosefta-text and additional Tannaite and Amoraic materials. I.3-5 compare the premises of our Mishnah paragraph with intersecting premises of different rules. I.6 then translates the process of Mishnah-criticism into a quest for a statement of a legal premise. I.7 extends and explores Mishnah's premises and principles by proposing a series of theoretical cases. II.1 seeks the scriptural basis for the rule of Mishnah and then aligns the rules with those of other Tannaite authorities.

**4:2**

A. A beast producing its firstborn that is in hard labor —

B. one cuts off the limbs [of the offspring] one by one and throws them to the dogs.
C. [If] the greater part of it came forth, lo, this is to be buried.
D. And it [the beast] is free of [the law of] the firstling.

I.1
A. *It was stated:* If one third [of a firstborn animal] came forth and he sold it to an idolater and then another third came forth — R. Huna said, "It is holy." Rabbah said, "It is not holy."

B. R. Huna said, "It is holy." *He reasons that it is retroactively holy. As soon as the major part came forth, the matter is clarified retroactively that from the start it was holy. And the one who bought [the first third], bought nothing.*

C. Rabbah said, "It is not holy." *He reasons that it becomes holy from the point [after the major part comes forth] onwards. And the one who bought [the first third] made a perfectly good purchase.*

D. *And they each are consistent with their own views elsewhere. For it was stated:* If one third [of a firstborn animal] came forth through a caesarian section and two thirds through the womb [in a normal birth] — R. Huna said, "It is not holy." Rabbah said, "It is holy."

E. R. Huna said, "It is not holy." *R. Huna is consistent with his view. For he said it is holy retroactively. And the first major portion [of the animal to come forth] does not come through the womb [by a normal birth process].*

F. Rabbah said, "It is holy." *Rabbah is consistent with his view. For he said that from this point onwards it is holy. And the majority [of the animal] does come forth through the womb.*

G. *And it is necessary to state both cases. For if we had been instructed in this one [the latter, we might argue that] in this one R. Huna stated matters because it is a lenient rule. But in that one [the former] that is a stricter rule, it would make sense to say that he agrees with Rabbah.* [Rashi explains otherwise.]

H. [70a] *And if it was stated only [the former, we might argue that] in this one alone Rabbah stated matters. But in this [other] one it makes sense to say that he agrees with R. Huna. It is necessary to state both.*

I.2
A. *It was taught in the Mishnah on Tannaite authority:* **A beast producing its firstborn that is in hard labor — one cuts off the limbs [of the offspring] one by one and throws them to the dogs [M. 4:2 A-B].** *Is it not the case that* he cuts off and puts aside [the limbs and later throws them to the dogs]? And if you say that it is holy retroactively, *it should be necessary then for him to bury them.*

B. *No. In this case what are we dealing with? Where he cuts off and throws [each one to the dogs]. But where he cuts off and puts aside [the limbs], what is the rule? They must be buried [when enough of the animal comes forth and it is retroactively a firstborn].*

C. *Why then was it taught in the latter text of the Mishnah:* **[If] the greater part of it came forth, lo, this is to be buried. And it [beast] is free of [the law of] the firstling [C-D]?**

D. *Let it be specified and taught therein [in the first text of the Mishnah]:* Under what circumstance? Where he cuts off and throws each limb [to the dogs]. But where he cuts off and puts them aside they must be buried. *This is in fact what was intended:* Under what circumstance? Where he cuts off and throws each limb [to the dogs]. But where he cuts off and puts them aside, it is as if the greater portion came forth and they must be buried.

I.3
A. *Raba posed a question:* In determining the status of the limbs did they follow the status of the majority or not? *What is the situation [that Raba refers to]? If you say that the case in question is one where the major part [of the animal] came forth, with the lesser part of a limb and he posed the question: This lesser part that is outside, do we say it follows the status of the major part of the limb [that is still inside]? Or do we say that it follows the status of the major part of the animal [that has already come forth]? [If this is the question then] it is obvious that we do not ignore the major part of the foetus and follow the greater part of the limb [to determine the status]!*

B. *Rather, [what is the situation that Raba refers to]? The case in question is one where half the animal came forth with a major part of a limb. And he posed the question: [For] this lesser part that is inside, what is the rule? Do we follow the status of the major part of the limb? [Then we could argue that the greater part of the animal had come forth.]*

C. *Come and take note:* **[If] the greater part of it came forth, lo, this is to be buried [C].** *What is meant by "the greater part?" If it means literally "the greater part," up to this point had we not been instructed [of the legal principle] that the greater part is equivalent to the whole? Rather must it not be the case that the question is where half the animal came forth with the greater part of the limb? No, it must be the case that the question is one where the major part of the animal came forth with the lesser part of a limb. And it makes the novel point that we do not ignore the greater part of the animal [that is outside] and follow the limb [whose greater part is inside the mother].*

D. *Raba posed a question: What is the law [with regard to the holiness of a firstborn] if he wrapped [the foetus during its birth] in a sheath? In a cloak? In its afterbirth? [The foetus in these cases does not come in contact with the birth canal.] 'In its afterbirth' is the natural manner [of birth, so why should this be a question]? Rather [it must mean, if he wrapped it] in the afterbirth of another [animal, what is the law]? If she wrapped it and brought it forth [i.e., either a woman wrapped her hands around (Rashi) or the female twin wrapped herself around (Tosafot)] what is the law?*

E. *What is the situation [of all these cases where the foetus was wrapped up during birth (Rashi)]? If it came forth head first [and then was wrapped], then it is born [by the time the rest of the animal comes forth]. Rather it must be that it came forth feet first.*

F. *[The Talmud poses several more questions.] If a weasel swallowed the foetus [in the mother's womb] and brought it forth, what is the law? Once he brought it forth it is outside [the womb and was not born naturally so is not a valid firstborn animal]. Rather it must be that it swallowed it and brought it forth and brought it back in and spit it up. And then it [the foetus] came forth on its own. What is the law?*

G. *If he attached together two wombs and it came forth from one and entered the other, what is the law? If it comes forth from its own is it* a firstborn? But if it comes forth from another womb is it not a firstborn? Or perhaps even if it comes forth from a womb that is not its own, is it a firstborn? These questions stand unresolved.

H.  R. Aha posed a question: If the walls of the womb expanded [so that the foetus did not touch them during its birth], what is the law? *Does the airspace of the womb render it holy and [in this case] we have that circumstance [and it has the status of a firstborn]? Or does the contact with the womb [during birth] render it holy and [in this case] we do not have that circumstance [and it does not have the status of a firstborn]?*

I.  Mar bar R. Ashi posed a question: If the walls of the womb were torn out what is the law? *If they were torn out, then they are not there [and what is the question]? Rather it must be that they were torn out and hung around the neck [of the mother]. What is the law? Does [the womb] in its proper place render it holy as a firstborn? But if it is not in its proper place, then it does not render it [the foetus] holy as a firstborn? Or perhaps even if it is not in its proper place does it render it holy?*

J.  R. Jeremiah posed a question to R. Zira: If the walls of the womb were mutilated, what is the law? *He said to him, "You have touched upon a question that has already been asked of us [in another form]. For R. Zira posed a question. And some say, R. Zira posed a question of R. Assi: If the remaining [wall area] was greater in size than the opening, and it came forth through the opening, or if the opening [in the wall area] was greater than the remaining [wall area] and it came forth through the [tear in the] remaining [area], what is the law?" On this point I had a question only with regard to [a case of a womb with] the opening greater than the remaining [area]. For some remaining [area of the wall of the womb] exists! But where it was mutilated [then it is as if no wall exists], we do not pose any question.*

I.1 contrasts the premise of our Mishnah paragraph with parallel concerns of different rules, working through the same problem in different ways. I.2 clarifies and spells out the implications of the rule of Mishnah and I.3 poses a series of questions probing the premises and principles of Mishnah.

#### 4:3 A-E [70b]

A. A beast, the foetus of which died in its womb,
B. and [that foetus] the shepherd put in his hand and touched —
C. whether in the case of an unclean beast or a clean beast—
D. he is clean.
E. R. Yosé the Galilean says, "In the case of an unclean beast, he is unclean, and in the case of a clean beast, he is clean."

#### I.1

A. *What is the basis for the view of the first Tanna? Said R. Hisda, "[It is based on a logical deduction] a fortiori: If [being in the womb of] the mother [when she is slaughtered] can have the effect of rendering it [the foetus] permitted for eating should it not have the effect of rendering it clean from the uncleanness of carrion?"*

B. *We have found [a logical basis] with regard to the case for a clean animal. What is the source [of argument] for the case of an unclean animal? [Slaughtering the mother has no effect on the offspring in her womb. So we can deduce nothing further.]*

C. [The verse states: "And if any animal of which you may eat dies, he who touches its carcass shall be unclean until the evening" (Lev. 11:39).] "And if any animal... dies," this refers to an unclean animal; "of which you may eat," this refers to a clean animal. The unclean animal was juxtaposed in the verse to the clean animal [to teach us the following]. What is the rule [in our case where the mother is slaughtered] for the clean animal? Its foetus is clean [of the uncleanness of carrion]. So too, for the unclean animal, its foetus is clean.

D. *And what is the basis for the view of R. Yosé the Galilean? Said R. Yitzhak, "Scripture stated, 'And all that go on their paws, among the animals that go on all fours, are unclean to you; whoever touches their carcass shall be unclean until the evening' (Lev. 11:27). I declared unclean to you [as carrion] all those animals that go on their paws."*

Bavli Hullin Chapter Four. Folios 68A-78A

E. *But what about this case of a foetus with uncloven hooves in the womb of a cow? Let it be deemed unclean. For it is like an animal that goes on its paws. [This specification of the verse refers to] those that go on their paws, among the animals that go on all fours. And this [case of a foetus with uncloven hooves in the womb of a cow] is a case of an animal that goes on all fours inside of an animal that goes on eight [counting each split hoof as two]!*

F. *[In accord with this logic] a cow [foetus] found in the womb of a camel should not be deemed unclean because it is a case of an animal that goes on eight found inside of an animal that goes on all fours.*

G. [The verse could have stated,] "That go." [Instead it stated,] "All that go," to include [in the law] the case of a foetus of a cow that was found in the womb of a camel.

H. *[Why not say] a foetus with uncloven hooves in the womb of a mother with uncloven hooves be deemed unclean [based on the verse]? For it is a case of an animal that goes on all fours found inside of an animal that goes on all fours. For this instance we apply the logical deduction a fortiori of R. Hisda.*

I. *R. Ahadaboy bar Ammi posed a contradiction to this: [Based on your logic] a foetus of a swine in the womb of a swine should not be deemed unclean. For it is an animal that goes on all eight inside of an animal that goes on all eight!*

J. But said R. Nahman bar Yitzhak, "From this [verse we derive that it is unclean], 'Or if any one touches an unclean thing, whether the carcass of an unclean beast or a carcass of unclean cattle or a carcass of unclean swarming things, [and it is hidden from him, and he has become unclean, he shall be guilty]' (Lev. 5:2)." And do we reason that the carcass of an unclean animal renders unclean and that [carcass] of a clean animal does not render unclean? So what does [the verse] refer to [by making this differentiation between clean and unclean carcasses]? [It implies] that the foetus in the womb of an unclean animal is unclean and one in a clean animal is clean.

K. *And after deducing this from the teaching of R. Nahman bar Yitzhak [J], why do we need the teaching of R. Yitzhak [D]? If not for the* teaching of R. Yitzhak, I would have reasoned all of it [the verse interpreted by Nahman bar Yitzhak] should go in accord with the view of Rabbi [see below, b. 71a]. It makes the novel point [applying part of the verse for our purposes here].

II.1
A. *It was taught on Tannaite authority:* Said R. Jonathan, "I remarked to Ben Azzai, 'We have learned that the carcass of a clean beast renders unclean as carrion, and the carcass of an unclean beast renders unclean as carrion, and that the carcass of an unclean wild animal renders unclean as carrion. Regarding the carcass of a clean wild beast we have not learned [that it renders unclean as carrion]. What is the source of this rule?'

B. "He remarked to me, '[It is from the verse:] And all that go on their paws, among the animals that go [on all fours, are unclean to you; whoever touches their carcass shall be unclean until the evening (Lev. 11:27)].' I remarked to him, 'But does it say, All animals? Does it not say, Among the animals? It comes to teach us regarding those that go on their paws of the animals [I.1 J].'

C. "He remarked to me, 'And what does Ishmael say in this regard?' I remarked to him, '[The verse states: And if any animal of which you may eat dies, he who touches its carcass shall be unclean until the evening (Lev. 11:39).] And if any animal... dies, this refers to an unclean animal; of which you may eat, this refers to a clean animal. We learned [the rules for] a wild animal are included in those of a beast; and for a beast in those for a wild animal; those for a clean wild animal in those for a clean beast; those for an unclean wild animal in those for an unclean beast; [71a] those for an unclean beast in those for an unclean wild animal; those for a clean beast in those for a clean wild animal.' And these are the words he [Ben Azzai] said to me, 'Too bad for Ben Azzai that he did not serve R. Ishmael.'"

D. *What is the source for the assertion that* wild animals are included in the rule of beasts? *As it is written,* "These are the animals you may eat: the ox, the sheep, the goat, the hart, the gazelle, the roebuck, the wild goat, the ibex, the antelope, and the mountain-sheep. Every animal that parts the hoof and has the hoof cloven in two, and chews the cud, among the animals, you may eat" (Deut. 14:4-6). *Lo, what is the case? The wild animal is included in the rule of the beast.*

E. *What is the source of the assertion that* beasts are included in the rule of wild animals? *As it is written,* "Say to the people of Israel, These are the living things which you may eat among all the [wild] beasts that are on the earth. Whatever parts the hoof and is cloven-footed and chews the cud, among the animals, you may eat" (Lev. 11:2-3). *Lo, what is the case? The beast is included in the rule of the wild animal.*

F. [In what regard is] the clean wild animal included in the rule of the clean beast? With regard to the [specification of the rules for the] tokens [of a clean animal].

G. [In what regard is] the unclean wild animal included in the rule of the unclean beast? With regard to the prohibition against cross breeding [Lev. 19:19: "You shall keep my statutes. You shall not let your cattle breed with a different kind; you shall not sow your field with two kinds of seed; nor shall there come upon you a garment of cloth made of two kinds of stuff."]

H. [In what regard is] the unclean beast included in the rule of the unclean wild animal? In accord with the view of Rabbi.

I. *As it was taught on Tannaite authority:* Rabbi says: I recite, "[Or if any one touches an unclean thing, whether the carcass of] an unclean [wild] beast." Why must it say, "Or a carcass of unclean cattle [or a carcass of unclean swarming things, and it is hidden from him, and he has become unclean, he shall be guilty]" (Lev. 5:2)?

J. It says here, "Unclean cattle." And it says further on, "[And if any one touches an unclean thing, whether the uncleanness of man or] an unclean beast [or any unclean abomination, and then eats of the flesh of the sacrifice of the Lord's peace-offerings, that person shall be cut off from his people]" (Lev. 7:21). [Rabbi assumes that unclean cattle are subsumed under the rule of unclean wild beasts. Thus the specification in Lev. 5:2 of unclean cattle is superfluous and may be used as a means of justifying an additional rule as follows.] Just as the case further on [the additional specification implies another prohibition, i.e., that a person with] uncleanness [may not eat] holy things, so too here [the additional specification implies another prohibition, i.e., that a person with] uncleanness [may not eat] holy things.

K. [In what regard] is the clean beast included in the rule of the clean wild animal? In regard to the rule regarding the formation [of an embryo]. *For it was taught in the Mishnah on Tannaite authority:* "She who produces [an abortion] like a beast, wild animal, or bird, whether [the species it resembles is] unclean or clean, if it is male, she should sit out [the days of uncleanness and cleanness required] for a male. And it if is female, she should sit out [the days of uncleanness and cleanness required] for a female. And if the sex [of the abortion] is not known, she should sit [out the days of uncleanness and cleanness] for a male and for a female," the words of R. Meir. And sages say, "Anything that does not bear [some aspect] of the human form is not deemed a foetus" [M. Nid. 3:2 G-K].

L. *But according to the view of the rabbis for what [specific teaching] do I need this verse [cf. above, I.1 J]? All of this follows in accord with the view of Rabbi.*

I.1 explores the scriptural and logical bases of the Mishnah. II.1 moves to a second-level issue out of the foregoing.

### 4:3 F-G

F. The woman whose foetus died in her womb, and [that foetus] the midwife put in her hand and touched —
G. the midwife is unclean with a seven-day uncleanness, and the woman is clean until the foetus will emerge.

I.1
A. Said Rabbah, "Just as an unclean object that is contained [inside a body] does not render unclean [the body], so also a clean object contained [inside a body] does not become unclean [if the body comes in contact with uncleanness]."

B. *What is the source [of the rule for] uncleanness that is contained? As it is written,* "[And if any animal of which you may eat dies, he who touches its carcass shall be unclean until the evening] and

Bavli Hullin Chapter Four. Folios 68A-78A          175

he who eats of its carcass shall wash his clothes [and be unclean until the evening; he also who carries the carcass shall wash his clothes and be unclean until the evening]" (Lev. 11:39-40). *Are we not dealing with a case where he ate [unclean food] close to sunset? And the Torah said that he is clean [even though undigested unclean food is contained inside him].*

C. *But perhaps that case is different [and does not prove the point]. [For the food inside him] is not fit for a stranger [to eat and therefore no longer carries the uncleanness of carrion].*

D. *This would settle the matter according to R. Yohanan who said, "[Regarding the uncleanness of carrion]: both for this [purpose of rendering persons unclean] and for that [purpose of rendering other foods unclean], as long as it is [fit for consumption] by a dog [it renders unclean]." Then this [use of the rule for carrion as proof of the principle of contained uncleanness] would make perfect sense.*

E. *But according to Bar Padda who said, "[Regarding the uncleanness of carrion, it transmits] stronger uncleanness [as long as it is fit for consumption] by a stranger. [It transmits] weaker uncleanness [as long as it is fit for consumption] by a dog." [We should have no proof of the principle of contained uncleanness from the rule of carrion] because it is not fit [when in the stomach for consumption] by a stranger [and therefore no longer unclean as carrion].*

F. *[We could argue that there is still a way of using the rule as proof of the principle.] We may allow that [food that was swallowed] is not fit [for consumption by] a stranger [if it was swallowed] in front of him. [But if it was swallowed] not in front of him, it might be fit [for his consumption, if for instance it was spit up intact and served to him]. [Hence we could prove the principle from this rule.]*

G. *Now we have found the source of the principle for uncleanness that was contained [inside a person's body, i.e., that it cannot be transmitted]. What is the source of the principle of cleanness [contained in a person's body, i.e., that a clean object inside cannot be made unclean]?*

H. *We derive it based on logic* a fortiori. *What is the case regarding a tightly sealed clay vessel? It does not prevent the unclean contents from rendering unclean [other objects].*

I. For the master said, "The uncleanness breaks forth and ascends up to the firmament [cf. M. Ohal. 7:1, 14:6-7]." [And we still say that the clay vessel] protects its clean contents from becoming unclean. [71b] [Regarding] a person who prevents the uncleanness inside him from rendering unclean [other objects], is it not logical to conclude that he protects the clean contents inside him from becoming unclean?

J. [But you could argue that it is not consistent to deduce this.] What is the case regarding a clay vessel? It cannot become unclean by contact with its outer surface. Will you say that a person [is subject to a stricter rule because] he does become unclean by contact with his outer surface?

K. *Are we speaking of a case where there is contact [of uncleanness] with his outer surface? We are speaking of a case where there is contact with his inner surface. And you may argue the opposite, that the rule for a clay vessel is stricter [than the rule for a person]. For [a clay vessel] renders unclean via its airspace [and a person does not]. [Hence we may say the original logic is sound.]*

L. *Now we have found [a source for the principles of uncleanness] contained that was swallowed [by a person] from above. What about [a source for the principles of] uncleanness that was inserted [inside a person] from below?*

M. *We derive it based on logic a fortiori. What is the case regarding food that was swallowed? Even though it does not putrefy, it prevents [the uncleanness from rendering unclean other objects]. Where it was inserted below, where it does putrefy, is it not logical to conclude that it prevents [the uncleanness from rendering unclean other objects]?*

N. But is it not the case that it putrefies below only when it enters above [and goes through the digestive process]? Even so, the putrefying below is substantial [whatever way it enters]. [Hence we may say the original logic is sound.]

O. *Now we have found [a source for the principles of uncleanness] contained that was swallowed by a person. What is the source for [the principles of uncleanness] contained that was swallowed by an animal?*

*We derive it based on logic a fortiori. What is the case regarding a person?* He renders unclean even while alive and still prevents [uncleanness] contained inside him [from rendering unclean other objects]. Regarding an animal that does not render unclean while it is still alive, is it not logical to conclude that it prevents [uncleanness] contained inside it [from rendering unclean other objects]?

P. [But you could argue that it is not consistent to deduce this.] What is the case regarding a person? He must linger in a house with a plague [in order for his clothing to contract uncleanness]. You may say regarding an animal [that its rule is stricter because] it does not need to linger in a house with a plague [before objects on it become unclean].

Q. *In what circumstance does this law apply?* For utensils that are upon it [that it is carrying]. [In that case] a person also need not linger [for the uncleanness to affect utensils upon him that he is carrying]. *As it was taught in the Mishnah on Tannaite authority:* **He who entered a house afflicted with the plague, with his garments over his shoulder, and his sandals and rings in his hands — he and they are unclean forthwith. He was dressed with his garments, with his sandals on his feet and his rings on his fingers — he is unclean forthwith. But they are clean unless he will remain for a time sufficient to eat a piece of bread — a piece of wheat bread, and not a piece of bread of barley bread — reclining and with a condiment** [M. Neg. 13:9].

R. *Said Raba, "Both of them [i.e., two principles regarding uncleanness that is contained, cf. A, above] were taught on Tannaite authority [so what does Rabbah's teaching in A add]? [The principle regarding] uncleanness that is contained was taught on Tannaite authority. And [the principle regarding] cleanness that was contained was taught on Tannaite authority."*

S. *[The principle regarding] uncleanness that is contained — as it was taught in the Mishnah on Tannaite authority:* **If one swallowed an unclean ring, he immerses, eats heave-offering, then vomited it up — it is unclean and renders him unclean** [M. Miq. 10:8 H-I].

T.     *[The principle regarding] cleanness that is contained — as it was taught in the Mishnah on Tannaite authority:* **If one swallowed a clean ring, entered the Tent of the corpse, was sprinkled and repeated the sprinkling and immersed and then vomited it up — lo, it is as it was [clean].**

U.     *What case then did Rabbah speak of [in his rule in A]? The case in question was one where:* One swallowed two rings, one that was unclean and one that was clean and the unclean one does not render unclean the clean one. [Since both are contained inside the body they can neither transmit nor contract uncleanness.]

V.     **[72a]** *But lo, [consider by way of contradiction to this the case of] a foetus and midwife that resembles [in its legal implications] the case of two rings.* **[The woman whose foetus died in her womb, and [that foetus] the midwife put in her hand and touched — the midwife is unclean with a seven-day uncleanness, and the woman is clean until the foetus will emerge [M. 4:3 F-G].]** *And yet the foetus does render unclean the midwife!*

W.     Rabbah [would have] said, "The case of the foetus is different since it is destined to come forth." [The rule concerning contained uncleanness does not apply to it.]

X.     Said Raba, "[You say that] the foetus is destined to come forth. Is not the ring also destined to come forth [from the animal through the natural process of elimination]?"

Y.     *Rather, said Raba, "A Pumbeditan knows the basis for this matter. And who is he? R. Joseph."* For said R. Joseph, said R. Judah, said Samuel, "This uncleanness was not ordained on the authority of the Torah, but [it was ordained] on the authority of the scribes."

Z.     *What does it mean:* [This uncleanness] was not ordained on the authority of the Torah, but [it was ordained] on the authority of the scribes? It means that you should not maintain [that the law in our Mishnah follows] in accord with the view of R. Aqiba who said, "A [dead] foetus in the womb of a woman is unclean." But [the law may follow] even in accord with the view of R. Ishmael who said, "A [dead] foetus in the womb of a woman is clean."

Bavli Ḥullin Chapter Four. Folios 68A-78A                                    179

> [Because in our case] they decreed for her [the midwife] uncleanness based on the authority of the rabbis.

AA. *What is the basis [for this decree]? Said R. Hoshaia, "They decreed it lest the foetus bring forth its head out of the birth canal."*

BB. *If this is the case then even the [pregnant] woman [herself should be deemed unclean]! [We say however that] the woman feels it [if the head of the foetus projects forth]. Then why would she not tell the midwife [that the head had emerged]? She is distracted [by the labor].*

I.2

A. *What is the view of R. Ishmael and what is the view of R. Aqiba [that we refer to above, I.1 Z]? As it was taught on Tannaite authority:* "'Whoever in the open field touches [one who is slain with a sword, or a dead body, or a bone of a man, or a grave, shall be unclean seven days]' (Num. 19:16) — this [reference to an open field] excludes the case of a [dead] foetus in the womb of a woman," the words of R. Ishmael. R. Aqiba says, "This [reference] comes to include [in the law] the covering and sides [boards of the coffin or stones of the grave]."

B. And R. Ishmael [will say that the references to] the covering and sides *are derived from a received tradition [and not from the words of the verse].*

C. *And from what source does R. Aqiba derive that a [dead] foetus in the womb of a woman is unclean based on the authority of the Torah? Said R. Hoshaia, "The verse said,* 'Whoever touches a dead person, [the body of any man who has died, and does not cleanse himself, defiles the tabernacle of the Lord, and that person shall be cut off from Israel; because the water for impurity was not thrown upon him, he shall be unclean; his uncleanness is still on him]' (Num. 19:13) — *what is a dead thing that is in a person [— playing on the words of the verse]? You will have to say that is a foetus that is in the womb of a woman."*

D. *And R. Ishmael [will say that this phrase in the verse] is needed [to teach]* that a quarter-*log* of blood that comes from a corpse renders unclean. For it says, "Whoever touches a dead person, the body of any man." *What is it from the body of any man that renders unclean? You will have to say that is a quarter-log of blood.*

E. *And R. Aqiba [does not need to derive this from the verse because he follows] in accord with his own view.* For he said, "Even a quarter-*log* of blood derived from two corpses renders unclean in a tent." *For it was taught on Tannaite authority:* What is the source of the rule that a quarter-*log* of blood derived from two corpses renders unclean in a tent? As it says, "He shall not go in to any dead body [plural in the Hebrew], [nor defile himself, even for his father or for his mother]" (Lev. 21:11) — [this implies that the rule pertains to a case of the blood of] two dead bodies that constitute one full measure [of a quarter-*log*].

I.1 identifies the principle behind the rule of Mishnah, seeks its scriptural basis, enters into a sustained inquiry of its premises and extends the discussion to related principles and their logical bases. I.2 enters into a second-level of the issue deriving from the preceding.

### 4:4

A. A beast that is in hard labor, and the young put forth its hoof (and) that one cut off, and afterward one slaughtered its dam —

B. [the hoof is unclean as carrion but] the meat [of the offspring in the womb] is clean.

C. [If] he slaughtered its mother and afterward cut it off—

D. "the meat [of the offspring] is in the status of that which has touched carrion [namely, the hoof, which, located outside the womb, is unaffected by the slaughter of the mother]," the words of R. Meir.

E. And sages say, "[It is in the status of that which has] touched *terefah* that has been slaughtered."

F. [72b] [They said to R. Meir,] "Just as we find in the case of the *terefah* that slaughtering it renders it clean, so the slaughtering of a beast should render the limb clean."

G. Said to them R. Meir, "No. If the slaughtering of a *terefah* animal has rendered it clean, it is something which is part of its body. But should it render the limb clean, which is not part of its body?"

| | | |
|---|---|---|
| | H. | How do we know concerning a *terefah* animal that slaughtering it renders it clean? |
| | I. | An unclean beast is prohibited to be eaten, so too a *terefah* beast is prohibited to be eaten. Just as [in the case of] an unclean beast slaughtering it does not render it clean, so in the case of a *terefah* beast, slaughtering it should not render it clean. |
| | J. | No. If you have so stated in the case of an unclean beast, that never had a moment when it was valid, will you say so in the case of a *terefah* beast, that had a moment when it was valid? |
| | K. | Take for yourself what you have brought [the implications of your own logic]! |
| | L. | Lo, what is born as a *terefah* from the womb — how should we know [the rule that slaughtering it renders it clean]? |
| | M. | No. If you have so stated in regard to the unclean beast, the species of which [animal] is not subject to slaughter, will you say so in the case of *terefah*, the species of which [animal] is subject to slaughter? |
| | N. | As to a live eight-month's birth, slaughtering it does not render it clean, because the like [of it] is not subject to slaughtering. |

I.1

A. *Why [in D-F do they rule it the foetus is unclean]? This should come under the principle of uncleanness that is concealed from view. And uncleanness that is concealed from view does not render unclean.*

B. *Let us say R. Meir [in D says it is unclean because he] follows in accord with his own view. As it was taught in the Mishnah on Tannaite authority:* **Three-by-three [finger-sized-cloth] that was divided is clean from *midras*-uncleanness but is unclean from the contact with *midras*-uncleanness [— the words of R. Meir (the Talmud adds this attribution)]. Said R. Yosé, "And with what *midras* did this have contact? But only if a *zab* has touched it is it unclean, on account of contact with the *zab*"** [M. Kel. 27:11].

C. *It was stated concerning this: Said Ulla,"This rule was taught only for a three-by-three cloth that was divided. But for three-by-three cloths* that come from a larger garment, at the time they are separated from their source, they contract uncleanness from their source. Here too at the time it separates from the limb, [the animal] contracts uncleanness from the limb."

D. Rabina said, "[The cases are not comparable.] A garment does not stand ready to be cut up. A foetus does stand ready to be cut up. [And we have the principle that] anything that stands ready for cutting [73a] is deemed to be already cut."

E. *In accord with whose view is this? In accord with the view of R. Meir. As it was taught on Tannaite authority in the Mishnah:* **All handles of utensils that are [too] long and that one is going to cut off — one immerses them up to the place of their proper measure** [the Talmud here gives these attributions: — **the words of R. Meir. And sages say...** ]. **R. Judah says, "[They are not clean] until one will immerse the whole object"** [M. Miq. 10:5 A-C].

F. *You could even maintain [that the rule of our Mishnah accords with] the view of the rabbis [i.e., Judah] that regarding the connections in [a bulk of solid] foods, we treat it as if it was a conglomeration of separate portions that touch one another.*

G. *According to the view of Ulla [C] it makes perfect sense why [the Mishnah] taught that he* **cut it off.** *[For if he did not, then it would not become unclean since this is a case of uncleanness that is concealed from view that does not render unclean (Rashi)].*

H. *But according to the view of Rabina [D] why [does Mishnah state]* **he cut it off?** *Since the former text of the Mishnah taught* **he cut it off,** *the latter text also taught* **he cut it off.**

II.1
A. **And sages say, "[It is in the status of that which has] touched terefah that has been slaughtered"** [M. 4:4 E]. *Does a terefah-animal that has been slaughtered render unclean? Yes. In accord with the view of the father of Samuel. For said the father of Samuel, "A terefah-animal that was slaughtered renders Holy Things unclean"* (b. 123b).

## III.1

A. [They said to R. Meir], "Just as we find in the case of the *terefah* that slaughtering it renders it clean, so the slaughtering of a beast should render the limb clean" [M. 4:4 F]. *It was taught on Tannaite authority:* Said to them R. Meir, "And what rendered this limb [of the offspring] clean from the uncleanness of carrion? The slaughter of its mother. If this is so, then let us permit it for eating." They said to him, "[In some instances, through the act of slaughter,] you can more effectively save what is not [a primary part of] the body than what is [a primary part of] the body. For we learned: [If] one cuts off part of the offspring which is in its womb — it [what is cut off] is permitted to be eaten. [If he cut off] part of the spleen or kidneys [of the beast itself], it is prohibited to be eaten [M. 4:1 D-F]."

B. *What is the implication of what is stated? Said Raba, and some say [said] Kadi,* "There is a lacuna in the text. And this is how you should teach the matter [of our Mishnah]: Said to them R. Meir, 'And what rendered this limb [of the offspring] clean from the uncleanness of carrion? The slaughter of its mother. If this is so, then let us permit it for eating.' They said to him, 'Let the rule of a *terefah*-animal prove the matter. For by slaughtering it you render it clean from the uncleanness of carrion, but you do not render it permitted for eating. [The slaughter therefore should render clean the limb.]'

C. "He said to them, 'No, [your argument is not consistent]. If the slaughter of a *terefah*-animal renders clean something that is part of the body [of the animal], should it render clean the limb, something that is not part of the body?' They said to him, '[In some instances, through the act of slaughter,] you can more effectively save what is not [a primary part of] the body than what is [a primary part of] the body.' For we learned: **[If] one cuts off part of the offspring which is in its womb — it [what is cut off] is permitted to be eaten. [If he cut off] part of the spleen or kidneys [of the beast itself], it is prohibited to be eaten [M. 4:1 D-F]."

D. *There is a Tannaite teaching that was taught also in this regard:* Said to them R. Meir, 'And what rendered this limb [of the offspring] clean from the uncleanness of carrion?' They said to him, 'The slaughter of its mother.' [He responded], 'If this is so, then let us permit it for eating.' They said to him, 'Let the rule of a *terefah*-animal prove the matter. For by slaughtering it you render it clean from the uncleanness of carrion, but you do not render it permitted for eating. [The slaughter therefore should render clean the limb.]'

E.  "He said to them, '[No, your argument is not consistent]. If the slaughter of a *terefah*-animal renders clean it and a limb that is dangling from it, [that is,] something that is part of the body [of the animal], should it render clean the [protruding limb of the] foetus, something that is not part of the body?' They said to him, '[In some instances, through the act of slaughter,] you can more effectively save what is not [a primary part of] the body than what is [a primary part of] the body.' For we learned: **[If] one cuts off part of the offspring which is in its womb — it [what is cut off] is permitted to be eaten. [If he cut off] part of the spleen or kidneys [of the beast itself], it is prohibited to be eaten [M. 4:1 D-F]**."

IV.1
A.  Said R. Simeon b. Laqish, "Just as the dispute [between Meir and sages in M. 4:4 D-E] pertains to the [protruding limbs of] foetuses, so the dispute pertains to [dangling] limbs [of the animal itself]."

B.  And R. Yohanan said, "The dispute [between them] pertains to the [protruding] limb of a foetus. But regarding the [dangling] limb of the animal itself, all agree that as far as the act of slaughter is concerned, it is considered to be detached."

C.  *Said R. Yosé b. R. Haninah, "What is the basis for the view of R. Yohanan? According to sages' view [the limb of a foetus is rendered clean from the uncleanness of carrion by the slaughter of the mother and the dangling limb of the mother is not, because] there is a redress for this one. [The limb of the foetus can be] put back [inside the mother]. But this one [for the dangling limb of the animal], there is no redress of putting it back."*

D.  *They posed an objection:* R. Meir said to them, "No! If the slaughter of a *terefah*-animal renders clean it and a limb that is dangling

Bavli Hullin Chapter Four. Folios 68A-78A

from it, [that is,] something that is part of the body [of the animal], should it render clean the [protruding limb of the] foetus, something that is not part of the body?" [III.1 E, above.]

E. [73b] This makes perfect sense according to the view of R. Simeon b. Laqish [who says in A that Meir and sages dispute with regard to both matters] that he [Meir] is stating matters in accord with their [sages] view. *[Meir would say], according to my view there is no difference [with regard to the law] between the protruding limb of the foetus and the dangling limb of the animal itself. They have the same status.*

F. But according to the view of R. Yohanan [who says in B that Meir and sages do not dispute over the case of a dangling limb of the animal itself] this [statement of R. Meir] leads to a *contradiction.*

G. *But if you wish to state the matter, this is how you should state the matter:* Said R. Simeon b. Laqish, "Just as the dispute [between Meir and sages in M. 4:4 D-E] pertains to the [protruding limbs of] foetuses, so the dispute pertains to [dangling] limbs [of the animal itself]."

H. And R. Yohanan said, "The dispute [between them] pertains to the [protruding] limb of a foetus. But regarding the [dangling] limb of the animal itself, all agree that as far as the act of slaughter is concerned, it is not considered to be detached."

I. *Said R. Yosé b. R. Haninah, "What is the basis for the view of R. Yohanan? According to R. Meir's view this [dangling limb] is part of the body of the animal and this [foetus] is not part of the body of the animal."*

IV.2
A. Said R. Yitzhak bar Joseph, said R. Yohanan, "All agree that as far as an animal that dies is concerned, it is considered to be detached. As far as the act of slaughter [is concerned], it is not considered to be detached."

B. *What situation are we dealing with? If you say [we are dealing] with the protruding limb of the foetus, we have a dispute [between Meir and* sages] over this! Rather it must be we are dealing with the dangling limb of the animal itself. But it was taught on Tannaite authority [explicitly] regarding the case of the animal that died and it was taught on Tannaite authority regarding the animal that was slaughtered.

C. *It was taught on Tannaite authority [explicitly] regarding the case of the animal that died:* "[If in the case of an animal with a dangling limb] the cattle died, the flesh requires preparation [to receive uncleanness]. The limb imparts uncleanness as a limb cut from a living beast, and it does not impart uncleanness as a limb of carrion," the words of R. Meir [M. 9:7 E-G].

D. *It also was taught on Tannaite authority regarding the animal that was slaughtered:* [The dangling limb and flesh in the case of cattle impart food uncleanness (when they are) in their place (attached). And they require preparation (i.e., wetting down, to receive uncleanness).] "[If] the cattle is slaughtered, they are deemed prepared through its blood [to receive uncleanness]," the words of R. Meir. And R. Simeon says, "They are not deemed prepared [to receive uncleanness, since the act of slaughter, not blood, renders meat susceptible, and these are unaffected by slaughter (M. 2:5)]" [M. 9:7 A-D].

E. *If I were to derive matters from this source I might have reasoned what does it mean,* **they are deemed prepared**? [It refers only to dangling] flesh. *But lo, it was taught,* **they [plural] are deemed prepared.** [You could say that] one case refers to flesh that separates [and dangles] from the animal itself, and one case refers to flesh that separates from the dangling limb [of the animal itself].

F. *And why would one case be more definite than the other? It might have made sense to maintain that since [the flesh that hangs from a dangling limb] would render unclean with a stronger form of uncleanness on account of its derivation [i.e., the limb itself], I would say that you should not need preparation [so as to become unclean]. It makes the novel point [that they do need it].*

### IV.3
A. *Said R. Joseph, "Take in hand the ruling of R. Yitzhak bar Joseph because Rabbah bar bar Hannah upholds his view."*

B. *For it was taught on Tannaite authority: "You shall not eat any flesh that is torn by beasts in the field" (Exod. 22:31) — this brings [under the rule] the limb and the flesh that are dangling from a beast, or a wild animal, or a bird that he slaughtered [to tell us] that they [the dangling parts] are prohibited. And said Rabbah bar bar Hannah, said R. Yohanan, [74a] "For these entities, there is a duty only to avoid them."* [This implies that with regard to slaughter they are deemed attached to the animal and in fact permitted.]

C. *R. Joseph sat [in session] before R. Huna and he sat and stated, "Said R. Judah, said Rab, 'If one ate such, he is subject to the punishment of flogging.' Said to him one of the rabbis, 'Pay no attention to him. This is what R. Yitzhak bar Samuel bar Marta said in the name of Rab: If one ate such, he is not subject to the punishment of flogging.'"*

D. *Said to him R. Huna, "On which authority shall we rely?" R. Joseph [angrily] turned away. He [Joseph] said to him, "What is the question? I stated matters regarding an animal that dies that [the dangling flesh] is considered to be detached. They stated matters regarding the act of slaughter, [that dangling flesh] is not considered to be detached."* [See above IV.2 A.]

E. *Said Raba, "What is the basis for this statement by the rabbis, that as far as an animal that dies is concerned, it is considered to be detached. As far as the act of slaughter [is concerned], it is not considered to be detached? As it is written, 'And anything upon which any of them falls when they are dead shall be unclean, [whether it is an article of wood or a garment or a skin or a sack, any vessel that is used for any purpose; it must be put into water, and it shall be unclean until the evening; then it shall be clean] (Lev. 11:32).'"* ["Falls when they are dead" implies that as far as an animal that dies is concerned it is considered to be detached.]

F. *What circumstance does [the verse] exclude? If you say it excludes the case of [creeping things] that are still alive, we derive this from the term, "Of their carcass."* ["And if any part of their carcass falls upon any seed for sowing that is to be sown, it is clean" (Lev. 11:37).] *Rather we may derive from this that as far as an animal that dies is concerned, it is considered to be detached. As far as the act of slaughter [is concerned], it is not considered to be detached.*

G. *Said R. Ada bar Ahavah to Raba, "But lo the verse stated matters with regard to creeping things."* He said to him, "If the matter does not pertain to creeping things that are not subject to the rules of slaughter, then you may teach that it pertains to beasts [that are subject to the rules of slaughter]." *And yet you still need that they [creeping things] be as if they had just died. [That is, if they are] moist they render unclean [other objects]. And if they are dried out, they do not render unclean. Two times it is written, "When they are dead"* (Lev. 11:31, 32). [So you may derive both principles.]

H. Said R. Hisda, "There is a dispute in the case of a limb of a live foetus [that protrudes from the mother]. But in the case of a limb of a dead foetus, all would agree that as far as the act of slaughter goes it is considered to be detached." And Raba said, "Just as there is a dispute in this case, there is a dispute in that case."

V.1
A. **As to a live eight-month's birth, slaughtering it does not render it clean, because the like [of it] is not subject to slaughtering [M. 4:4 N].** *But lo it was taught on Tannaite authority:* [The case of] a live eight-month's birth will decide the matter. For even though the like of it is subject to slaughtering, the act of slaughter does not render it clean. [This teaching implies that the act of slaughter does not render clean a *terefah*-animal either.]

B. Said R. Kahana, "The like of it is subject to slaughtering by virtue of [an instance where one slaughtered] its mother [before it was born]." *And [what is the basis for the view of] our Tanna [in the Mishnah here]? He does not raise a question based on the assumption that the mother is the like [of a live eight-month's birth]. But [the basis for] that Tanna who does raise a question [based on that assumption] what is his basis for the view that slaughtering a* terefah-*animal renders it clean [of the uncleanness of carrion]?*

C. *He may derive this from what R. Judah said in the name of Rab. For said R. Judah, said Rab, and some say that this was taught in a Tannaite teaching: Scripture stated,* "And if from among any animal [of which you may eat dies, he who touches its carcass shall be unclean until the evening" (Lev. 11:39); "From among" implies] some of the animals render unclean and some of the animals do

*Bavli Ḥullin Chapter Four. Folios 68A-78A*

not render unclean. And which is it [that does not render unclean]? It is a *terefah*-animal that was slaughtered.

**V.2**

A. R. Hoshaia *posed a question:* If one inserted his hand into the womb of an animal and slaughtered a live nine-month-old foetus what is the law? *You may pose the question to R. Meir. And you may pose the question to the rabbis [of our Mishnah, D-E].*

B. *You may pose the question to R. Meir — on the point R. Meir stated that an animal born live [from a slaughtered mother] needs to be slaughtered [before one can eat it, was that] only in the circumstance where it emerged [from the womb]? But where it is still in the mother's womb, [might we argue that] slaughtering it will not render it permitted? Or perhaps even in accord with the view of the rabbis [might we argue that] through four organs the Torah allowed it to be rendered valid [i.e., the two of the mother or the two of the foetus]?*

C. Said R. Hananiah, "Come and take note: **Lo, what is born as a terefah from the womb [M. 4:4 L]** — *now if you hold the view [that slaughtering in the womb is effective] we find that it had a moment when it was valid. For if he wanted he could have put in his hand and slaughtered it."*

D. Said to him Raba, "Teach the matter [that the case was where] it was formed as a terefah-*animal from the womb. And we find this in the case of an animal that has five legs."*

I.1 analyzes the reasoning of Mishnah's authorities and invokes Tannaite complements in establishing the premises. II.1 gives a principle in support of one view of Mishnah. III.1 then continues the exposition of the Mishnah-paragraph on its own terms. IV.1 extends the dispute of Mishnah to another related issue and works out the implications. IV.2 continues the foregoing, extending it to a second-level issue and IV.3 provides further inquiry into the theme. V.1 returns to the subject of Mishnah and explores its assumptions. V.2 concludes with a secondary matter.

### 4:5

A. He who slaughters a beast and found in it an eight-months' birth, living or dead, or a dead nine-months' birth,

B. tears it out and removes its blood.

C. "[If] he found a live nine-months' birth, it requires slaughtering.

D. "And it is liable to the rule concerning *it and its young* [Lev. 22:28, which are not to be slaughtered on the same day]," the words of R. Meir.

E. And sages say, "The slaughtering of its mother renders it clean."

F. [74b] R. Simeon Shezuri says, "Even if [it grew to the] age of eight years and ploughs a field — the slaughtering of its mother renders it clean."

G. [If] one cut [into a beast] and found in it a living nine-months' birth, it requires slaughtering,

H. because its mother has not been slaughtered.

### I.1

A. Said R. Eleazar, Said R. Oshaia, "They followed this line [of reasoning discussed in the Mishnah] only with regard to [the need to perform on the offspring an act of] slaughtering."

B. *What does this come to exclude? It excludes [from that which is permitted in the offspring by virtue of the mother] the forbidden fats and the sinew of the hip [of the offspring].*

C. *Which forbidden fats [do we refer to in this statement]? If you say it refers to the fat of the foetus, concerning this there is a dispute. For it was taught on Tannaite authority:* "[The prohibition of the sinew of the hip] applies to the foetus, and its fat is prohibited," the words of R. Meir [M. 7:1D]. R. Judah says, "It does not apply to the foetus. Its fat is permitted" [M. 7:1E-F][T. 7:1 A-B].

D. And said R. Eleazar, said R. Oshaia, "The dispute pertains to a case of a live nine-months' birth. And R. Meir follows in accord with his view [that it must be slaughtered] and R. Judah with his view."

E. *Rather [it refers to] forbidden fats of the sinew. [But in this too] there is a dispute. For it was taught on Tannaite authority:* "As to the sinew of the hip: One digs after it in every place in which it is located and removes it. And he cuts away its fat from its root," the words of R. Meir [cf. M. 7:2B]. R. Judah says, "One removes it [merely] from the cap of the hip bone" [cf. M. 7:2C and T. 7:4 A-B].

F. *Rather if you state the matter [of A], state it as follows:* Said R. Eleazar, said R. Oshaia, "They followed this line [of reasoning discussed in the Mishnah] only with regard to matters pertaining to eating [the animal]." This excludes [from their concern in M.] one who interbreeds with the animal (Lev. 19:19) or plows with it [in a forbidden fashion, Deut. 22:10. These prohibitions pertain to the animal according to both views (Rashi).]

II.1
A. Said R. Simeon b. Laqish, "According to the authority who permits the fats, he would also permit the blood [of this animal]. According to the authority who prohibits the fats, he would also prohibit the blood."

B. And R. Yohanan said, "Even according to the authority who permits the fats, he would prohibit the blood."

C. *R. Yohanan raised an objection to the view of R. Simeon b. Laqish:* [The Mishnah states explicitly in B that one] **tears it out and removes its blood!**

D. Said R. Zira, "[R. Yohanan intended in his statement] to say that [it is prohibited, but that he who eats the blood of this animal] is not subject to the punishment of extirpation."

E. *In accord with which authority do we state this matter? If you wish to say it is in accord with the view of R. Judah, this could only be with regard to the blood that flows [from the animal]. As it was taught on Tannaite authority:* **The blood that flows [out after the initial lifeblood spurts out] is subject only to a warning [but there is no penalty for eating it]. R. Judah says, "[One who eats it] is subject to the penalty of extirpation"** [T. Ker. 2:19 B-C].

F. R. Pappa, the son of R. Sala the pious interpreted before R. Pappa, "R. Judah interprets [that it could have stated] 'blood' but instead stated, '[Moreover you shall eat] no blood whatever, [whether of fowl or of animal, in any of your dwellings]' (Lev. 7:26). [From this you may derive that] *in any instance where one is liable [to the punishment of extirpation] for the life-blood, he is liable for the blood that flows. And in any instance where one is not liable for the life-blood [e.g., for the foetus], he is not liable for the blood that flows.*

**III.1**

A. *They raised a question:* What is the rule [for whether one may redeem a first-born ass] with a live birth [of a lamb] from a slaughtered mother? *According to the view of R. Meir you should have no question. Because since he says that you must slaughter it, it is a perfectly good lamb. Where will you have a question? In accord with the view of the rabbis who said that the act of slaughter for the mother renders it clean.*

B. *What does it mean that the act of slaughter for the mother renders it clean? Is it like meat in a basket [and is not called a lamb anymore]? Or perhaps because it runs back and forth, we may call it a lamb [and redeem with it a first born ass]?*

C. Mar Zutra said, "They do not redeem [with it]." And R. Ashi said, "They do redeem [with it]."

D. Said R. Ashi to Mar Zutra, "What is your view? You derived [from the common use in the verses of the word] 'lamb' for this matter and for the matter of the paschal lamb." [The verses are: "Every firstling of an ass you shall redeem with a **lamb**, or if you will not redeem it you shall break its neck. Every first-born of man among your sons you shall redeem" (Exod. 13:13); "Your **lamb** shall be without blemish, a male a year old; you shall take it from the sheep or from the goats" (Exod. 12:5).]

E. But if you accept this then you should say, just as there [for the paschal lamb] you must have a male, without blemish and a year old, so here too [with regard to the redemption of the firstling] you must have a male, without blemish, a year old. It says, "You shall redeem." "You shall redeem" includes [other animals].

Bavli Hullin Chapter Four. Folios 68A-78A

F. If [it writes] "You shall redeem" [and] "You shall redeem" includes [other animals], then why not even all other kinds of animals [even the live birth from the slaughtered mother]? [No. You could not go that far. Because] if so, what good would it do to derive anything [from the common use in the verses of the word] 'lamb'.

**IV.1**

A. *They raised a question:* What is the law with regard to counting for this [live birth from a slaughtered mother] first- and second-remove uncleanness.

B. R. Yohanan said, "They count for it first- and second-remove uncleanness." And R. Simeon b. Laqish said, "They do not count for it first- and second-remove uncleanness." It is considered to be analogous to a nut that is enclosed in its shell.

C. *R. Simeon b. Laqish posed a question to R. Yohanan:* "**The meat [of the offspring] is in the status of that which has touched carrion [namely, the hoof, which, located outside the womb, is unaffected by the slaughter of the mother],**" **the words of R. Meir. And sages say, "[It is in the status of that which has] touched** *terefah* **that has been slaughtered**" [M. 4:4]. It makes perfect sense according to my view because I reasoned that they are like one body. That is why the foetus is made susceptible to uncleanness by virtue of the blood of the mother [that comes forth during the act of slaughter]. But according to your view, with what [liquid] does it become susceptible to uncleanness?

D. He [Yohanan] said to him, "With the act of slaughter itself and in accord with the view of R. Simeon [cf. M. 2:5 E]."

E. *R. Yohanan posed a question to R. Simeon b. Laqish:* If it [the live birth from a slaughtered mother] passed through a river, it became susceptible to uncleanness [by virtue of the water]. If it went to a cemetery, it became unclean [by virtue of passing over graves]. *This makes perfect sense according to my view. For I maintain that they are two separate bodies. Because of this you say if it was rendered susceptible, then yes [it can become unclean]. But if it was not rendered susceptible, then no [it cannot become unclean]. But according to your view that they [mother and foetus] are like one body, lo [the* foetus] is rendered susceptible by the blood of the mother [that comes forth during the act of slaughter].

F. [75a] [We can avoid this objection by stipulating that the case here is one of] an act of slaughter that is dry [i.e., no blood spurts on the animal] and not in accord with the view of R. Simeon [M. 2:5 E].

G. *Who is the Tannaite authority behind the rule [in E]:* If it [the live birth from a slaughtered mother] passed through a river, it became susceptible to uncleanness [by virtue of the water]. If it went to a cemetery, it became unclean [by virtue of passing over graves]? Said R. Yohanan, "It is R. Yosé the Galilean."

H. *As it was taught on Tannaite authority:* R. Simeon b. Eleazar says in the name of R. Yosé the Galilean, "It is susceptible to uncleanness as food and imparts uncleanness as food and requires preparation [to be susceptible to uncleanness]." Rabbi (the Talmud's version: sages) says, "It does not impart uncleanness as food, because it is alive, and that which is alive does not impart the uncleanness as food" [T. 4:6 B-C].

I. And R. Yohanan holds in accord with his view elsewhere. For said R. Yohanan, "R. Yosé the Galilean and the House of Shammai said the same thing." *R. Yosé the Galilean, as we just stated. The House of Shammai, as it was taught in the Mishnah on Tannaite authority:* Fish — from what point do they receive uncleanness? The House of Shammai say, "When they are caught." And the House of Hillel say, "When they die." R. Aqiba says, "If they could not live" [M. Uqsin 3:8 A-D].

J. *What [case] between them [do they dispute]?* Said R. Yohanan, "The dispute between them is [over the case of a fish that is] making fluttering motions [even though it is dead]."

K. R. Hisda posed a question: If tokens [of defects] that render an animal *terefah* appeared in a fish, what is the law? *This will be a question according to the authority who holds the view that a terefah is considered to be alive and according to the authority who holds the view that a* terefah *is not considered to be alive* [cf. above, b. 42a, M. 3:1 I.1 C-H].

L. *This will be a question according to the authority who holds the view that a* terefah *is considered to be alive [as follows]. A beast has a lot of life [so even when it is* terefah *it still is considered alive]. But a fish does not have a lot of life [so if it is* terefah*] it is not [considered alive]. Or perhaps even according to the authority who holds the view that a* terefah *is not considered to be alive, this concern applies only to a beast that falls into the category of [a living thing that requires] slaughtering. But [in the case of] a fish that does not fall into the category of [a living thing that requires] slaughtering, it would make sense to say that it is not [considered to be alive]. The question stands unresolved.* (Rashi has a variant reading.)

### IV.2

A. If it aborted the foetus [what is the status of the fat of the aborted foetus]? R. Yohanan said, "Its fat has the same status of that of the beast [its mother]." And R. Simeon b. Laqish said, "Its fat has the same status of that of a wild animal."

B. R. Yohanan said, "Its fat has the same status of that of the beast [its mother]." [Coming out of the womb of the mother and coming into] *the air causes it to [take on the status of a beast].* And R. Simeon b. Laqish said, "Its fat has the same status of that of a wild animal." [Coming to complete term] *in [the expected number of] months causes it to [take on the status of a beast. And this one did not come to term].*

C. *There are those who say that in any case where it did not come to term in the expected number of months of gestation, it is as if nothing at all occurred. [The animal is deemed neither a beast nor a wild animal.]*

D. *[In accord with this view] they dispute in a case where he inserted his hand into the womb of the beast and tore off forbidden fat of a live nine-month-old foetus and ate it.* R. Yohanan [would have] said, "Its fat has the same status as that of a beast. [Coming to complete term] in months *causes* it to [take on the status of a beast. And this one did come to term.]" And R. Simeon b. Laqish [would have] said, "Its fat has the same status as that of a wild animal. [Coming to complete term] in months and [coming out of the womb of the mother] into the *air cause* it to [take on the status of a beast. And this one did not come out.]"

E. *R. Yohanan [could have] raised an objection to the view of R. Simeon b. Laqish, "In the same manner that, 'the two kidneys with the fat that is on them' stated in connection with the guilt-offering [which must be a male] rules out from the category that [fat] of a foetus. So too in any instance it rules out from the category that of a foetus." [The verses are: "And all its fat shall be offered, the fat tail, the fat that covers the entrails, the two kidneys with the fat that is on them at the loins, and the appendage of the liver which he shall take away with the kidneys" (Lev. 7:3-4).]*

F. *Now it makes perfect sense in accord with my view why we need a verse to exclude [the fat]. But according to your view, why do we need a verse [to exclude it]? He [would have] said to him, "The basis for my view [to begin with] is also this verse."*

G. *And there are those that say [there is an alternative version of this matter]. R. Simeon b. Laqish [could have] raised an objection to the view of R. Yohanan, "In the same manner that, 'the two kidneys with the fat that is on them' stated in connection with the guilt-offering [which must be a male] rules out from the category that [fat] of a foetus. So too in any instance it rules out from the category that of a foetus."*

H. *Now it makes perfect sense in accord with my view why the Torah excluded [the fat]. But according to your view, let it be brought near [on the altar]! He [would have] said to him, "It is on account of it being [analogous to a substance that] is lacking in that it did not reach its prescribed term. [They must wait for seven days before offering it.]"*

V.1
A. Said R. Ammi, "He who slaughters a *terefah*-animal and found in it a live nine-months' birth, in accord with the view of the one who prohibits [in the same case, but where the mother is not a *terefah*-animal, i.e., Meir in M. 4:5 D], he should permit [the slaughter and consumption of the offspring in this case, since the status of the mother has no bearing on the offspring]. And in accord with the view of the one who permits [in the same case, but where the mother is not a *terefah*-animal, i.e., sages in M. 4:5 E], he should prohibit [the slaughter and consumption of the offspring, since the status of the mother is applicable to the offspring]."

B. Raba said, "In accord with the view of the one who permits [in the same case, but where the mother is not a *terefah*-animal, i.e., sages in M. 4:5 E], he also should permit [the slaughter and consumption of the offspring]. *Through four organs the Torah rendered [the offspring] valid.*" [That is, either through the proper slaughter of the mother or through the proper slaughter of the offspring itself.]

C. Said R. Hisda, "He who slaughters a *terefah*-animal and found in it a live nine-months' birth, [75b] it must be slaughtered and it is liable to the priestly gifts of the shoulder, the cheeks and the maw (Deut. 18:3). But it if dies, it is clean of imparting uncleanness through carriage [i.e., that conveyed to one who carries it]."

D. Said to him Raba, "It must be slaughtered — *in accord with whose view is this?* In accord with the view of R. Meir [M. 4:5 C-D]. But it if dies, it is clean of imparting uncleanness through carriage — *in accord with whose view is this?* In accord with the view of the rabbis.

E. "*And according to your logic, [consider the same objection to] that which R. Hiyya taught [in Tosefta on Tannaite authority]*: **He who slaughters a *terefah*-animal and found in it a live nine-month-old birth — it requires slaughtering and is liable for [priestly] gifts. And if it died, it is clean of imparting uncleanness through carriage, because the slaughter of its dam renders it clean [T. 4:8 A-B].**

F. "It must be slaughtered — *in accord with whose view is this?* In accord with the view of R. Meir [M. 4:5 C-D]. But it if dies, it is clean of imparting uncleanness through carriage — *in accord with whose view is this?* In accord with the view of the rabbis.

G. "Lo, *this is not a contradiction. R. Hiyya stated matters in the case where they found it had already died. But according to your reasoning [R. Hisda], it should be a contradiction.*"

H. *He [Hisda] said to him, "According to my reasoning it also is not contradiction. Through four organs the Torah rendered [the offspring]* valid." [That is, either through the proper slaughter of the mother or through the proper slaughter of the offspring itself.]

I. *When R. Zira departed [to Israel] he found R. Assi sitting and stating this teaching (Rashi: Assi found Zira). He said to him, "Well put! And so too did R. Yohanan state the matter."* [He said,] *"May we derive that R. Simeon b. Laqish disputed him?"*

J. [We do not know because] *he [Simeon b. Laqish] hesitated and was silent [at the time Yohanan stated his view]. And there is a version that he was drinking at the time and was silent.*

VI.1
A. **R. Simeon Shezuri says, "Even if [it grew to the] age of eight years and ploughs a field — the slaughtering of its mother renders it clean" [M. 4:5 F].** *This is the same as the view of the first Tanna.*

B. Said R. Kahana, "[The case of] where it walked away on the ground is a matter of dispute between them [i.e., between the first Tanna and Simeon]." [Sages would require slaughter in that instance on the authority of the rabbis.]

C. *Said R. Mesharshayya, "According to the view of those who say we take into account the seed of the father [in determining the status of the progeny], if an offspring that was born alive after the slaughter of the mother mates with a normal cow, there is no redress for the offspring."*

D. Said Abayye, "All would agree that an animal with an uncloven hoof that was an offspring that was born alive after the slaughter of the mother is permitted. What is the basis for this view? People can identify anything that is unusual."

E. *Another version:* Said Abayye, "All would agree that an animal with an uncloven hoof, that was an offspring of a cow with an uncloven hoof, that was born alive [after the slaughter of the mother] is permitted. What is the basis for this view? People can identify anything that is in two ways unusual."

Bavli Hullin Chapter Four. Folios 68A-78A

VI.2

A. Said Ziri, said R. Haninah, "The law follows in accord with R. Simeon b. Shezuri." And so R. Simeon b. Shezuri would permit its offspring and the offspring of that offspring down through all the generations of offspring.

B. R. Yohanan said, "It [an offspring that was born alive after the slaughter of the mother] is permitted. Its offspring is prohibited."

C. *Ada bar Habo had an offspring that was born alive after the slaughter of the mother that a wolf attacked. He came before R. Ashi [for a ruling]. He said to him, "Go and slaughter it." He said to him, "Lo said Ziri, said R. Hanina, 'The law follows in accord with R. Simeon b. Shezuri.' And so R. Simeon b. Shezuri would permit its offspring and the offspring of that offspring down through all the generations of offspring. And even R. Yohanan stated matters only with regard to its [subsequent] offspring. But regarding it [the original offspring] he did not dispute [that it was permitted without any act of slaughter]."*

D. *He said to him, "R. Yohanan [held his own view but he] stated matters in accord with the words of R. Simeon Shezuri."*

E. But lo, said Rabin bar Hanina, said Ulla, said R. Hanina, "The law follows in accord with the view of R. Simeon Shezuri." And not only that but in every place in our Mishnah that R. Simeon Shezuri taught, the law follows in accord with his view.

F. *He said to him, "I reason in accord with this that was stated by R. Jonathan: The laws follows in accord with R. Simeon Shezuri with regard to an endangered person and the tithe of heave-offering of demai."*

G. An endangered person — *as it was taught in the Mishnah on Tannaite authority:* **At first they would rule: He who goes forth in fetters and stated, "Write a writ of divorce for my wife" — lo, they are to write and deliver [the writ of divorce to his wife]. They reverted to rule: [That is the rule] even in the case of one who went out on a voyage or set forth with a caravan. R. Simeon Shezuri says, "Even in the case of one who is on the point of death"** [M. Tebul Yom 4:5 C-E].

H. Tithe of heave-offering of *demai* — *as it was taught in the Mishnah on Tannaite authority:* [Regarding heave-offering of the tithe of *demai* that returned to its place [that fell back into the now-tithed *demai*-produce from which it was originally separated, thus rendering the entire mixture prohibited to a non-priest] — R. Simeon of Sezur says, "Even on a weekday he inquires of him [the vendor] and eats at his word" [M. Demai 4:1 K-M].

I-II explore various extensions of the rules of Mishnah. III-IV inquire into intersecting rules, based on the principles of the rule of Mishnah, cite complementary Tannaite rules and work through the problem in different ways. V.1 continues the inquiry into the premises of Mishnah. VI.1 reverts to the text and extends the rule of Mishnah. VI.2 further clarifies the position of Simeon b. Shezuri.

### 4:6 [76a]

A. A beast, the [hind] legs of which are cut off below the knee, is valid.
B. [If they are cut off] above the knee, it is invalid.
C. And so [if] the juncture of the thigh sinews was removed [it is invalid].
D. [If] the bone broke [but was not cut off], if most of the meat remains, slaughtering it renders it [the broken leg] clean.
E. And if not, slaughtering it does not render it clean [and the broken leg cannot be eaten, but the rest of the beast is valid].

### I.1

A. Said R. Judah, said Rab, said R. Hiyya, "Below, [means] below the knee. Above, [means] above the knee. About which [part of the leg beneath the] joint did they speak? The [part of the leg beneath the] joint that is sold with the head [as waste]." [See Cashdan, p. 419, for a discussion of the anatomical reference.]

B. Ulla said [to] R. Oshaia, "[It is the joint] whose location is recognizable in a camel."

C. Said Ulla to R. Judah, "It makes perfect sense, in accord with my view, for I maintain that, '[It is the joint] whose location is recognizable in a camel,' that it is taught [in M. 4:6 C], **And so**

Bavli Ḥullin Chapter Four. Folios 68A-78A

[if] the juncture of the thigh sinews was removed [it is invalid]. But in accord with your view, what is the purpose of [teaching], **And so [if] the juncture of the thigh sinews was removed [it is invalid]?**"

D. He said to him, "[We need to specify this for the cases where] the bone [was removed] but not the juncture of the thigh sinews, or where the juncture of the thigh sinews [was removed] but not the bone."

E. [Ulla replied,] "*But lo it was taught* [in M.], **cut off.**" *He [Judah] was silent. After he [Ulla] departed, he [Judah] said, "On what basis did I not say to him, 'Below, [means] below the knee. Above, [means] above the juncture of the thigh sinews'? He further said, 'Did I not say [something] to him? And he said to me, It was taught,* **cut off***. Here too [he would say to me], It was taught [in B of M.],* **[If they are cut off] above the knee, [it is invalid].**'"

F. *R. Pappa taught [a version of A] as follows:* Said R. Judah, said Rab, said R. Hiyya, "Below, [means] below the knee and the juncture of the thigh sinews. Above, [means] above the knee and the thigh sinews. And so too if the juncture of the thigh sinews was removed."

G. And [the identification of] the knee itself is in accord with Ulla in the name of R. Oshaia [B].

H. *But is there such a case where if he cuts it off [on the leg] higher, it lives. But if he cuts it off lower, it dies?*

I. Said R. Ashi, "Can you compare [defects that render animals] *terefot* to one another? We do not say concerning [defects that render animals] *terefot* that this one resembles that one. For lo you may cut from this place [on the animal] and it will die. You may cut from here [an identical amount in another place on the animal] and it will live [b. 48b, XIV.1 I]."

II.1
A. *And this is the juncture of the thigh sinews.* [Said] Rabbah, said R. Ashi, "Beyond the point of adhesion [of the sinews to the bone up to the place the sinews separate (Rashi)]." [Said] Rabbah bar R. Huna, said

R. Ashi, "Within the point of adhesion [of the sinews to the bone up to the joint]." [Said] Raba the son of Rabbah bar R. Huna, said R. Assi, "That part above the heel."

B. *A certain rabbi was sitting before R. Abba and he sat and stated [that the juncture of the thigh sinews included the sinews on] the heel itself. Said to him R. Abba, "Pay him no heed! [He is too strict (Rashi).] This is what R. Judah said, 'Where the butchers separate them [the sinews from the bone, i.e., above the heel].'" And likewise: [Said] Rabbah the son of Rabbah bar R. Huna, said R. Assi.*

C. Said R. Judah, said Samuel, "The juncture of the thigh sinews that they spoke of is the place where the sinews join up to what point?" *Said a certain rabbi to him, and R. Jacob was his name, "When I was in the house of R. Judah he said to us, 'Hear from me a matter that I heard from a great man. And who was this? Samuel. The juncture of the thigh sinews that they spoke of is the place where the sinews join. And from the point they join up to the place that they spread apart.'"*

D. *And how far is this?* Said Abayye, "Four fingers in an ox." *And in a small animal what is the measure?* Said Abayye, "Where they protrude, that is the juncture of the thigh sinews. Where they recede, that is not the juncture of the thigh sinews. Where they are hard, that is the juncture of the thigh sinews. Where they are soft, that is not the juncture of the thigh sinews. Where they are thick, that is the juncture of the thigh sinews. Where they are thin, that is not the juncture of the thigh sinews. Where they are white, that is the juncture of the thigh sinews. Where they are not white, that is not the juncture of the thigh sinews."

E. [76b] Mar bar R. Ashi said, "Wherever they are clear, even if they are not white [that is the juncture of the thigh sinews]."

F. Said Amemar in the name of R. Zebid, "[The juncture of the thigh sinews consists of] three tendons. One is thick and two are thin. If the thick one is severed, the major part of the thigh structure is gone. If the thin ones are severed, the majority of the thigh tendons are gone. [In either case it is terefah.]"

G. *Mar bar R. Ashi taught this matter as a lenient rule: If the thick one is severed, lo there is still a majority [of the tendons intact]. If the thin ones are severed, lo there is still the major part [of the thigh structure intact]. [In either case it is valid.]*

**II.2**
A. *In fowl — [the juncture of the thigh sinews consists of] sixteen tendons. If one of them is severed, it is* terefah.

B. *Said Mar bar R. Ashi, "I was attending my father and they brought before him a bird [for a ruling]. And he inspected it and found fifteen tendons. One of them was different from the rest of them. He split it open and found that it was two [tendons cleaving together]."*

**II.3**
A. Said R. Judah, said Rab, "The juncture of the thigh sinews about which they spoke [render the animal terefah if they sever] the major part of them. What does 'the major part' mean? The major part of one of them. *When I spoke of these matters before Samuel he said to me, "What is the case? There are three [tendons]. If one is severed completely, lo, there are two. The basis for this reasoning is that there are two [remaining]. Lo, if there are not two remaining, then no [it would not be valid]."*

B. *And this is in dispute with the view of Rabbinai. For said Rabbinai, said Samuel, "The juncture of the thigh sinews — even if there remained intact only as much as a [thickness of a] wool strand, it is valid."*

C. *And there is another version: What does 'the major part' mean? The major part of each one of them. When I spoke of these matters before Samuel, he said to me, "What is the case? There are three [tendons]. [Even if the major part of each is severed] lo there is one third of each one [intact]."*

D. *And this supports the view of Rabbinai. For said Rabbinai, said Samuel,* "The juncture of the thigh sinews — even if there remained intact only as much as a [thickness of a] wool strand, it is valid."

III.1
A. **[If] the bone broke [but was not cut off], if most of the meat remains, slaughtering it renders it [the broken leg] clean [M. 4:6 D].** Said Rab, "[If it broke] above the knee, if most of the flesh is intact, both [the limb and the animal] are permitted. And if not, both are prohibited. [If it broke] below the knee, if most of the flesh is intact, both are permitted. And if not, the limb is prohibited, but the [rest of the] animal is permitted."

B. And Samuel said, "[If it broke] whether above or below [the knee], if most of the flesh is intact, both are permitted. And if not, the limb is prohibited, but the [rest of the] animal is permitted."

C. R. Nahman raised a contradiction to the view of Samuel: They will say, "Its limb is in the garbage and yet it is permitted!"

D. Said R. Aha bar R. Huna to R. Nahman, "In accord with the view of Rab they may also say, 'Its limb is in the garbage and yet it is permitted!'"

E. He said to him, "Here is what you should say, 'Its vital limb is in the garbage and yet it is permitted!'"

F. *They sent from there [Israel]: The law follows in accord with the view of Rab. Subsequently they sent that it was in accord with the view of Samuel. Subsequently they sent that it was in accord with the view of Rab and that the limb itself renders unclean through carriage.*

G. *R. Hisda posed an objection [to this last statement]:* [This argument was advanced in the course of a discussion above,] 'No, [your argument is not consistent]. If the slaughter of a *terefah*-animal renders clean it and a limb that is dangling from it, [that is,] something that is part of the body [of the animal], should it render clean the [protruding limb of the] foetus, something that is not part of the body' [b. 73a, M. 4:4, III.1 E]? [Based on this we should conclude that the dangling limb should not render unclean through carriage.]

H. *Said to him Rabbah, "Why go so far in search of questions? You may pose an objection from the rule of the Mishnah:* **'[If] the cattle is**

Bavli Hullin Chapter Four. Folios 68A-78A

slaughtered, they are deemed prepared through its blood [to receive uncleanness],' the words of R. Meir. And R. Simeon says, 'They are not deemed prepared [to receive uncleanness, since the act of slaughter, not blood, renders meat susceptible, and these are unaffected by slaughter (M. 2:5)]' [M. 9:7 C-D]."

I. He said to him, "You could rebut this objection based on the Mishnah as it was rebutted." [See above, b. 73b, M. 4:4, IV.2.]

J. When R. Zira departed [for Israel] he found R. Jeremiah sitting and stating this tradition [of Rab in A]. He said to him, "Very well! So too did Arioch proclaim in Babylonia!"

K. Who is Arioch? Samuel. But lo, he disputed [the view of Rab]! Samuel retracted his view so as to accord with that of Rab.

**IV.1**
A. *Our rabbis taught on Tannaite authority:* If the bone was broken and it extrudes [through the skin], if the hide and the flesh cover the major part of it, it is permitted. And if not, it is prohibited.

B. And how much is the major part? *When R. Dimi came, [he brought this teaching:] said R. Yohanan, "The major part in thickness." And some say concerning it, "The major part of its circumference." Said R. Pappa, "Therefore they require the major part of its thickness and the major part of its circumference."*

C. Said Ulla, said R. Yohanan, "The hide, lo it is the same as the flesh." Said R. Nahman to Ulla, "But why does the master not say that the hide combines together with the flesh? For lo, it was taught [in A], 'The hide and the flesh.'" He [Ulla] said to him, "We taught the version, 'The hide or the flesh.'"

D. Another version: [Said Ulla], said R. Yohanan, "The hide, lo it combines together with the flesh." Said R. Nahman to Ulla, "But why does the master not say that we deem that the hide completes [the minimum prescribed measure] together with the flesh in order to render a strict ruling?"

E. He [Ulla] said to him, "I know of a case of a young pigeon that was in the house of R. Yitzhak [that had a bone extruding through the skin and hide and flesh covered it] and it was a case where the hide combined with the flesh [to make the minimum measure]. And they brought it before R. Yohanan [for a ruling]. And he declared it valid."

F. He [Nahman] said to him, "You stated that it was a young pigeon. A [case of a] young pigeon that is tender is a different circumstance."

G. [A bird that had a bone extruding through the skin and flesh covered it together with] these tender sinews. They brought it before Rabbah [=Raba] [for a ruling]. Said Rabbah [=Raba], "What should we suspect? First of all, R. Yohanan said that [one who eats] sinews that are going to become hard [from the Paschal lamb of a certain fellowship] [77a] are counted [as having been part of the group] of that Paschal lamb on account of [eating] it. [That implies that the sinews are deemed to be flesh, cf. b. Pes 84a.]

H. And furthermore [we have a principle that] the Torah had mercy on the money of an Israelite [b. 49b].

I. Said R. Pappa to Rabbah [=Raba], "[We must take into account the view of] R. Simeon b. Laqish [who disputes the view of R. Yohanan in b. Pes. 84a and holds that the sinews are not deemed to be flesh]. And [we are dealing here with] a prohibition [of an animal that is terefah] that is based on the authority of the Torah. And you say, 'What should we suspect?'"

J. He [Raba] was silent. And why was he silent? Lo, did Raba not say that the law follows in accord with the view of R. Simeon b. Laqish in these three [specified cases, not including ours, per b. Yeb. 36a]?

K. This one is different because R. Yohanan retracted his view regarding the matter in deference to the view of R. Simeon b. Laqish. For he said to him, "Stop annoying me. I teach this as a personal view."

IV.2
A. There was [a case of a bird] whose bone was broken and extruded outside the skin. A fragment [of the bone] was taken away from it. They brought it before Abayye [for a ruling]. He delayed [ruling on the matter] for three festivals. Said to him R. Ada bar Matna, "Go before Raba the son of R. Joseph bar Hama [for a ruling] because he is as sharp as a tack [and will find a way to permit the use of the bird]."

B. He said, "Consider that it was taught on Tannaite authority [in IV.1 A], 'If the bone was broken and it extrudes [through the skin].' What difference does it make to me if [a piece] fell away or if it is still there?"

C. Said Rabina to Raba, "What is the law in the case of [flesh around an extruding bone] that must be gathered up [to constitute the minimum needed to cover it]? What is the law in the case of [flesh around an extruding bone] that was shredded? What is the law in the case of [flesh around an extruding bone] that was putrefied?"

D. What is the definition of [flesh around an extruding bone] that was putrefied? Any instance [of non-vital tissue] that the physician would scrape away [to help restore the living flesh][M. 3:1, XXVII.3 D, b. 53b].

E. They posed to them a question: What is the law in the case of [flesh around an extruding bone] that was pierced? What is the law if it was peeled away [from the bone]? What is the law if it was slit? What is the law if the inner third [layer of the flesh] was removed?

F. Come and take note: For said Ulla, said R. Yohanan, "The hide, lo it is the same as the flesh [IV.1 C]." [Certainly it should be sufficient in these cases where flesh remains in addition to the skin.] Perhaps [this is not a fair assumption] because the bone holds on to its own [skin but not on to the flesh in these cases].

G. Said R. Ashi, "When I was in the house of R. Pappi he posed a question to us, 'What is the law if it [flesh] was sliced off like a ring [around a bone]?' And we answered him by making reference to this. For said R. Judah, said Rab, 'This matter I asked of the sages and the physicians and they said [there is a ruling that] they may cut around with a bone [scalpel] and it will form a scab and heal up. But if one cuts with an iron [scalpel] it will inflame the flesh and infect the wound.'"

H. Said R. Pappa, "It is the case that the bone causes its own [skin to adhere and this is the beginning of healing through the formation of a scab]."

I.1 begins with an exercise in Mishnah-criticism that clarifies the correct reading and meaning before us. II.1 further clarifies Mishnah's terms and rules. II.2-3 extend the rule of Mishnah and defines it. III.1 analyzes a dispute based on the rule of Mishnah. IV.1 cites a Tannaite complement to M and clarifies its meaning. Finally, IV.2 adds cases related to the foregoing and examines their premises.

### 4:7

A. He who slaughters the beast and found in it an afterbirth —
B. [slaughtering the mother renders it clean, so] a robust person will eat it.
C. But it is subject to neither the uncleanness of foods nor [if the beast dies] the uncleanness of carrion.
D. [If] he gave thought to it [for use as food], it imparts the uncleanness of foods [M. Uqsin 3:1], but not the uncleanness of carrion.
E. An afterbirth, part of which emerged, is prohibited to be eaten.
F. It is a token of [the birth of] an offspring in a woman, and the token of [the birth of] an offspring in a beast.
G. A beast which, producing its first born, dropped an afterbirth —
H. one should throw it to the dogs.
I. And in the case of Holy Things, it is to be buried.
J. They do not bury it at the crossroads.
K. And they do not hang it on a tree,
L. because of [the prohibition against imitating] the ways of the Amorites.

I.1
A. *What is the source of these assertions? As it was taught by our rabbis on Tannaite authority:* "Every animal [that parts the hoof and has the hoof cloven in two, and chews the cud, among the animals], it you may eat" (Deut. 14:6) — this [phrasing of the verse has extraneous words and thereby] includes in the rule the afterbirth. You might infer that even if part of it [the foetus] came out [it, the afterbirth, should be permitted as it is a different entity]. It comes to teach [to the contrary by the addition of the word], "it [you may eat]." "It [you may eat]" and not its afterbirth.

B. *Consider* [that this is stated in an explicit rule]: There is only an afterbirth where there is a foetus [i.e., they have the same status,

b. B.Q. 11a]. *Why then do I need to infer the rule from a verse? The verse is merely a secondary support.*

II.1
A. **But it is subject to neither the uncleanness of foods nor [if the beast dies] the uncleanness of carrion [M. 4:7 C].** *R. Yitzhak bar Nappaha posed a question: What is the law regarding the hide of an ass that was boiled [until it softened]? To which [law is he referring]? If [the question refers] to the law of rendering foods unclean, this was taught on Tannaite authority.* **[77b]** *If [the question refers] to the law of rendering unclean as carrion, this was taught on Tannaite authority.*

B. *With regard to rendering foods unclean — as it was taught on Tannaite authority:* The hide and the afterbirth [of unclean animals] do not render foods unclean. Hide that was boiled and an afterbirth that he intended [to eat from these animals] do render foods unclean [b. Erub. 28b].

C. *With regard to the law of [these parts of the animal] rendering unclean as carrion, this also was taught on Tannaite authority:* "[And if any animal of which you may eat dies, he who touches] its carcass [shall be unclean until the evening]" (Lev. 11:39) — and not [one who touches] its hide, and not its sinews, and not its horns, and not its hooves.

D. And said Rabbah bar bar Hannah, "It was necessary to teach this only [to exclude these parts of the animal from the law of the uncleanness of carrion] where he stewed them in a pot [to make them edible]."

E. It is consistent to conclude that [the question was posed in A in reference to] the law of rendering foods unclean. And [even though the matter is stated explicitly] the case of the hide of an ass *is different* [from the ordinary case of hides] because it is disgusting.

III.1
A. **An afterbirth, part of which emerged, is prohibited to be eaten [M. 4:7 E].** Said R. Eleazar, "They taught this only in the case where there is no foetus with it [i.e., with that part that remains in the womb of the mother]. But where there is a foetus with it,

they do not suspect that there is another foetus [and that it came out with the first part of the afterbirth]."

B. And R. Yohanan said, "Whether there is not or is a foetus with it, we do suspect that there is another foetus."

C. *Is this accurate? For lo, said R. Jeremiah, "R. Eleazar stated a strict rule."*

D. *But if you wish to state the matter [correctly], here is how you should state the matter:* Said R. Eleazar, "They taught this only in the case where it was not attached to the foetus. But where it was attached to the foetus, they do not suspect that there is another foetus."

E. And R. Yohanan said, "For our purposes we rule [in this manner] only where there is an afterbirth without a foetus. But where there is a foetus with it, whether it is attached to the foetus or it is not attached to the foetus, we do not suspect that there is another foetus."

F. *And this is consistent with what R. Jeremiah said, "R. Eleazar stated a strict rule."*

G. *There is a Tannaite teaching in accord with the view of R. Eleazar:* One who aborts [a foetus that looks like] a kind of beast, or wild beast, or fowl, and the afterbirth is [aborted] with it — as long as it is attached to [the foetus], we do not suspect that there is another foetus. If it was not attached to the [foetus], lo I apply to this case the strict rule of [assuming that there were] two foetuses. [One foetus may have been a female and she would have to observe fourteen days of uncleanness on account of that abortion.] For I say, perhaps the [other] foetus of that afterbirth dissolved. Or perhaps the afterbirth of [this animal-like] foetus dissolved.

IV.1
A. **A beast which, producing its first born, dropped an afterbirth — one should throw it to the dogs [M. 4:7 G-H].** *What is the basis for this rule?* Said R. Iqa the son of R. Ammi, "[We have a principle:] The majority of animals give birth to a firstling that is

holy. And a minority of animals give birth to a firstling that is not holy." *And what is that [animal that is not holy]?* [A sheep or a goat that gave birth to] a similar [species of animal. See M. Bekh. 2:5.]

B. And all those that give birth, give birth half the time to males and half the time to females. *You may add the minority of cases of [a sheep or a goat that give birth to] a similar [species] to the half that are [normally born] female. And the chances of a [normal] male birth will then be in the minority.* [This is the logical basis for our rule in the Mishnah.]

V.1

A. **And in the case of Holy Things, it is to be buried [M. 4:7 I].** *What is the basis for this rule? The majority of offspring of holy animals are holy.*

VI.1

A. **They do not bury it at the crossroads [M. 4:7 J].** Abayye and Raba both said, "Anything that is done to heal, may not classified as a [prohibited] practice of the Amorites. [Anything] that is not done to heal, may be classified as a [prohibited] practice of the Amorites."

B. *But lo it was taught on Tannaite authority:* A tree that drops all its fruits off may be tinted red or have stones heaped on it.

C. *Now it makes perfect sense to say that one may heap on it stones* **[78a]** *because this will weaken its [excessive] power [and heal it of its dysfunction]. But why should they permit it to be tinted red? [This appears to be a magical practice.] In order that people will see it and seek mercy for it [through prayer].*

D. *As was taught on Tannaite authority:* "[The leper who has the disease shall wear torn clothes and let the hair of his head hang loose, and he shall cover his upper lip] and cry, 'Unclean, unclean'" (Lev. 13:45). He does this to inform the public [of his malady] so that the public will seek mercy for him [through prayer].

E. And likewise anyone who is afflicted in some way must inform the public so that the public will seek mercy for him [through prayer].

F. *Said Rabina, "In accord with whose view [are we permitted] to hang a basket [of dates] on a tree [that drops its fruit]? In accord with this Tannaite authority [of B]."*

I.1 provides scriptural basis for the rules of Mishnah. II-VI clarify the meaning and underlying principles of Mishnah.

# 4

# Bavli Ḥullin Chapter Five

# Folios 78A-83B

|     |    | 5:1 |
|-----|----|-----|
|     | A. | [The prohibition against slaughtering on the same day] "it and its young" (Lev. 22:28) applies (1) in the Land and outside the Land, (2) in the time of the Temple and not in the time of the Temple, (3) in the case of unconsecrated beasts and in the case of consecrated beasts. |
|     | B. | How so? |
| I   | C. | He who slaughters it and its offspring, (1) which are unconsecrated, (2) outside [the Temple courtyard] — both of them are valid. And [for slaughtering] the second he incurs forty stripes. |
| II  | D. | [He who slaughters] (1) Holy Things (2) outside — [for] the first is he liable to extirpation, and both of them are invalid, and [for] both of them he incurs forty stripes. |
| III | E. | [He who slaughters] (1) unconsecrated beasts (2) inside [the Temple courtyard] — both of them are invalid, and [for] the second he incurs forty stripes. |
| IV  | F. | [He who slaughters] (1) Holy Things (2) inside — the first is valid, and he is exempt [from any punishment], and [for] the second he incurs forty stripes, and it is invalid. |

## 5:2

V A. [He who slaughters] (1) unconsecrated beasts and (2) Holy Things *outside* [the Temple courtyard], the first is valid, and he is free [on its account of the penalty of extirpation], and [for] the second he incurs forty stripes, and it is invalid.

VI B. [He who slaughters] (1) Holy Things and (2) unconsecrated beasts *outside*, [for] the first he is liable to extirpation, and it is invalid. And the second is valid. And [for] both of them he incurs forty stripes.

VII C. [He who slaughters] (1) unconsecrated beasts and (2) Holy Things *inside* [the Temple], both of them are invalid. And [for] the second he incurs forty stripes.

VIII D. [He who slaughters] (1) Holy Things and (2) unconsecrated beasts *inside*, the first is valid. And he is free [on its account of the penalty of extirpation]. And [for] the second he incurs forty stripes, and it is invalid.

IX E. [He who slaughters] unconsecrated beasts (1) outside and (2) inside, the first is valid, and he is free [of the penalty of extirpation]. And [for the second] he incurs forty stripes, and it is invalid.

X F. [He who slaughters] Holy Things (1) outside and (2) inside, [for] the first he is liable to extirpation, and both of them are invalid. And [for] both of them he incurs forty stripes.

XI G. [He who slaughters] unconsecrated beasts (1) inside and (2) outside, the first is invalid. And he is free [of the penalty of extirpation]. And [for] the second he incurs forty stripes. And it is valid.

XII H. [He who slaughters] Holy Things (1) inside and (2) outside, the first is valid. And he is free [of the penalty of extirpation]. And [for] the second he incurs forty stripes, and it is invalid.

I.1

A. *Our rabbis taught on Tannaite authority: Based on what source do we say that* [the prohibition against slaughtering on the same day] "it and its young" applies to Holy Things? It comes to teach us [in the verse], "When a bull or sheep or goat is born, [it shall remain seven days with its mother; and from the eighth day on it shall be acceptable as an offering by fire to the Lord]" (Lev. 22:27). And it is written after that, "And whether the mother is a cow or a ewe, you shall not kill both her and her young in one day" (Lev. 22:28). This teaches us that [the prohibition against slaughtering on the same day] "it and its young" applies to Holy Things.

B. But it should makes sense to maintain [that the prohibition does apply] to Holy Things and not to unconsecrated beasts. [The repetition of the introductory phrase] "[And whether the mother is] a cow" breaks in to the matter. [The added phrase in the second verse suggests it deals with a separate subject.]

C. But then it should make sense to maintain [that the prohibition does apply] to unconsecrated beasts and not to Holy Things. It is written, "And [whether the mother is] a cow." The conjunctive-*vav* ["And"] adds on to the original matter. [The conjunction suggests that the second verse stipulates the prohibition in the case of the first and second circumstances.]

D. If this is so [that there is a conjunction between the rules for Holy Things and unconsecrated beasts, then we should reason as follows]: What is the case with regard to Holy Things? A hybrid animal may not [become Holy]. So too with regard to [the prohibition against slaughtering on the same day] "it and its young" — a hybrid animal should not be [subject to the rule].

E. Why then was this taught on Tannaite authority: **[The prohibition against slaughtering on the same day] "it and its offspring" applies to hybrid animals and to the *koy* [T. 5:1 A]**? And moreover, it is written [in the verse], "a sheep." And said Raba, [78b] "This is a basic principle. Anywhere it says 'sheep' it is only to exclude [from the rule] a hybrid animal."

F. [But we do include a hybrid in the rule.] Scripture said, "or" to include [in the rule] a hybrid animal. [But is this the case?] *This use of "or" is needed in order to indicate a separation of the cases. For you might have said that it makes sense to maintain that until one slaughters [both] a cow and its offspring and a sheep and its offspring [on the same day] he is not liable to punishment. It comes to make the novel point [that we separate the cases].*

G. *We could derive that we separate the cases from [the term] "its offspring." [The word "or" then would be extraneous and could be used to include a hybrid in the rule.] But we still need ["or"] in accord with what was taught on Tannaite authority:* If it stated, "A cow or a ewe and its offspring" I would have said [you are not liable] until you slaughter a cow, a ewe and the offspring [of one of them]. It comes to teach us, "And whether the mother is a cow or a ewe, [you shall not kill] both her and her young [in one day]."

H. *Is it not the case that we derive [that conclusion from the word] "or?" No. [It is just as reasonable to conclude that] we derive it from [the word] "it."*

I. *This would settle the matter in accord with the view of the rabbis who say that the word "it" is extraneous. But in accord with the view of Hananiah who does not say the word "it" is extraneous, based on what then would I conclude that we should separate the cases?*

J. *To separate the cases he does not need a scriptural basis. For he reasons in accord with the view of R. Jonathan. As it was taught on Tannaite authority:* "For every one who curses his father or [lit. 'and'] his mother [shall be put to death; he has cursed his father or his mother, his blood is upon him]" (Lev. 20:9). [From this verse] I could deduce that [he is liable] only if he [curses] his father and his mother. What is the source of the rule for [one who curses] his father, but not his mother, or his mother, but not his father?

K. *It comes to teach us [the additional phrase], "He has cursed his father or his mother." "[He is liable if] he cursed his father [or if] he cursed his mother," the words of R. Oshaia. R. Jonathan says, "This implies [that he is liable if he curses] the two of them at the same time. And it implies [that he is liable if he curses] one of them unless Scripture specifies [that they be] 'together.'"*

L. *What is [the view of] Hananiah and what is [the view of] the rabbis [referred to in I above]? As it was taught on Tannaite authority:* [The prohibition against slaughtering on the same day] "it and its young" applies to females but not to males [i.e., dams, but not sires and their offspring]. Hananiah says, "It applies to both males and females."

M. *What is the basis for the view of the rabbis? As it was taught on Tannaite authority:* You might want to infer that [the prohibition against slaughtering on the same day] "it and its young" applies to both males and females. But it is logical [to argue that this is not the case]. You are liable here [for transgressing the prohibition against slaughtering on the same day] and you are liable for [taking the mother from the nest in the presence of the offspring, as it is written, "If you chance to come upon a bird's nest, in any tree or on the ground, with young ones or eggs and the mother sitting upon the young or upon the eggs, you shall not take] the mother with the young" (Deut. 22:6). What is the case where you are liable for [taking] "the mother with the young"? It is for females and not for males. So too the case where you are liable here [for the prohibition against slaughtering on the same day it is logical to argue that] it is for females and not for males.

N. No. [This is not the case.] You may say regarding [the prohibition of taking] "the mother with its young" that [the rule] does not apply to [birds that are] already captured as it does to those that are not already captured. You will say that [with regard to the prohibition against slaughtering on the same day] "it and its young" [the parameters of the law are different] because it equates [the cases of animals that are] already captured and animals that are not already captured.

O. It comes to teach [the word], "It." [He needs to slaughter] one [parent] and not two. Now that Scripture has separated the cases I am warranted to draw a logical conclusion [in the other direction]. He is liable here [if he slaughters the mother and offspring on the same day] and he is liable in the case where he takes "the mother with its young." What is the case? Where he is liable for taking "the mother with its young" [the prohibition applies] to females and not to males. So too where he is liable here [if he slaughters the mother and offspring on the same day], [he is liable] for females and not for males [i.e., for the mother and offspring].

P. And if you wish, you may say [that the verse specifies the prohibition for] "its young" [and that implies] one [animal] whose young trails after it [i.e., the mother], that excludes a male [parent] whose young do not trail after it.

Q. What does it mean: 'And if you wish, you may say'? *Will you maintain that "it" [masculine pronoun] implies it is a male? Lo it says, "its young." [And that implies] one [animal] whose young trails after it [i.e., the mother], that excludes a male [parent] whose young do not trail after it.*

R. [79a] And in accord with the view of Hananiah [in L] it is written [both] "it" [masculine pronoun] that implies it is a male. And it is written "its young" [that implies] one [animal] whose young trails after it [i.e., the mother] a female. Therefore the rule applies to both males and females.

S. Said R. Huna bar Hiyya, said Samuel, "The law follows in accord with the view of Hananiah." *And Samuel is consistent with his view elsewhere. For it was taught in the Mishnah on Tannaite authority:* **R. Judah says, "All offspring of a [female] horse, even though their sires are asses, are permitted [to mate] with one another... But the offspring of a [female] ass are prohibited [to mate] with the offspring of a [female] horse" [M. Kil. 8:4 C, E].**

T. And said R. Judah, said Samuel, "These are the words of R. Judah who said that we do not take into account the seed of the sire [to determine the category of the offspring]." But sages say, "All the varieties of mules are one category."

U. *And who is the authority behind the view of sages? It is Hananiah who said, "We do take into account the seed of the sire." And this one that is the offspring of a horse and a [female] ass or this one that is the offspring of an ass and a [female] horse, they are all one category. [This implies that the law follows in accord with Hananiah.]*

I.2
A. *They posed a question: Is it obvious to R. Judah that we do not take into account the seed of the sire? Or perhaps does he have some doubt about it? What difference does it make [with regard to the law]? [The difference is whether we] permit the offspring [of a female horse and an ass, i.e., a mule] to mate with [the species of] its mother. If you say that*

it is obvious [that we do not take into account the seed of the sire], then we should permit the offspring to mate with its mother. But if you say that he has some doubt, then we should prohibit the offspring to mate with the mother.

B. *What is the law? Come and take note:* **R. Judah says, "All offspring of a [female] horse, even though their sires are asses, are permitted [to mate] with one another"** [M. Kil. 8:4 C]. *What is the situation? If you say that the sire of this one is an ass and the sire of that one is an ass, do you need to spell this out [that it is permitted]? Rather is it not the case that the sire of this one is a horse and the sire of that one is an ass? And it was taught that they are,* **"permitted [to mate] with one another."** *It seems [logical to conclude] that it is obvious [that we do not take into account the seed of the sire in the determination of the offspring].*

C. *No. It is consistent to say that the sire of this one is an ass and the sire of that one is an ass. And what [about the objection that] was stated, "Do you need to spell this out?" [It was necessary to state the matter in accord with this reasoning]. What might I have maintained? The side [of the animal that derives from the] horse mates with [the side of the animal that derives from the] ass. Or the side of [the animal that derives from] the ass mates with [the side of the animal that derives from the] horse. It makes the novel point [that with regard to the law we do not suppose this to be the case].*

I.3
A. *Come and take note:* **A [female] mule that was in heat — they mate with it neither a horse nor an ass [but] only with its own species** [T. Kil. 1:8 A-B]. *And if you say that it is obvious [that we do not take into account the seed of the sire in the determination of the offspring], then why not mate it with the species of the mother? [They cannot do this because] they do not know what is the species of the mother.*

B. *But lo it was taught,* **"but only with its own species"** *[implying that they know the parentage]. This is how you should state matters:* **They mate with it neither a horse nor an ass** *— because they do not know its species.*

C. *So why do they not inspect its tokens [to determine the parentage]? For Abayye said, "If it has a thick voice, it is the offspring of a she-ass. if it has a thin voice, it is the offspring of a [female] horse." And said R. Pappa, "If it has big ears and a short tail, it is the offspring of a she-ass. If it has small ears and a long tail, it is the offspring of a [female] horse."*

D. *In this case what are we dealing with? [An animal that is] mute and mutilated [and accordingly they could not inspect its tokens to determine the parentage].*

E. *What is the result [of our inquiry begun at I.2 A]? Come and take note: For said R. Huna the son of R. Joshua, "All agree that it is prohibited [to mate] the offspring with [the species of] its mother." We derive from this the conclusion that he [Judah] has some doubt [about whether we take into account the seed of the sire]. We derive it.*

I.4
A. *Said R. Abba to his servant, "When you hitch up the mules to the wagon, look for those that are alike [in their ears and tails] and hitch them up for me." It seems [logical to conclude] that he reasons that we do not take into account the seed of the sire* **[79b]** *and that the [determination of parentage through these] tokens is based on the authority of the Torah.*

I.5
A. Our rabbis taught on Tannaite authority: **[The prohibition against slaughtering on the same day] "it and its offspring" applies to hybrid animals and to the** *koy***. R. Eleazar [b. reads Eliezer] says, "To the hybrid of a ewe and a goat — it applies. But to that of a** *koy* **it does not apply" [T. 5:1].**

B. Said R. Hisda, "What is the [parentage of the] *koy* that is the subject of the dispute between R. Eliezer and sages? It is that offspring that comes out of the union of a goat and a [female] deer."

C. What is the situation? If you maintain that a goat mated with a [female] deer and she gave birth and he slaughtered her and her offspring [on the same day] — lo, said R. Hisda, "All agree [in the case

*Bavli Ḥullin Chapter Five. Folios 78A-83B* 221

where] she [the mother] is a deer and her offspring is a goat, that he [who slaughters them on the same day] is free [of any liability for slaughtering the mother and offspring on the same day]. The [basis for this is the assumption that] Torah stated [the prohibition in the case of] a sheep and its offspring and not in the case of a deer and its offspring."

D. Rather it must be maintained that a [male] deer mated with a female [goat] and she gave birth and he slaughtered her and her offspring [on the same day] — lo, said R. Hisda, "All agree [in the case where] she [the mother] is a goat and her offspring is a deer, that he [who slaughters them on the same day] is liable [for slaughtering the mother and offspring on the same day.] [The basis for this is the assumption that] the Torah stated [the prohibition in the case of] a sheep and any kind of offspring from it at all [including a deer]."

E. It is consistent to maintain that [the case is one where] a goat mated with a [female] deer. And she gave birth to a female offspring. And that female offspring gave birth to a male offspring. And he slaughtered her and her offspring [on the same day]. Our rabbis reasoned in accord with the principle that we do take into account the seed of the sire. And the specification that it be a sheep [to be liable to the prohibition means] even if it is partly a sheep. And R. Eliezer reasoned in accord with the principle that we do not take into account the seed of the sire. And the specification that it be a sheep [to be liable to the prohibition means] we do not say that [an animal that is] partly a sheep [is included].

F. But why not stipulate that the dispute [hinges on whether the authorities hold the principle that] they take into account the seed of the sire as in the dispute between Hananiah and the rabbis [I.1 U]? [And say that according to Eliezer it does not apply to males and according to the rabbis it does apply (Rashi).]

G. If we stipulate that they disputed regarding this [principle], I would have reasoned that in this case even the rabbis agreed that the specification that it be a sheep [means] we do not say that [an animal that is] partly a sheep [is included in the prohibition]. It makes the novel point [that this is not the case].

H. But lo it was taught in the Mishnah on Tannaite authority: **A koy... they may not slaughter it on a festival. But if one slaughters it** [on a festival], they do not cover up its blood [since it is only partly a wild animal, cf. M. 6:1 and M. Bik. 2:9 C-D]. *In that case what are we dealing with? If we maintain that it is a case of a goat that mated with a [female] deer and it gave birth, then in accord with the views of both the rabbis and R. Eliezer he should be permitted to slaughter it and obligated to cover its blood. [The Torah stipulated (Lev. 17:13) that one must cover the blood of] a deer and that means even [an animal that is] partly a deer.*

I. *Rather it must be that it is a case of a deer that mated with a [female] goat and it gave birth. If we hold in accord with the view of the rabbis, then he should be permitted to slaughter it and obligated to cover its blood [since in regard to the law, it is part wild animal]. And if we hold in accord with the view of R. Eliezer, then he should be permitted to slaughter it and not obligated to cover its blood [since in regard to the law, it is not a wild animal at all].*

J. *It is consistent to maintain that it is a case of deer that mated with a [female] goat. And the rabbis were in doubt whether or not we take into account the seed of the sire. And since we say that the rabbis were in doubt about this, [is it fair to assume that] R. Eliezer holds the view that it is obvious [that we do not take into account the seed of the sire in the determination of the offspring]?*

K. *And [consider] what was taught on Tannaite authority:* **[The requirement to give to the priest] the shoulder, the two cheeks, and the maw [M. Hul. 10:1 A] applies to hybrid beasts and to the *koy*. R. Eleazar says, "To the hybrid beast born of the ewe and the goat it does apply. To that of the *koy* — it is exempt from the gifts. [He who lays claim against his fellow must bring proof of the validity of his claim]"** [T. 9:1]. *What case are we dealing with? If we maintain that it is a case of a goat that mated with a [female] deer and gave birth, it makes perfect sense in accord with the view of R. Eliezer that it be exempt [from the gifts]. He would reason that the specification that it be a sheep [to be liable to the prohibition means] we do not say that [an animal that is] partly a sheep [is included].*

L. *But in accord with the view of the rabbis, let it be the case that the specification that it be a sheep [to be liable to the prohibition means we do say that an animal that is] partly a sheep [is included]. It makes*

*Bavli Ḥullin Chapter Five. Folios 78A-83B*

perfect sense that they do not give half [of the gifts that derive from the deer to the Priest]. Regarding the other half [of the gifts that derive from the sheep] let us say to him [the Priest] that he should bring evidence that we do take account of the seed of the sire and take [the gifts].

M. Rather it must be [that the case is] a deer that mated with a [female] goat and it gave birth. It makes perfect sense in accord with the view of the rabbis. What is he obligated to give? Half of the gifts. But in accord with the view of R. Eliezer let him be obligated to give all of the gifts! [We do not take into account the seed of the sire.]

N. It is consistent to say [that the case is] a deer that mated with a [female] goat and it gave birth. And R. Eliezer is also in doubt as to whether or not we take into account the seed of the sire. But if according to the view of the rabbis we are in doubt about this, and according to the view of R. Eliezer we are in doubt about this, then in what case do they dispute?

O. [They dispute over the issue of whether] the specification that it be a sheep [to be liable to the prohibition means] we say that [an animal that is] partly a sheep [is included]. The rabbis reason that the specification that it be a sheep [to be liable to the prohibition means] we do say that [an animal that is] partly a sheep [is included]. And R. Eliezer reasons that the specification that it be a sheep [to be liable to the prohibition means] we do not say that [an animal that is] partly a sheep [is included].

P. Said R. Pappa, "Therefore with regard to the matter of covering the blood and gifts [to the Priest] we find only [that the obligation applies for a koy in the case of] a deer that mated with a [female] goat. For both in accord with the view of the rabbis and of R. Eliezer there is a doubt about whether or not we take into account the seed of the sire. And they dispute over whether or not we say the specification that it be a sheep [to be liable to the prohibition means] that [an animal that is] partly a sheep [is included]."

Q. Regarding the matter of [the prohibition of slaughtering on the same day] "it and its young" we find that [they dispute] both in the case of a goat that mated with a [female] deer and in the case of a deer that mated with a [female] goat.

R.    *In the case of a goat that mated with a [female] deer [they dispute] regarding the prohibition. For the rabbis reason that perhaps we do take account of the seed of the sire and that the specification that it be a sheep [to be liable to the prohibition means] we do say that [an animal that is] partly a sheep [is included] and it is prohibited.*

S.    *And R. Eliezer reasons that we allow also that we take account of the seed of the sire but that the specification that it be a sheep [to be liable to the prohibition means] we do not say that [an animal that is] partly a sheep [is included].*

T.    *And in the case of a deer that mated with a [female] goat [they dispute] regarding whether they flog [the violator]. The rabbis reason that we allow that we take account of the seed of the sire and that the specification that it be a sheep [to be liable to the prohibition means] we do say that [an animal that is] partly a sheep [is included] and they flog him.*

U.    *And R. Eliezer reasons that there is a prohibition [against slaughtering them on the same day] but they do not flog him [for violating it]. There is a prohibition because perhaps we do not take account of the seed of the sire and then this [animal] is a perfectly complete sheep. They do not flog him because perhaps we do take account of the seed of the sire and the specification that it be a sheep [to be liable to the prohibition means] we do not say that [an animal that is] partly a sheep [is included].*

I.6

A.    Said R. Judah, "The *koy* is another category of creature unto itself. And the sages did not decide whether it is a kind of beast or a kind of wild animal."

B.    Said R. Nahman, "The *koy* is the wild ram." *And this accords with the Tannaite [dispute]:* The *koy* is the wild ram. And some say that it is the offspring of the goat that mates with the [female] deer. R. Yosé says, "The *koy* is another category of creature unto itself. And the sages did not decide whether it is a kind of beast or a kind of wild animal." Rabban Simeon b. Gamaliel says, "It is a kind of beast and the people of Bet Doshai raised many flocks of them" [cf. T. Bekh. 2:9].

**I.7**

A. Said R. Zira, said R. Safra, said R. Hamnuna, "These goats of Lebanon are valid to be brought upon the altar." *He reasons regarding this in accord with what R. Yitzhak said, "Scripture enumerated ten kinds of beasts [that are valid for slaughtering and eating]." And no more. And these [goats], since they were not understood to be classed together with the wild beasts, we derive from this that they are [in the general category of] goat.*

B. *R. Aha bar Jacob raised a contradiction to this: It makes sense to say that [the verse], "The hart, the gazelle, [the roebuck, the wild goat, the ibex, the antelope, and the mountain-sheep]" (Deut. 14:5) — is a specification [of the rule]. [The verse], "Every animal [that parts the hoof and has the hoof cloven in two, and chews the cud, among the animals, you may eat]" (Deut. 14:6) — is a general rule. [Where there is] a specification and a general rule, it is the case that the general rule adds on to the specification.*

C. *There are many [kinds of beasts that are valid that are not enumerated by Scripture]. If this is the case, then why do I need these specifications [in the verse at all]?*

D. *R. Aha the son of R. Iqa raised a contradiction: But perhaps [this goat of Lebanon] is a kind of the wild goat (Deut. 14:5). Said R. Aha the son of Raba to R. Ashi, but some say that R. Aha the son of R. Avya said to R. Ashi, "Perhaps it is a kind of antelope or mountain-sheep." Said R. Hanan to R. Ashi, "Amemar permitted [them to eat] the fat [of these goats, as if they were wild beasts]."*

E. *Abba the son of R. Minyamin bar Hiyya posed a question to R. Huna bar Hiyya, "These goats of Lebanon, what is the law regarding whether they may be brought upon the altar?"*

F. *He said to him, "On this point R. Yosé and the rabbis disputed only with regard to the wild ox." As it was taught in the Mishnah on Tannaite authority:* **A wild ox is [considered] a kind of domesticated animal. And R. Yosé says, "[It is considered] a kind of wild animal"** *[M. Kil. 8:6 A-B].*

G. *For the rabbis reason that since "wild ox" was translated into the Aramaic equivalent of "goat of Lebanon," it is deemed to be a* [domesticated] beast. And R. Yosé reasons that since it was understood to be classed together with those wild beasts, it is a kind of wild beast. But these [goats of Lebanon] according to all views are a kind of goat.

H. R. Aha the son of R. Iqa raised a contradiction: But perhaps they are a kind of "wild goat"? Said Rabina to R. Ashi, "But perhaps they are a kind of 'antelope' or 'mountain-sheep'"? Said R. Nahman to R. Ashi, "Amemar permitted [them to eat] the fat [of these goats, as if they were wild beasts]."

II.1
A. How so? He who slaughters [it and its offspring, (1) which are unconsecrated, (2) outside [the Temple courtyard] — both of them are valid. And [for slaughtering] the second he incurs forty stripes] [M. 5:1 B-C]. Said R. Oshaia, "The entire Mishnah does not accord with the view of R. Simeon."

B. *In what way is this the case? Since it teaches,* [He who slaughters] (1) Holy Things (2) outside — [for] the first is he liable to extirpation, and both of them are invalid, and [for] both of them he incurs forty stripes [M. 5:1 D]. *Consider and take note that R. Simeon said, "An act of slaughter that is improper, is not deemed a valid act of slaughter."*

C. [80b] [On the basis of this principle we may reason that] *the first [animal he slaughtered] he just killed it [because the act was not deemed valid]. The second one should be acceptable inside [the Temple]. He should be liable to extirpation [for slaughtering it outside] as well.*

D. [He who slaughters] (1) unconsecrated beasts (2) inside [the Temple courtyard] — both of them are invalid, and [for] the second he incurs forty stripes [M. 5:1 E]. *Consider and take note that R. Simeon said, "An act of slaughter that is improper, is not deemed a valid act of slaughter."*

E. [On the basis of this principle we may reason that] *the first [animal he slaughtered] he just killed it [because the act was not deemed valid]. For the second one then why should he incur forty stripes?*

F. [He who slaughters] (1) Holy Things (2) inside — the first is valid, and he is exempt [from any punishment], and [for] the second he incurs forty stripes, and it is invalid [M. 5:1 F]. *Consider and take note that R. Simeon said, "An act of slaughter that is improper, is not a valid act of slaughter."*

G. [On the basis of this principle we may reason that] *the slaughter of Holy Things is also deemed improper. For as long as he did not sprinkle the blood [on the altar], the meat is not permitted [for eating]. For the second one then why should he incur forty stripes?*

H. *Rather we must derive from this [line of reasoning] that the law does not follow in accord with R. Simeon. But this is obvious. But because we deal here with an act of slaughtering Holy Things we needed to state the matter. I might have thought that it makes sense to say that this act of slaughter of a Holy Thing is a proper act. For lo, if he pierced [the organs] and sprinkled the blood, the meat would not be permitted [for eating]. And now that he performed an act of slaughter [and sprinkled the blood], the meat is permitted and it is a proper act of slaughter. It makes the novel point [that this is not the case].*

II.2
A. And should he not incur stripes also on account of [offering a sacrifice] at the wrong time? *For it was taught on Tannaite authority:* On what basis do they rule that all invalid [animals that are offered as sacrifices] of oxen or sheep are subsumed under the prohibition [established by the phrase], "It cannot be accepted" (Lev. 22:23)? It comes to teach [in the verse], "A bull or a lamb which has a part too long or too short you may present for a freewill offering; but for a votive offering it cannot be accepted" (Lev. 22:23). This teaches us about the invalid [animals that are offered as sacrifices] of oxen or sheep that they are subsumed under the prohibition [established by the phrase], "It cannot be accepted." [Why then does the Mishnah not specify that he be liable for stripes for this violation?]

B. *What was understood [as pertinent to the Mishnah] were the prohibitions against slaughtering it and its offspring on the same day. Other prohibitions were not understood [as pertinent to the concerns of the Mishnah here].*

C. *But this is not so. For lo, [the case of slaughtering]* **Holy Things outside** *involves other prohibitions and it was understood [as pertinent* to the Mishnah]. *For it was taught in the Mishnah:* **[He who slaughters] (1) Holy Things (2) outside — [for] the first is he liable to extirpation, [and both of them are invalid], and [for] both of them he incurs forty stripes [M. 5:1 D].** *Now it makes perfect sense [that he incurs stripes for slaughtering] the second one on account of the prohibition against slaughtering it and its offspring on the same day. [And the Mishnah is justified in specifying it.] But for the first one, why does he incur stripes? Is it not because of the prohibition against slaughtering [Holy Things] outside? [Why then does the Mishnah specify it?]*

D. [We can explain it as follows.] *In any instance where there is no prohibition against slaughtering it and its offspring on the same day, it is understood that the other prohibitions are not [pertinent to the concerns of Mishnah]. And in any instance where there is a prohibition against slaughtering it and its offspring on the same day, it is understood that the other prohibitions are [pertinent to the concerns of Mishnah].*

E. R. Zira said, "Leave out [of our discussion] the prohibition of [offering a sacrifice] at the wrong time. For Scripture **[81a]** has linked that [prohibition] to a positive commandment." [That puts it into a different category of prohibition.]

F. *What is the basis for this assertion? For Scripture stated,* "[When a bull or sheep or goat is born, it shall remain seven days with its mother]; and from the eighth day on it shall be acceptable [as an offering by fire to the Lord]" (Lev. 22:27). "From the eighth day on" — yes [it is acceptable]. From before this time — no [it is not acceptable]. [That makes this into] a prohibition that derives from a positive commandment, that is deemed itself to be a positive commandment.

G. *But do we not need this [verse] in accord with [the view of] R. Aptoriqi? For R. Aptoriqi raised in contradiction [the following]: It is written,* "It shall remain seven days with its mother." *Lo, [this implies that] at night [after the seventh day] it is fit. And it is written,* "From the eighth day on it shall be acceptable." "From the eighth day on" — yes [it is acceptable]. From the night [before] — no [it is not acceptable].

H. *Lo, what then is the case? At night [it is fit] to be sanctified. On the day [it is fit] to be accepted. It is written in another verse [along the same lines], "You shall do likewise with your oxen and with your sheep: seven days it shall be with its dam; on the eighth day you shall give it to me" (Exod. 22:30).*

II.3
A. Said R. Hamnuna, "R. Simeon used to say, 'The prohibition against slaughtering it and its offspring on the same day does not apply to Holy Things.'" *What is the basis for this assertion? It is based on the fact that R. Simeon said, "An act of slaughter that is improper, is not deemed a valid act of slaughter."* [Above, II.1 B.]

B. [Any act of] slaughtering Holy Things is [by definition] an act of slaughter that is improper [and is therefore not a valid act of slaughter].

C. *Raba objected:* [With regard to the] prohibition against slaughtering it and its offspring on the same day for animals that are Holy Things slaughtered outside — R. Simeon says, "The second one is subject to a prohibition." For R. Simeon used to say, "Any [sacrifice slaughtered outside] that it is proper to bring after its specified time is subject to a prohibition [that incurs stripes] but is not subject to the punishment of extirpation." And sages say, "Any act that is not subject to the punishment of extirpation is not subject to a negative prohibition [that incurs stripes]."

D. *And what is difficult for us is the case of [both mother and offspring that were slaughtered on the same day] that were Holy Things outside [the Temple and the ruling is that] for [slaughtering] the second one he violates a prohibition. [But this is not logical on the following basis.] The first one he just killed [because the act of slaughter was not deemed valid]. The second one would have been accepted inside [as a valid sacrifice]. He therefore should be liable also to the punishment of extirpation [for slaughtering a Holy Thing outside].*

E. *But Raba said, and some say Kadi [said] that there is a lacuna in the text. And this is how you should teach matters: The case is both [mother and offspring that were slaughtered on the same day] that were Holy Things outside [the Temple and the ruling is that] according to* the view of the rabbis for [slaughtering] the first he is subject to the punishment of extirpation. The second is rendered invalid but he is exempt from the prohibition against slaughtering outside. According to the view of R. Simeon, for [slaughtering] both of them he is subject to the punishment of extirpation.

F. *If [he slaughtered] one outside and one inside, according to the view of the rabbis, for the first one [the act of slaughter is valid] and he is subject to the punishment of extirpation. For the second one, it [the act of slaughter] is invalid and he is exempt [from punishment]. According to the view of R. Simeon, the second one is valid.*

G. *If [he slaughtered] one inside and one outside, according to the view of the rabbis, for the first one [the act of slaughter] is valid and he is exempt from punishment. For the second one, it [the act of slaughter] is invalid and he is exempt [from punishment]. According to the view of R. Simeon, for the second he is subject to a prohibition.*

H. *And if you wished to conclude that the prohibition against slaughtering it and its offspring on the same day does not apply to Holy Things, then why is the second one subject to a prohibition? Should he not also be liable for the punishment of extirpation?*

I. *Rather said Raba, "Here is how R. Hamnuna stated matters. The punishment of stripes for slaughtering it and its offspring on the same day does not apply to Holy Things. Because as long as he has not sprinkled the blood, he has not rendered the meat permitted [for eating]. At the time that he slaughters [any warning he receives that the act he is about to perform is prohibited] is a warning subject to doubt. [Perhaps he will not sprinkle the blood.] And [we have a principle that] any warning that is subject to doubt is not deemed a valid warning."*

J. *And Raba is consistent with his view elsewhere. For said Raba, "If she [the mother] was an unconsecrated beast, and the offspring was a Peace-offering — if he slaughtered the unconsecrated beast and then slaughtered the Peace-offering, he is exempt [from violating the prohibition against slaughtering it and its offspring on the same day]. If he slaughtered the Peace-offering and then slaughtered the unconsecrated beast, he is liable." [There is no longer a doubtful warning.]*

Bavli Hullin Chapter Five. Folios 78A-83B       231

K.  And said Raba, "If she is an unconsecrated beast and the offspring is a Burnt-offering, there is no question that where he slaughtered the unconsecrated beast and afterward slaughtered the Burnt-offering that he is exempt. [81b] But even where he first slaughtered the Burnt-offering and then slaughtered the unconsecrated beast, he is exempt. Because the first act of slaughtering is not one that will lead to any eating."

L.  But [contrary to this, said] R. Jacob, said R. Yohanan, "The consumption [of meat] on the altar is deemed a valid act of 'eating.'" *What is the basis for this view?* For Scripture stated, "If any of the flesh of the sacrifice of his Peace-offering is eaten [on the third day, he who offers it shall not be accepted, neither shall it be credited to him; it shall be an abomination, and he who eats of it shall bear his iniquity]" (Lev. 7:18). The verse states matters [in emphatic terms that suggest] two acts of eating — whether the eating done by a person or the 'eating' done by the altar — [that they are equivalent].

I.1 engages in a detailed analysis of the scriptural basis for the rule of Mishnah. This leads eventually to the citation of an intersecting secondary rule regarding the legal ramifications of the genetic relation of the sire to the offspring, a subject developed at I.2. I.3-4 move to a tertiary level of discourse. I.5 returns to the primary thematic level citing a relevant Tosefta-text. In this long and tight composition, the framers make reference to the secondary premises [e.g., at F] and work through all the alternatives. I.6 cites a brief secondary expansion on the subject of the *koy*-animal. I.7 discusses a tertiary concern. II.1 engages in the familiar process of clarifying the authorship of Mishnah. II.2 presents an ostensible Tannaite contradiction to the rule of Mishnah. II.3 picks up on a principle evoked in II.1 and seeks to align the Tannaite premises.

### 5:3 A-I

A. (1) He who slaughters [a beast], and it turns out to be *terefah*,

B. (2) he who slaughters a beast for idolatrous purpose,

C. (3) and he who slaughters a cow [to be burned] for purification [water], and an ox which is to be stoned, and a heifer whose neck is to be broken [none of these is eaten] —

D. R. Simeon declares exempt [from punishment for violating the prohibition against slaughtering it and its offspring on one day].

E. And sages declare liable.

F. (1) He who slaughters [a beast], and it is made carrion by his own deed,

G. (2) he who pierces [the windpipe],

H. (3) and he who tears out [the windpipe]

I. is exempt on account of violating the prohibition against slaughtering it and its offspring on one day.

I.1
A. Said R. Simeon b. Laqish, "They taught this rule [that he is liable] only where he slaughtered the first one for idolatrous purposes and the second one for consumption at his table. But where he slaughtered the first one for his table and the second one for idolatrous purposes, he is exempt from punishment because of the principle that [with regard to his liability to punishment] *the greater [violation] overrides the lesser [violation and cancels its punishment]*."

B. Said to him R. Yohanan, "Even little schoolchildren know this. But there are times when even if he slaughtered the first for his table and the second for idolatrous purposes that he is liable. The case in question may be one where they warned him about the prohibition of slaughtering it and its offspring on the same day but they did not warn him about the prohibition of [slaughtering the animal for] idolatrous purposes."

C. And R. Simeon b. Laqish said, "Since where they warned him [about idolatry] he is exempt [from the punishment for the lesser violation of slaughtering it and its offspring on the same day], where they did not warn him [about idolatry], he is also exempt [from the lesser punishment]."

D. *And they [Yohanan and Simeon] are consistent with their views elsewhere. For when R. Dimi came [from Israel] he said,* "Those who inadvertently violated a prohibition [that had he violated deliberately he would have been] subject to the death penalty, and those who inadvertently violated a prohibition [that had he violated deliberately he would have been] subject to stripes, and [he violated] another act [involving a monetary payment] — R. Yohanan says he is liable [to pay]. And R. Simeon b. Laqish says he is exempt [from paying]."

E. R. Yohanan says he is liable because lo, they did not warn him [about the greater punishment]. And R. Simeon b. Laqish says he is exempt because since where they warn him [about the greater punishment] he is exempt, where they do not warn him, he also is exempt.

F. *And it is necessary [to teach both rules in the cases of C and of D]. For if we had been instructed in this [first case, we would say that] in this case does R. Simeon b. Laqish state [that he is exempt]. But in the other it would make sense to say that he agrees with the view of R. Yohanan. And if we had been instructed in this [second case, we would say that] in this case does R. Yohanan state [that he is liable]. But in the other it would make sense to say that he agrees with the view of R. Simeon b. Laqish. It is necessary [to teach both rules].*

II.1
A. And is [the slaughter of] **a cow [to be burned] for purification [water] [M. 5:3 C]** an act of slaughter that is invalid? *But lo, it was taught on Tannaite authority:* **R. Simeon says, "A cow [for purification] renders foodstuffs and liquid unclean if there was [at least] a moment when it was fit" [T. Parah 7:9 A].**

B. [82a] And said R. Simeon b. Laqish, "R. Simeon used to say that a cow could be redeemed even when it was laying upon the pile of wood [after it was already slaughtered. Therefore the act is valid. Cf. M. Parah 3:9]."

C. Said R. Shaman bar Abba, said R. Yohanan, "The cow of purification is not supposed to be in our Mishnah."

II.2
A. And is the [slaughter of] **a heifer whose neck is to be broken [M. 5:3 C]** an act of slaughter that is invalid? *But lo, it was taught in the Mishnah on Tannaite authority:* **[If] the murderer was found before the neck of the heifer was broken, it [simply] goes forth and pastures in the herd [M. Sotah 9:7 A].** [If it is then slaughtered, it is valid.]

B. Said R. Simeon b. Laqish in the name of R. Yannai, "The heifer whose neck is to broken is not supposed to be in our Mishnah."

C. But did R. Yannai say this? But lo, said R. Yannai, "I learned that there was some limitation to this rule. But I forgot what it was. *But the associates turned out to say, 'When it is taken down to the rugged valley, it is rendered prohibited.'"*

D. *And if you have it [listed in our Mishnah] teach as follows: This one [the rule in M. Sotah] refers to [the heifer] before it went down [into the rugged valley and is still valid for eating]. And this one [the rule in our Mishnah] refers to [the heifer] after it went down [into the rugged valley and is no longer valid].*

E. *Said R. Phineas the son of R. Ammi, "I taught in the name of R. Simeon b. Laqish, 'The heifer whose neck is to be broken is not supposed to be in our Mishnah."*

F. *Said R. Ashi, "When I was in the house of R. Pappi we had a question as to whether R. Simeon b. Laqish said this."*

G. *But lo, it was stated:* The birds [for the sacrifices] of the leper — from what time do they become prohibited? R. Yohanan said, 'From the time they are slaughtered.' R. Simeon b. Laqish said, 'From the time they are taken [as a sacrifice]' [b. Qid. 57a].

H. *And we say, "What is the basis for the view of R. Simeon b. Laqish? He derives if from the common use of the term 'take' [with regard to the birds of the leper and with regard to] the heifer whose neck is broken."* [The verses are: "The priest shall command them to *take* for him who is to be cleansed two living clean birds and cedarwood and scarlet stuff and hyssop" (Lev. 14:4); "And the elders of the city which is nearest to the slain man shall *take* a heifer which has never been worked and which has not pulled in the yoke" (Deut. 21:3).]

I. Rather said R. Hiyya bar Abba, said R. Yohanan, "The heifer whose neck is to be broken is not supposed to be in our Mishnah."

Bavli Ḥullin Chapter Five. Folios 78A-83B

I.1 analyzes the premises of the rule of Mishnah. II.1-2 are an interesting exercise in Mishnah-criticism. The units cite relevant Tannaite sources and criticize the working of the Mishnah-paragraph.

### 5:3 J-L

J. Two who purchased, [one] a cow, and [the other] its offspring —
K. that one who purchased the first slaughters first.
L. But if the second did it first, he has acquired the right [to do so].

I.1
A. Said R. Joseph, "*The Mishnah taught this with regard to the legal rights* [of the purchasers and not with regard to the prohibition itself (Rashi)]."

B. *It was taught on Tannaite authority: If the second one [slaughters his animal] first, lo he is astute and he gains an advantage. He is astute in that he did not violate a prohibition. And he gains an advantage in that he gets to eat meat [that day].*

I.1 identifies Mishnah's operative principle.

### 5:3 M-Q

I  M. [If] he slaughtered a cow and afterward its two offspring, he incurs eighty stripes.
II N. [If] he slaughtered its two offspring and afterward slaughtered it, he incurs forty stripes.
III O. [If] he slaughtered it, its daughter, its granddaughter, he incurs eighty stripes.
IV P. [If] he slaughtered it and its granddaughter and afterward slaughtered its daughter, he incurs forty stripes.
Q. Sumkhos says in the name of R. Meir, "He incurs eighty stripes."

I.1
A. *Why is this the case [that he is liable in N]? The Torah stated, "It and its offspring"* (Lev. 22:28) *and not "Its offspring and it." No. You cannot have concluded that. For it was taught on Tannaite authority: [From the verse], "It and its offspring" I may derive only [that it*

is prohibited to slaughter in order], "It and its offspring." What is the source [of the prohibition of slaughtering in the reverse order], It and its mother? When it says, "[And whether the mother is a cow or a ewe], you (plural) shall not kill [both her and her young in one day]" (Lev. 22:28). Lo, here you have reference to two [people who are liable to punishment].

B. Lo, what is the case? Where one person slaughtered the cow and one person slaughtered its mother and one person slaughtered its offspring, the last two are liable [for transgressing the prohibition against slaughtering it and its offspring on the same day].

C. [82b] *But is this phrase not needed for defining the prohibition itself? If that is all [that Scripture intended] it should have written, "You (singular) shall not kill." Why does it say, "You (plural) shall not kill"? But we still would need to state it [in the plural]. For if the Torah had written, "You (singular) shall not kill" I would have reasoned that if one [person slaughtered both animals then] yes [he would be liable for violating the prohibition]. But if two [people slaughtered, each slaughtering one animal then] no [neither would be liable]. The Torah [therefore] wrote, "You (plural) shall not kill." This implies that even two [people who each slaughtered one animal are liable].*

D. If this is the case, *then let [the Torah] write, "They shall not kill." Why does it say, "You (plural) shall not kill"? We derive from this two [rules. Two may slaughter and it may be in either order].*

II.1
A. **[If] he slaughtered it and its granddaughter and afterward slaughtered its daughter, he incurs forty stripes. Sumkhos says in the name of R. Meir, "He incurs eighty stripes" [M. 5:3 P-Q].** Said Abayye to R. Joseph, "What is the basis for the view of Sumkhos? Does Sumkhos reason in accord with the view that one who ate two olive-bulks of forbidden fat in one inadvertent violation is liable to bring two sin-offerings [b. Shab. 93b]?

B. *"And it is logical to conclude that we may be instructed of this [opinion of Sumkhos] in general [wherever there is a possibility of multiple transgressions]. And the reason that it makes the novel point [of specifying his view] in regard to our rule is to apprise you of the*

*Bavli Ḥullin Chapter Five. Folios 78A-83B*

authority of the opinion of the rabbis. For even though [he commits the act of slaughter on] two separate entities, the rabbis exempted him [of the additional forty stripes].

C. "Or perhaps Sumkhos reasons in accord with the view that one who ate two olive-bulks of forbidden fat in one inadvertent violation is liable to bring only one sin-offering. *But here the basis for his view [that he incurs the penalty of eighty stripes] is because [he commits the act of slaughter on] two separate entities.*"

D. He [Joseph] said to him, "Yes. He holds the view that one who ate two olive-bulks of forbidden fat in one inadvertent violation is liable to bring two sin-offerings."

E. *Why do we draw this conclusion? Based on what was taught on Tannaite authority:* One who plants seeds of diverse kinds, [and again plants seeds] of diverse kinds, incurs the penalty of stripes. *What does it mean that he* incurs the penalty of stripes? *If you say that it means he incurs the penalty of one set of stripes, that is obvious [and need not be stated]. And furthermore, what does it mean [by repeating]* of diverse kinds, of diverse kinds?

F. *But it is obvious that it means he incurs the penalty of two sets of stripes. What case are we dealing with? If you say that the case is where he [sowed them] one after another and with two [separate] warnings [that the act is prohibited], this was taught on Tannaite authority:* **A Nazirite who was drinking wine all day long is liable for only one [violation]. If they said to him, "Do not drink it," and he drank it, [and again they said to him], "Do not drink it," and he drank it, he is liable for each and every one [M. Makkot 3:7].**

G. *But it is obvious then that we are dealing with a case where he sows them all at once and with one warning. In accord with whose opinion is this? If we say in accord with the opinion of the rabbis that dispute the view of Sumkhos, let us now consider the matter. What is the case there [in our Mishnah]? There are separate entities and the rabbis exempted him [from multiple punishments]. Here [where he sows all at once] is it not more logical to conclude [that he be exempt from multiple punishments]?*

H. *Then rather do we not interpret [the rule stated in E] in accord with the view of Sumkhos? No. It is consistent to say that we interpret in accord with the view of the rabbis. And it makes the novel point of teaching us about one matter incidental to another, [that is that] there are two types of diverse kinds. And this serves to disclaim the view of R. Oshaia.*

I. *For said R. Oshaia, "[One is not liable for violating the prohibition of sowing diverse kinds] until he sows wheat, barley and grape seeds in one throw" [b. Qid. 39a]. It makes the novel point [here] that if he sowed wheat and grape seeds or barley and grape seeds he also would be liable.*

II.2
A. *Come and take note:* **[If] he ate two sinews from two thighs from two beasts, he incurs eighty stripes. R. Judah says, "He incurs only forty stripes"** [T. 7:5 E-F]. *What is the situation? If we say that [he ate in two acts] one after the other and he received two warnings, then what is the basis for the view of R. Judah? [Each time he eats] it is a warning that is subject to doubt. [Judah holds the view that only one of the thighs is prohibited and we do not know which one. Each warning then is subject to doubt.] And we learned of [a principle that] R. Judah held. For he said, "Any warning that is subject to doubt is not a valid warning"* [M. 5:1, II.3 I, b. 81a].

B. *For it was taught on Tannaite authority:* **[Concerning a son who is not certain which of two men is his father]: If he struck one [man who might be his father] and then he struck the other [who might be his father]; if he cursed one and then he cursed the other [he is exempt from punishment. But] if he hit them both at the same time; or if he cursed both of them at the same time, he is liable [to the death penalty in accord with Exod. 21]. R. Judah says, "[If he hit them] at the same time he is liable. [If he hit them] one after the other, he is exempt"** [cf. T. Yeb. 12:7 H-K, for a variant version].

C. *But it is obvious that we deal with a case where he did both acts [of eating the thigh] at the same time and he had one warning. And in accord with whose view is that of the first Tanna? If we say in accord with the opinion of the rabbis that dispute the view of Sumkhos, let us now consider the matter. What is the case there [in our Mishnah]?*

*There are separate entities and the rabbis exempted him [from multiple punishments]. Here [where he performs the acts all at once] is it not more logical to conclude [that he be exempt from multiple punishments]?*

D. *Then rather do we not interpret [the rule] in accord with the view of Sumkhos? No. It is consistent to say that we interpret that it is a case [where he performed the acts] one after the other and it is in accord with the view of the rabbis. And this Tanna reasons in accord with the view of another Tanna, in accord with R. Judah who said that a warning that is subject to doubt is a valid warning.*

E. *As it was taught on Tannaite authority:* [The verse says:] "And you shall let none of it remain until the morning, anything that remains until the morning you shall burn" (Exod. 12:10). **[83a]** "The verse comes to connect a commandment to a prohibition to tell us that they do not incur stripes for violating it [i.e., for letting it remain past the appointed time]," the words of R. Judah. R. Jacob says, "This is not the reason [that they do not incur stripes for violating it]. But it is because [violating] the prohibition [of leaving over the sacrifice] does not require an overt act. And [we have a principle that for violating] any prohibition that does not require an overt act, they do not incur stripes."

II.3

A. **Come and take note: [If] he ate two sinews from two thighs from two beasts, he incurs eighty stripes. R. Judah says, "He incurs only forty stripes" [T. 7:5 E-F].** *What is the situation? If we say that [he ate in two acts] one after the other and he received two warnings, then what is the basis for the view of R. Judah who says he incurs forty stripes and no more? But it is obvious that the case is that he ate them [both] at once and with one warning. And in accord with whose view is that of the first Tanna? If we say in accord with the opinion of the rabbis that dispute the view of Sumkhos, let us now consider the matter. What is the case there [in our Mishnah]? There are separate entities and the rabbis exempted him [from multiple punishments]. Here [where he performs the acts all at once] is it not more logical to conclude [that he be exempt from multiple punishments]?*

B. Then rather do we not interpret [the rule] in accord with the view of Sumkhos? No. It is consistent to say that we interpret that it is a case [where he performed the acts] one after the other and [how do we respond to] what was stated, "What is the basis for the view of R. Judah [who says he incurs forty stripes and no more?]" The case in question must be on where there was not an olive's bulk.

C. For it was taught on Tannaite authority: [If] he ate it and it does not contain an olive's bulk, lo, this one is liable [M. Hul. 3:3 B]. R. Judah declares exempt until there will be an olive's bulk therein [T. 7:5 C-D].

I.1 explores the premises of the scriptural and logical bases of Mishnah's rules. II.1 identifies the operative principle of the view of Sumkhos in Mishnah and explores its application to secondary cases. II.2 then cites a related rule from a Tosefta-text and seeks to align its views with those of our Mishnah. II.3 continues this inquiry.

### 5:3 R-V

R. At four seasons in the year does he who sells a beast to his fellow have to inform him, "Its mother did I sell for slaughter, its daughter did I sell for slaughter," and these are they: (1) On the eve of the last festival day of the Festival [of Sukkot;] (2) on the eve of the first festival day of Passover; (3) on the eve of Aseret [Shabuot], (4) and on the eve of the New Year.

S. And in accord with the opinion of R. Yosé the Galilean, "Also on the eve of the Day of Atonement in Galilee."

T. Said R. Judah,"Under what circumstances? When there is no space of time [between sales]. But if there is a space of time [between sales] he does not need to inform him."

U. And R. Judah agrees in the case of one who sells the dam to the bridegroom and the daughter to the bride, that he needs to inform him.

V. For it is certain that both will slaughter [them] on the same day.

### 5:4

A. At these four seasons do they force the butcher to slaughter [an animal] against his will.

- B. Even if it was an ox worth a thousand denars, and the purchaser has only one denar, they force him to slaughter it.
- C. Therefore if it dies, the loss is that of the customer.
- D. But on the rest of the days of the year, it is not so.
- E. Therefore if it dies, the loss is that of the seller.

I.1
- A. *It was taught on Tannaite authority:* If they did not inform him, he may go and slaughter and does not have refrain [from slaughtering in any way].

II.1
- A. Said R. Judah, "Under what circumstances? When there is no space of time [between sales]. But if there is a space of time [between sales] he does not need to inform him." And R. Judah agrees in the case of one who sells the dam to the bridegroom and the daughter to the bride, that he needs to inform him. For it is certain that both will slaughter [them] on the same day [M. 5:3 T-V]. *Why must I teach,* the dam to the bridegroom and the daughter to the bride? *This teaches us a novel point about one matter incidental to another. That is, it is normal that the house of the bridegroom makes a more elaborate [celebration] than the house of the bride. [Because the Mishnah speaks of a case where the bridegroom slaughter the dam and the bride slaughter the offspring.]*

III.1
- A. At these four seasons do they force the butcher to slaughter [an animal] against his will [M. 5:4 A]. *But lo, he did not yet draw it [the animal toward him as a means of acquiring possession]. [Therefore the customer should not take any loss contrary to C.]* Said R. Huna, said Rab, "[We deal with a case where] he did draw it to him."

- B. *If this is so then consider the last text of the Mishnah:* **But on the rest of the days of the year, it is not so. Therefore if it dies, the loss is that of the seller [D-E].** *But lo [why is this the case]? He already drew it to him [thus acquiring it]!*

- C. Said R. Samuel bar Yitzhak, "It is consistent to say that he did not draw it to him. And the case in question is one where he became the owner through the action of another party."

D. **At these four seasons,** since it is a benefit for him [to own the animal, we act in accord with the principle,] they may accept a benefit on behalf of a person [even] in his absence. But during **the rest of the days of the year,** since it is a loss to him [they do not accept it on his behalf in accord with the principle,] they may not accept a loss on behalf of a person in his absence.

E. R. Eleazar says, said R. Yohanan, "**At these four seasons** the sages supported their words with the authority of the Torah." For said R. Yohanan, "On the basis of the law of the Torah money effects acquisition [of title in a transfer of property while a formal act of drawing does not (b. Bekh. 13b)]." And on what basis did they [the rabbis] say that an act of drawing effects acquisition? It is a decree [to protect the buyer] lest he [the seller] say to him, "Your wheat was burned up in a fire in the attic."

I.1 extends the rule of Mishnah. II.1 derives a minor point from a criticism of the Mishnah-paragraph. III.1 is a brief inquiry into the premises of Mishnah.

### 5:5

A. [Concerning the phrase], "One day" which is stated in connection with "it and its young" [with regard to the law this means] the day [accords] with the preceding night.

B. This did Simeon b. Zoma expound: "It is stated with reference to the works of creation, 'One day' (Gen. 1:5), and it is stated with reference to 'it and its young,' 'One day' (Lev. 22:28). Just as 'One day' stated with reference to the works of creation means [as to the law] the day [accords] with the preceding night, so 'One day' stated with reference to 'it and its young' [means] the day [accords] with the preceding night."

I.1

A. *Our rabbis taught on Tannaite authority:* R. Simeon b. Zoma expounded this: Because the entire context [of the rules of our prohibition] speaks only about Holy Things, and because in regard to Holy Things the night follows the day, you might infer that even here that is the case [that the night follows the day]. [Therefore] it is stated here, 'One day' and stated with reference to the works of creation, 'One day.' **Just as 'One day' stated with reference to the works of creation means [as to the law] the day [accords] with the preceding night, so 'One day' stated with reference to 'it and its young' [means] the day [accords] with the preceding night.**

B. [83b] Rabbi says, "'One day' means [to specify] the special requirement of the one day on which you must announce [four times a year that you sold the mother to be slaughtered, warning thereby the buyer of the offspring not to slaughter it on that day]." Based on this [teaching] they said, **At four seasons in the year does he who sells a beast to his fellow have to inform him, ["Its mother did I sell for slaughter, its daughter did I sell for slaughter"]** [M. 5:3 R].

I.1 clarifies the premise of the Mishnah.

# 5

## Bavli Ḥullin Chapter Six

## Folios 83B-89B

### 6:1

A. [The requirement to] cover up the blood applies in the Land and abroad, (2) in the time of the Temple and not in the time of the Temple, (3) in the case of unconsecrated beasts, but not in the case of Holy Things.

B. And it applies (4) to a wild beast and a bird, (5) to that which is captive and to that which is not captive.

C. And it applies (6) to a *koy*, because it is a matter of doubt [whether it is wild or domesticated].

D. And they do not slaughter it [a *koy*] on the festival. But if one has slaughtered it, they do not cover up its blood.

### I.1

A. *On what basis does [the rule] not apply to Holy Things? Do you say it is on account of the view of R. Zira?* For said R. Zira, "One who slaughters must put dust below and dust above [the blood]. For it says, '[Any man also of the people of Israel, or of the strangers that sojourn among them, who takes in hunting any beast or bird that may be eaten] shall pour out its blood and cover it in dust' (Lev. 17:13). It does not say 'with dust,' but it does say, 'in dust.' This teaches us that the one who slaughters must put dust below and dust above [the blood]."

B. *And here [in the case of Holy Things] it is not possible [to cover it above and below with dust]. What are his options? If he puts [dust on* the altar] and declares it null [he thereby violates the prohibition against] adding on to the structure [of the altar]. And it is written [that you cannot change the structures of the Temple], "And this he made clear by the writing from the hand of the Lord concerning it, all the work to be done according to the plan" (I Chron. 28:19).

C. *If he does not declare it null, then it [the dust underneath] will interpose [between the blood and the altar and invalidate the sacrifice].*

D. *Let it be the case then that below it is not possible [to cover the blood of a Holy Thing with dust]. But above it is possible to cover it with dust [in accord with the following]. Was it [the following] not taught on Tannaite authority?* R. Jonathan b. Joseph says, "If one slaughtered a wild animal and afterward one slaughtered a beast, he is exempt from the obligation to cover the blood [of the wild animal since the blood of the beast covers it]. [If one slaughtered] a beast and afterward [one slaughtered] a wild animal, he is liable to cover the blood [of the wild animal even though the blood of the beast lies beneath it." [Here too he should have to cover with dust above it even if he does not place dust below it.]

E. And this accords with the principle of R. Zira. For said R. Zira, "For anything that is suitable for mixing, the absence of the act of mixing does not impede [the effectiveness of the mixture]. And for anything that is not suitable for mixing, the absence of the act of mixing does impede [the effectiveness of the mixture] [b. Men. 103b, b. B.B. 81b]." [In these cases it would have been suitable to put dust below the wild animal's blood. For Holy Things it would not be suitable to put dust below because it would invalidate the sacrifice.]

F. *But why not let him scrape it [the blood off the altar, move it away], and cover it? And [in accord with this] was it not taught on Tannaite authority in the Mishnah:* **Blood that splashes and what is on the knife, one is liable to cover it up [M. 6:6 A-B]?** *It seems logical to conclude that implies he may scrape it off and cover it. Here too let us scrape it off and cover it.*

G. If we are dealing with Holy Things brought upon the altar, *that is indeed the case. In our case what are we dealing with?* With Holy Things that are consecrated property of the Temple treasury [that may not be eaten by anyone until they are redeemed. Thus the act of slaughter accomplishes no change in the status of the animal as food and is invalid.]

H. [84a] *But why not let him redeem it and then cover the blood [since the act of slaughter would then be valid]? [You cannot do this because] you need to assess and appraise [the value of the animal by bringing it to a priest before you redeem it]. And in accord with whose view is this? If you say that it is in accord with the view of R. Meir who said that all cases [of Holy Things] fall under the rule of having to be assessed and appraised, lo he said, "An act of slaughter that is improper, is a valid act of slaughter."* [He must cover the blood in any case.]

I. *And if it is in accord with the view of R. Simeon who said [cf. b. 80a], "An act of slaughter that is improper, is not a valid act of slaughter," lo, he said that all cases do not fall under the rule of having to be assessed and appraised.*

J. Said R. Joseph, "It is in accord with the view of Rabbi. And he concurs with both Tannaite authorities. With regard to an act of slaughter that is improper he holds in accord with the view of R. Simeon [that it is not a valid act of slaughter]. And with regard to the need to assess and appraise [before redeeming the animal] he holds in accord with the view of R. Meir [that all cases fall under the rule]."

K. *And another possibility: The entire matter is in accord with the views of R. Simeon. This case is different [from the ordinary case] because Scripture said, "[He] shall pour out [its blood] and cover it [with dust]" (Lev. 17:13). [This subsumes under the rule] any [Holy Thing] that is lacking only pouring and covering. This excludes that which is lacking pouring, redeeming and covering.*

L. *But now that you have reached this point in the argument, you should maintain even regarding* Holy Things *[i.e., birds] that are consecrated to the altar [that the rule applies only to] that which is lacking only pouring and covering. This excludes that which is lacking pouring, scraping and covering.*

M. Mar bar R. Ashi said, "Scripture said, 'Any beast or bird' (*ibid.*). Just as a wild beast cannot be consecrated [to the altar], so too [we cannot refer here to] a bird that is consecrated to the altar." If [you wish to argue against this you may say] what is the case regarding wild animals? There are none of its kind that can be consecrated. So too regarding birds [we refer only to those] whose kind cannot be consecrated. This would exclude turtle doves and young pigeons whose kind can be consecrated.

N. No [this is not a valid argument]. [Birds] must be like wild animals [in all respects with regard to the law for the logic of the argument to hold]. What is the case with regard to wild animals? You do not distinguish [between kinds that are and are not consecrated]. So too for birds you should not distinguish [between kinds that are and are not consecrated]. [In any case we deal here with unconsecrated birds (Rashi).]

**II.1**

A. *Jacob the heretic said to Raba, "We have the principle that a wild animal is included under the rule for beasts with regard to the tokens [of cleanness] [cf. b. 71a]. It would make sense to maintain also that the beast is included under the rule for wild animals with regard to [the obligation] to cover [the blood]."*

B. *He said to him, "On your account Scripture stated, '[Only you shall not eat the blood]; you shall pour it out upon the earth like water' (Deut. 12:16)." What is the case regarding water? You do not have to cover it up. So too this [blood of a beast] you also do not have to cover it up.*

C. *But on this basis we should infer that they may immerse in it [i.e., in a pool filled with blood to remove uncleanness]. Scripture stated, "Nevertheless a spring or a cistern holding water shall be clean; [but whatever touches their carcass shall be unclean]" (Lev. 11:36). These [pools of water] yes [do render objects clean through immersion]. Other kinds [of pools] do not.*

D. *But it would makes sense to maintain that this concern applies to exclude other kinds of liquids that are not compared to water. But blood that is compared to water should be also [valid for immersion]. [This is not the case because] two exclusions were written in the verse: a spring of water and a cistern of water. But it would make sense to say that both of these exclude other liquids [as valid]. One excludes water that* streamed [into a pool] and one excludes water that was gathered to be held [in a pool]. [This is not the case because] three exclusions were written in the verse: a spring of water, a cistern of water, and a holding of water.

### III.1

A. *Our rabbis taught on Tannaite authority:* "[Any man also of the people of Israel, or of the strangers that sojourn among them], who takes in hunting [any beast or bird that may be eaten shall pour out its blood and cover it with dust]" (Lev. 17:13). I have only [the rule that he cover the blood] for those that he "takes in hunting." What is the basis [for the rule] for those that are already taken and make themselves ready, such as geese and chickens? It comes to teach, "in hunting" implying any way [he takes them they are subject to the rule]. If so what does it come to teach by stating "who takes"? The Torah taught proper behavior. For a person should eat meat only after this kind of [extensive] preparation. [One should not eat meat often lest he become poor (Rashi).] [Cf. T. Arak. 4:28.]

### III.2

A. *Our rabbis taught on Tannaite authority:* "When the Lord your God enlarges your territory, [as he has promised you, and you say, 'I will eat flesh,' because you crave flesh, you may eat as much flesh as you desire]" (Deut. 12:20). The Torah taught proper behavior. A person should eat meat only when he craves it.

B. You might infer that a person may buy meat from the market place [any time he desires] and eat it. It comes to teach, "[If the place which the Lord your God will choose to put his name there is too far from you], then you may kill any of your herd or your flock, [which the Lord has given you, as I have commanded you; and you may eat within your towns as much as you desire]" (Deut. 12:21).

C. You might infer that he may kill all his herd and eat it or kill all his flock and eat it. It comes to teach, "Of your herd" — and not all your herd; "[Of] your flock" — and not all your flock. [Cf. T. Arak. 4:26.]

D. Based on this said R. Eleazar b. Azariah, "Whoever has a *maneh* should buy a *litra* of vegetables for his stew. If he has ten *manehs* he should buy a *litra* of fish for his stew. If he has fifty *manehs* he should buy a *litra* of meat for his stew. If he has one hundred *manehs* they should cook up a stew for him every day." [Cf. T. Arak. 4:27.]

E. *And for the others [who have less than a hundred] when should they [cook up a stew]? On every Sabbath eve.*

F. Said Rab, "We must show concern for the words of an elder [i.e., for the view of Eleazar and make do on a modest diet]." Said R. Yohanan, "Abba [Rab] was from a healthy family [who could thrive on this diet]. But we [are not]. Whoever has a penny in his pocket should run and take it to the storekeeper [and not wait in accord with Eleazar's teaching]." Said R. Nahman, "But we [are not like that]. We borrow to eat."

## III.3

A. [We have this related exposition about self-sufficiency based on these two verses in Proverbs: "The lambs will provide your clothing, and the goats the price of a field. There will be enough goats' milk for your food, for the food of your household and maintenance for your maidens" (Prov. 27:26-27).] "The lambs will provide your clothing," [means] from the shearing of your lambs you should make your clothes. "And the goats the price of a field," [means] a person in general may sell his field to buy goats. But he may not sell his goats to buy a field. "There will be enough goats' milk" [means] it is enough if a person sustains himself through the milk of goats and lambs that are in his household. "For your food, for the food of your household" [means] your food should take precedence over the food for your household.

B. "And maintenance for your maidens" — said Mar Zutra the son of R. Nahman, "Provide maintenance for your maidens. From this stipulation the Torah taught us proper behavior. For a person should not teach his child [to expect to have] meat and wine."

*Bavli Hullin Chapter Six. Folios 83B-89B* 251

C. Said R. Yohanan, **[84b]** "A person who wishes to become wealthy should breed small animals." Said R. Hisda, "What is the implication of that which is written, 'The increase of your cattle' (Deut. 7:13)? [It means that breeding cattle] increases the wealth of the owners."

D. *And said R. Yohanan, "It is better to drink a cup of magical potion than to drink a cup of warm water. And this concern applies to [water in] a metal vessel. But we do not have this concern regarding a clay vessel. And we say this only regarding a metal vessel that had no roots [of herbs and spices] in it. But if it had roots in it we do not have this concern. And we say this only where they put no roots in it and where they did not boil [the water first]. But where they did boil it we do not have this concern."*

E. And said R. Yohanan, "If a person's father left him money and he wants to lose it, let him wear linen garments and use glass utensils and hire workers but not sit with them [to oversee them]. Let him wear linen garments [such as] *Roman linen.* And let him use glass utensils [such as] *white glassware.* And let him hire workers but not sit with them [such as] *those that work with oxen who can cause great loss [if not supervised properly]."*

**III.4**
A. R. Avira expounded, sometimes he said this in the name of R. Ammi and sometimes he said this in the name of R. Assi, "What is the meaning of what is written, 'It is well with the man who deals generously and lends, who conducts his affairs with justice' (Ps. 112:5)? A person should always eat and drink [on a standard] lower than his means. And he should dress and clothe himself in accord with his means. And he should respect his wife and children [on a standard that is] beyond his means. For they depend on him and he depends on the one who spoke and brought the world into being."

B. R. Ayna expounded *at the gate of the house of the Exilarch:* "One who slaughters [a bird] on the Sabbath on behalf of a person who is ill is liable to cover [the blood with dust]." *Rabbah said to them,* "Mute him!" He meant, "Take his amora away from him."

C. *For it was taught on Tannaite authority* [T. 6:1 C-6:3, with some variations]: R. Yosé says, "As to a *koy*: they do not slaughter it on the festival, because it is a matter of doubt, but if they have slaughtered it, they do not cover up its blood" [M. Hul. 6:1 C-D].

D. This is based on an argument *a fortiori*. [Said R. Yosé], "Now [consider that] for circumcision, in a case that is certain it overrides the Sabbath, [while] what is a matter of doubt... does not override the festival. [Then concerning] the covering up of the blood, [that in a case that is certain] does not override the Sabbath, logically in a matter of doubt [surely it] should not override the festival."

E. They said to him, "The sounding of the shofar in the provinces [when the New Year falls on a Sabbath day] will prove [the contrary].... For even though when it is a matter of certainty, it does not override the Sabbath, [but] when it is a matter of doubt, it [still] does override the festival."

F. Answered [R. Hiyya the son of] R. Eleazar Haqqappar Beribbi, "Now the distinctive reason that circumcision [in a matter of doubt] does not override the festival [is that when it is certainly required it does not override the nights of festivals]. But will you say so in the case of the covering up of the blood, [for when it is certainly required], it overrides the nights of festival. [Since when it is certainly required it overrides the nights of a festival, it is logical that when it is a matter of doubt it should override the festival.]"

G. Said R. Abba, "This is one of the matters to which R. Hiyya did say there is no answer, and R. Eleazar Haqqappar Beribbi supplied the answer."

H. *It was taught there [D] in any case:* [Then concerning] the covering up of the blood, [that in a case that is certain] does not override the Sabbath, what is the case of a matter of certainty regarding the covering up of the blood that does not override the Sabbath? Is it not the case of one who slaughters on the Sabbath on behalf of a person who is ill?

Bavli Ḥullin Chapter Six. Folios 83B-89B    253

I.  *But perhaps this is where he violated the prohibition and slaughtered [on the Sabbath]. [No, this cannot be.] It must be a case that is comparable to the case of circumcision [on the Sabbath]. Just as for circumcision he is permitted [to perform the act] so too for the case of covering the blood it must be where he was permitted [to slaughter the animal. Accordingly, it must be that he did it for a person who was ill].*

J.  [Reverting now to E above]: **They said to him, "The sounding of the shofar in the provinces [when the New Year falls on a Sabbath day] will prove [the contrary].... For even though when it is a matter of certainty, it does not override the Sabbath, [but] when it is a matter of doubt, it [still] does override the festival."** What is the case of a matter of doubt? *If we say there is a doubt about whether it is a weekday or a festival day, let us now consider the matter. If it overrides a day that is certainly a festival day, is there any question that it overrides a day about which there is a doubt whether it is a weekday or a festival day?*

K.  [85a] *Rather [the case must be] where there is a doubt whether [the person who blows the shofar] is a man of a woman. And R. Yosé is consistent with his view elsewhere. For he said that a person who is certainly a woman also may sound the shofar. [Accordingly there is not question about this case of doubt while the question remains about the law in a case of doubt for a koy.]*

L.  *For it was taught on Tannaite authority:* The sons of Israel may lay their hands [on the sacrifice]. But the daughters of Israel may not lay their hands. [The verse is: "He shall lay his hand upon the head of the burnt offering, and it shall be accepted for him to make atonement for him" (Lev. 1:4).] R. Yosé and R. Simeon say, "Women are permitted to lay their hands [on the sacrifice]." [And for Yosé the principle may be extended to instruct us that women may sound the shofar.]

M.  Said Rabina, "But according to what the rabbis said [that a woman cannot sound the shofar] there is another form of refutation [in this logical argument]. What is the case regarding the sounding of the shofar? Where it is certain [that it is the festival], it overrides the Sabbath in the Temple. What can you say regarding the covering of the blood where there is no case at

N. [Consider again the previous text at F]: **Answered [R. Hiyya the son of] R. Eleazar Haqqappar Beribbi, "Now the distinctive reason that circumcision [in a matter of doubt] does not override the festival [is that when it is certainly required it does not override the nights of festivals].** *Is it just on festival nights that circumcision is not practiced? Is it practiced on other nights? [No.] Rather [this is how you should state the matter]:* What is the case regarding circumcision? It is not practiced at night as it is during the day. What can you say about the covering of the blood? It is practiced at night just as it is during the day.

O. [Repeating G]: **Said R. Abba, "This is one of the matters to which R. Hiyya did say there is no answer, and R. Eleazar Haqqappar Beribbi supplied the answer."**

I.1 identifies the premise and logic of the rule of Mishnah in a sustained inquiry. II.1 explores a second level of issues. III.1-4 add related insight on the value of moderation. The unit concludes citing the relevant Tosefta-text and exploring its premises.

### 6:2

A. (1) He who slaughters [a wild beast or a bird] and it turns out to be *terefah*,
B. (2) he who slaughters for the purpose of idolatry,
C. (3) he who slaughters an unconsecrated [wild animal or bird] inside [the Temple] or consecrated ones outside [M. 5:1],
D. (4) a wild beast and a bird which are to be stoned —
E. R. Meir declared liable [for the covering up of the blood] [M. 5:3].
F. And sages declare free [of the liability].
G. (1) He who slaughters [a wild beast or a bird] and it is made carrion by his own deed,
H. (2) he who pierces [the windpipe],
I. (3) he who tears out [the windpipe],
J. is free [of the obligation] to cover up [the blood].

## I.1

A. Said R. Hiyya bar Abba, said R. Yohanan, "Rabbi concurred with the words of R. Meir regarding the prohibition against slaughtering it and its offspring on the same day. And he repeated it here attributing it to the sages. And [he concurred with the words] of R. Simeon regarding the obligation to cover the blood. And he repeated it here, attributing it to the sages."

B. *On what basis* did R. Meir [rule as he did] regarding the prohibition against slaughtering it and its offspring on the same day? Said R. Joshua b. Levi, "He derived it from the common use of the word 'slaughter' [in our case and in the case of sacrifices that were] slaughtered outside [the Temple]." [The verses are: "If any man of the house of Israel kills (i.e., slaughters) an ox or a lamb or a goat in the camp, or kills (slaughters) it outside the camp" (Lev. 17:3). And whether the mother is a cow or a ewe, you shall not kill (slaughter) both her and her young in one day" (Lev. 22:28).] What is the case there? We consider an improper act of slaughter to be a valid act of slaughter. So too here an improper act of slaughter is a valid act of slaughter.

C. And R. Simeon *on what basis* [did he dispute this view]? Said R. Mani bar Patish, "He derived it from the verse, [When Joseph saw Benjamin with them, he said to the steward of his house, 'Bring the men into the house], and slaughter an animal and make ready, [for the men are to dine with me at noon'] (Gen. 43:16). What is the case there? It is a proper act of slaughter [that he instructed them to perform]. So too here it must be a proper slaughter [to be deemed a valid act]."

D. *And why does R. Meir not derive [the same conclusion] from,* "slaughter an animal"? [He does not because he holds the view that] we may deduce a conclusion from the common use of the word 'slaughter' [šḥt]. But we cannot deduce a conclusion from the use of 'slaughter' [šḥt] based on the use of [a different root], 'slaughter an animal' [ṭbḥ].

E. *What difference does it make [that we have different terms here]? Lo, it was taught on Tannaite authority by the House of R. Ishmael: [The verse says],* "And the priest shall come again [on the seventh day, and look; and if the disease has spread in the walls of the house]

(Lev. 14:39).... Then the priest shall go [and look; and if the disease has spread in the house, it is a malignant leprosy in the house; it is unclean]" (Lev. 14:44). [The term] "come again" is common to [the term] "go" [as far as deducing conclusions regarding the rules].

F. [This objection based on the teaching of the house of R. Ishmael is not applicable to our circumstance.] *Their concern applies where there is no identical term* [to compare to in another verse for the purposes of making a deduction concerning the law]. *But where there is an identical term, we must derive any inference from the [verse with the] identical term.*

G. *And why does R. Simeon not deduce a conclusion from the common use of the term in the verse concerning the slaughter of sacrifices outside the Temple [as in B above]? [He holds the view that] we deduce a conclusion from one [case of the slaughter of] an unconsecrated animal to another [such case]. But we do not deduce a conclusion for one [case of the slaughter of] an unconsecrated animal from a [case of the slaughter of] a consecrated animal.*

H. *But [does this not pose a difficulty then according to the view of] R. Meir? [He would answer], does not the prohibition against slaughtering it and its offspring on the same day apply to consecrated animals? This is the basis for what R. Hiyya said [in A],* "Rabbi concurred with the words of R. Meir regarding the prohibition against slaughtering it and its offspring on the same day. And he repeated it here attributing it to the sages."

I. *On what basis* did R. Meir [rule as he did] regarding the obligation to cover the blood? Said R. Simeon b. Laqish, "He derived it from the common use of the word 'pour' [in our case and in the case of sacrifices that were] slaughtered outside [the Temple]." [The verses are: "Any man also of the people of Israel, or of the strangers that sojourn among them, who takes in hunting any beast or bird that may be eaten shall pour out its blood and cover it with dust" (Lev. 17:13). "[... and does not bring it to the door of the tent of meeting, to offer it as a gift to the Lord before the tabernacle of the Lord, bloodguilt shall be imputed to that man]; he has shed (poured) blood; [and that man shall be cut off from among his people]" (Lev. 17:4).] What is the case there? We consider an improper act of slaughter to be a valid act of slaughter. So too here an improper act of slaughter is a valid act of slaughter.

J. And [what will] R. Simeon [respond to this line of reasoning]? *It is written, "That may be eaten."* [You cannot compare this to the case of a consecrated animal.]

K. And [what will] R. Meir [respond to this]? This [phrase] *comes to exclude* an unclean bird [from the obligation]. [But you can make other comparisons.]

L. And [what will] R. Simeon [respond to this]? *What is the basis for excluding an unclean bird? It is because it is not permitted for eating. A* terefah-*bird also is not permitted for eating [but according to Meir it is still subject to the obligation]. This is the basis for what R. Hiyya said [in A],* "Rabbi concurred with the words of R. Simeon regarding the obligation to cover the blood. And he repeated it here, attributing it to the sages."

I.2
A. Said R. Abba [85b], "Not for every matter did R. Meir say that an improper act of slaughter is a valid act of slaughter. R. Meir would agree that it does not render [the animal] permitted for eating. And not for every purpose did R. Simeon say that an improper act of slaughter is not a valid act of slaughter. R. Simeon would agree that it renders [the animal] clean of the uncleanness of carrion."

B. Said the master, "[We learned], 'Not for every matter did R. Meir say that an improper act of slaughter is a valid act of slaughter. R. Meir would agree that it does not render [the animal] permitted for eating.' *But this is obvious! Is an animal that is* terefah *permitted [to be eaten] on account of an act of slaughter?"* No. *It is necessary [to state the matter for clarification of the law in the case of] one who slaughtered a* terefah-*animal and found in it a live nine-month old foetus. You might have concluded that it makes sense to say that since R. Meir said, "An improper act of slaughter is a valid act of slaughter," that the slaughter of the mother will be effective [for the offspring] and it will not need its own act of slaughter. It makes the* novel point [that, "It does not render the animal permitted for eating"].

C. *But is this a proper line of reasoning? Lo, did not R. Meir say, "A live birth from a [properly] slaughtered animal needs [its own act of] slaughter." [It is surely obvious that his view would be that the offspring needs its own act of slaughter in the case of a live birth from an animal that was itself subjected to an improper act of slaughter.] No. It is necessary [to state the matter]. For Rabbi reasons in accord with the view of R. Meir and he reasons in accord with the view of the rabbis.*

D. *He reasons in accord with the view of R. Meir who said, "An improper act of slaughter is a valid act of slaughter." And he reasons in accord with the view of the rabbis who said, "The act of slaughter of its mother renders it clean." [Accordingly you might conclude] that the slaughter of the mother will be effective [for the offspring] and it will not need its own act of slaughter. It makes the novel point [that, "It does not render the animal permitted for eating"].*

E. *[Returning to Abba's statement at A]: "And not for every purpose did R. Simeon say that an improper act of slaughter is not a valid act of slaughter. R. Simeon would agree that it renders [the animal] clean of the uncleanness of carrion." But this is obvious! For said R. Judah, said Rab, and some say that this was taught in a Tannaite teaching: Scripture stated, "And if from among any animal [of which you may eat dies, he who touches its carcass shall be unclean until the evening" (Lev. 11:39); "from among" implies] some of the animals render unclean and some of the animals do not render unclean. And which is it [that does not render unclean]? It is a terefah-animal that was slaughtered (b. 74a, V.1 C).*

F. *But it is necessary [to state the rule to exclude a case where] he slaughtered a terefah-animal and it was an unconsecrated animal [slaughtered] in the Temple court. For it was taught on Tannaite authority: He who slaughters a terefah-animal, and likewise he who slaughters [an apparently normal animal] and it is found to be a terefah, both of them unconsecrated animals [slaughtered] in the Temple court — R. Simeon permits them to derive from them* benefit. And the sages prohibit. *You might have concluded that it makes sense to say that since R. Simeon said they are permitted to derive from them benefit, it seems logical to conclude that this is not deemed an act of slaughter in any respect. It would make sense to maintain then that it [the slaughter] does not render it [the animal] clean from the uncleanness of carrion. It comes to make the novel point [that, "It renders the animal clean of the uncleanness of carrion"].*

G. *Said R. Pappa to Abayye, "Does R. Simeon reason in accord with the view that [the slaughter of] an unconsecrated animal in the Temple court [is prohibited] on the authority of the Torah?" He said to him, "Yes. For it was taught in the Mishnah on Tannaite authority:* **R. Simeon says, 'Unconsecrated beasts that are slaughtered in the Temple courtyard are to be burned. And so: A wild animal that is slaughtered in the Temple courtyard'** [M. Tem. 7:4 F-G]. *This makes perfect sense if you say that [it is prohibited] on the authority of the Torah. That is why we decree [a prohibition] for a wild animal incidental to [the prohibition] for a beast. But if you say that [it is prohibited] on the authority of the rabbis [to begin with, then we have the following situation]. A beast [that is not consecrated is prohibited to be slaughtered in the Temple court] on what basis? [We decree against it] lest perhaps [this will lead to confusion and] they come to eat Holy Things outside [the Temple]. This itself would be a decree [of the rabbis]. Would we then go and establish [another] decree to extend this [original] decree?" [We would not. Hence, according to Simeon, since we do make a decree it must be that he holds the view that the original prohibition is based on the authority of the Torah.]*

II.1
A. *Worms infested the flax of R. Hiyya. He came before Rabbi [for advice]. He said to him, "Take a bird and slaughter it over the vat of water [that the flax is soaking in]. For they will smell the blood and leave the flax."*

B. *Now how could he act in accord with this advice? Lo, was it not taught on Tannaite authority:* He who slaughters and needs to use the blood, he is liable to cover it. What must he do [to kill it in order to use the blood without covering it]? Either he stabs it or he rips out its organs [b. 27b].

C. *When R. Dimi came [from Israel] he said [in order to use the blood without having to cover it], "Go and render it terefah," is what he [Rabbi] said to him [Hiyya]." When Rabin came [from Israel] he said, "Go and stab it," is what he said to him.*

D. *According to the authority [Dimi] who holds the view [that he told him], "Go and render it terefah," why did he not tell him to, "Go and stab it?" And if you wish to maintain it is because he holds the view that, "The Torah did not prescribe the procedures of slaughtering for fowl" (b. 4a, Zahavy, Hullin, vol. I, p. 28), [therefore] stabbing it is the same as slaughtering it [and he would be liable to cover the blood if he did this], but lo, it was taught on Tannaite authority: Rabbi says, "'As I have commanded you' (Deut. 12:21) — this teaches us that Moses was commanded concerning [the requirement to slaughter by cutting] the gullet and the windpipe [and the requirement to slaughter] the majority of one organ for a bird and the majority of two organs for a beast" [b. 28a, Zahavy, Hullin, vol. I, p. 151]. [Accordingly, this cannot be the explanation.]*

E. **[86a]** *[The reason he told him to render it terefah is] he stated matters in the most efficient way. It was not efficient for him to say, "Go and stab it," for that is not an act of slaughtering at all. But [in telling him], "Go and render it terefah," it might have made sense to maintain that an improper act of slaughter is deemed an act of slaughter and it is necessary to cover the blood. It makes the novel point [that it is not necessary] in accord with R. Hiyya bar Abba.*

F. *And the authority who holds the view [Rabin] that he told him, "Go and stab it," why did he not tell him, "Go and render it terefah?" And if you wish to maintain that it is because he holds the view that an improper act of slaughter is a valid act of slaughter, but lo, said R. Hiyya bar Abba, said R. Yohanan, "Rabbi concurred with the words [of R. Meir regarding the prohibition against slaughtering it and its offspring on the same day. And he repeated it here attributing it to the sages. And he concurred with the words] of R. Simeon regarding the obligation to cover the blood. And he repeated it here, attributing it to the sages" [I.1 A, above]. [Accordingly, this cannot be the explanation.]*

G. *[The reason he told him to stab it is] he stated matters in the most efficient way. It was not efficient for him to say, "Go and render it terefah," because an improper act of slaughter is not deemed an act of slaughter. But [in telling him], "Go and stab it," it might have made sense to maintain [as at D above] that, "The Torah did not prescribe the procedures of slaughtering for fowl" (b. 4a, vol. I, p. 28), [therefore] stabbing it is the same as slaughtering it, and he should be liable to cover the blood. It comes to make the novel point [that there are procedures for the fowl], 'As I have commanded you' (Deut. 12:21).*

H. *But how is it possible that worms infested his [Hiyya's] flax [A, above]? Lo, did not Rabin bar Abba say, and some say that is was R. Abin bar Sheba, "When the residents of the diaspora came up [to Israel] the meteorites, earthquakes, winds and thunderstorms ceased. And their wine did not sour and their flax did not suffer an infestation. And the sages attributed this to [the merits of] R. Hiyya and his children" (b. Suk. 20a)?*

I. *Their merit helped protect the rest of the world. It did not work for them. And this accords with what R. Judah said in the name of Rab. For said R. Judah, said Rab, "Every day a heavenly echo goes forth and says, 'The entire world derives its sustenance on account of [the merit of] Hanina [b. Dosa] my son [cf. b. Ta'an. 24b-25a]. And for Hanina my son [the ascetic] it is enough if he has a qab of carob from one Sabbath even to the next."*

I.1 aligns various views of Mishnah and sets forth a sustained inquiry into the scriptural and logical bases for the rule. I.2 takes up the premises of the preceding and explores them independent of the criticism of our Mishnah-text. II.1 has no bearing on the elucidation of the Mishnah until F relates the inquiry to I.1 A.

6:3
A. **A deaf-mute, an imbecile, and a minor who slaughtered, and others oversee them [M. 1:1] are liable to cover up [the blood].**
B. **[If they did so] all by themselves, they are free of liability to cover up [the blood].**
C. **And so with regard to the matter of, "It and its offspring:"**

D. [if] they have slaughtered and others oversee them, it is prohibited to slaughter [the offspring] after them.
E. [If they did so] all by themselves,
F. R. Meir permits [one] to slaughter [the offspring] after them.
G. And sages prohibit.
H. But they agree that if one has slaughtered [the offspring after the deaf-mute, imbecile, or minor has slaughtered the dam], he does not incur forty stripes.

I.1
A. And for the rabbis *what difference is there between the first text [of the Mishnah], where they did not dispute, and the last text [of the Mishnah], where they did dispute? In [respect to the ruling of] the first text if we say that they are* liable to cover the blood, *people will say that their act of slaughter is fine and will come to eat from what they slaughtered.*

B. *But from [the ruling] of the last text I also [would conclude] that because the rabbis say that it is prohibited to slaughter [the second animal] after they [slaughtered the first], people will say that their act of slaughter is fine and will come to eat from what they slaughtered.*

C. *[The cases are different.] In the [case presented in] last text people will say [he does not slaughter the second animal] because he does not need any more meat [and not because the act of slaughter for the first one was valid].*

D. *But then in the [case presented in] the first text people will say that [he covers the blood] to clean up his yard [and not because he is liable to do so].*

E. *[This may be true. But] if he slaughtered at a trash heap, will you be able to say this? Or if he sought a ruling [from a court as to whether he was liable to cover the blood and they ruled that he was liable] will you be able to say [that their act of slaughter in general is not fine]?*

F. *But then according to your logic in the [case presented in the] last text, if he sought a ruling [and was told not to slaughter the second animal] will you be able to say [that their slaughter in general is not fine]?*

G. *Rather it must be the case that the rabbis disputed the entire matter [both cases]. But they postponed until R. Meir had presented the whole matter and then they disputed his view.*

H. *Now the view of the rabbis makes perfect sense because it presents a stringency [in a case of doubt]. But what is the basis for the view of R. Meir?*

I. Said R. Jacob, said R. Yohanan, "R. Meir used to declare one who ate from what they slaughtered liable on account of [eating] carrion." *What is the basis for this view?* Said R. Ammi. "It is because the majority of their actions are flawed."

J. Said R. Pappa to R. Huna the son of R. Joshua, and some say R. Huna the son of R. Joshua said to R. Pappa, "*Why specify that a majority [of their actions are flawed]? Even if a minority [are flawed] it also would be the case [that we should declare the animal carrion]. For lo, R. Meir shows concern for the minority [b. 6a, Zahavy, Hullin, vol. I, p. 37]. Now you combine this minority [of cases] together with the presumption [that the animal is forbidden for eating until it is properly slaughtered], and you have undermined the majority [of cases where they would perform a proper act of slaughter]."*

K. *For it was taught in the Mishnah on Tannaite authority:* **A child [who is unclean] who is found at the side of the dough and the dough is in his hand — R. Meir declares clean. And sages declare unclean, for it is the way of the child to slap [dough]** [M. Toh. 3:8 A-D]. *And we say what is the basis for the view of R. Meir. He reasons that the majority of children slap and a minority do not slap. And the dough itself retains a presumption of cleanness. You combine* **[86b]** *the minority together with the presumption, and you have undermined the majority.*

L. [Carrying this reasoning further]: If they said that it is clean in a case of doubt with regard to uncleanness, they should accordingly say that it is permitted in a case of doubt with regard to a prohibition. [Therefore in our case, Meir permits them to slaughter the second animal, even though he shows concern for a minority of cases, and they might have slaughtered it properly, since we say that the majority of their actions are flawed and the presumption is that the animal is forbidden until slaughtered (Rashi)].

II.1
A. Rabbi taught in accord with the view of R. Meir. And Rabbi taught in accord with the view of sages. *Which of these was his last [and definitive ruling]?*

B. *Come and take note: R. Abba the son of R. Hiyya bar Abba and R. Zira were standing in the market place of Caesarea near the door of the house of study. R. Ammi came out and found them there. He said to them, "Did I not instruct you that during the session of the house of study you should not stand outside lest there be those who need to know a tradition and there be trouble [because they cannot ascertain in your absence what is the tradition]?"*

C. *R. Zira went in. R. Abba did not go in. They were sitting and asking [in the session], "Which of these was his last [and definitive ruling]?" Said to them R. Zira, "I did not know [that this question was under discussion]. I could have asked the elder [R. Abba]. Perhaps he heard from his father and his father heard from R. Yohanan [which one was the definitive ruling]. For R. Hiyya bar Abba used to review his learning before R. Yohanan every thirty days."*

D. *What was the outcome of the issue? Come and take note:* R. Eleazar sent to the diaspora [to Babylonia], "Rabbi taught in accord with the view of R. Meir." But lo, he also taught in accord with the rabbis. But it must be that you derive from this that this was his definitive ruling. We do derive this conclusion.

I.1 identifies the nature and premises of the dispute of Mishnah. II.1 turns to the second-level issue of what is the definitive rule that derives from the Mishnah?

### 6:4 A-D

A. (1) [If] one has slaughtered a hundred wild beasts in one place, a single covering up of the blood [serves] for all of them.

B. (2) [If one has slaughtered] a hundred birds in one place, a single covering up of the blood [serves] for all of them.

C. (3) [If one has slaughtered] a wild beast and a bird in one place, a single covering up of the blood [serves] for all of them.

D. R. Judah says, "[If] one has slaughtered a wild beast, he should cover up [its blood], and afterward let him slaughter the bird."

I.1
A. *Our rabbis taught on Tannaite authority:* ["Any man also of the people of Israel, or of the strangers that sojourn among them, who takes in hunting any beast or bird that may be eaten shall pour out its blood and cover it in dust" (Lev. 17:13).] "Any beast" means any number of beasts, whether many or few. "Any... bird" means any number of birds, whether many or few.

B. *Based on this they said,* (1) [If] one has slaughtered a hundred wild beasts in one place, a single covering up of the blood [serves] for all of them. (2) [If one has slaughtered] a hundred birds in one place, a single covering up of the blood [serves] for all of them. (3) [If one has slaughtered] a wild beast and a bird in one place, a single covering up of the blood [serves] for all of them [M. 6:4 A-C].

C. **R. Judah says, "[If] one has slaughtered a wild beast, he should cover up [its blood], and afterward let him slaughter the bird."** [M. 6:4 D]. As it is written, "Any beast or bird."

D. They said to him, "Lo, it is written, 'For the life of every creature is the blood of it; [therefore I have said to the people of Israel, You shall not eat the blood of any creature, for the life of every creature is its blood; whoever eats it shall be cut off]' (Lev. 17:14)."

E. *What did they answer him? This is what the rabbis said to him,* "This word 'or' [as in 'Any beast or bird'] is needed to separate [beast from bird, i.e., that you do not need to slaughter both to be liable to cover the blood.]" And R. Judah [holds the view that] we derive that they separate [beast from bird] from the words 'its blood' in the verse. And the rabbis [hold the view that] the words 'its blood' mean all blood [is forbidden]. As it is written, "For the life of every creature is the blood of it."

## II.1

A. Said R. Hanina, "R. Judah would agree that with regard to reciting a blessing [over the acts of slaughtering a beast and a bird, M. 6:4 D], that he recites only one blessing [even though the act of covering the blood interposes]."

B. *Said Rabina to R. Aha the son of Raba, and some say R. Aha the son of Raba said to R. Ashi, "How is this different from [the ruling of the students of Rab]?" For R. Brona and R. Hananel, students of Rab, were sitting at a dinner. R. Yeba the elder was standing near them. They said to him, "Let us recite the blessing [after the meal]." Then they said to him, "Let us have something to drink." R. Yeba the elder said to them, "This is what Rab said, 'As soon as one says, Let us recite the blessing, [the meal is over and] it is prohibited for him to drink wine [unless he recites another blessing before drinking].'"*

C. *Here too, as soon as he gets involved in covering the blood, he is liable to recite another blessing [for his next act of slaughter].*

D. *[87a] But are these cases comparable? There [regarding the meal] it is impossible for him to drink [more wine] and to recite the blessing [over the meal] at the same time. Here [in the case of slaughtering] it is possible for him to slaughter with one hand and to cover the blood with the other at the same time.*

I.1 establishes a scriptural basis for the rule of Mishnah. II.1 examines a second-level issue — regulations for reciting blessings over acts of slaughter and covering the blood.

### 6:4 E-G

E. [If] he slaughtered [a wild beast or a bird] and he did not cover up [its blood] and another person saw him, he [the other person] is liable to cover up [the blood].

F. [If] he covered up [the blood] and it became uncovered, he is free of liability to cover it up [again].

G. [If] the wind [blew dirt and] covered it up [and it became uncovered], he is liable to cover it up.

## I.1

A. *Our rabbis taught on Tannaite authority: "[He] shall pour out its blood and cover it with dust" (Lev. 17:13) [means] the one who* pours it out should cover it. [If] he slaughtered [a wild beast or a bird] and he did not cover up [its blood] and another person saw him, on what basis is he [the other person] liable to cover up [the blood]? As it says, "Therefore I have said to the people of Israel" (Lev. 17:14). This is an admonition to all the people of Israel.

B. *Another Tannaite teaching:* "[He] shall pour out its blood and cover it with dust" (Lev. 17:13) [means] with what he poured it out he should cover it. He should not cover it [by kicking dust on it] with his foot. For he should not subject the commandments to derision. [Cf. T. 6:10.]

C. *Another Tannaite teaching:* "[He] shall pour out its blood and cover it with dust" (Lev. 17:13) [means] the one who poured it out should be the one who covers it.

D. Once [*m'sh b*] a person slaughtered and his associate went ahead and covered the blood. And Rabban Gamaliel declared him [the associate] liable to give him [the person who slaughtered] ten gold coins.

E. *They posed a question: Was this compensation for [depriving him of] performing a commandment or of reciting a blessing? In what case is there a practical difference [between these alternative explanations]? In [the case of one who goes ahead and deprives his associate of] reciting the blessing over the meal. If you say it is compensation for the performance of a commandment, then it is one [commandment that he deprived him of fulfilling]. But if you say that it is compensation for the recitation of a blessing, then here there are four [blessings that he deprived him of reciting]. Which is it?*

F. *Come and take note:* A certain Sadducee said to Rabbi, "The one who formed the mountains did not create the winds. And the one who created the winds did not form the mountains. *For it is written,* 'For lo, he who forms the mountains, and creates the wind' (Amos 4:13)."

G. *He said to him,* "Fool! Look at the end of the verse, '[For lo, he who forms the mountains, and creates the wind, and declares to man what is his thought; who makes the morning darkness, and

H. *He said to him, "Give me three days and I will return with a decisive refutation." Rabbi sat and fasted for three days. When he was about to eat they said to him, "A Sadducee is at the gate." He said, "They gave me poison for food" (Ps. 69:21).*

I. He said to him, "Rabbi, I bring you good tidings. He [the other one] could not find an answer and he threw himself off the roof and died." He said to him, "Do you wish to dine with me?" He said to him, "Yes."

J. After they ate and drank he [Rabbi] said to him, "Would you prefer to drink the cup [of wine over which you will recite] the blessings? Or would you rather have forty gold coins?" He said to him, "I would rather drink the cup over which one recites the blessings." A heavenly echo went forth and proclaimed, "The cup of wine over which one recites the blessings is worth forty gold coins."

K. Said R. Yitzhak, "They still consider that family [of the opponent of Rabbi] among the greatest in Rome. And they call it the family of Bar Luianus."

II.1
A. **[If] he covered up [the blood] and it became uncovered, he is free of liability to cover it up [again] [M. 6:4 F].** Said R. Aha the son of Raba to R. Ashi, "Why is this different from the obligation to return a lost object?" For said the master, "You shall take them back to your brother" (Deut. 22:1) [means] even a hundred times.

B. He said to him, "There, no exclusion is written in the verse. Here, an exclusion is written in the verse: '[And he shall] cover it with dust.'"

III.1
A. **[If] the wind [blew dirt and] covered it up [and it became uncovered], he is liable to cover it up [M. 6:4 G].** Said Rabbah bar bar Hannah, said R. Yohanan, "They taught this matter only

where it again became uncovered. But where it did not again become uncovered, his is exempt from the obligation to cover it."

B. *But who cares if it again became uncovered? Lo, the [obligation] was already deferred [when the wind covered it]. Said R. Pappa, "This means that there is no deferral for the performance of commandments."*

C. *And how is this different from what was taught on Tannaite authority: One who slaughters, and the blood is absorbed into the ground, he is liable to cover the blood? That is where the outline [of the blood] is visible.*

I.1 sets forth a scriptural basis for the rules of Mishnah and several further expositions of the verse in A-C. D-K move to a second-level issue derivative of the primary consideration of the nature of the commandment to cover the blood. II.1 contrasts the premise of the Mishnah-paragraph with an intersecting premise of a different rule. III.1 engages in a brief criticism of the premise of the rule of the Mishnah.

### 6:5
A. Blood that was mixed with water,
B. if it has the appearance of blood,
C. one is liable to cover it up.
D. [If] it was mixed with wine, they regard it as if it were water.
E. [If] it was mixed up with blood of a [domesticated] beast [87b] or with blood of a wild beast, they regard it as if it were water.
F. R. Judah says, "Blood does not annul blood."

### 6:6
A. Blood that splashes and that is on the knife,
B. one is liable to cover it up.
C. Said R. Judah, "Under what circumstances? When there is there only that blood. But [if] there is there blood other than that, he is free [of the liability] to cover it up."

I.1
A. *It was taught there in the Mishnah on Tannaite authority:* **Blood that was mixed with water, if it [the mixture] has the appearance of**

blood, it is valid. [If] it was mixed with wine, they regard it as if it were water [and if the mixture is blood-color, it is valid]. [If] it [blood of Holy Things] was mixed with the blood of a beast or with the blood of a fowl [that was unconsecrated], they regard it as if it were water. R. Judah says, "Blood [under any circumstances] does not annul blood" [M. Zeb. 8:6].

B. Said R. Hiyya bar Abba, said R. Yohanan, "They taught this rule [of M. 6:7 A-C] only where the water fell into the blood. But where the blood fell into the water, as each [drop falls in] it is annulled."

C. Said R. Pappa, "To the matter of covering the blood, this rule does [of B] not apply. [We have a principle that] you do not defer commandments."

D. Said R. Judah, said Samuel, "With any reddish [mixture of blood and water] they may attain atonement [through its use in the sacrificial rite], and they may render [foods] susceptible to uncleanness, and they are liable to cover it [after slaughtering an animal]."

E. *What novel point does this make? That they may attain atonement was taught elsewhere on Tannaite authority. That they are liable to cover it was taught elsewhere on Tannaite authority. We need [to stipulate the rule to teach] that they may render [foods] susceptible [with this mixture].*

F. *But it also [was taught on Tannaite authority that both liquids render susceptible]. [Accordingly] if it is deemed blood it surely renders susceptible. And if it is deemed water it surely renders susceptible.*

G. *No [this is not a valid line of reasoning]. We need to [stipulate it explicitly for a case where] he mixed it with rain water. [That renders susceptible only if subject to active intention that it be put on the foods.] But rainwater also will render susceptible because when he takes it and pours it [into the blood] he has demonstrated his intention [to use it].*

H. *No [this is not a valid line of reasoning]. [We may be dealing with a case where] the mixture occurred by itself [i.e., the rain water fell into the blood]. [We need then to stipulate the rule, as E says, for this case.]*

I. *R. Assi of Nehar Bil says, "[This rule applies] to the clear liquid of the blood itself. [If it has the appearance of blood it can render foods susceptible to uncleanness.]"*

J. R. Jeremiah of Difti said, "[One who drinks such liquid] is subject to the punishment of extirpation. And that is only where there is an olive's bulk of [congealed] blood [in with the clear liquid of the blood itself]."

I.2
A. *In a Tannaite tradition it was taught:* [A mixture of water with blood from a corpse] renders unclean in a tent as long as there is a quarter-*log* [of blood in the mixture].

B. *It was taught there on Tannaite authority:* Every liquid substance that exudes from a corpse is clean except for its blood. [And blood] as long as it is reddish in appearance, it renders objects unclean [that are together with it] in a tent [cf. T. Ahilot 4:9; T. Maksh. 3:15].

C. *But is it the case that,* Every liquid substance from a corpse is clean [except for its blood]? *They raised a contradiction:* **The liquids [that exude from] the *tebul-yom* are like the liquids that he touches: [88a] these and those are not susceptible to uncleanness. All other sources of uncleanness, whether minor or major — the liquids that exude from them are like liquids that he touches: these and those are in the first remove of uncleanness, except for the liquid that [itself] is a Father of Uncleanness [M. Tebul Yom 2:1].**

D. *What is meant by* **minor,** *and what is meant by* **major**? *Is it not the case that* **minor** *[means] a dead creeping thing and a zab, and that* **major** *[means] a corpse? No.* **Minor** *[means] a dead creeping thing, and* **major** *[means] a zab. [And liquid from a corpse is not included in the rule.]*

E. *What is the difference with regard to the law between the zab for whom the rabbis issued a decree [regarding the liquids that issue from him], and a corpse for which the rabbis did not issue a decree? For a zab, because people do not avoid contact with him, the rabbis issued a decree. For a corpse, because people do avoid contact with it, the rabbis did not issue a decree.*

II.1
A. **Blood that splashes and that is on the knife, [one is liable to cover it up] [M. 6:6 A-B].** *Our rabbis taught on Tannaite authority:* "And cover it [with dust]" (Lev. 17:13) — this teaches us that, **Blood that splashes and that is on the knife, one is liable to cover it up. Said R. Judah, "Under what circumstances? When there is there only that blood. But [if] there is there blood other than that, he is free [of the liability] to cover it up."**

B. *Another Tannaite teaching:* "And cover it with dust" (Lev. 17:13) — this teaches us that he is liable to cover up all of its blood. Based on this they said, Blood that spurts and that is on the sides [of the neck where it is slaughtered], one is liable to cover it up.

C. Said Rabban Simeon b. Gamaliel, "Under what circumstances? Where he did not cover the life-blood [that spurts out at the time of slaughter]. But where he did cover the life-blood, he is exempt from the obligation to cover [this other blood]."

D. *Concerning what interpretation of law do they dispute? The rabbis reason that [when the Torah says], "its blood" it means every bit. R. Judah reasons that [when the Torah says], "its blood" it means any partial amount. And Rabban Simeon b. Gamaliel reasons that "its blood" means the special blood [that spurts out at the time of slaughter].*

I.1 clarifies the premises of Mishnah. I.2 progresses to a second-level issue, but II.1 reverts to the Mishnah-text and sets forth the scriptural and logical bases for the rules.

### 6:7

A. With what do they cover up [the blood], and with what do they not cover up the blood?

B. They cover up the blood (1) with fine dung and (2) with fine sand and (3) with lime and (4) with [pieces of] potsherd and (5) with brick and (6) with the plug of a jar [both (5,6)] of which one has crushed.

C. But they do not cover up the blood either (1) with coarse dung or (2) with coarse sand or (3) with a brick or (4) with the plug of a jar neither [(3,4)] of which one has crushed.

D. And one should not turn a utensil over on it.

E. A general principle did Rabban Simeon b. Gamaliel state: "With something in which one grows plants, they cover it up, and with something in which one does not grow plants, they do not cover it up."

I.1
A. *What is the definition of* "**fine sand**"? Said Rabbah bar bar Hannah, said R. Yohanan, "Any [sand] that the potter does not have to crush up [before using it]."

B. *And there is a version that teaches this regarding the last text of the Mishnah [C]:* **But they do not cover up [the blood] either (1) with coarse dung or (2) with coarse sand.** *What is the definition of* "**coarse sand**"? Said Rabbah bar bar Hannah, said R. Yohanan, "Any [sand] that the potter does have to crush up [before using it]."

C. *What is the difference between the versions? The difference between them is where he doesn't really have to [crush it up] because it crumbles on its own. [According to the first version they may use it. According to the second, they may not (Rashi).]*

II.1
A. *Our rabbis taught on Tannaite authority:* "And cover it [with dust]" (Lev. 17:13) — you might infer that he may cover it with stones or that he may overturn a vessel on it. It comes to teach us, "With dust." I only have [derived from this that he may cover it] with dust. What is the source that includes [in the rule that he may cover it], **(1) with fine dung and (2) with fine sand** and with crushings of stones, and crushings of shards, and fine scrapings of flax, [88b] and fine sawdust, **and (3) with lime and (4) with [pieces of] potsherd and (5) with brick and (6) with the**

plug of a jar [both (5,6)] of which one has crushed? It comes to teach, "And cover it."

B. You might infer that I include even, (1) **with coarse dung or** (2) **with coarse sand or** with crushings of metal vessels, or (3) **with a brick or** (4) **with the plug of a jar neither [(3,4)] of which one has crushed,** or with flour or bran or coarse bran. It comes to teach, "With dust."

C. And why would you see fit to include these and exclude those? After Scripture included some with its usage and excluded others with its usage I see fit to include all those [substances] that are a kind of "dust." And I see fit to exclude all those [substances] that are not a kind of "dust."

D. *It makes sense to maintain as follows:* "And cover it" is a general rule; "With dust" is a specification. Where there is a general rule and a specification we only have in the general rule what is found in the specification. *What is [a kind of] "dust" is [included]. Any other substance is not [included].*

E. Said R. Mari, "Because we have here a general rule that must be qualified by a specification [your conclusion is not warranted]. For the principle is that any general rule that must be qualified by a specification is not subject to [the ordinary method of] interpretation of a general rule and a specification."

II.2
A. R. Nahman bar R. Hisda expounded, "They may cover [the blood] only with a substance in which you may plant and things will grow."

B. Said Raba, "What a boorish thing to say!" Said R. Nahman bar Yitzhak to Raba, "What is so boorish about that? I said it and I said it based on this Tannaite teaching: If one was travelling in the wilderness and had no dust to cover it — he should scrape a gold *denar* and cover it [with the scrapings]. [The desert sand is not valid.] If one was travelling on a ship and had no dust to cover it — he should burn his cloak and cover it [with the ashes]."

C. *Now it makes sense to say* he should burn his cloak and cover it [because] *we do find that ashes are called "dust."* [Cf. Num 19:17, "For the unclean they shall take some ashes (the word is 'dust') of the burnt sin offering, and running water shall be added in a vessel."] *But what is the source of the assertion that [scrapings of] a gold denar [are called dust]?* Said R. Zira, "[It is based on the verse], '[Its stones are the place of sapphires], and it has dust of gold' (Job 28:6)."

### II.3

A. *Our rabbis taught on Tannaite authority:* "They may cover [the blood] only with dust," the words of the House of Shammai. And the House of Hillel say, "We find ashes that are called dust. As it says, 'For the unclean they shall take some ashes (the word is 'dust') of the burnt sin-offering, and running water shall be added in a vessel' (Num. 19:17)."

B. *And [how do we interpret this in accord with the view of] the House of Shammai? [They would say that ashes might be called] "the dust of the burnt sin-offering" but they would not be called ordinary dust.*

### III.1

A. *It was taught on Tannaite authority:* Add to them [that may be used to cover the blood] soot, stibium, and dust from chiselling [Rashi: from the grindstone]. And some say, "Even orpiment."

### IV.1

A. Said Raba, "As a reward for what Abraham our forefather said, '[Abraham answered, Behold, I have taken upon myself to speak to the Lord], I who am but dust and ashes' (Gen. 18:27), his descendants merited two commandments, the ashes of the Red Heifer and the dust given to the *sotah*-woman [suspected of infidelity]."

B. *And why do we not include with them [that on his merit they were given the commandment] to cover the blood with dust? For that there it is valid [to eat the animal even if he does not cover the blood. Accordingly] there is a commandment [to cover it]. But there is no benefit [directly derived from the action].*

C. Said Raba, "As a reward for what Abraham our forefather said, [89a] 'That I would not take a thread or a sandal-thong or anything that is yours, lest you should say, I have make Abram rich' (Gen. 14:23), his descendants merited two commandments, the thread of blue [of the fringes on a garment] and the thong of the *tefillin*."

D. *Now it makes perfect sense [that there is merit in the commandment to wear] the thong of the* tefillin. *It is written,* "And all the peoples of the earth shall see that you are called by the name of the Lord; and they shall be afraid of you" (Deut. 28:10). *And it was taught on Tannaite authority:* R. Eliezer the great says, "These [promises] refer to the *tefillin* for the head." [The peoples will see from the *tefillin* that you are called by the name of the Lord.]

E. *But why [do we ascribe merit] to the thread of blue? For it was taught on Tannaite authority:* R. Meir says, "How different is blue from among all the colors. For blue is the color of the sea. And the sea is the same color as the firmament. And the firmament is the same color as the sapphire stone. And the sapphire stone is the same color as the throne of glory."

F. *As it is written,* "And they saw the God of Israel; and there was under his feet as it were a pavement of sapphire stone, like the very heaven for clearness" (Exod. 24:10). *And it is written,* "And above the firmament over their heads there was the likeness of a throne, in appearance like sapphire; and seated above the likeness of a throne was a likeness as it were of a human form" (Ezek. 1:26).

V.1
A. Said R. Abba, "How severe is the sin of a theft of something that is consumed. For even the completely righteous cannot return it. As it says, 'I will take nothing but what the young men have eaten, [and the share of the men who went with me; let Aner, Eshcol, and Mamre take their share]' (Gen. 14:24)."

B. Said R. Yohanan in the name of R. Eleazar b. R. Simeon, "Everywhere you find the words of R. Eliezer the son of R. Yosé the Galilean, make your ear like a funnel [to receive them]."

## Bavli Hullin Chapter Six. Folios 83B-89B

C. [He said], "It was not because you were more in number than any other people that the Lord set his love upon you and chose you, for you were the fewest of all peoples" (Deut. 7:7). Said the Holy One Blessed be He to Israel, "I adore you. For even at the time that I bestow upon you greatness, you humble yourselves before me.

D. "I bestowed greatness upon Abraham and he said before me, 'I am but dust and ashes' (Gen. 28:27). [I bestowed greatness upon] Moses and Aaron and they said, 'What are we? Your murmurings are not against us but against the Lord' (Exod. 16:8). [I bestowed greatness upon] David and he said, 'But I am a worm, and no man' (Ps. 22:6).

E. "But the idolaters are not [humble] like this. I bestowed greatness upon Nimrod and he said, 'Come let us build ourselves a city, and a tower with its top in the heavens, and let us make a name for ourselves...' (Gen. 11:4). [I bestowed greatness upon] Pharaoh and he said, 'Who is the Lord?' (Exod. 5:2). [I bestowed greatness upon] Sennacherib and he said, 'Who among all the gods of the countries have delivered their countries out of my hand, that the Lord should deliver Jerusalem out of my hand?' (II Kings 18:35). [I bestowed greatness upon] Nebuchadnezzar and he said, 'I will ascend above the heights of the clouds, I will make myself like the Most High' (Isa. 14:14). [I bestowed greatness upon] Hiram king of Tyre and he said, 'I am a god, I sit in the seat of the gods, in the heart of the seas' (Ezek. 28:2)."

V.2

A. Said Raba, and some say said R. Yohanan, "What Moses and Aaron said was more [humble] than what Abraham said. For Abraham *it was written*, 'I am but dust and ashes.' But for Moses and Aaron *it was written*, 'What are we?'"

B. And said Raba, and some say R. Yohanan, "The world continues to exist because of [the merit of that humble utterance of] Moses and Aaron. *It is written there*, 'What are we (*nhnw mh*)?' *And it is written here*, 'He stretches out the north over the void, and hangs the earth upon nothing (*blymh*)' (Job 26:7)." [The pericope makes a play on the words.]

C. Said R. Ila, "The world continues to exist because of [the merit of] a person who controls himself (*bwlm*) in a time of contention. As it says, '[He] hangs the earth upon nothing (*blymh*)' (Job 26:7)." [Another play on the words.]

D. R. Abbahu said, "The world continues to exist because of [the merit of] a person who completely abases himself. As it says, 'And underneath are the everlasting arms' (Deut. 32:27)." [Those who make themselves low, support the world (Cashdan).]

E. Said R. Yitzhak, "*Why is it written,* 'Did you indeed decree what is right, you gods [or: in silence]? Did you judge the sons of men uprightly?' (Ps. 58:1). What should a person's vocation be in this world? He should make himself mute. You might infer that he do so even with regard to the words of the Torah. It comes to teach, 'Decree what is right' [or: speak righteousness, i.e. Torah]. You might infer that he then will become haughty. It comes to teach, 'Judge the sons of men uprightly' [or: evenly, i.e., with moderation]."

**VI.1**
A. Said R. Zira, "They may cover the blood with the dust of a condemned city (cf. Deut. 13)."

B. *But why may he do this? It is prohibited to derive benefit from [the city] (Deut. 13:18)! Said Ziri, "It was only necessary to state this on account of the dust of the earth. As it is written,* 'You shall gather all its spoil into the midst of its open square, and burn the city and all its spoil with fire' (Deut. 13:16). *This refers to whatever needs only to be gathered and burned. It excludes whatever needs to be uprooted, gathered and burned."* [Accordingly, one may use the dust of the earth of the city.]

C. *But Raba said, "Fulfilling the commandments does not give one any benefits."* [Accordingly, to fulfill the commandment of covering the blood, one may use the dust from the city.]

D. *Rabina sat and he stated this tradition. R. Rahumi raised an objection to Rabina. A shofar that was used for idolatry, he should not sound it* [on the new year to fulfill the commandment]. *Is it the case that if he sounded it, he did not fulfill the commandment?*

*Bavli Ḥullin Chapter Six. Folios 83B-89B* 279

No, if he sounded it, he did fulfill the commandment. A lulab that was used for idolatry, he should not take it [on Sukkot]. *Is it the case that if he took it, he did not fulfill the commandment?* No, if he took it, he did fulfill the commandment.

E. *But lo, it was taught on Tannaite authority: If he sounded it, he did not fulfill the commandment. If he took it, he did not fulfill the commandment.*

F. Said R. Ashi, *"Are these cases [i.e., shofar and lulab of idolatry, and dust from a condemned city] comparable? There [in the cases of lulab and shofar]* **[89b]** *we need a measurable object [to fulfill the commandment]. And we have a principle that using it for idolatry [figuratively] 'shatters it into particles.' [With regard to the law, it is considered as if it does not fulfill the minimum size requirements for fulfilling the commandments.] Here [with regard to dust for covering the blood] the more it is shattered into particles, the better it is to use for covering [the blood]."*

I.1 defines the terms of Mishnah. II.1 finds a scriptural basis for the rule of Mishnah. II-III give further inquiries extending the rule of Mishnah. IV.1 adds secondary materials with no bearing on the elucidation of Mishnah but developed out of the general theme of the discussion. This continues at V.1-2 with homilies on the same general theme. VI.1 concludes with a rule related to Mishnah in a brief appendix.

# Abbreviations

**A. Z.:** Abodah Zarah
**alt.:** alternative reading
**Arak.:** Arakhin
**B., b.:** Talmud Babli
**B. B.:** Baba Batra
**B. M.:** Baba Mesia
**B. Q.:** Baba Qamma
**Bekh.:** Bekhorot
**Ber.:** Berakhot
**Bes.:** Besah
**Bik.:** Bikkurim
**Chron.:** Chronicles
**Dan.:** Daniel
**Deut.:** Deuteronomy
**Ed.:** Eduyot
**Erub.:** Erubin
**Ex., Exod.:** Exodus
**Ezek.:** Ezekiel
**Gen.:** Genesis
**Git.:** Gittin
**Ḥul.:** Ḥullin
**Isa.:** Isaiah
**Jer.:** Jeremiah
**Josh.:** Joshua
**Judg.:** Judges
**Kel.:** Kelim
**Ker.:** Keritot
**Kil.:** Kilayim
**Lam.:** Lamentations
**Lev.:** Leviticus
**Lewysohn:** L. Lewysohn, *Zoologie des Talmuds*, Frankfurt, 1858
**M.:** Mishnah
**M. Q.:** Mo'ed Qatan
**m'sh:** formal introduction to a tale

**Mak.:** Makkot
**Maksh.:** Makshirin
**Men.:** Menaḥot
**Miq.:** Miqvaot
**MS:** manuscript
**Nasi:** prince, officer
**Neg.:** Nega'im
**Nid.:** Niddah
**Num.:** Numbers
**Ohal.:** Ohalot
**Pes.:** Pesahim
**Prov.:** Proverbs
**Ps.:** Psalms
**Qid.:** Qiddushin
**Qoh.:** Qohelet, Ecclesiastes
**R.:** Rabbi
**RSV:** Revised Standard Version
**Sam.:** Samuel
**San., Sanh.:** Sanhedrin
**Shab.:** Shabbat
**Suk.:** Sukkah
**T., Tos.:** Tosefta
**Ta'an:** Ta'anit
**Tem.:** Temurah
**Tefillin:** phylacteries
**Ter.:** Terumot
**Toh.:** Tohorot
**Tos.:** Tosefta
**V:** Vienna ms. of Tosefta
**var.:** variant reading
**Y.:** Yerushalmi, Talmud of the Land of Israel, the Palestinian Talmud
**Yeb.:** Yebamot
**Zeb.:** Zebaḥim
**Zech.:** Zechariah

# Transliterations

| | | | | | | |
|---|---|---|---|---|---|---|
| א | = | ʾ | ל | = | l |
| ב | = | b | ם, מ | = | m |
| ג | = | g | ן, נ | = | n |
| ד | = | d | ס | = | ś |
| ה | = | h | ע | = | ʿ |
| ו | = | w | ף, פ | = | p |
| ז | = | z | ץ, צ | = | ṣ |
| ח | = | ḥ | ק | = | q |
| ט | = | ṭ | ר | = | r |
| י | = | y | שׁ | = | š |
| ך, כ | = | k | שׂ | = | s |

ת = t

# Index of Biblical and Talmudic References

**Biblical References**

Amos
3:8, 120
4:13, 267-8
7:2, 123

Daniel
4:9, 116

Deuteronomy
2:23, 125
2:9, 125
3:9, 126
7:13, 251
7:7, 277
12:16, 248
12:17, 160
12:20-1, 249
12:21, 260
13:16, 278
13:18, 278
14:4-6, 172-3
14:5-6, 225
14:6, 158, 163, 208
14:7, 124
14:13, 136
14:21, 6
18:3, 6, 197
18:4, 7
21:3, 234
22:1, 268
22:6, 217
22:6-7, 7
22:10, 191
23:4, 132
28:10, 276
32:27, 278
32:6, 103

Exodus
3:14, 132
5:2, 277
12:5, 192
12:10, 239
13:13, 192
16:8, 277
22:30, 229
22:31, 3n, 20, 47, 155, 187
23:19, 6
23:31, 159
24:10, 276
34:26, 6

Ezekiel
1:26, 276
4:14, 32
28:2, 277

Genesis
1:5, 242
1:11, 122
1:12, 124
1:14, 123
1:16, 123
2:1, 122
2:5, 124
11:4, 277
12:3, 57
14:1, 142
14:23, 276
14:24, 276
18:27, 275
21:23, 125
28:27, 277
43:16, 255
47:21, 126

I Samuel
17:5, 147
17:14, 123

I Chronicles
28:19, 246

II Kings
18:35, 277

Isaiah
13:21, 141
14:14, 277
42:21, 147
43:20, 142

Job
2:6, 24
16:13, 24
26:7, 277-8
28:6, 275
28:7, 137
42:15, 154
42:30, 154

Joshua
13:3, 124

Judges
17:6, 108

Lamentations
4:3, 141

Leviticus
1:14, 126
1:4, 253
3:3, 57-8
5:2, 171, 173
7:3-4, 196
7:18, 231
7:21, 173
7:26, 192
9:23, 131
11:2, 20
11:2-3, 173
11:3, 116
11:7, 118
11:9-10, 148
11:11, 154
11:13, 126, 127, 136
11:14, 135
11:15, 134, 129
11:16, 135, 141
11:17, 133
11:18, 133
11:19, 133, 135
11:21, 116, 143, 145-6
11:22, 143, 145-6
11:27, 170, 172
11:32, 187-8
11:36, 248
11:37, 187
11:39, 170, 172, 175, 188, 209, 258
11:41, 140, 151-2
11:42, 154
11:47, 21
13:25, 135
13:45, 211
14:4, 234
14:39, 256
14:44, 256
15:2, 68
17:3, 255
17:4, 256
17:13, 222, 245, 247, 249, 255-6, 265, 266-7, 272-3
17:14, 265, 267
19:19, 173, 191
20:9, 216
21:11, 180
22:23, 227
22:27, 214-5, 228
22:28, 5, 9, 190, 213, 215, 235-6, 242, 255
27:9, 165

Micah
1:8, 141

283

## Numbers
6:23, 57
6:27, 57
19:6, 131
19:13, 179
19:16, 179
19:17, 275
21:26, 125
28:15, 123

## Proverbs
6:6-8, 107
12:21, 116
15:27, 33
18:20, 119
27:26-27, 250

## Psalms
22:6, 277
36:6, 133
58:1, 278
69:21, 268
69:31, 121-2
104:3, 121
104:31, 122
112:5, 251
128:2, 34

## Qohelet
2:14, 29
7:12, 115

## Song of Songs
5:11, 134

## Zechariah
10:4, 103
10:8, 134

## Mishnah

### Bekhorot
2:5, 211
6:1, 45
6:7, 112
7:6, 132
8:1, 155

### Bikkurim
2:9, 222
3:3, 90

### Demai
4:1, 200

### Eduyot
5:1, 109

### Kelim
2:2, 91
19:2, 90
27:9-10, 9

### Kilayim
8:4, 218-19
8:6, 225

### Makkot
3:7, 237

### Menahot
12:3, 4

### Miqvaot
10:5, 182
10:8, 177

### Negaim
13:9, 177

### Niddah
3:2, 174
5:3, 68
6:9, 147

### Ohalot
2:3, 22, 74
7:1, 176
14:6-7, 176

### Parah
3:9, 233
9:3, 130
9:7, 233

### Tebul Yom
2:1, 271
4:5, 199

### Temurah
1:3, 163
6:5, 109-110
7:4, 259
8:4, 59

### Tohorot
1:2, 113
3:8, 263

### Uqsin
3:1, 208
3:8, 194

### Zebahim
2:2, 96
4:6, 4
8:6, 10, 270

## Tosefta

### Hullin
3:1, 39
3:2, 64
3:6, 21, 94
3:7, 95
3:11, 66
3:15, 99
3:19, 115
3:20, 117
3:21, 118
3:22, 142, 143
3:23-24, 139
3:25, 143
4:3, 157
4:6, 194
4:8, 197
5:1, 215, 220
6:1-3, 252
7:1, 190
7:2, 163
7:4, 191
7:5, 238-9
9:1, 222
9:13, 37
9:14, 57

### Ahilot
4:9, 271

### Arakhin
4:26, 249
4:28, 249
4:29, 250

### Bekhorot
2:9, 224

### Eduyot
1:5, 32

### Kelim B. M.
9:3, 92

### Keritot
2:19, 191

### Kilayim
1:8, 219

### Makhshirin
3:15, 271

### Parah
7:9, 233

### Sukkah
2:3, 29

### Terumot
7:12, 60
9:5, 141

### Yebamot
4:7, 33
10:4, 51
12:7, 238

### Zebahim
2:3, 96-7

## Babylonian Talmud

### Abodah Zarah
39a, 147

### Baba Batra
81b, 246

Index

Baba Qamma
11a, 209

Bekhorot
13b, 242
51a, 150

Besah
6b, 69
26b, 69

Erubin
28b, 209

Gittin
68b, 133

Menahot
103b, 246

Mo'ed Qatan
21b, 62

Niddah
40a, 69

Pesahim
84a, 206

Qiddushin
39a, 238
57a, 234

Sanhedrin
22b, 132

Shabbat
93b, 236
136a, 69

Sukkah
20a, 261

Ta'anit
24b-25a, 261

Temurah
11b, 165

Yebamot
36a, 206

**Avot deRabbi Nathan**
2, 33

# General Index

Aaron, 277
Abahu, 55
Abayye, 26, 28, 40, 59, 63, 64, 66, 79, 81, 84, 103, 111, 118, 126, 131, 132-136, 141-143, 161, 198, 202, 206, 211, 220, 236, 259
Abba, 29, 38, 39, 48, 56, 61, 62, 65, 86, 105, 202, 220, 225, 233, 234, 250, 252, 254, 255, 257, 258, 260, 261, 264, 270, 276
Abbahu, 91, 101, 115, 119, 120, 136, 137, 147, 278
Abbuha, 30
Abimi, 49, 137, 158
Abimi the son of R. Abbahu, 137
Abin, 39, 90, 92, 261
Abina, 64, 65, 124
Abraham, 125, 275-277
Abram, 276
Ada, 42, 55, 134, 188, 199, 206
Ada bar Ahavah, 42, 188
Ada bar Habo, 199
Ada bar Manyomi, 55
Ada bar Matna, 206
Ada bar R. Nathan, 55
Ada bar Shimi, 134
Aha bar Abba, 56
Aha bar Ava, 64-5
Aha bar Jacob, 100, 108, 110, 225
Aha bar R. Huna, 204
Aha the son of R. Avya, 225
Aha the son of R. Iqa, 225, 226
Aha the son of Raba, 49, 107, 225, 266, 268
Ahadaboy bar Ammi, 171
Ahai, 119, 120, 145
Amemar, 38, 45, 64, 70, 71, 82, 108-110, 129, 133, 202, 225, 226
Ammi, 43, 52, 53, 56, 61, 83, 113, 171, 196, 210, 234, 251, 263, 264
Amora, amoraic, 14, 21, 22, 25, 85, 165, 251
Amorites, 125, 126, 208, 211
Amram, 76
Amraphel, 142
Anan, 99

Anatomy: abdominal cavity, 77, 83, 84; abomasum, 57, 58; afterbirth, 4, 9, 156, 168, 208-210; aorta, 11, 38, 87; back, 9, 66, 68, 80-82, 103, 107, 113, 120, 121, 124, 150, 152, 154, 168, 184, 192, 200, 268; backbone, 19, 39, 88, 95, 96; belly, 11, 19, 24, 36, 57, 64, 75, 87, 103, 121, 154; birth canal, 168, 179; bone, 6, 21, 35, 99, 100, 104, 111, 179, 191, 200-202, 204, 205, 206, 207; brain, 11, 19, 37, 85, 87, 88, 99, 100, 104; bronchial tubes, 11, 19, 38, 48, 49, 53, 56, 87; cheeks, 6, 7, 197, 222; colon, 53; cranium, 37; crop, 102, 126; cyst, 45; diaphragm, 43; ductus choledocus, 54; dura mater, 37; ear, 45, 276; entrails, 57, 58, 196; falciform ligament, 42; fat, 6, 27, 38, 57-61, 119, 163, 190, 191, 195, 196, 225, 226, 236, 237; femur, 23, 88, 89, 103-106; flesh, 3, 6, 9, 20, 31, 32, 47, 51, 54, 83, 84, 96, 118, 153, 159, 173, 186, 187, 204-207, 231, 249; gall-bladder, 19, 22, 24, 25, 42, 43, 51, 55; gizzard, 25, 26, 97, 101, 126, 132; gullet, 2, 3, 11, 19, 25-28, 30, 31, 84, 86, 97, 102, 260; heart, 11, 19, 38, 39, 87, 88, 101, 115, 277; hilum, 92; hoof, 4, 6, 9, 69, 96, 117-119, 121, 122, 124, 155-160, 163, 164, 171-173, 180, 193, 198, 208, 209, 225; horn, 6, 118-122, 209; intestine, 11, 53, 61, 62, 87; intestines, 19, 24, 56, 61-63, 70, 83-85, 97, 100-103, 112; jaw, 30, 31, 88, 93; juncture of the thigh-sinews, 21; kidneys, 12, 24, 52, 86, 88, 92, 97, 155, 163, 164, 183, 184, 196; knee, 4, 21, 105, 200, 201, 204; legs, 4, 9, 21, 67, 102, 103, 105, 112, 115, 116, 132, 143-146, 189, 200; ligaments, 89; liver, 11, 19, 25, 38, 41-43, 47, 49, 51, 54, 55, 87, 88, 100, 101, 196; lobes of the lung, 45, 50; lung, 2, 11, 12, 19, 36, 38, 39, 43-56, 63, 84, 87, 93, 94, 97, 103, 104; lungs, 38, 43, 46, 52, 94, 104; maw, 6, 7,

57, 197, 222; mediastal cavity, 38; medulla, 39; mucal sieve, 64; neck, 2, 11, 36, 83, 85, 87, 169, 192, 231, 233, 234, 272; nerves, 40, 41; occipital condyles, 37; parenchyma pulmonis, 43; pericardium, 60; pharynx, 11, 28, 30, 86; portal vein, 55; rectum, 11, 60, 63, 87, 113; reticulum, 12, 54, 65, 66, 87, 112; ribs, 12, 19, 72-75, 87, 104; sacral nerves, 41; sciatic nerve, 2, 5, 6, 8, 86; sciatica, 67; shoulder, 6, 7, 177, 197, 222; sinew of the hip, 5, 163, 190, 191; skeleton, 22, 74; skull, 23, 34, 74, 75, 88, 98, 108; socket, 23, 74, 75, 88, 89; spinal cord, 11, 19, 37, 39-41, 87,88; spine, 22, 40, 67, 68, 72, 74, 75; spleen, 23, 88, 92, 93, 155, 163, 183, 184; stibium, 275; stomach, 2, 6, 19, 22, 64-66, 88, 115, 116, 142, 175; teeth, 80, 98, 117, 120, 125; tendons, 202, 203; throat, 2-4, 70; thyroid, 2; ulcerations of the lung, 11, 87; vena cava inferior, 38; vertebra, 22, 37, 73-75; villi, 30; white calyces, 92; windpipe, 2, 3, 11, 19, 31, 34-36, 38, 63, 64, 84, 86, 88, 97, 102, 106, 260; womb, 4, 9, 49, 68, 88, 92, 94, 102, 155, 157, 158, 160, 161, 163, 164, 166, 168-171, 174, 178-181, 183, 184, 189, 193, 195, 209

Animals: antelope, 119, 120, 172, 225, 226; ass, 118, 121, 192, 209, 218-220; bull, 121, 122, 214, 227, 228; camel, 117, 118, 124, 171, 200; cat, 76-79, 81, 83; cattle, 3, 4, 6, 10, 19, 31, 76, 88, 116-119, 171, 173, 186, 204, 251; deer, 115, 119, 120, 220-224; dog, 3, 9, 79, 81-83, 115, 166, 167, 175, 208, 210; ewe, 5, 67, 79, 215, 216, 220, 222, 255; fox, 79; gazelle, 172, 225; goat, 76, 77, 119, 123, 172, 192, 211, 214, 220-226, 228, 250, 255; hart, 172, 225; heifer, 231, 233, 234, 275; hide, 6, 12, 22, 88, 94-97, 153, 205-207, 209; horse, 218-220; hybrid animal, 215; ibex, 172, 225; jackals, 141, 142; Karkuz goat, 119; kids, 78; koy-animal, 16, 215, 220-224, 231, 245, 252, 253; lambs, 76-78, 250; lion, 20, 76, 80-82, 120; marten, 76, 77; mountain-sheep, 172, 225, 226; mule, 219; ox, 6, 28-30, 64, 69, 119, 121, 122, 172, 202, 225, 231, 241, 255; rams, 67, 68, 94; roebuck, 172, 225; serpent, 60, 140; sheep, 6, 7, 77, 78, 172, 192, 211, 214, 215, 221-229; snake, 60, 114, 115, 154; swine, 118, 171; tiger, 120; weasel, 76, 78, 97, 98, 102, 168; wild ass, 118; wild goat, 172, 225, 226; wolf, 20, 56, 76, 77, 199

Antigonus, 83, 96, 101
Aptoriqi, 141, 228
Aqiba, 3, 6, 9, 57, 58, 95, 178-180, 194
Aramean, 103
Arioch, 142, 205
Arnon, 125
Ashdod, 124
Ashi, 26, 43, 46, 49, 50, 54, 55, 64, 67, 69-71, 75, 78, 79, 82-84, 93, 101, 106, 107, 109, 110, 112, 129, 141, 153, 164, 169, 192, 199, 201-203, 207, 225, 226, 234, 247, 266, 268, 279
Ashkelon, 124
Asi, 73
Asia Minor, 49
Assi, 31, 43, 52, 56, 64, 65, 96, 113, 124, 131, 139, 169, 198, 202, 251, 271
Assi of Nehar Bil, 271
Avira, 23, 66, 92, 251
Avvim, 124, 125
Avya, 28, 46, 61, 64, 225
Ayn Ibl, 108
Azariah, 250
Azzai, 172

Babylonia, 137, 205
Bar Luianus, 268
Bar Padda, 175
Bar Qappara, 37
Be Huzai, 40, 158
Be Ilai, 120
Bed, 90
Belteshazzar, 116
Ben Pazzi, 41
Ben Zakkai, 72, 73
Ben Zoma, 242
Benjamin, 65, 76, 255
Benjamin bar Yefet (Yapet), 65, 76
Beribbi, 77, 78, 101, 104, 252, 254
Bet Doshai, 224
Betera, 86
Bibi, 28, 56, 84, 103, 134
Bibi Bar Abayye, 28, 84, 103, 134

Birds, 7, 8, 12, 14, 76, 78, 79, 82, 87, 100, 103, 127, 128, 131, 133, 134, 135-139, 155, 234, 248, 264, 265; black woodpecker, 131; bustard, 133; buzzard, 136; chicken, 77, 78, 114; cormorant, 133; cuckoo, 135; dove, 130, 135, 140, 164; eagle, 126-128; falcon, 20. 135-137; gannet, 133; geese, 100, 249; green flamingo, 132; hawk, 20, 76, 77, 79, 135; hen, 100, 101, 106, 107, 131-133; heron, 135; hoopoe, 133, 135; hummingbird, 142; kite, 135, 136; lapwing, 132; lark, 131; linnet, 131; magpie, 134; moor-cock, 131, 132; moor-hen, 131, 132; mountain chaffinch, 131; osprey, 127-129, 133; ostriches, 141, 142; parrot, 132; partridge, 131; pelican, 133; penguin, 132; pigeon, 130, 132, 205, 206; pink flamingo, 132; raven, 127-129, 134, 135, 140, 143; redwing thrush, 132; rehaba-doves, 130; screech owl, 133; sea crow, 134; sea-mew, 132; stock pigeon, 132; stork, 135; swallow, 129, 130, 148, 151; talon, 116, 142; tasil-dove, 130; turtle doves, 126, 128, 248; vulture, 127-129, 133, 134; white jay, 131; wings, 7, 41, 71, 72, 102, 104, 116, 121, 143, 144; wood lark, 131; wren, 131

Birth: caesarian section, 68, 69, 166; midwife, 174, 178, 179

Blessing, 17, 57, 266-268

Blood, 2-6, 8, 10, 17, 26, 44, 45, 47, 66, 77, 78, 81, 83, 112, 114, 141, 162, 179, 180, 186, 190-194, 205, 216, 222, 223, 227, 230, 245-249, 251-257, 259-262, 264-267, 269-273, 275, 278

Bloodguilt, 256

Bridegroom, 240, 241

Broken ribs, 12, 87

Brona, 266

Butcher, 52, 55, 64, 112, 240, 241

Caesar, 120, 121
Caesarea, 264
Caphtor(im), 125
Cappadocia, 47
Carrion, 3, 4, 6, 8, 9, 73, 99, 137-139, 157, 161, 170, 172, 175, 180, 183, 184, 186, 193, 208, 209, 232, 254, 257-259, 263
Case of doubt, 27, 119, 253, 263

Cashdan, E., 28, 30, 37-39, 42, 43, 47, 49, 51, 54, 60, 71, 75, 115, 117, 130, 133, 135, 143, 200, 278
Chameleon, 133
Circumcision, 47, 252-254
Coins: gordian dinar, 89; issur, 34, 35, 84, 88-90, 106; Italian issar, 88, 89, 106; sela, 90, 95; shekels, 147
Commandments, 267, 269, 270, 275, 276, 278, 279
Cosmology: creation, 242, 243; firmament, 176, 276; heaven, 276
Court: temple, 161, 258, 259; law, 262
Cud, 117, 118, 124, 163, 172, 173, 208, 225

Daniel bar Qatina, 130
David, 123, 277
Dimi, 40, 70, 79, 205, 232, 260
Dimi bar Yitzhak, 40
Disease: leprosy, 121, 135, 256
Diverse kinds, 237, 238
Divine presence, 120
Dosa, 119
Dostai the father of R. Aptoriqi, 141

Eiblayim, 96
Ekron, 124
Elam, 142
Eleazar, 21, 22, 34, 35, 40, 52, 60, 63, 65, 94-96, 99, 101, 108, 116, 142, 143, 190, 191, 194, 209, 210, 220, 222, 242, 250, 252, 254, 264, 276
Eleazar b. Antigonus, 96, 101
Eleazar b. Azariah, 250
Eleazar b. R. Yannai, 96, 101
Eleazar b. R. Simeon, 52, 276
Eleazar bar Sadoq, 142
Eleazar Haqqappar Beribbi, 101, 252, 254
Eleazar the scribe, 94
Eliakim, 52
Eliezer, 4, 96, 109-111, 129, 130, 143, 220-224, 276
Eliezer b. Judah, 96
Ellasar, 142
Eschatology: Messiah, 134; Redemption, 192
Exilarch, 115, 119, 251

Fats, 11, 13, 87, 119, 154, 162, 190, 191; forbidden fat, 27, 60, 195, 236, 237

Festivals, 69, 206, 221, 240, 245, 252-254; Day of Atonement, 240; Lulab, 279; new moon, 123; New year, 240, 252, 253, 278; Passover, 240; Passover seder, 8; Shofar, 252, 253, 278, 279; Sukkot, 240

First fruits, 6, 7, 90, 159

Firstling, 7, 33, 45, 69, 166, 167, 192, 210, 211

Fish: anthias, 147; aphis fish, 147; clean fish, 14, 147, 154, 155; colas, 147; fins and scales, 116, 138, 147-150, 154; swordfish, 147; scomber, 147; tunny, 147

Foetus, 4, 5, 110, 158, 160, 163, 164, 167-171, 174, 178, 179, 181, 182, 184, 185, 188-190, 193, 195, 196, 204, 208-210, 257

Foods, 1, 2, 4-6, 8, 54, 59, 107, 163, 175, 176, 186, 194, 247, 250, 268; bread, 177; chicken, 38, 49-51; dates, 111, 152; eggs, 2, 7, 13, 14, 108-110, 114, 115, 138-140, 155, 217; figs, 152; fruit, 34, 65, 119, 122; herbs, 251; honey, 59, 60, 115; liquids, 11, 59, 87, 248, 270-272; meat, 1, 2, 4, 6, 8, 10, 32, 33, 41, 69, 86, 154, 155, 157, 180, 186, 192, 193, 200, 204, 205, 227, 230, 235, 249, 250, 262; nuts, 115; vinegar, 59; water, 5, 44, 48, 50, 52, 59, 70, 93, 94, 99, 100, 111, 114, 115, 130, 133, 142, 147, 149, 179, 187, 248, 249, 251, 259, 269-271, 275; wine, 7, 59, 132, 152, 159, 237, 250, 261, 266, 268-270. See also vegetables

Foreigner, 6

Fringes on a garment, 276

Fruits, 34, 65, 119, 122; caperberries, 115; dates, 111, 152; figs, 152

Gabihah of be Katil, 141

Gamaliel, 61, 62, 88, 89, 108, 142, 224, 267, 272, 273

Gath, 124

Geniva, 30, 64, 65

Gentile, 4-6, 139

Goria, 34

Grape vines, 152

Habiba, 67

Halafta, 106, 107

Hama, 29, 34, 51, 128, 140, 206

Hamnuna, 225, 229, 230

Hanan, 83, 124, 135, 225

Hanan bar R. Hisda, 135

Hanan bar Raba, 83, 124

Hananel, 266

Hanania, 36, 161

Hananiah, 120, 121, 189, 216, 218, 221

Hanina, 36, 46, 48, 52, 61, 64, 75, 104, 106, 122, 199, 261, 266

Hanina bar Pappa, 122

Haninah, 83, 184, 185, 199

Haninah b. Antigonus, 83

Hanna the money changer, 89

Hannah, 23, 25, 31-33, 35, 37, 40, 51, 72, 83, 94, 95, 186, 187, 209, 268, 273

Heave-offering, 177, 199, 200

Heavenly echo, 29, 30, 261, 268

Helbo, 34

Heresy, heretic, 248

Hermon, 126

Heshbon, 125

Hezekiah, 104, 141

Hillel, House of, 22, 29, 74, 75, 194, 275

Hinnena, 60

Hisda, 33, 62, 70, 76, 77, 117, 118, 124, 135, 152, 170, 171, 188, 194, 197, 204, 220, 221, 251, 274

Hiyya, 24, 36, 38, 39, 42, 56, 61, 62, 65, 69, 83, 85, 101, 106, 112, 126, 197, 200, 201, 218, 225, 234, 252, 254-257, 259, 260, 261, 264, 270

Hiyya bar Abba, 56, 61, 62, 65, 234, 255, 260, 264, 270

Hiyya bar Ashi, 69, 106

Hiyya bar Joseph, 36, 39, 85

Hoshaiah, 179, 189

House of R. Ishmael, 20, 21, 117, 118, 144, 146, 147, 149, 164, 255, 256

Huna, 39, 41, 46, 50, 55, 56, 60, 64, 66, 67, 70, 80, 84, 99, 104, 105, 108, 111, 112, 132, 137, 151, 152, 166, 167, 187, 201, 202, 204, 218, 220, 225, 241, 263

Huna bar Hinnena, 60

Huna bar Hiyya, 218, 225

Huna bar Judah, 55

Huna Mar bar Avya, 46

Huna the son of R. Joshua, 41, 60, 84, 220, 263

Idi, 31, 55, 106, 153

Idolatry, 4, 254, 278, 279

Ila, 76, 278
Ilai, 63, 120
Ilfa, 83, 161
Immersion in water, 44, 48, 182, 248
Incision, 11, 86, 87, 157, 158
Insects: cricket, 143-147; fly, 71, 72, 82, 111, 131; gnat, 111, 112; grasshopper, 143-146; locusts, 4, 6, 8, 14, 116, 131, 137, 143, 155; maggots, 153, 154; mites, 152; mosquitoes, 152; worm, 14, 49, 56, 111, 133, 151-153, 155, 259, 261, 277
Intention (legal principle), 4, 96, 97, 270
Iqa the son of R. Ammi, 210
Isa, 141, 142, 147, 277
Ishmael, 20-22, 57, 58, 64, 96, 113, 117, 118, 144-147, 149, 164, 172, 178, 179, 255, 256
Isi b. Judah, 137
Israel, 5, 57, 98, 99, 103, 106, 107, 123, 125, 126, 137, 173, 179, 245, 249, 253, 255, 256, 265, 267, 276, 277
Israel, Land of, 126, 137

Jacob, 5, 39, 64, 75, 96, 100, 106, 108, 110, 123, 202, 225, 231, 239, 248, 263
Jacob bar Idi, 106
Jacob bar Nahmani, 64, 75
Jeremiah, 34, 37, 38, 40-42, 52, 53, 56, 70, 75, 105, 141, 161, 169, 205, 210, 271
Jeremiah bar Abba, 38, 56, 105
Jeremiah of Difti, 271
Jerusalem, 2, 8, 144, 159, 161, 277
Jonah, 28
Jonathan, 36, 124, 172, 199, 216, 246
Jonathan b. Joseph, 246
Joseph, 24-26, 29, 36, 39, 42, 43, 47-52, 54, 56, 65, 79, 83, 85, 86, 100, 101, 115, 120, 125, 153, 178, 185-187, 206, 235, 236, 246, 247, 255
Joseph bar Dostai, 56
Joseph bar Hama, 29, 206
Joseph bar Manyomi, 43, 49, 50
Joseph the trapper, 86
Joshua, 30, 35, 37, 40, 41, 56, 60, 64, 84, 100-102, 106, 109-111, 120, 121, 122, 220, 255, 263
Joshua b. Hananiah, 120, 121
Joshua b. Levi, 35, 37, 40, 56, 64, 100-102, 106, 122, 255
Judah, 7, 12, 19, 20, 22, 24, 30, 34, 40, 49, 52, 55, 64, 65, 68-70, 74, 76, 83, 86, 87, 95, 96, 98, 99, 102-104, 107, 113, 115, 116, 120-122, 129-135, 137, 143, 150, 155, 159, 162, 163-165, 178, 182, 187, 188, 190-192, 200-203, 207, 218, 219, 224, 238-241, 258, 261, 265, 266, 269, 270, 272
Judah b. Betera, 86
Judah b. R. Simeon, 52
Judea, 129

Kadi, 183, 229
Kaftorim, 125
Kahana, 27, 31, 47, 55, 61, 73, 77-79, 84, 120, 188, 198
Kefar Akkum, 96
King David, 123
Knife, 5, 27, 47, 49, 131, 132, 246, 269, 272

Lacuna in a text, 183, 229
Laqish, 20, 36, 41, 52, 85, 88, 89, 98, 123, 125, 184, 185, 191, 193, 195, 196, 198, 206, 232-234, 256
Levi, 35, 37, 40, 56, 64, 98-102, 104, 106, 122, 255
Leviathan, 154
Lewysohn, L., 143, 153
Lod, 102
Logical argument: a fortiori, 122, 161, 170, 171, 175-177, 252

Maimonides, 3
Majority (legal principle), 28, 29, 31, 32, 34, 35, 38, 39, 72-75, 80, 83, 104, 166, 167, 202, 203, 210, 211, 260, 263
Malokh of Arabia, 56
Mamre, 276
Mani bar Patish, 52, 255
Manyomi(n), 43, 49, 50, 55, 59
Mar bar Hiyya, 38, 112
Mar bar R. Ashi, 112, 169, 202, 203, 247
Mar bar R. Idai, 134
Mar Judah, 49
Mar the son of R. Joseph, 54
Mar the son of Rabina, 29
Mar Zutra, 26, 33, 50, 55, 56, 70, 130, 192, 250
Mar Zutra the son of R. Mari, 55, 56
Mar Zutra the son of R. Nahman, 250
Mari, 28, 55, 56, 274
Mari bar Mar Uqba, 28
Matna, 23, 52, 74, 75, 88, 89, 100, 206

Mattiah bar Judah, 150
Mauling (by a beast), 12, 20, 24, 26, 27, 76-85, 87
Mehoza, 111
Meir, 5, 9, 10, 88, 92-95, 103, 138, 157, 162-165, 174, 180-186, 189, 190, 191-193, 196, 197, 205, 235, 236, 247, 254-258, 260, 262-264, 276
Menashe, 68
Menstrual uncleanness, 91
Meremar, 46, 132
Mesharshayya, 56, 63, 107, 153, 162, 198
Meshullam, 45, 108
Mina, 112
Minyamin bar Hiyya, 225
Miracles, 24-25
Mishnah, 1, 2, 7, 8, 10-17, 20-23, 25, 31, 33, 38, 42, 48, 51, 58, 59, 66, 76, 77, 86-90, 97, 102, 105, 106, 109, 110, 112, 113, 114, 116, 154-158, 163-165, 167, 169, 174, 177, 178, 180-182, 188, 189, 191, 194, 199, 200, 204, 205, 207, 208, 211, 212, 218, 221, 225-228, 231, 233-235, 240-243, 246, 254, 259, 261, 263, 264, 266, 269, 272, 273, 279; Mishnaic law, 1, 2, 8
Moab, 125
Moses, 21, 24, 124, 260, 277
Mourning customs, 61, 62, 87, 141

Nahman, 25, 30, 35, 38, 43, 49, 50, 52, 53, 57-60, 62, 64, 68, 69, 84, 85, 90, 95, 99, 101, 121, 124, 128, 129, 157, 158, 171, 172, 204, 205, 224, 226, 250, 274
Nahman bar Pappa, 124
Nahman bar R. Hisda, 274
Nahman bar Yitzhak, 57-59, 64, 95, 101, 157, 158, 171, 274
Nahmani, 35, 37, 57, 64, 75
Nathan, 32, 39, 46-48, 55, 64, 112
Nathan bar Shila, 112
Nazirite, 237
Nebuchadnezzar, 277
Negative prohibition, 229
Nehardea, 64, 65, 70, 98
Nehemiah, 50, 70, 98
Nehorai, 95, 106
Nehuniah, 92
Neusner, J., 1, 3, 7, 8, 147, 150
Nimrod, 277
Nivli, 39

Olive trees, 152
Ono, 102
Orpiment, 275
Oshaia, 57, 75, 95, 98, 112, 190, 191, 200, 201, 216, 226, 238

Pappa, 23, 24, 26, 31, 35, 41, 42, 59, 60, 63, 70, 86, 92, 111, 122, 124, 125, 132, 135, 143, 192, 201, 205-207, 220, 223, 259, 263, 269, 270
Pappa bar Abba, 86
Pappa, the son of R. Sala the pious, 192
Pappi, 28, 45, 50, 84, 207, 234
Parah, 130, 233
Parasites, 153
Patriarch, 34, 41, 123
Pazzi, 37, 41, 123
Pharaoh, 277
Phineas, 234
Phineas the son of R. Ammi, 234
Pinhas, 8
Plants: asafoetida, 114, 115; crocus, 47; crowfoot, 114, 115; hyssop, 131, 234; oleander, 114, 115
Prayer: Tefillin, 276
Presumptive status (legal principle), 81
Pumbedita, 42, 89, 104; Pumbeditan, 178
Punishments: extirpation, 96, 97, 191, 213, 214, 226, 228-230, 271; flogging, 187; forty stripes, 5, 10, 213, 214, 226-228, 235, 236, 238-240, 262; stripes, 5, 10, 213, 214, 226-228, 230, 232, 235-240, 262
Purities: uncleanness, 2, 4, 6-8, 7-9, 27, 75, 91, 96, 113, 128, 140, 170, 173-179, 181-184, 186, 188, 193, 194, 197, 205, 208, 209, 210, 257-259, 263, 270, 271; minimum quantity, 113

Qahaty, Pinhas, 8
Qatina, 130

Rab, 23, 24, 28-32, 34, 36-40, 43, 58, 59, 64, 68-70, 73-76, 78, 80-83, 85, 92, 96, 98, 99, 103-106, 111, 115, 116, 125, 132, 135, 137, 138, 143, 145, 155, 159, 160, 187, 188, 200, 201, 203-205, 207, 241, 250, 258, 261, 266
Raba, 23, 25, 28-30, 36, 43-47, 49, 50, 52, 59, 60, 63, 64, 68, 75, 83, 89, 90, 92, 100, 103, 107, 113, 124, 131, 135, 140, 161, 167,

# Index

168, 177, 178, 183, 187-189, 197, 202, 206, 207, 211, 215, 225, 229-231, 248, 266, 268, 274-278
Rabbah, 23, 25, 26, 30-33, 35, 37, 38, 40, 42, 43, 51, 56, 64, 65, 72, 74, 75, 80, 83, 94, 95, 102, 104, 159, 166, 167, 174, 177, 178, 186, 187, 201, 202, 204, 206, 209, 251, 268, 273
Rabbah bar Abbuha, 30
Rabbah bar bar Hannah, 23, 25, 31-33, 35, 37, 40, 51, 72, 83, 94, 95, 186, 187, 209, 268, 273
Rabbah bar R. Huna, 64, 80, 104, 201, 202
Rabbah bar R. Shila, 23, 74, 75
Rabbah bar Tahlifa, 38, 56
Rabbah bar Yitzhak, 38
Rabban (honorific title), 61, 88, 108, 142, 224, 267, 272, 273
Rabbi, 27, 39, 42, 64, 66, 85, 101, 102, 106, 108, 112, 124, 136, 137, 172, 173, 174, 194, 202, 243, 247, 255-260, 264, 267, 268
Rabbinai, 203
Rabin, 49, 58, 199, 260, 261
Rabin bar Hanina, 199
Rabin bar Sheba, 49
Rabina, 29, 30, 43, 44, 47, 50, 51, 55, 67, 110, 112, 122, 131, 140, 149, 150, 153, 182, 207, 212, 226, 253, 266, 278
Rabinowitz, L., 3
Rafram, 46, 55
Rahumi, 278
Rakhish bar Pappa, 23, 24, 92
Rami bar Ezekiel, 30
Rashi (Commentary of Solomon b. Isaac), 21, 42, 55, 113, 132, 138, 140, 141, 152, 168, 182, 191, 195, 198, 201, 202, 221, 235, 248, 249, 264, 273
Rehaba, 130
Religious obligation (commandment), 17, 90, 148, 228, 239, 267, 269, 275, 276, 278, 279; negative commandment, 148; positive commandment, 228
Resh Laqish, 41, 85
Rodents: bat, 133, 134; mole, 134
Rome, 120, 121, 131, 251, 268

Sabbath, 44, 102, 250-253, 261; Sabbath eve, 250
Sadducee, 267, 268
Safra, 66, 79, 225

Sama the son of Raba, 47
Samuel, 13, 22, 23, 28-31, 37-41, 43, 51, 55, 62, 64, 69, 70, 74, 75, 81, 82-84, 95, 98, 99, 101, 103, 104, 111, 114-116, 119, 120, 123, 132, 138, 152, 159, 178, 182, 187, 202-205, 218, 241, 270
Samuel bar Nahmani, 37
Samuel bar Hiyya, 101
Samuel bar Yitzhak, 103, 241
Samuel the son of R. Abbahu, 119, 120
Satyrs, 141
Scripture, 1, 3, 13, 29, 33, 114, 118, 133, 134, 137, 151, 155, 159, 163, 164, 170, 188, 215-217, 225, 228, 231, 236, 247, 248, 258, 274; prophets, 103
Sennacherib, 277
Sepphoris, 64, 66, 112
Shaman bar Abba, 233
Shammai, House of, 22, 29, 74, 75, 194, 275
Sheba, 49, 261
Sheshet, 58, 59, 153
Sheshet the son of R. Idi, 153
Shila, 23, 64, 74, 75, 112
Shimi, 62, 79, 134, 164
Shimi bar Ashi, 79, 164
Shimi bar Hiyya, 62
Shinar, 142
Shisha the son of R. Idi, 31, 153
Shizbi, 100, 114
Sidon, 60; Sidonians, 126
Sihon, 125
Simai, 102
Simeon, 4, 5, 10, 15, 19-22, 36-38, 40, 42, 48, 52, 56, 58-62, 69, 85, 88, 89, 94-96, 98, 99, 106-108, 123, 125, 142, 158, 160, 164, 165, 184-186, 190, 191, 193-196, 198-200, 205, 206, 224, 226, 227, 229, 230, 232-234, 242, 247, 253, 255-260, 272, 273, 276
Simeon b. Eleazar, 21, 22, 40, 60, 94, 95, 99, 108, 142, 194
Simeon b. Gamaliel, 61, 62, 88, 89, 108, 142, 224, 272, 273
Simeon b. Halafta, 106, 107
Simeon b. Laqish, 20, 36, 52, 85, 88, 89, 98, 123, 125, 184, 185, 191, 193, 195, 196, 198, 206, 232-234, 256
Simeon bar Yohai, 164
Simeon b. Eliakim, 52
Simeon b. Judah, 96

Simeon b. Pazzi, 37, 123
Simeon b. Zoma, 242
Simeon bar Rabbi, 42
Simeon of Sezur, 200; Simeon Shezuri, 190, 198, 199; Simeon b. Shezuri, 15, 199, 200
Sirion, 126
Slaughtering, 2, 3, 5, 9-11, 30, 36, 66, 67, 86, 103, 163, 180, 181, 183, 184, 188-190, 195, 197, 198, 200, 204, 213, 214, 215-217, 220, 221, 223-232, 236, 241, 255, 256, 260, 261, 266, 270
Solomon, 108
Sumkhos, 16, 235-240

Tabot, 30, 60
Tahlifa, 38, 56, 124
Tahlifa bar Abina, 124
Tammuz, 107, 115, 120
Tamrata, 129
Tanhum(a), 93
Tanna, 21, 22, 31, 77, 89, 123, 141, 145, 146, 152, 170, 188, 198, 238, 239; Tannaitic view, 21, 90; Tannaite teaching, 12, 14-16, 22-25, 32, 33, 36, 38, 39, 42, 44, 45, 47, 49, 51, 57, 59-62, 68, 74-79, 91, 94-97, 99, 101, 102, 103, 108-110, 112, 113, 117, 118, 126, 129, 133, 134, 136-140, 142, 143, 147-149, 151-154, 156, 157, 163, 164, 165, 167, 172-174, 177-183, 186-191, 194, 197, 199, 200, 205, 207-212, 214-218, 220-222, 224, 225, 227, 231, 233, 235, 237-242, 246, 247, 249, 252, 253, 255, 258-260, 263, 265-267, 269-276, 279
Tarfon, 95
Temple, 2-4, 10, 133, 161, 213, 214, 226, 229, 245, 246, 253, 256, 258, 259; burnt-offering, 4, 96, 164, 165, 231; cow of purification, 233; paschal lamb, 192, 206; peace-offering, 173, 230, 231; Priest, 2, 6, 7, 32, 57, 131, 134, 135, 156, 234, 247, 255, 256; Sacrifice, 1, 4, 6, 14, 128-130, 155, 173, 231, 246; sin-offering, 159, 237, 275
Temple treasury, 246
Tiberias, 52
Tithes, 159, 164; demai, 199-200; second tithes, 159
Tokens of animals, 4, 13, 14, 116-119, 126, 128, 138-140, 145, 146, 154, 155, 173, 194, 220, 248

Torah, 4, 11, 20, 59, 86, 116, 117, 124-128, 131, 133, 134, 138, 139, 141, 145-147, 175, 178, 179, 189, 196, 197, 206, 220, 221, 222, 235, 236, 242, 249, 250, 259-261, 272, 278

Ulla, 24, 27, 41, 48, 72, 73, 159, 181, 182, 199-201, 205, 207
Uncleanness, 2, 4, 6-8, 7-9, 27, 75, 91, 96, 113, 128, 140, 170, 173, 174, 175-179, 181-184, 186, 188, 193, 194, 197, 205, 208, 209, 210, 257-259, 263, 270, 271; *midras*, 181; *zab*, 181, 271, 272
Upper Galilee, 129
Uqba, 28, 51, 128, 140
Uqba bar Hama, 51, 128, 140
Usha, 8

Vegetables, 250; cabbages, 131; cucumber, 111, 152; lentils, 71, 152

Weather: rains, 121; winds, 261, 267
Wild beast, 3, 5, 6, 10, 13, 58, 118, 119, 154, 172, 210, 226, 245, 247, 254, 265-267, 269
Women, 9, 27, 47, 120, 156, 168, 174, 178, 179, 208, 253, 275
Writ of divorce, 199

Yannai, 41, 61, 96, 101, 234
Yannai b. R. Ishmael, 96
Yavneh, 49; Yavnean, 8
Yeba the Elder, 266
Yemar, 67, 100
Yitzhak, 24, 25, 35, 37, 38, 40, 51-53, 56-59, 64, 69, 84, 95, 101, 103, 138, 157, 158, 170-172, 185-187, 205, 209, 225, 241, 268, 274, 278
Yitzhak b. R. Joseph, 24, 25
Yitzhak bar Ammi, 56
Yitzhak bar Joseph, 51, 52, 101, 185, 186
Yitzhak bar Nahmani, 35, 37, 57
Yitzhak bar Samuel, 69, 84, 187
Yitzhak bar Samuel bar Marta, 69, 84, 187
Yitzhak Nappaha, 53
Yohai, 164
Yohanan (bar Nappaha), 24, 25, 36, 48, 51, 52, 55, 58, 61-64, 69, 72, 73, 85, 88-91, 95, 96, 98, 100, 104, 106, 113, 133, 134, 138, 159, 160, 164, 175, 184, 185, 187, 191, 193-196, 198, 199, 205-207, 210,

231-234, 242, 250, 251, 255, 260, 263, 264, 268, 270, 273, 276, 277
Yosé, 6, 9, 22, 24, 45, 64, 66, 75, 90, 92, 100, 104, 106, 108, 116, 143, 154, 164, 165, 170, 181, 184, 185, 194, 224-226, 240, 252, 253, 276
Yosé b. Hanina(h), 64, 75, 104, 184, 185
Yosé b. Nehorai, 106
Yosé b. Durmasqet, 154
Yosé b. (Ha-)Meshullam, 45, 108
Yosé b. Joshua, 100
Yosé b. R. Judah, 22, 24
Yosé bar Abin, 90, 92
Yosé bar Zabeda, 92
Yosé of Medea, 66
Yosé the Galilean, 6, 170, 194, 240, 276

Zadok, 102
Zakkai, 72, 73
Zebid, 34, 84, 202
Zeriqa(n), 43, 53
Zira, 28, 34, 38, 42, 56, 58, 61, 83, 93, 105, 119, 130, 138, 139, 169, 191, 198, 205, 225, 228, 245, 246, 264, 275, 278
Ziri, 63, 72, 89, 98, 199, 278
Zutra, 26, 33, 50, 55, 56, 70, 130, 192, 250

# Brown Judaic Studies

| | | |
|---|---|---|
| 140001 | *Approaches to Ancient Judaism I* | William S. Green |
| 140002 | *The Traditions of Eleazar Ben Azariah* | Tzvee Zahavy |
| 140003 | *Persons and Institutions in Early Rabbinic Judaism* | William S. Green |
| 140004 | *Claude Goldsmid Montefiore on the Ancient Rabbis* | Joshua B. Stein |
| 140005 | *The Ecumenical Perspective and the Modernization of Jewish Religion* | S. Daniel Breslauer |
| 140006 | *The Sabbath-Law of Rabbi Meir* | Robert Goldenberg |
| 140007 | *Rabbi Tarfon* | Joel Gereboff |
| 140008 | *Rabban Gamaliel II* | Shamai Kanter |
| 140009 | *Approaches to Ancient Judaism II* | William S. Green |
| 140010 | *Method and Meaning in Ancient Judaism I* | Jacob Neusner |
| 140011 | *Approaches to Ancient Judaism III* | William S. Green |
| 140012 | *Turning Point: Zionism and Reform Judaism* | Howard R. Greenstein |
| 140013 | *Buber on God and the Perfect Man* | Pamela Vermes |
| 140014 | *Scholastic Rabbinism* | Anthony J. Saldarini |
| 140015 | *Method and Meaning in Ancient Judaism II* | Jacob Neusner |
| 140016 | *Method and Meaning in Ancient Judaism III* | Jacob Neusner |
| 140017 | *Post Mishnaic Judaism in Transition* | Baruch M. Bokser |
| 140018 | *A History of the Mishnaic Law of Agriculture: Tractate Maaser Sheni* | Peter J. Haas |
| 140019 | *Mishnah's Theology of Tithing* | Martin S. Jaffee |
| 140020 | *The Priestly Gift in Mishnah: A Study of Tractate Terumot* | Alan. J. Peck |
| 140021 | *History of Judaism: The Next Ten Years* | Baruch M. Bokser |
| 140022 | *Ancient Synagogues* | Joseph Gutmann |
| 140023 | *Warrant for Genocide* | Norman Cohn |
| 140024 | *The Creation of the World According to Gersonides* | Jacob J. Staub |
| 140025 | *Two Treatises of Philo of Alexandria: A Commentary on* De Gigantibus *and* Quod Deus Sit Immutabilis | Winston/Dillon |
| 140026 | *A History of the Mishnaic Law of Agriculture: Kilayim* | Irving Mandelbaum |
| 140027 | *Approaches to Ancient Judaism IV* | William S. Green |
| 140028 | *Judaism in the American Humanities I* | Jacob Neusner |
| 140029 | *Handbook of Synagogue Architecture* | Marilyn Chiat |
| 140030 | *The Book of Mirrors* | Daniel C. Matt |
| 140031 | *Ideas in Fiction: The Works of Hayim Hazaz* | Warren Bargad |
| 140032 | *Approaches to Ancient Judaism V* | William S. Green |
| 140033 | *Sectarian Law in the Dead Sea Scrolls: Courts, Testimony and the Penal Code* | Lawrence H. Schiffman |
| 140034 | *A History of the United Jewish Appeal: 1939-1982* | Marc L. Raphael |
| 140035 | *The Academic Study of Judaism* | Jacob Neusner |
| 140036 | *Woman Leaders in the Ancient Synagogue* | Bernadette Brooten |
| 140037 | *Formative Judaism I: Religious, Historical, and Literary Studies* | Jacob Neusner |
| 140038 | *Ben Sira's View of Women: A Literary Analysis* | Warren C. Trenchard |
| 140039 | *Barukh Kurzweil and Modern Hebrew Literature* | James S. Diamond |
| 140040 | *Israeli Childhood Stories of the Sixties: Yizhar, Aloni, Shahar, Kahana-Carmon* | Gideon Telpaz |
| 140041 | *Formative Judaism II: Religious, Historical, and Literary Studies* | Jacob Neusner |
| 140042 | *Judaism in the American Humanities II: Jewish Learning and the New Humanities* | Jacob Neusner |

| | | |
|---|---|---|
| 140043 | Support for the Poor in the Mishnaic Law of Agriculture: Tractate Peah | Roger Brooks |
| 140044 | The Sanctity of the Seventh Year: A Study of Mishnah Tractate Shebiit | Louis E. Newman |
| 140045 | Character and Context: Studies in the Fiction of Abramovitsh, Brenner, and Agnon | Jeffrey Fleck |
| 140046 | Formative Judaism III: Religious, Historical, and Literary Studies | Jacob Neusner |
| 140047 | Pharaoh's Counsellors: Job, Jethro, and Balaam in Rabbinic and Patristic Tradition | Judith Baskin |
| 140048 | The Scrolls and Christian Origins: Studies in the Jewish Background of the New Testament | Matthew Black |
| 140049 | Approaches to Modern Judaism I | Marc Lee Raphael |
| 140050 | Mysterious Encounters at Mamre and Jabbok | William T. Miller |
| 140051 | The Mishnah Before 70 | Jacob Neusner |
| 140052 | Sparda by the Bitter Sea: Imperial Interaction in Western Anatolia | Jack Martin Balcer |
| 140053 | Hermann Cohen: The Challenge of a Religion of Reason | William Kluback |
| 140054 | Approaches to Judaism in Medieval Times I | David R. Blumenthal |
| 140055 | In the Margins of the Yerushalmi: Glosses on the English Translation | Jacob Neusner |
| 140056 | Approaches to Modern Judaism II | Marc Lee Raphael |
| 140057 | Approaches to Judaism in Medieval Times II | David R. Blumenthal |
| 140058 | Midrash as Literature: The Primacy of Documentary Discourse | Jacob Neusner |
| 140059 | The Commerce of the Sacred: Mediation of the Divine Among Jews in the Graeco-Roman Diaspora | Jack N. Lightstone |
| 140060 | Major Trends in Formative Judaism I: Society and Symbol in Political Crisis | Jacob Neusner |
| 140061 | Major Trends in Formative Judaism II: Texts, Contents, and Contexts | Jacob Neusner |
| 140062 | A History of the Jews in Babylonia I: The Parthian Period | Jacob Neusner |
| 140063 | The Talmud of Babylonia: An American Translation XXXII: Tractate Arakhin | Jacob Neusner |
| 140064 | Ancient Judaism: Debates and Disputes | Jacob Neusner |
| 140065 | Prayers Alleged to Be Jewish: An Examination of the Constitutiones Apostolorum | David Fiensy |
| 140066 | The Legal Methodology of Hai Gaon | Tsvi Groner |
| 140067 | From Mishnah to Scripture: The Problem of the Unattributed Saying | Jacob Neusner |
| 140068 | Halakhah in a Theological Dimension | David Novak |
| 140069 | From Philo to Origen: Middle Platonism in Transition | Robert M. Berchman |
| 140070 | In Search of Talmudic Biography: The Problem of the Attributed Saying | Jacob Neusner |
| 140071 | The Death of the Old and the Birth of the New: The Framework of the Book of Numbers and the Pentateuch | Dennis T. Olson |
| 140072 | The Talmud of Babylonia: An American Translation XVII: Tractate Sotah | Jacob Neusner |
| 140073 | Understanding Seeking Faith: Essays on the Case of Judaism II: Literature, Religion and the Social Study of Judiasm | Jacob Neusner |
| 140074 | The Talmud of Babylonia: An American Translation VI: Tractate Sukkah | Jacob Neusner |
| 140075 | Fear Not Warrior: A Study of 'al tira' Pericopes in the Hebrew Scriptures | Edgar W. Conrad |

| | | |
|---|---|---|
| 140076 | Formative Judaism IV: Religious, Historical, and Literary Studies | Jacob Neusner |
| 140077 | Biblical Patterns in Modern Literature | Hirsch/Aschkenasy |
| 140078 | The Talmud of Babylonia: An American Translation I: Tractate Berakhot | Jacob Neusner |
| 140079 | Mishnah's Division of Agriculture: A History and Theology of Seder Zeraim | Alan J. Avery-Peck |
| 140080 | From Tradition to Imitation: The Plan and Program of Pesiqta Rabbati and Pesiqta deRab Kahana | Jacob Neusner |
| 140081 | The Talmud of Babylonia: An American Translation XXIII.A: Tractate Sanhedrin, Chapters 1-3 | Jacob Neusner |
| 140082 | Jewish Presence in T. S. Eliot and Franz Kafka | Melvin Wilk |
| 140083 | School, Court, Public Administration: Judaism and its Institutions in Talmudic Babylonia | Jacob Neusner |
| 140084 | The Talmud of Babylonia: An American Translation XXIII.B: Tractate Sanhedrin, Chapters 4-8 | Jacob Neusner |
| 140085 | The Bavli and Its Sources: The Question of Tradition in the Case of Tractate Sukkah | Jacob Neusner |
| 140086 | From Description to Conviction: Essays on the History and Theology of Judaism | Jacob Neusner |
| 140087 | The Talmud of Babylonia: An American Translation XXIII.C: Tractate Sanhedrin, Chapters 9-11 | Jacob Neusner |
| 140088 | Mishnaic Law of Blessings and Prayers: Tractate Berakhot | Tzvee Zahavy |
| 140089 | The Peripatetic Saying: The Problem of the Thrice-Told Tale in Talmudic Literature | Jacob Neusner |
| 140090 | The Talmud of Babylonia: An American Translation XXVI: Tractate Horayot | Martin S. Jaffee |
| 140091 | Formative Judaism V: Religious, Historical, and Literary Studies | Jacob Neusner |
| 140092 | Essays on Biblical Method and Translation | Edward Greenstein |
| 140093 | The Integrity of Leviticus Rabbah | Jacob Neusner |
| 140094 | Behind the Essenes: History and Ideology of the Dead Sea Scrolls | Philip R. Davies |
| 140095 | Approaches to Judaism in Medieval Times III | David R. Blumenthal |
| 140096 | The Memorized Torah: The Mnemonic System of the Mishnah | Jacob Neusner |
| 140097 | Knowledge and Illumination | Hossein Ziai |
| 140098 | Sifre to Deuteronomy: An Analytical Translation I: Pisqaot 1-143. Debarim, Waethanan, Eqeb | Jacob Neusner |
| 140099 | Major Trends in Formative Judaism III: The Three Stages in the Formation of Judaism | Jacob Neusner |
| 140101 | Sifre to Deuteronomy: An Analytical Translation II: Pisqaot 144-357. Shofetim, Ki Tese, Ki Tabo, Nesabim, Ha'azinu, Zot Habberakhah | Jacob Neusner |
| 140102 | Sifra: The Rabbinic Commentary on Leviticus | Neusner/Brooks |
| 140103 | The Human Will in Judaism | Howard Eilberg-Schwartz |
| 140104 | Genesis Rabbah I: Genesis 1:1 to 8:14 | Jacob Neusner |
| 140105 | Genesis Rabbah II: Genesis 8:15 to 28:9 | Jacob Neusner |
| 140106 | Genesis Rabbah III: Genesis 28:10 to 50:26 | Jacob Neusner |
| 140107 | First Principles of Systemic Analysis | Jacob Neusner |
| 140108 | Genesis and Judaism | Jacob Neusner |
| 140109 | The Talmud of Babylonia: An American Translation XXXV: Tractates Meilah and Tamid | Peter J. Haas |
| 140110 | Studies in Islamic and Judaic Traditions I | Brinner/Ricks |

| | | |
|---|---|---|
| 140111 | Comparative Midrash: The Plan and Program of Genesis Rabbah and Leviticus Rabbah | Jacob Neusner |
| 140112 | The Tosefta: Its Structure and its Sources | Jacob Neusner |
| 140113 | Reading and Believing | Jacob Neusner |
| 140114 | The Fathers According to Rabbi Nathan | Jacob Neusner |
| 140115 | Etymology in Early Jewish Interpretation: The Hebrew Names in Philo | Lester L. Grabbe |
| 140116 | Understanding Seeking Faith: Essays on the Case of Judaism I: Debates on Method, Reports of Results | Jacob Neusner |
| 140117 | The Talmud of Babylonia: An American Translation VII: Tractate Besah | Alan J. Avery-Peck |
| 140118 | Sifre to Numbers: An American Translation and Explanation I: Sifre to Numbers 1-58 | Jacob Neusner |
| 140119 | Sifre to Numbers: An American Translation and Explanation II: Sifre to Numbers 59-115 | Jacob Neusner |
| 140120 | Cohen and Troeltsch: Ethical Monotheistic Religion and Theory of Culture | Wendell S. Dietrich |
| 140121 | Goodenough on the History of Religion and on Judaism | Neusner/Frerichs |
| 140122 | Pesiqta deRab Kahana I: Pisqaot 1-14 | Jacob Neusner |
| 140123 | Pesiqta deRab Kahana II: Pisqaot 15-28 and Introduction to Pesiqta deRab Kahana | Jacob Neusner |
| 140124 | Sifre to Deuteronomy: Introduction | Jacob Neusner |
| 140126 | A Conceptual Commentary on Midrash Leviticus Rabbah: Value Concepts in Jewish Thought | Max Kadushin |
| 140127 | The Other Judaisms of Late Antiquity | Alan F. Segal |
| 140128 | Josephus as a Historical Source in Patristic Literature through Eusebius | Michael Hardwick |
| 140129 | Judaism: The Evidence of the Mishnah | Jacob Neusner |
| 140131 | Philo, John and Paul: New Perspectives on Judaism and Early Christianity | Peder Borgen |
| 140132 | Babylonian Witchcraft Literature | Tzvi Abusch |
| 140133 | The Making of the Mind of Judaism: The Formative Age | Jacob Neusner |
| 140135 | Why No Gospels in Talmudic Judaism? | Jacob Neusner |
| 140136 | Torah: From Scroll to Symbol Part III: Doctrine | Jacob Neusner |
| 140137 | The Systemic Analysis of Judaism | Jacob Neusner |
| 140138 | Sifra: An Analytical Translation I | Jacob Neusner |
| 140139 | Sifra: An Analytical Translation II | Jacob Neusner |
| 140140 | Sifra: An Analytical Translation III | Jacob Neusner |
| 140141 | Midrash in Context: Exegesis in Formative Judaism | Jacob Neusner |
| 140143 | Oxen, Women or Citizens? Slaves in the System of Mishnah | Paul V. Flesher |
| 140144 | The Book of the Pomegranate | Elliot R. Wolfson |
| 140145 | Wrong Ways and Right Ways in the Study of Formative Judaism | Jacob Neusner |
| 140146 | Sifra in Perspective: The Documentary Comparison of the Midrashim of Ancient Judaism | Jacob Neusner |
| 140148 | Mekhilta According to Rabbi Ishmael: An Analytical Translation I | Jacob Neusner |
| 140149 | The Doctrine of the Divine Name: An Introduction to Classical Kabbalistic Theology | Stephen G. Wald |
| 140150 | Water into Wine and the Beheading of John the Baptist | Roger Aus |
| 140151 | The Formation of the Jewish Intellect | Jacob Neusner |
| 140152 | Mekhilta According to Rabbi Ishmael: An Introduction to Judaism's First Scriptural Encyclopaedia | Jacob Neusner |

| | | |
|---|---|---|
| 140153 | Understanding Seeking Faith: Essays on the Case of Judaism III: Society, History, and Political and Philosophical Uses of Judaism | Jacob Neusner |
| 140154 | Mekhilta According to Rabbi Ishmael: An Analytical Translation II | Jacob Neusner |
| 140155 | Goyim: Gentiles and Israelites in Mishnah-Tosefta | Gary P. Porton |
| 140156 | A Religion of Pots and Pans? | Jacob Neusner |
| 140157 | Claude Montefiore and Christianity | Maurice Gerald Bowler |
| 140158 | The Philosophical Mishnah III: The Tractates' Agenda: From Nazir to Zebahim | Jacob Neusner |
| 140159 | From Ancient Israel to Modern Judaism I: Intellect in Quest of Understanding | Neusner/Frerichs/Sarna |
| 140160 | The Social Study of Judaism I | Jacob Neusner |
| 140161 | Philo's Jewish Identity | Alan Mendelson |
| 140162 | The Social Study of Judaism II | Jacob Neusner |
| 140163 | The Philosophical Mishnah I: The Initial Probe | Jacob Neusner |
| 140164 | The Philosophical Mishnah II: The Tractates' Agenda: From Abodah Zarah Through Moed Qatan | Jacob Neusner |
| 140166 | Women's Earliest Records | Barbara S. Lesko |
| 140167 | The Legacy of Hermann Cohen | William Kluback |
| 140168 | Method and Meaning in Ancient Judaism | Jacob Neusner |
| 140169 | The Role of the Messenger and Message in the Ancient Near East | John T. Greene |
| 140171 | Abraham Heschel's Idea of Revelation | Lawerence Perlman |
| 140172 | The Philosophical Mishnah IV: The Repertoire | Jacob Neusner |
| 140173 | From Ancient Israel to Modern Judaism II: Intellect in Quest of Understanding | Neusner/Frerichs/Sarna |
| 140174 | From Ancient Israel to Modern Judaism III: Intellect in Quest of Understanding | Neusner/Frerichs/Sarna |
| 140175 | From Ancient Israel to Modern Judaism IV: Intellect in Quest of Understanding | Neusner/Frerichs/Sarna |
| 140176 | Translating the Classics of Judaism: In Theory and In Practice | Jacob Neusner |
| 140177 | Profiles of a Rabbi: Synoptic Opportunities in Reading About Jesus | Bruce Chilton |
| 140178 | Studies in Islamic and Judaic Traditions II | Brinner/Ricks |
| 140179 | Medium and Message in Judaism: First Series | Jacob Neusner |
| 140180 | Making the Classics of Judaism: The Three Stages of Literary Formation | Jacob Neusner |
| 140181 | The Law of Jealousy: Anthropology of Sotah | Adriana Destro |
| 140182 | Esther Rabbah I: An Analytical Translation | Jacob Neusner |
| 140183 | Ruth Rabbah: An Analytical Translation | Jacob Neusner |
| 140184 | Formative Judaism: Religious, Historical and Literary Studies | Jacob Neusner |
| 140185 | The Studia Philonica Annual 1989 | David T. Runia |
| 140186 | The Setting of the Sermon on the Mount | W.D. Davies |
| 140187 | The Midrash Compilations of the Sixth and Seventh Centuries I | Jacob Neusner |
| 140188 | The Midrash Compilations of the Sixth and Seventh Centuries II | Jacob Neusner |
| 140189 | The Midrash Compilations of the Sixth and Seventh Centuries III | Jacob Neusner |
| 140190 | The Midrash Compilations of the Sixth and Seventh Centuries IV | Jacob Neusner |
| 140191 | The Religious World of Contemporary Judaism: Observations and Convictions | Jacob Neusner |
| 140192 | Approaches to Ancient Judaism VI | Neusner/Frerichs |
| 140193 | Lamentations Rabbah: An Analytical Translation | Jacob Neusner |
| 140194 | Early Christian Texts on Jews and Judaism | Robert S. MacLennan |
| 140196 | Torah and the Chronicler's History Work | Judson R. Shaver |

| | | |
|---|---|---|
| 140197 | *Song of Songs Rabbah: An Analytical Translation I* | Jacob Neusner |
| 140198 | *Song of Songs Rabbah: An Analytical Translation II* | Jacob Neusner |
| 140199 | *From Literature to Theology in Formative Judaism* | Jacob Neusner |
| 140202 | *Maimonides on Perfection* | Menachem Kellner |
| 140203 | *The Martyr's Conviction* | Eugene Weiner/Anita Weiner |
| 140204 | *Judaism, Christianity, and Zoroastrianism in Talmudic Babylonia* | Jacob Neusner |
| 140205 | *Tzedakah: Can Jewish Philanthropy Buy Jewish Survival?* | Jacob Neusner |
| 140206 | *New Perspectives on Ancient Judaism I* | Neusner/Borgen/Frerichs/Horsley |
| 140207 | *Scriptures of the Oral Torah* | Jacob Neusner |
| 140208 | *Christian Faith and the Bible of Judaism* | Jacob Neusner |
| 140209 | *Philo's Perception of Women* | Dorothy Sly |
| 140210 | *Case Citation in the Babylonian Talmud: The Evidence Tractate Neziqin* | Eliezer Segal |
| 140211 | *The Biblical Herem: A Window on Israel's Religious Experience* | Philip D. Stern |
| 140212 | *Goodenough on the Beginnings of Christianity* | A.T. Kraabel |
| 140213 | *The Talmud of Babylonia: An American Translation XXI.A: Tractate Bava Mesia Chapters 1-2* | Jacob Neusner |
| 140214 | *The Talmud of Babylonia: An American Translation XXI.B: Tractate Bava Mesia Chapters 3-4* | Jacob Neusner |
| 140215 | *The Talmud of Babylonia: An American Translation XXI.C: Tractate Bava Mesia Chapters 5-6* | Jacob Neusner |
| 140216 | *The Talmud of Babylonia: An American Translation XXI.D: Tractate Bava Mesia Chapters 7-10* | Jacob Neusner |
| 140217 | *Semites, Iranians, Greeks and Romans: Studies in their Interactions* | Jonathan A. Goldstein |
| 140218 | *The Talmud of Babylonia: An American Translation XXXIII: Temurah* | Jacob Neusner |
| 140219 | *The Talmud of Babylonia: An American Translation XXXI.A: Tractate Bekhorot Chapters 1-4* | Jacob Neusner |
| 140220 | *The Talmud of Babylonia: An American Translation XXXI.B: Tractate Bekhorot Chapters 5-9* | Jacob Neusner |
| 140221 | *The Talmud of Babylonia: An American Translation XXXVI.A: Tractate Niddah Chapters 1-3* | Jacob Neusner |
| 140222 | *The Talmud of Babylonia: An American Translation XXXVI.B: Tractate Niddah Chapters 4-10* | Jacob Neusner |
| 140223 | *The Talmud of Babylonia: An American Translation XXXIV: Tractate Keritot* | Jacob Neusner |
| 140224 | *Paul, the Temple, and the Presence of God* | David A. Renwick |
| 140225 | *The Book of the People* | William W. Hallo |
| 140226 | *The Studia Philonica Annual 1990* | David Runia |
| 140227 | *The Talmud of Babylonia: An American Translation XXV.A: Tractate Abodah Zarah Chapters 1-2* | Jacob Neusner |
| 140228 | *The Talmud of Babylonia: An American Translation XXV.B: Tractate Abodah Zarah Chapters 3-5* | Jacob Neusner |
| 140230 | *The Studia Philonica Annual 1991* | David Runia |
| 140231 | *The Talmud of Babylonia: An American Translation XXVIII.A: Tractate Zebahim Chapters 1-3* | Jacob Neusner |
| 140232 | *Both Literal and Allegorical: Studies in Philo of Alexandria's Questions and Answers on Genesis and Exodus* | David M. Hay |
| 140233 | *The Talmud of Babylonia: An American Translation XXVIII.B: Tractate Zebahim Chapters 4-8* | Jacob Neusner |

| | | |
|---|---|---|
| 140234 | The Talmud of Babylonia: An American Translation XXVIII.C: Tractate Zebahim Chapters 9-14 | Jacob Neusner |
| 140235 | The Talmud of Babylonia: An American Translation XXIX.A: Tractate Menahot Chapters 1-3 | Jacob Neusner |
| 140236 | The Talmud of Babylonia: An American Translation XXIX.B: Tractate Menahot Chapters 4-7 | Jacob Neusner |
| 140237 | The Talmud of Babylonia: An American Translation XXIX.C: Tractate Menahot Chapters 8-13 | Jacob Neusner |
| 140238 | The Talmud of Babylonia: An American Translation XXIX: Tractate Makkot | Jacob Neusner |
| 140239 | The Talmud of Babylonia: An American Translation XXII.A: Tractate Baba Batra Chapters 1 and 2 | Jacob Neusner |
| 140240 | The Talmud of Babylonia: An American Translation XXII.B: Tractate Baba Batra Chapter 3 | Jacob Neusner |
| 140241 | The Talmud of Babylonia: An American Translation XXII.C: Tractate Baba Batra Chapters 4-6 | Jacob Neusner |
| 140242 | The Talmud of Babylonia: An American Translation XXVII.A: Tractate Shebuot Chapters 1-3 | Jacob Neusner |
| 140243 | The Talmud of Babylonia: An American Translation XXVII.B: Tractate Shebuot Chapters 4-8 | Jacob Neusner |
| 140244 | Balaam and His Interpreters: A Hermeneutical History of the Balaam Traditions | John T. Greene |
| 140245 | Courageous Universality: The Work of Schmuel Hugo Bergman | William Kluback |
| 140246 | The Mechanics of Change: Essays in the Social History of German Jewry | Steven M. Lowenstein |
| 140247 | The Talmud of Babylonia: An American Translation XX.A: Tractate Baba Qamma Chapters 1-3 | Jacob Neusner |
| 140248 | The Talmud of Babylonia: An American Translation XX.B: Tractate Baba Qamma Chapters 4-7 | Jacob Neusner |
| 140249 | The Talmud of Babylonia: An American Translation XX.C: Tractate Baba Qamma Chapters 8-10 | Jacob Neusner |
| 140250 | The Talmud of Babylonia: An American Translation XIII.A: Tractate Yebamot Chapters 1-3 | Jacob Neusner |
| 140251 | The Talmud of Babylonia: An American Translation XIII.B: Tractate Yebamot Chapters 4-6 | Jacob Neusner |
| 140252 | The Talmud of Babylonia: An American Translation XI: Tractate Moed Qatan | Jacob Neusner |
| 140253 | The Talmud of Babylonia: An American Translation XXX.A: Tractate Hullin Chapters 1 and 2 | Tzvee Zahavy |
| 140254 | The Talmud of Babylonia: An American Translation XXX.B: Tractate Hullin Chapters 3-6 | Tzvee Zahavy |
| 140255 | The Talmud of Babylonia: An American Translation XXX.C: Tractate Hullin Chapters 7-12 | Tzvee Zahavy |
| 140256 | The Talmud of Babylonia: An American Translation XIII.C: Tractate Yebamot Chapters 7-9 | Jacob Neusner |
| 140257 | The Talmud of Babylonia: An American Translation XIV.A: Tractate Ketubot Chapters 1-3 | Jacob Neusner |
| 140258 | The Talmud of Babylonia: An American Translation XIV.B: Tractate Ketubot Chapters 4-7 | Jacob Neusner |
| 140259 | Jewish Thought Adrift: Max Wiener (1882-1950) | Robert S. Schine |
| 140260 | The Talmud of Babylonia: An American Translation XIV.C: Tractate Ketubot Chapters 8-13 | Jacob Neusner |

| | | |
|---|---|---|
| 140261 | The Talmud of Babylonia: An American Translation XIII.D: Tractate Yebamot Chapters 10-16 | Jacob Neusner |
| 140262 | The Talmud of Babylonia: An American Translation XV. A: Tractate Nedarim Chapters 1-4 | Jacob Neusner |
| 140263 | The Talmud of Babylonia: An American Translation XV.B: Tractate Nedarim Chapters 5-11 | Jacob Neusner |
| 140264 | Studia Philonica Annual 1992 | David T. Runia |
| 140265 | The Talmud of Babylonia: An American Translation XVIII.A: Tractate Gittin Chapters 1-3 | Jacob Neusner |
| 140266 | The Talmud of Babylonia: An American Translation XVIII.B: Tractate Gittin Chapters 4 and 5 | Jacob Neusner |
| 140267 | The Talmud of Babylonia: An American Translation XIX.A: Tractate Qiddushin Chapter 1 | Jacob Neusner |
| 140268 | The Talmud of Babylonia: An American Translation XIX.B: Tractate Qiddushin Chapters 2-4 | Jacob Neusner |
| 140269 | The Talmud of Babylonia: An American Translation XVIII.C: Tractate Gittin Chapters 6-9 | Jacob Neusner |
| 140270 | The Talmud of Babylonia: An American Translation II.A: Tractate Shabbat Chapters 1 and 2 | Jacob Neusner |
| 140271 | The Theology of Nahmanides Systematically Presented | David Novak |
| 140272 | The Talmud of Babylonia: An American Translation II.B: Tractate Shabbat Chapters 3-6 | Jacob Neusner |
| 140273 | The Talmud of Babylonia: An American Translation II.C: Tractate Shabbat Chapters 7-10 | Jacob Neusner |
| 140274 | The Talmud of Babylonia: An American Translation II.D: Tractate Shabbat Chapters 11-17 | Jacob Neusner |
| 140275 | The Talmud of Babylonia: An American Translation II.E: Tractate Shabbat Chapters 18-24 | Jacob Neusner |
| 140276 | The Talmud of Babylonia: An American Translation III.A: Tractate Erubin Chapters 1 and 2 | Jacob Neusner |
| 140277 | The Talmud of Babylonia: An American Translation III.B: Tractate Erubin Chapters 3 and 4 | Jacob Neusner |
| 140278 | The Talmud of Babylonia: An American Translation III.C: Tractate Erubin Chapters 5 and 6 | Jacob Neusner |
| 140279 | The Talmud of Babylonia: An American Translation III.D: Tractate Erubin Chapters 7-10 | Jacob Neusner |
| 140280 | The Talmud of Babylonia: An American Translation XII: Tractate Hagigah | Jacob Neusner |
| 140281 | The Talmud of Babylonia: An American Translation IV.A: Tractate Pesahim Chapter 1 | Jacob Neusner |
| 140282 | The Talmud of Babylonia: An American Translation IV.B: Tractate Pesahim Chapters 2 and 3 | Jacob Neusner |

## Brown Studies on Jews and Their Societies

| | | |
|---|---|---|
| 145001 | American Jewish Fertility | Calvin Goldscheider |
| 145002 | The Impact of Religious Schooling: The Effects of Jewish Education Upon Religious Involvement | Harold S. Himmelfarb |
| 145003 | The American Jewish Community | Calvin Goldscheider |
| 145004 | The Naturalized Jews of the Grand Duchy of Posen in 1834 and 1835 | Edward David Luft |
| 145005 | Suburban Communities: The Jewishness of American Reform Jews | Gerald L. Showstack |

| | | |
|---|---|---|
| 145007 | *Ethnic Survival in America* | David Schoem |
| 145008 | *American Jews in the 21st Century: A Leadership Challenge* | Earl Raab |

## Brown Studies in Religion

| | | |
|---|---|---|
| 147001 | *Religious Writings and Religious Systems I* | Jacob Neusner, et al |
| 147002 | *Religious Writings and Religious Systems II* | Jacob Neusner, et al |
| 147003 | *Religion and the Social Sciences* | Robert Segal |

3 6877 00078 2598

**DATE DUE**

BM 499.5 .E4 1984 v.30:B

37057

Talmud.
 Tractate ≥Hullin

DEMCO